Celtic
Mythology

This edition published 1999 by Geddes & Grosset, an imprint of
Children's Leisure Products Limited, based on a text by Charles Squire

© 1999 Children's Leisure Products Limited, David Dale House, New
Lanark ML11 9DJ, Scotland

Reprinted 2001

Cover photograph of a page from the Book of Kells, courtesy of Trinity
College Library, Dublin. Cover illustrations by John Marshall

ISBN 1 85534 299 5

Printed and bound in Indonesia

Contents

List of Illustrations

Introduction

The Celts are much less well known to us than the Greeks and the Romans, although theirs was a great civilisation in its own way. Unlike the Romans, they were not empire-builders, being very much a tribal society, so they did not make an impact in this way.

A major problem for those who seek to know more about the Celts is the lack of contemporary written history or literature. It is known that they had the ability to write, but they appear not to have done so. It has been suggested that, perhaps, this was part of their social and religious culture and that the druids, or priests, had put them under some kind of taboo not to write things down.

Because of this, theirs was very much an oral tradition. Their culture is rich in marvellous legends, but these were handed down by word of mouth and so tend to have several variations, as do many of the Celtic names. It was not until comparatively recently that our knowledge of the Celts has been extended, thanks to archaeology. We have learnt far more about the lifestyle of the Celts from what has been dug up than from that which has been written down.

Because they believed that a dead person simply travelled to the Otherworld, Celtic graves contained not only corpses but many of the appurtenances that were needed in the mortal world and were thought to be needed in the Otherworld. These appurtenances, which include carts, wagons, even horses, as well as dishes, tools and jewellery, have led us to have a greater understanding of the Celts and to appreciate that they were not so primitive as many of us might have believed.

This book, by describing some of the customs as well as some of the legends of the Celts, seeks to add to the reader's knowledge of a people who are still, to a great extent, enveloped in mystery.

Part One

The Mythology of the British Islands

Chapter 1

THE INTEREST AND IMPORTANCE OF CELTIC MYTHOLOGY

The earliest legendary and poetic records of any country are of great interest and value, not only to its inhabitants but to the wider world. The classical myths of Greece form a sufficient example. In three ways they influenced the destiny of the people that created them and the country of which they were the imagined theatre. First, in the period in which they were still fresh, belief and pride in them were powerful enough to bring scattered tribes together into confederation. Secondly, they gave inspiration to sculptors and poets to produce an art and literature unsurpassed, if not unequalled, by any other age or race. Lastly, when 'the glory that was Greece' had faded and her people had, by dint of successive invasions, perhaps even ceased to have any right to call themselves Greeks, they passed over into the literatures of the modern world and so gave Greece a poetic interest that still makes a small country of greater account in the eyes of the world than many other countries far superior to it in extent and resources.

This permeating influence of Greek classical mythology, apparent in all civilised countries, has acted especially on the countries of the British Isles. From almost the very dawn of English literature, Greek stories of gods and heroes formed a large part of the stock in trade of British poets. The inhabitants of Olympus, the dwelling place of the Greek gods, occupy under their better-known Latin names almost as great a space in English poetry as they did in that of the countries to which they were native. From Chaucer onwards, they have captivated the imagination of poets and their listeners alike. The magic cauldron of classical myth fed, like the Celtic Grail, all who came to it for sustenance.

At last, however, its potency became somewhat exhausted. Alien and exotic to English soil, it degenerated slowly into a convention. In the shallow hands of minor poets of the eighteenth century its figures became mere puppets. When every wood had become a 'grove' and every country girl a 'nymph', one could only expect to find Venus in the ballroom armed with patch and powder puff, Mars shouldering a musket and Apollo inspiring the poet's own trivial strains. The affectation killed – and fortunately – a mode of expression that had become obsolete. Smothered by ridicule and abandoned to the trite vocabulary of inferior writers, classical mythology became a subject that only the greatest poets could afford to handle.

But mythology is so vital to literature that, deprived of the store of legends native to southern Europe, imaginative writers looked for a fresh impulse. They turned their eyes to the north. Inspiration was sought not from Olympus but from Asgard, the dwelling place of the Norse gods. Moreover, it was believed that the fount of primeval poetry issuing from Scandinavian and Germanic mythology was truly that of the British Isles and that we were rightful heirs of it by reason of the Anglo-Saxon in our blood. So, indeed, we are, but it is not our sole heritage. There must also run much Celtic – that is, truly British – blood in our veins.[1] Matthew Arnold was probably right in asserting in his book *The Study of Celtic Literature* that while we owe to our Anglo-Saxon heritage the more practical qualities that were most manifest in the building up of the British Empire, we have inherited from the Celtic side the poetic vision that has made English literature the most brilliant since the Greek.

We have the right, therefore, to claim a new spiritual possession, and a splendid one it is. Celtic mythology has little of the heavy crudeness that repels one in Germanic and Scandinavian stories. It is as beautiful and graceful as the Greek and, unlike the Greek, which is the reflection of a Mediterranean climate quite different from our Temperate Zone, it is our own. Gods should, surely, seem the inevitable outgrowth of the land they move in. How strange

---

[1] 'There is good ground to believe,' wrote E. W. B. Nicholson in the preface to his *Keltic Researches*, 'that Lancashire, West Yorkshire, Staffordshire, Worcestershire, Warwickshire, Leicestershire, Rutland, Cambridgeshire, Wiltshire, Somerset, and part of Sussex, are as Keltic as Perthshire and North Munster; that Cheshire, Shropshire, Herefordshire, Monmouthshire, Gloucestershire, Devon, Dorset, Northamptonshire, Huntingdonshire, and Bedfordshire are more so – and equal to North Wales and Leinster; while Buckinghamshire and Hertfordshire exceed even this degree and are on a level with South Wales and Ulster. Cornwall, of course, is more Keltic than any other English county, and as much so as Argyll, Inverness-shire, or Connaught.'

Apollo would appear naked among icebergs or fur-clad Thor striding under groves of palms. But the Celtic gods and heroes are the natural inhabitants of a British landscape, not seeming foreign and out of place in a scene where there is no vine or olive but shading in with our home-grown oak and bracken, gorse and heath.

Thus we gain an altogether fresh interest in the beautiful spots of our own islands, especially those of the wilder and more mountainous west, where the older inhabitants of the land lingered longest. Saxon conquest obliterated much in eastern Britain and changed more, but in the West of England, in Wales, in Scotland, and especially in legend-haunted Ireland, the hills and dales still hold memories of the ancient gods of the ancient race. Here and there in South Wales and the West of England are regions – once mysterious and still romantic – that the British Celts held to be the homes of gods or out-posts of the Otherworld. In Ireland, not only is there scarcely a place that is not connected in some way with the traditional exploits of the Red Branch champions or of Fionn and his mighty men, but the old deities are still re-membered, dwindled into fairies perhaps but keeping the same attributes and often the same names. Wordsworth's complaint, in a sonnet written in 1801, that while Pelion and Ossa, Olympus and Parnassus are 'in immortal books enrolled', not one English mountain, 'though round our sea-girt shore they rise in crowds', had been 'by the Celestial Muses glorified' doubtless seemed true to his own generation. Thanks to the scholars who unveiled the ancient Gaelic and British mythologies, it need not be so for ours. On Ludgate Hill in London, as well as on many less famous hills, once stood the temple of the British Zeus. A mountain not far from Betws-y-Coed in Wales was the British Olympus, the court and palace of our ancient gods.

It may well be doubted, however, whether Wordsworth's contemporaries would have welcomed the mythology that was their own by right of birth as a substitute for that of Greece and Rome. The inspiration of classical culture, which Wordsworth was one of the first to break with, was still powerful. How some of its adherents would have held their sides and roared at the very no-tion of a British mythology. Yet, all the time, it had long been secretly leaven-ing English ideas and ideals, no less potently because they were disguised un-der forms that could readily be appreciated. Popular fancy had rehabilitated the old gods, long before banned by the priests' bell, book and candle, under various disguises. They still lived on in legend as kings of ancient Britain reigning in a fabulous past earlier in time than Julius Caesar – such were King Lud, founder of London, King Lear, whose legend was immortalised by Shakespeare, King Brennius, who conquered Rome, as well as many others who are found filling parts in old dramas, for example mystery plays. They still lived on as long-dead saints of the early churches of Ireland and Britain. Their wonderful attributes and adventures are in many cases only those of their original namesakes, the old gods, told afresh. And they still lived on in another and a yet more potent way. Myths of Arthur and his cycle of gods passed into the hands of the Norman storytellers to reappear as the romances of King Arthur and his Knights of the Round Table. Thus spread over civilised Europe, their influence was immense, and their primal poetic impulse is still resonant in our literature, playing a particularly strong part in works by nine-teenth-century poets like Tennyson and Swinburne.

This diverse influence of Celtic mythology on English poetry and romance was eloquently set out by Charles Elton in his *Origins of English History*. 'The religion of the British tribes,' he writes, 'has exercised an important influence upon literature. The medieval romances and the legends which stood for his-tory are full of the "fair humanities" and figures of its bright mythology. The elemental powers of earth and fire, and the spirits which haunted the waves and streams, appear again as kings in the Irish annals or as saints and hermits in Wales. The Knights of the Round Table, Sir Kay and Tristan and the bold Sir Bedivere, betray their mighty origin by the attributes they retained as heroes of romance. It was a goddess . . . who bore the wounded Arthur to the peaceful valley. "There was little sunlight on its woods and streams, and the nights were dark and gloomy for want of the moon and stars." This is the country of Oberon and of Sir Huon of Bordeaux. It is the dreamy forest of Arden. In an older mythology, it was the realm of a King of Shadows, the country of Gwyn ap Nudd, who rode as Sir Guyon in *The Fairie Queene* –

> And knighthood took of good Sir Huon's hand,
> When with King Oberon he came to Fairyland.'

To trace Welsh and Irish kings and saints and hermits back to 'the elemen-tal powers of earth and fire, and the spirits that haunted the woods and streams' of Celtic imagination and to disclose primitive pagan deities under the medieval and Christian trappings of 'King Arthur's Knights' will necessarily fall within the scope of this volume. But meanwhile the reader may be asking what evidence there is that apocryphal British kings like Lear and Lud and Irish saints like Bridget are really disguised Celtic gods, or that the *Morte D'Arthur*, with its love of Launcelot and the queen, and its quest of the Holy Grail, was ever anything more than an invention of the Norman romance writers. He or she will want to know what facts we really possess about this supposed Celtic mythology, alleged to have furnished their prototypes, and of what real antiquity and value are our authorities for it.

The answer to his question will be found in the next chapter.

Chapter 2

THE SOURCES OF OUR KNOWLEDGE OF CELTIC MYTHOLOGY

Charles Elton touched on a part only of the material on which we may draw to reconstruct the ancient mythology of the British Isles. Luckily, we are not wholly dependent on the difficult tasks of resolving the fabled deeds of apocryphal Irish and British kings who reigned earlier than St Patrick or before Julius Caesar into their original form of Celtic myths, of sifting the attributes and miracles of doubtfully historical saints or of separating the primitive pagan elements in the legends of Arthur and his Knights from the embellishments added by the Norman romance writers. We have, in addition to these sources – which we may for the present put on one side as secondary – a mass of genuine early writings that, although post-Christian in the form in which they now exist, nonetheless descend from the preceding pagan age. These are contained in vellum and parchment manuscripts long preserved from destruction in great houses and monasteries in Ireland, Scotland and Wales, and only during the nineteenth century brought to light, copied and translated by patient scholars who grappled with the long-obsolete dialects in which they were transcribed.

Many of these volumes are curious miscellanies. Usually a single record of a great house or monastic community, everything was copied into it that the scholar of the family or brotherhood thought to be best worth preserving. Hence they contain diverse material. There are translations of portions of the Bible and of the classics, and of such then popular books as Geoffrey of

Monmouth's and Nennius' histories of Britain; lives of famous saints, together with works attributed to them; poems and romances of which, under a thin disguise, the old Gaelic and British gods are the heroes; together with treatises on all the subjects then studied – grammar, prosody, law, history, geography, chronology and the genealogies of important chiefs.

The majority of these documents were put together during a period that, roughly speaking, lasted from the beginning of the twelfth century to the end of the sixteenth. In Ireland, in Wales and, apparently, also in Scotland, it was a time of literary revival after the turmoil of the previous epoch. In Ireland, the Norsemen, after long ravaging, had settled down peacefully, while in Wales, the Norman Conquest had rendered the country for the first time comparatively quiet. The scattered remains of history, lay and ecclesiastical, of science and of legend were gathered together.

Of the Irish manuscripts, the earliest, and, for our purposes, the most important, on account of the great store of ancient Gaelic mythology which, in spite of its dilapidated condition, it still contains, is in the possession of the Irish Academy. Unluckily, it is reduced to a fragment of one hundred and thirty-eight pages, but this remnant preserves a large number of romances relating to the old gods and heroes of Ireland. Among other things, it contains a complete account of the epic saga called the *Táin Bó Cuailgne*, the 'Raiding of the Cattle of Cooley', in which the hero, Cúchulainn, performed his greatest feats. This manuscript is called the Book of the Dun Cow, from the tradition that it was copied from an earlier book written on the skin of a favourite animal belonging to St Ciaran, who lived in the seventh century. An entry on one of its pages reveals the name of its scribe, one Maelmuiri, whom we know to have been killed by robbers in the church of Clonmacnois in the year 1106.

Far more voluminous and only a little less ancient is the Book of Leinster, which is said to have been compiled in the early part of the twelfth century by Fionn Mac Gorman, Bishop of Kildare. This also contains an account of Cúchulainn's mighty deeds, which supplements the older version in the *Táin Bó Cuailgne*. Of somewhat less importance from the point of view of the student of Gaelic mythology come the Book of Ballymote and the Yellow Book of Lecan, belonging to the end of the fourteenth century, and the Books of Lecan and of Lismore, both attributed to the fifteenth century. Besides these six great collections, there survive many other manuscripts that also contain ancient mythical lore. In one of these, dating from the fifteenth century, is to be found the story of the Battle of Magh Tuireadh, or Moytura, fought between the gods of Ireland and their enemies, the Fomorii, or demons of the deep sea.

The Scottish manuscripts, preserved in the Advocates' Library in Edinburgh, date back in some cases as far as the fourteenth century, although the majority of them belong to the fifteenth and sixteenth. They corroborate the Irish documents, add to the Cúchulainn saga and make a more special subject of the other heroic cycle, that which relates the no less wonderful deeds of Fionn, Oisín and the Fianna. They also contain stories of other characters who, more ancient than either Fionn or Cúchulainn, are the Tuatha Dé Danaan, the god tribe of the ancient Gaels.

The Welsh documents cover about the same period as the Irish and the Scottish. Four of these stand out from the rest as most important. The oldest is the Black Book of Caermarthen, which dates from the third quarter of the twelfth century; the Book of Aneurin, which was written late in the thirteenth; the Book of Taliesin, assigned to the fourteenth; and the Red Book of Hergest, compiled by various persons during that century and the one following it. The first three of these 'Four Ancient Books of Wales' are small in size and contain poems attributed to the great traditional bards of the sixth century, Myrddin, Taliesin and Aneurin. The last – the Red Book of Hergest – is far larger. In it are to be found Welsh translations of the British Chronicles; the often mentioned triads – verses celebrating famous traditional persons or things; ancient poems attributed to Llywarch Hên; and, of priceless value to any study of our subject, the so-called Mabinogion, in which large parts of the old Celtic mythology of the British Isles are worked up into romantic form.

The whole bulk, therefore, of the native literature bearing upon the mythology of the British Islands may be attributed to a period that lasted from the beginning of the twelfth century to the end of the sixteenth. But even the start of this period will no doubt seem far too late a day to give authenticity to material that ought to have vastly preceded it. The date, however, merely marks the final amalgamation of the contents of the manuscripts into the form in which they now exist without bearing at all upon the time of their authorship. As they are copies of ancient poems and tales from much older manuscripts, these books no more fix the period of the original composition of their contents than the presence of a portion of the *Canterbury Tales* in a modern anthology of English poetry would assign Chaucer to the present time.

This has been proved both directly and inferentially. In some instances – as in that of an elegy upon St Columba in the Táin Bó Cuailgne, the Book of the Dun Cow – the dates of authorship are actually given. In others, we may depend upon evidence that, if not quite so absolute, is nearly as convincing. Even where the writer does not state that he is copying from older manuscripts, it is obvious that this must have been the case from the glosses in his version. The scribes of the earlier Gaelic manuscripts very often found, in the documents from which they themselves were copying, words so archaic as to be unintelligible to the readers of their own period. To render them comprehensible, they were obliged to insert marginal notes that explained these obsolete words by reference to other manuscripts more ancient still. Often the medieval copyists have ignorantly moved these notes from the margin into the text, where they remain, like philological fossils, to give evidence of previous forms of life. The documents from which they were taken have perished, leaving the medieval copies as their sole record. In the Welsh Mabinogion the same process is apparent. Peculiarities in the existing manuscripts show plainly enough that they must have been copied from some more archaic text. Besides this, they are, as they at present stand, obviously made up of earlier tales pieced together. Almost as clearly as the Gaelic manuscripts, the Welsh point us back to older and more primitive forms.

The ancient legends of the Gael and the Briton are thus shown to have been no mere inventions of scholarly monks in the Middle Ages. We have now to trace, if possible, the date, not necessarily of their first appearance as stories but of their first appearance in writing in approximately the form in which we have them now.

Circumstantial evidence can be adduced to prove that the most important portions both of Gaelic and British early literature can be safely relegated to a period of several centuries prior to their now existing record. Our earliest version of the episode of the *Táin Bó Cuailgne*, which is the nucleus and centre of the ancient Gaelic heroic cycle of which Cúchulainn, *fortissimus heros Scotorum*, is the principal figure, is found in the twelfth-century Book of the Dun Cow. But legend tells us that at the beginning of the seventh century the saga had not only been composed but had actually become so obsolete as to have been forgotten by the bards. Their leader, one Seanchan Torpeist, a historical character and chief bard of Ireland at that time, obtained permission from the saints to call Fergus, Cúchulainn's contemporary and a chief actor in the 'Raid', from the dead and received from the resurrected hero a true and full version. This tradition, dealing with a real person, surely shows that the story of the *Táin* was known before the time of Seanchan and probably preserves the fact either that his version of Cúchulainn's famous deeds became the accepted one or that he was the first to put it in writing. An equally suggestive consideration approximately fixes for us the earliest appearance of the Welsh mythological prose tales called the 'Mabinogion' or, more correctly, the 'Four Branches of the Mabinogi'. In none of these is there the slightest mention, or apparently the least knowledge, of Arthur, around whom and whose supposed contemporaries centres the mass of British legend as it was transmitted by the Welsh to the Normans. These mysterious mythological records must in all probability, therefore, antedate the Arthurian cycle of myth, which was already appearing in the sixth century. On the other hand, the characters of the 'Four Branches' are mentioned without comment – as though they were people with whom no one could fail to be familiar – in the supposed sixth-century poems contained in those 'Four Ancient Books of Wales' in which are found the first meagre references to the British hero.

Such considerations as these push back, with reasonable certainty, the existence of the Irish and Welsh poems and prose tales, in something like their present shape, to a period before the seventh century.

But this, again, means only that the myths, traditions and legends were current at that to us early, but to them, in their actual substance, late date, in literary form. A mythology must always be far older than the oldest verses and stories that celebrate it. Elaborate poems and sagas are not made in a day or in a year. The legends of the Gaelic and British gods and heroes could not have sprung, like Athena from the head of Zeus, full-born out of some poet's brain. The bard who first put them into artistic shape was setting down the primitive traditions of his race. We may therefore venture to describe them as not of the twelfth century or of the seventh but as of a prehistoric and immemorial antiquity.

Internal evidence bears this out. An examination of both the Gaelic and British legendary romances shows, under embellishing details added by later hands, an inner core of primeval thought that brings them into line with the similar ideas of other races in the earliest stage of culture. Their 'local colour' may be that of their last 'editor' but their 'plots' are pre-medieval, pre-Christian, prehistoric. The characters of early Gaelic legend belong to the same stamp of imagination that created Olympian and Titan, Aesir and Jötun. We must go far to the back of civilised thought to find parallels to such a story as that in which the British sun god, struck by a rival in love with a poisoned spear, is turned into an eagle from whose wound great pieces of carrion are continually falling (*see* Chapter 18 'The Gods of the British Celts').

This aspect of the Celtic literary records was clearly seen and eloquently expressed by Matthew Arnold in his *Study of Celtic Literature*. He was referring to the Welsh side, but his image holds good equally for the Gaelic. 'The first thing that strikes one,' he says, 'in reading the *Mabinogion* is how evidently the medieval storyteller is pillaging an antiquity of which he does not fully possess the secret: he is like a peasant building his hut on the site of Halicarnassus or Ephesus; he builds, but what he builds is full of materials of which he knows not the history, or knows by a glimmering tradition merely: stones "not of this building", but of an older architecture, greater, cunninger, more majestical.' His heroes 'are no medieval personages: they belong to an older, pagan, mythological world'. So, too, with the figures, however reconciled with history, of the three great Gaelic cycles: that of the Tuatha Dé Danaan, of the heroes of Ulster, of Fionn and the Fianna. Their divinity outshines their humanity; through their masks may be seen the faces of gods.

Yet, gods as they are, they had taken on the semblance of mortality by the time their histories were fixed in the form in which we have them now. Their earliest records, if those could be restored to us, would doubtless show them as eternal and undying, changing their shapes at will but not passing away. But the post-Christian copyists, whether Irish or Welsh, would not countenance this. Hence we have the singular paradox of the deaths of Immortals. There is hardly one of the figures of either the Gaelic or the British pantheon whose demise is not somewhere recorded. Usually they fell in the unceasing battles between the gods of darkness and of light. Their deaths in earlier cycles of myth, however, do not preclude their appearance in later ones. Only, indeed, with the closing of the lips of the last mortal who preserved his tradition can the life of a god be truly said to end.

Chapter 3

WHO WERE THE ANCIENT BRITONS?

Before proceeding to recount the myths of the 'Ancient Britons', it will be well to decide what people exactly we mean by that loose but convenient phrase. We have, all of us, vague ideas of Ancient Britons, recollected doubtless from our schoolbooks. There we saw their pictures as, painted with woad, they paddled coracles or drove scythed chariots through legions of astonished Romans. Their druids, white-bearded and wearing long, white robes, cut the mistletoe with a golden sickle at the time of the full moon or, less innocently employed, made bonfires of human beings shut up in gigantic figures of wickerwork.

Such picturesque details were little short of the sum total, not only of our own knowledge of the subject but also of that of our teachers. Practically all their information concerning the ancient inhabitants of Britain was taken from the Commentaries of Julius Caesar. So far as it went, it was no doubt correct, but it did not go far. Caesar's interest in our British ancestors was that of a general who was his own war correspondent rather than that of an exhaustive and painstaking scientist. It has been reserved for modern archaeologists, philologists and ethnologists to give us a fuller account of the Ancient Britons.

The inhabitants of our islands before the Roman invasion are generally described as 'Celts'. But they must have been largely a mixed race, and the people with whom they mingled must have modified to some – and perhaps to a large – extent their physique, their customs and their language.

Speculation has run somewhat wild over the question of the composition of the Early Britons. But out of the clash of rival theories there emerges one that may be considered as scientifically established. We have certain proof of two distinct human stocks in the British Islands at the time of the Roman

Conquest. The earliest of these two races would seem to have inhabited our islands from the most ancient times and may, for our purpose, be described as aboriginal. They were the people who built the long barrows and who are variously called by ethnologists the Iberian, Mediterranean, Berber, Basque, Silurian or Euskarian race. In physique they were short, swarthy, dark-haired, dark-eyed and long-skulled. Their language belonged to the group called Hamitic, the surviving types of which are found among the Gallas, Abyssinians, Berbers and other North African tribes, and they seem to have come originally from some part either of eastern, northern or central Africa. Spreading from there, they were probably the first people to inhabit the Valley of the Nile and sent offshoots into Syria and Asia Minor. The earliest Greeks found them in Greece under the name of Pelasgians, the earliest Latins in Italy as the Etruscans and the Hebrews in Palestine as the Hittites. They spread northward through Europe as far as the Baltic and westward along the Atlas chain to Spain, France and our own islands. In many countries they reached a comparatively high level of civilisation, but in Britain their development must have been early checked. We can discern them as an agricultural rather than a pastoral people, still in the Stone Age, living in tribes on hills the summits of which they fortified elaborately and the slopes of which they cultivated on what is called the 'terrace system'. They held our islands until the coming of the Celts, who fought with the aborigines, dispossessed them of the more fertile parts, subjugated them, even amalgamated with them, but certainly never destroyed them. In the time of the Romans they were still practically independent in South Wales. In Ireland they were long unconquered and are found as allies rather than serfs of the Gaels, ruling their own provinces and preserving their own customs and religion. Nor, in spite of all the successive invasions of Great Britain and Ireland, are they yet extinct or so merged as to have lost their type, which is still the predominant one in many parts of the west both of Britain and Ireland and is believed by some ethnologists to be generally on the increase all over England.

The second of the two races was the exact opposite of the first. They were the tall, fair, light-haired blue- or grey-eyed, broad-headed people called, popularly, the Celts, who belonged in speech to the Aryan family, their language finding its affinities in Latin, Greek, Teutonic, Slavic, the Zend of Ancient Persia and the Sanskrit of ancient India. Their original home was probably somewhere in Central Europe, along the course of the upper Danube or in the region of the Alps. The round barrows in which they buried their dead or deposited their burnt ashes differ in shape from the long barrows of the earlier race. They were in a higher stage of culture than the Iberians and introduced into Britain bronze and silver and, perhaps, some of the more lately domesticated animals.

Both Iberians and Celts were divided into numerous tribes, but there is nothing to show that there was any great diversity among the former. It is otherwise with the Celts, who were separated into two main branches which came over at different times. The earliest were the Goidels or Gaels, the second the Brythons or Britons. Between these two branches there was not only a dialectical but probably also a considerable physical difference. Some anthropologists even postulate a different shape of skull. Without necessarily admitting this, there is reason to suppose a difference of build and of colour of hair. With regard to this, we have the evidence of Latin writers – of Tacitus, who tells us in *Agricola* that the 'Caledonians' of the north differed from the southern Britons in being larger-limbed and redder-haired, and of Strabo, who described the tribes in the interior of Britain in *Geographica* as taller than the Gaulish colonists on the coast, with hair less yellow and limbs more loosely knit. Equally do the classical authorities agree in recognising the Silures of South Wales as an entirely different race from any other in Britain. The dark complexions and curly hair of these Iberians seemed to Tacitus to prove them to be immigrants from Spain.

The nineteenth-century scholar John Rhys also put forward evidence to show that the Goidels and the Brythons had already separated before they first left Gaul for our islands, finding them as two distinct peoples there. We do not expect so much nowadays from 'the merest schoolboy' as we did in Macaulay's time, but even the modern descendant of that paragon could probably tell us that, according to Julius Caesar, all Gaul was divided into three parts, one of which was inhabited by the Belgae, another by the Aquitani and the third by those who called themselves Celtae but were termed Galli by the Romans, and that they all differed from one another in language, customs and laws. Of these, Professor Rhys identified the Belgae with the Brythons and the Celtae with the Goidels, the third people, the Aquitani, being non-Celtic and non-Aryan, part of the great Hamitic-speaking Iberian stock. The Celtae, with their Goidelic dialect of Celtic, which survives today in the Gaelic languages of Ireland, Scotland and the Isle of Man, were the first to come over to Britain, pushed forward, probably, by the Belgae, who, Caesar tells us, were the bravest of the Gauls. Here they conquered the native Iberians, driving them out of the fertile parts into the rugged districts of the north and west. Later came the Belgae themselves, compelled by press of population, and they, bringing better weapons and a higher civilisation, treated the Goidels as they had treated the Iberians. Thus harried, the Goidels probably combined with the Iberians against what was now the common foe and became to a large degree amalgamated with them. The result was that during the Roman domination the British Islands were roughly divided with regard to race as follows: the Brythons, or second Celtic race, held all Britain south of the Tweed, with the exception of the extreme west, while the first Celtic race, the Goidelic, had most of Ireland as well as the Isle of Man, Cumberland, the West Highlands, Cornwall, Devon and North Wales. North of the Grampians lived the Picts, who were probably more or less Goidelicised Iberians, the aboriginal race also holding out, unmixed, in South Wales and parts of Ireland.

It is now time to decide what, for the purposes of this book, it will be best to call the two different branches of the Celts and their languages. With such familiar terms as 'Gael' and 'Briton', 'Gaelic' and 'British' ready to our hands, it seems pedantic to insist upon the more technical 'Goidel' and 'Brython', 'Goidelic' and 'Brythonic'. The difficulty is that the words 'Gael' and 'Gaelic' have been so long popularly used to designate only the modern Goidels of Scotland and their language that they may create confusion when also applied to the people and languages of Ireland and the Isle of Man. Similarly, the words 'Briton' and 'British' have come to mean the people of the whole of the British Islands, although they at first signified only the inhabitants of England, Central Wales, the Lowlands of Scotland and the Brythonic colony in Brittany. The words 'Goidel' and 'Brython', however, with their derivatives, are so clumsy that it will probably prove best to use the neater terms. In this volume, therefore, the Goidels of Ireland, Scotland and the Isle of Man are our Gaels and the Brythons of England and Wales are our Britons.

We get the earliest accounts of the life of the inhabitants of the British Islands from two sources. The first is a foreign one, that of the Latin writers. But the Romans really knew only the southern Britons, whom they describe as similar in physique and customs to the Continental Gauls, with whom, indeed, they considered them to be identical. At the time they wrote, colonies of Belgae were still settling upon the coasts of Britain opposite to Gaul. Roman

information grew scantier as it approached Hadrian's Wall, and of the northern tribes they seem to have had only such knowledge as they gathered
through occasional warfare with them. They describe them as entirely barbarous, naked and tattooed, living by hunting alone, without towns, houses or
fields, without government or family life, and regarding iron as an ornament
of value, as other, more civilised peoples regarded gold. As for Ireland, it never
came under their direct observation, and we are entirely dependent on native
writers for information as to the manners and customs of the Gaels there. It
may be considered convincing proof of the authenticity of the descriptions of
life contained in the ancient Gaelic manuscripts that they corroborate so completely the observations of the Latin writers on the Britons and Gauls. Reading
the two side by side, we may largely reconstruct the common civilisation of
the Celts.

Roughly speaking, one may compare it with the civilisation of the Greeks
as described by Homer. Both peoples were in the tribal and pastoral stage of
culture in which the chiefs are the great cattle owners round whom their less
wealthy fellows gather. Both wear much the same kind of clothing, use the
same kind of weapons and fight in the same manner – from the war chariot, a
vehicle already obsolete even in Ireland by the first century of the Christian
era. Battles are fought single-handedly between chiefs, the ill-armed common
people contributing little to their result and less to their history. Such chiefs
are said to be divinely descended – sons, even, of the immortal gods. Their
tremendous feats are sung about by the bards, who, like the Homeric poets,
were privileged persons, inferior only to the warlord. Ancient Greek and Ancient Celt had very much the same conceptions of life, both as regards this
world and the next.

We may gather much detailed information of the early inhabitants of the
British Islands from various authorities. Their clothes, which consisted, according to the Latin writers, of a blouse with sleeves, trousers fitting closely
round the ankles and a shawl or cloak fastened at the shoulder with a brooch,
were made either of thick felt or of woven cloth dyed with various brilliant
colours. The writer Diodorus tells us that they were crossed with little squares
and lines, 'as though they had been sprinkled with flowers'. They were, in fact,
like 'tartans', and we may believe Marcus Terentius Varro, who tells us that
they 'made a gaudy show'. The men alone seem to have worn hats, which were
of soft felt, the women's hair being uncovered and tied in a knot at the back of

the neck. In time of battle, the men also dispensed with any head-covering, brushing their abundant hair forward into a thick mass and dyeing it red with a soap made of goat's fat and beech ashes until they looked (says Cicero's tutor, Posidonius, who visited Britain about 110 BC) less like human beings than wild men of the woods. Both sexes were fond of ornaments, which took the form of gold bracelets, rings, pins and brooches, and of beads of amber, glass and jet. Their knives, daggers, spear heads, axes and swords were made of bronze or iron; their shields were the same round target used by the Highlanders at the battle of Culloden; and they seem also to have had a kind of lasso to which a hammer-shaped ball was attached and which they used as the gauchos of South America use their *bola*. Their war chariots were made of wicker, the wooden wheels being armed with sickles of bronze. These were drawn either by two or four horses and were large enough to hold several persons in each. Standing in these, they rushed along the enemy's lines, hurling darts and driving the scythes against all who came within reach. The Romans were much impressed by the skill of the drivers, who, according to Caesar, 'could check their horses at full speed on a steep incline, and turn them in an instant, and could run along the pole, and stand on the yoke, and then get back into their chariots again without a moment's delay'.

With these accounts of the Roman writers we may compare the picture of the Gaelic hero Cúchulainn, as the ancient Irish writers describe him dressed and armed for battle. Glorified in the *Táin Bó Cuailgne*, he still wears essentially the same costume and equipment that the classical historians and geographers described more soberly. 'His gorgeous raiment that he wore in great conventions' consisted of 'a fair crimson tunic of five plies and fringed, with a long pin of white silver, gold-enchased and patterned, shining as if it had been a luminous torch which for its blazing property and brilliance men might not endure to see. Next his skin, a body vest of silk, bordered and fringed all round with gold, with silver, and with white bronze, which vest came as far as the upper edge of his russet-coloured kilt. . . . About his neck were a hundred linklets of red gold that flashed again, with pendants hanging from them. His head gear was adorned with a hundred mixed carbuncle jewels, strung.' He carried 'a trusty special shield, in hue dark crimson, and in its circumference armed with a pure white silver rim. At his left side a long and golden-hilted sword. Beside him, in the chariot, a lengthy spear; together with a keen, aggression-boding javelin, fitted with hurling thong, with rivets of white bronze.' Another passage of Gaelic saga, *Tochmarc Emire*, 'The Wooing of Emer', an old Irish romance, describes his chariot. It was made of fine wood, with wickerwork, moving on wheels of white bronze. It had a high rounded frame of creaking copper, a strong curved yoke of gold and a pole of white silver with mountings of white bronze. The yellow reins were plaited, and the shafts were as hard and straight as sword blades.

In same way the ancient Irish writers glorified the halls and fortresses of their mythical kings. Like the palaces of Priam, of Menelaus and of Odysseus, they gleam with gold and gems. Conchobar, or Conachar, the legendary King of Ulster in its golden age, had three such 'houses' at Emain Macha. Of the one called the 'Red Branch', we are told that in 'The Wooing of Emer' that it contained nine compartments of red yew, partitioned by walls of bronze, all grouped around the king's private chamber, which had a ceiling of silver and bronze pillars adorned with gold and carbuncles. But the far less magnificent accounts of the Latin writers have, no doubt, more truth in them than such lavish pictures. They described the Britons they knew as living in villages of beehive huts, roofed with fern or thatch, from which, at the approach of an enemy, they retired to the local *dún*. This, according to Caesar, far from being elaborate, merely consisted of a round or oval space fenced in with palisades and earthworks and situated either on the top of a hill or in the middle of a not easily traversable morass. The remains of such strongholds can still be seen in many parts of England – notable ones are the 'castles' of Amesbury, Avebury and Old Sarum in Wiltshire, St Catherine's Hill near Winchester and St George's Hill in Surrey – and it is probable that, in spite of the Celtic praisers of past days, the 'palaces' of Emain Macha and of Tara were very like them.

The Celtic customs were, like the Homeric, those of the primitive world. All land (although it may have theoretically belonged to the chief) was cultivated in common. This community of possessions is stated by Caesar to have extended to their wives, but the imputation cannot be said to have been proved. On the contrary, in the stories of both branches of the Celtic race, women seem to have taken a higher place in men's estimation and to have enjoyed far more personal liberty than among the Homeric Greeks. The idea may have arisen from a misunderstanding of some of the curious Celtic customs. Descent seems to have been traced through the maternal rather than through the paternal line, a very un-Aryan procedure that some believe to have been borrowed from another race. Parental relationship was still further lessened by the custom of sending children to be brought up outside the family in which they were born so that they had foster parents to whom they were as much, or even more, attached than to their natural ones.

Their political state, mirroring their family life, was not less primitive. There was no central tribunal. Disputes were settled within the families in which they occurred, while in the case of more serious clashes, the injured party or his nearest relation could kill the culprit or exact a fine from him. As families increased in number, they became petty tribes, often at war with one another. A defeated tribe had to recognise the sovereignty of the head man of the conquering tribe, and a succession of such victories exalted him into the position of a chief of his district. But even then, although his decision was the whole of the law, he was little more than the mouthpiece of public opinion.

Chapter 4

The Religion of the Ancient Britons and Druidism

The ancient inhabitants of Britain – the Gaelic and British Celts – have been already described as forming a branch of what are roughly called the Aryans. This name has, however, little reference to race and really signifies the speakers of a group of languages that can be all shown to be connected and to descend remotely from a single source – a hypothetical mother tongue spoken by a hypothetical people whom we term Aryan or, more correctly, Indo-European. This primeval speech probably evolved on some part of the great plain that stretches from the mountains of Central Europe to the mountains of Central Asia and spread, superseding or amalgamating with the tongues of other races, until branches of it were spoken over almost the whole of Europe and a great portion of Asia. All the various Latin, Greek, Slavic, Germanic and Celtic languages are Aryan, as well as Persian and other Asiatic dialects derived from the ancient Zend and the numerous Indian languages that trace their origin to Sanskrit.

Not very long ago, it was supposed that this common descent of language involved a common descent of blood. A real brotherhood was enthusiastically claimed for all the principal European nations, who were also invited to recognise Hindus and Persians as their long-lost cousins. Since then, it has been conceded that while the Aryan speech survived, although greatly modified, the Aryan blood might well have disappeared, diluted beyond recognition by crossing with the other races whom the Aryans conquered or among whom they more or less peacefully settled. As a matter of fact, there are no European nations – perhaps no people at all except a few remote savage tribes – that are not made up of the most diverse elements. Aryan and non-Aryan long ago blended inextricably to form new peoples by their fusion.

But just as the Aryan speech influenced the new languages and the Aryan customs the new civilisations, so we can still discern in the religions of the Aryan-speaking nations similar ideas and expressions pointing to an original source of mythological concepts. Hence, whether we investigate the mythology of the Hindus, the Greeks, the Germans or the Celts, we find the same mythological groundwork. In each, we see the powers of nature personified and endowed with human form and attributes, although bearing, with few exceptions, different names. Like the Vedic Brahmans, the Greek and Latin poets and the Norse scalds, the Celtic bards – whether Gaels or Britons – imagined the sky, the sun, the moon, the earth, the sea and the dark underworld, as well as the mountains, the streams and the woods, to be ruled by beings like their own chiefs but infinitely more powerful. Every passion, as war and love, and every art, as poetry and smithcraft, had its divine founder, teacher and exponent, and of all these deities and their imagined children, they wove the poetical and allegorical romances that form the subject of the present volume.

Like other nations, too, whether Aryan or non-Aryan, the Celts had, besides their mythology, a religion. It was not enough to tell tales of shadowy gods. They had to be made visible by sculpture housed in groves or temples, served with ritual and propitiated with sacrifices if they were to bestow their favours. Every cult had to have its priests living by the altar.

The priests of the Celts are well known to us by name as the 'druids' – a word derived from a root, DR, which signifies a tree, and especially the oak, in several Aryan languages. This is generally taken as proving that they paid special veneration to the king of trees. It is true that the mistletoe – that strange parasite on the oak – was prominent among their 'herbs of power' and played a part in their ritual, but this is equally true of other Aryan nations. It was held by the Norse to be sacred to the god Balder, while the Romans believed it to be the 'golden bough' that gave access to Hades.

The accounts both of the Latin and Gaelic writers give us a fairly complete idea of the nature of the druids and especially of the high estimation in which they were held. They were at once the priests, the physicians, the wizards, the diviners, the theologians, the scientists and the historians of their tribes. All spiritual power and all human knowledge were vested in them, and they ranked second only to the kings and chiefs. They were freed from all contribution to the state, whether by tribute or service in war, so that they might the better apply themselves to their divine offices. Their decisions were absolutely final, and those who disobeyed them were laid under a terrible excommunication or boycott. Classical writers tell us how they lorded it in Gaul, where, no doubt, they borrowed splendour by imitating their more civilised neighbours. Men of the highest rank were proud to cast aside the insignia of mere mortal honour to join the company of those who claimed to be the direct mediators with the sky god and the thunder god, and who must have resembled the ecclesiastics of medieval Europe in the days of their greatest power, combining, like them, spiritual and temporal dignities and possessing the highest culture of their age. Yet it was not among these druids of Gaul, with their splendid temples and vestments and their elaborate rituals, that the metropolis of druidism was to be sought. We learn from Caesar that the Gallic druids believed their religion to have come to them originally from Britain and that it was their practice to send their 'theological students' across the Channel to learn its doctrines at their purest source. To trace a cult backwards is often to take a retrograde course in culture, and it was no doubt in Britain – which Pliny the Elder tells us 'might have taught magic to Persia' – that the sufficiently primitive and savage rites of the druids of Gaul were preserved in their still more savage and primitive forms. It is curious corroboration of this alleged British origin of druidism that the ancient Irish also believed their druidism to have come from the sister island. Their heroes and seers are described as only gaining the highest knowledge by travelling to Alba (*see* Chapter 12, 'The Irish Iliad'). However this may be, we may take it as certain that this druidism was the accepted religion of the Celtic race.

Certain scholars look deeper for its origin, holding its dark superstitions and savage rites to bear the stamp of lower minds than those of the poetic and manly Celts. Professor Rhys inclines to see three forms of religion in the British Islands at the time of the Roman invasion: the 'druidism' of the Iberian aborigines, the pure polytheism of the Brythons, who, having come later into the country, had mixed but little with the natives, and the mingled Aryan and non-Aryan cults of the Goidels, who were already largely amalgamated with them. But many authorities dissent from this view, and, indeed, we are not obliged to postulate borrowing from tribes in a lower state of culture to explain primitive and savage features underlying a higher religion. The Aryan nations must have passed, equally with all others, through a state of pure savagery, and we know that the religion of the Greeks, in many respects so lofty, sheltered features and legends as barbarous as any attributable to the Celts.

Celtic Worship, from a drawing by E. Wallcousins

Of the famous teaching of the druids we know little, owing to their habit of never allowing their doctrines to be put into writing. Caesar, however, roughly records its scope. 'As one of their leading dogmas,' he says, 'they inculcate this: that souls are not annihilated but pass after death from one body to another, and they hold that by this teaching men are much encouraged to valour, through disregarding the fear of death. They also discuss and impart to the young many things concerning the heavenly bodies and their movements, the size of the world and of our earth, natural science, and of the influence and power of the immortal gods.' The Romans seem to have held their wisdom in some awe, although it is not unlikely that the druids themselves borrowed whatever knowledge they may have had of science and philosophy from the classical culture. That their creed of transmigration was not, however, merely taken over from the Greeks seems certain from its appearance in the ancient Gaelic myths. Not only the shape-changing common to the magic stories of all nations but actual reincarnation was in the power of privileged beings. We know from 'The Wooing of Emer' that the hero Cúchulainn was urged by the men of Ulster to marry because they knew 'that his rebirth would be of himself' and they did not wish so great a warrior to be lost to their tribe. Another legend, from the *Táin Bó Cuailgne*, tells how the famous Fionn Mac Cumhaill was reborn after two hundred years as an Ulster king called Mongan.

Such ideas, however, belonged to the metaphysical side of druidism. Far more important to the practical primitive mind are ritual and sacrifice, by the due performance of which the gods are persuaded or compelled to grant earth's increase and length of days to men. Among the druids, this humouring of the gods took the shape of human sacrifice. 'The whole Gaulish nation,' says Caesar, 'is to a great degree devoted to superstitious rites; and on this account those who are afflicted with severe diseases, or who are engaged in battles and dangers, either sacrifice human beings for victims, or vow that they will immolate themselves, and these employ the druids as ministers for such sacrifices because they think that, unless the life of man be repaid for the life of man, the will of the immortal gods cannot be appeased. They also ordain national offerings of the same kind. Others make wickerwork images of vast size, the limbs of which they fill with living men and set on fire.'

We find evidence of similarly awful customs in pagan Ireland. Among the oldest Gaelic records are tracts called *Dinnsenchus*, in which famous places are enumerated together with the legends relating to them. Such topographies are found in several of the great Irish medieval manuscripts and therefore, of course, received their final transcription at the hands of Christian monks. But these ecclesiastics rarely tampered with compositions in elaborate verse. Nor can it be imagined that any monastic scribe could have invented such a legend as this one, which describes the practice of human sacrifice among the ancient Irish. The poem (which is found in the Books of Leinster, of Ballymote, of Lecan and in a document called the Rennes manuscript) records the reason why a spot near the present village of Ballymagauran in County Cavan received the name of Magh Slecht, the 'Plain of Adoration'.[1]

'Here used to be
A high idol with many fights,
Which was named the Cromm Cruach;
It made every tribe to be without peace.

''Twas a sad evil!
Brave Gaels used to worship it.
From it they would not without tribute ask
To be satisfied as to their portion of the hard world.

'He was their god,
The withered Cromm with many mists,
The people whom he shook over every host,
The everlasting kingdom they shall not have.

'To him without glory
They would kill their piteous, wretched offspring
With much wailing and peril,
To pour their blood around Cromm Cruach.

'Milk and corn
They would ask from him speedily
In return for one-third of their healthy issue:
Great was the horror and the scare of him.

[1] Three verses omitted here will be found later as a note to Chapter 12, 'The Irish Iliad'.

'To him
Noble Gaels would prostrate themselves,
From the worship of him, with many manslaughters,
The plain is called "Magh Slecht".

.   .   .   .

'They did evil,
They beat their palms, they pounded their bodies,
Wailing to the demon who enslaved them,
They shed falling showers of tears.

.   .   .   .

'Around Cromm Cruach
There the hosts would prostrate themselves;
Though he put them under deadly disgrace,
Their name clings to the noble plain.

'In their ranks (stood)
Four times three stone idols;
To bitterly beguile the hosts,
The figure of the Cromm was made of gold.

'Since the rule
Of Herimon[1], the noble man of grace,
There was worshipping of stones
Until the coming of good Patrick of Macha.

'A sledge-hammer to the Cromm
He applied from crown to sole,
He destroyed without lack of valour
The feeble idol which was there.'

Such, we gather from a tradition that we may take as authentic, was human sacrifice in early Ireland. According to the quoted verse, one third of the healthy children were slaughtered, presumably every year, to wrest from the powers of nature the grain and grass upon which the tribes and their cattle subsisted. In a prose *dinnsenchus* preserved in the Rennes manuscript, there is a slight variant. ''Tis there,' (at Magh Slecht), it runs, 'was the king idol of Erin, namely the Crom Croich, and around him were twelve idols made of stones, but he was of gold. Until Patrick's advent he was the god of every folk that colonised Ireland. To him they used to offer the firstlings of every issue and the chief scions of every clan.' The same authority also tells us that these sacrifices were made at Hallowe'en, which took the place in the Christian calendar of the heathen *Samhain* – 'Summer's End' – when the sun's power waned and the strength of the gods of darkness, winter and the underworld grew great.

Who, then, was this bloodthirsty deity? His name, Cromm Cruach, means the 'Bowed One of the Mound' and was evidently applied to him only after his fall from godhead. According to the Tripartite Life of St Patrick, a fifteenth-century combination of three very ancient Gaelic manuscripts, it relates to the tradition that, at the approach of the all-conquering St Patrick, the 'demon' fled from his golden image, which thereupon sank forward in the earth in homage to the power that had come to supersede it. But from another source we glean that the word *cromm* was a kind of pun upon *cenn*, and that the real title of the 'king idol of Erin' was *Cenn Cruach*, 'Head' or 'Lord' of the Mound. This suggests that he was probably the Gaelic heaven god, worshipped, like the Hellenic Zeus, upon 'high places', natural or artificial. At any rate, we may see in him the god most revered by the Gaels, surrounded by the other twelve chief members of their pantheon.

It would appear probable that the Celtic state worship was what is called 'solar'. All its chief festivals related to points in the sun's progress, the equinoxes having been considered more important than the solstices. It was at the spring equinox (called 'Beltane' by the Celts) in every nineteenth year that, we learn from Diodorus the Sicilian, a writer contemporary with Julius Caesar, Apollo himself appeared to his worshippers and was seen harping and dancing in the sky until the rising of the Pleiades. The other corresponding festival was 'Samhain', the autumn equinox. As Beltane marked the beginning of summer, so Samhain recorded its end. The summer solstice was also a great Celtic feast. It was held at the beginning of August in honour of the god called Lugus by the Gauls, Lugh by the Gaels and Lleu by the Britons – the pan-Celtic

---

[1]   The first King of the Sons of Mil Espaine. The name is more usually spelt Eremon.

Apollo, and, probably, when the cult of the war god had fallen from its early prominence, the chief figure of the common pantheon.

It was doubtless at Stonehenge that the British Apollo was thus seen harping and dancing. That marvellous structure well corresponds to Diodorus's description of a 'magnificent temple of Apollo', which he locates 'in the centre of Britain'. 'It is a circular enclosure,' he says, 'adorned with votive offerings and tablets with Greek inscriptions suspended by travellers upon the walls. The rulers of the temple and city are called "Boreadce"[1], and they take up the government from each other according to the order of their tribes. The citizens are given up to music, harping and chanting in honour of the sun.' Stonehenge, therefore, was a sacred religious centre, equally revered by and equally belonging to all the British tribes – a Rome or Jerusalem of our ancient paganism.

The same great gods were, no doubt, adored by all the Celts, not only of Great Britain and Ireland but of Continental Gaul as well. Sometimes they can be traced by name right across the ancient Celtic world. In other cases, what is obviously the same personified power of nature is found in various places with the same attributes but with a different title. Besides these, there must have been a multitude of lesser gods, worshipped by certain tribes alone, to whom they stood as ancestors and guardians. 'I swear by the gods of my people' was the ordinary oath of a hero in the ancient Gaelic sagas. The aboriginal tribes must also have had their gods, whether it is true or not that their religion influenced the Celtic druidism. We can see in the almost nameless spirits of well and river, mountain and wood – shadowy remnants of whose cults survive today – members of a swarming pantheon of the older Iberians. These local beings would in no way conflict with the great Celtic nature gods, and the two worships could exist side by side, both even claiming the same priest. It needs the stern faith of monotheism to deny the existence of the gods of others. Polytheistic nations have seldom or never risen to such a height. In their dealings with a conquered people, the conquerors naturally held their own gods to be the stronger. Still, it could not be denied that the gods of the conquered were on their own ground. They knew, so to speak, the country and might have unguessed powers of doing evil! What if, to avenge their wor-

---

[1]   It has been suggested that this title is an attempt to reproduce the ancient British word for 'bards'.

Portion of the circles, Stonehenge

shippers and themselves, they were to make the land barren and useless to the conquerors? As a result, conquering pagan nations have usually been quite ready to stretch out the hand of welcome to the gods of their new subjects, to propitiate them by sacrifice and even to admit them within the pale of their own pantheon.

This raises the question of the exact nationality of the gods whose stories we are about to tell. Were they all Aryan or did any of the greater aboriginal gods climb up to take their place among the Gaelic tribe of the goddess Danu or the British children of the goddess Don? Some of the Celtic gods have seemed to scholars to bear signs of a non-Aryan origin. The point, however, is very obscure. Neither does it much concern us. Just as the diverse gods of the Greeks – some Aryan and Hellenic, some pre-Aryan and Pelasgian, some imported and Semitic – were all gathered into one great divine family, so we may consider as members of one national Olympus all these gods whose legends make up 'The Mythology of the British Islands'.

Part Two

THE GAELIC GODS AND THEIR STORIES

Chapter 5

THE GODS OF THE GAELS

Of the two Celtic races that settled in our islands, it is the earlier, the Gaels, that has best preserved its old mythology. It is true that we have in few cases such detailed accounts of the Gaelic gods as we have of the Hellenic deities from the Greek poets, of the Indian Devas from the Rig Veda, or of the Norse Aesir from the Eddas. Yet nonetheless we may draw from the ancient Irish manuscripts quite enough information to enable us to see their figures with some clearness. We find them, as might have been anticipated, very much like the divine hierarchies of other Aryan peoples.

We also find them separated into two opposing camps, a division common to all the Aryan religions. Just as the Olympians struggled with the Giants, the Aesir fought the Jötuns and the Devas the Asuras, so there is warfare in the Gaelic spiritual world between two superhuman hosts. On one side are ranged the gods of day, light, life, fertility, wisdom and good; on the other, the demons of night, darkness, death, barrenness and evil. The first were the great spirits symbolising the beneficial aspects of nature and the arts and intelligence of humans; the second were the hostile powers thought to be behind such baneful manifestations as storm and fog, drought and disease. The first are ranged as a divine family round a goddess called Danu, from whom they took their well-known name of *Tuatha Dé Danaan*, 'Tribe' or 'Folk of the Goddess Danu'. The second owned allegiance to a female divinity called Domnu. Their king, Indech, is described as her son, and they are all called 'Domnu's gods'. The word 'Domnu' appears to have signified the abyss or the deep sea, and the same idea is also expressed in their better-known name of 'Fomorii', derived from two Gaelic words meaning 'under sea'. The waste of water seems always to have impressed the Celts with the sense of primeval ancientness. It was connected in their minds with vastness, darkness and monstrous births –

the very antithesis of all that was symbolised by the earth, the sky and the sun.

The Fomorii therefore were held to be more ancient than the gods before whom they were, however, destined to fall in the end. Offspring of 'Chaos and Old Night', they were, for the most part, huge and deformed. Some had only one arm and one leg apiece, while others had the heads of goats, horses, or bulls. The most famous, and perhaps the most terrible of them all, was Balor, whose father is said to have been one Buarainech, that is, the 'cow-faced', and who combined in himself the two classical roles of the Cyclops and the Medusa. Although he had two eyes, one was always kept shut, for it was so venomous that it slew anyone on whom its look fell. This malignant quality of Balor's eye was not natural to him but was the result of an accident. Urged by curiosity, he once looked in at the window of a house where his father's sorcerers were preparing a magic potion, and the poisonous smoke from the cauldron reached his eye, infecting it with so much of its own deadly nature as to make it disastrous to others. Neither god nor giant seems to have been exempt from its dangers, so that Balor was allowed to live only on condition that he kept his terrible eye shut. On days of battle he was placed opposite the enemy, the lid of the destroying eye was lifted up with a hook, and its gaze withered all who stood before it. The memory of Balor and his eye still lingers in Ireland: the 'eye of Balor' is the name for what the folk culture of other countries call the 'evil eye'. Stories are still told of *Balar Beimann*, or 'Balor of the Mighty Blows', and 'Balor's Castle' is the name of a curious cliff on Tory Island. This island off the coast of Donegal was the Fomorian outpost on earth, their real abode being in the cold depths of the sea.

This rule, however, as to the hideousness of the Fomorii had its exceptions. Elathan, one of their chiefs, is described in the fifteenth-century Harleian manuscript in the British Library as of magnificent presence – a Miltonic prince of darkness. 'A man of fairest form,' it says, 'with golden hair down to his shoulders. He wore a mantle of gold braid over a shirt interwoven with threads of gold. Five golden necklaces were round his neck, and a brooch of gold with a shining precious stone thereon was on his breast. He carried two silver spears with rivets of bronze, and his sword was golden-hilted and golden-studded.' Nor was his son less handsome. His name was Bres, which means 'beautiful', and we are told that every beautiful thing in Ireland, 'whether plain, or fortress, or ale, or torch, or woman, or man', was compared with him, so that men said of them, 'that is a Bres'.

Balor, Bres and Elathan are the three Fomorian personages whose figures, seen through the mists of antiquity, show clearest to us, but they are only a few out of many, nor are they the oldest. We can learn, however, nothing but a few names of any ancestors of the Gaelic giants. This is equally true of the Gaelic gods. Those we know are evidently not without parentage but the names of their fathers are no more than shadows following into oblivion the figures they designated. The most ancient divinity of whom we have any knowledge is Danu herself, the goddess from whom the whole hierarchy of gods received its name of Tuatha Dé Danaan. She was also called Anu or Ana,[1] and her name still clings to two well-known mountains near Killarney, which, although now called simply 'The Paps', were known formerly as the 'Paps of Ana'. She was the universal mother; 'well she used to cherish the gods', says the commentator of a ninth-century Irish glossary attributed to Cormac, King-Bishop of Chasel. Her husband is never mentioned by name, but one may assume him, from British analogies, to have been Bíle, known to Gaelic tradition as a god of Hades, a kind of Celtic Pluto from whom sprang the first men. Danu herself probably represented the earth and its fruitfulness, and one might compare her with the Greek Demeter. All the other gods are, at least by title, her children. The greatest of these would seem to have been Nuada, called Argetlámh, or 'He of the Silver Hand'. He was at once the Gaelic Zeus, or Jupiter, and their war god, for among primitive nations to whom success in war is all-important the god of battles is the supreme god. Among the Gauls, Camulus, whose name meant 'Heaven', was identified by the Romans with Mars, and other such instances come readily to the mind. He possessed an invincible sword, one of the four chief treasures of the Tuatha Dé Danaan over whom he was twice king, and there is little doubt that he was one of the most important gods of both the Gaels and the Britons, for his name is spread over the whole of the British Isles, which we may surmise the Celts conquered under his auspices. We may picture him as a more savage Mars, delighting in battle and slaughter, and, like his Gaulish affinities, Teutates and Hesus, of whom the Latin poet Lucan tells us in *Pharsalia*, worshipped with human sacrifices shared in by his female consorts, who, we may imagine, were not more merciful than himself or than that Gaulish Taranis whose cult was 'no gentler

---

[1] 'In Munster was worshipped the goddess of prosperity, whose name was Ana, and from her are named the Two Paps of Ana over Luachair Degad.' From *Coir Anmann*, the 'Choice of Names', a sixteenth-century tract.

than that of the Scythian Diana' and who completes Lucan's triad as a fit companion to the 'pitiless Teutates' and the 'horrible Hesus'. Of these warlike goddesses there were five – Fea, the 'Hateful', Nemain, the 'Venomous', Badb, the 'Fury', Macha, a personification of 'battle', and, over all of them, the Morrigan, or Morrígú, the 'Great Queen'. This supreme war goddess of the Gaels, who resembles a fiercer Hera, perhaps symbolised the moon, considered by early races to have preceded the sun and worshipped with magical and cruel rites. She is represented as going fully armed and carrying two spears in her hand. As with Ares and Poseidon in the Iliad, her battle cry was as loud as that of ten thousand men. Wherever there was war, either among gods or men, she, the great queen, was present, either in her own shape or in her favourite disguise, that of a 'hoodie' or carrion crow. An old poem shows her inciting a warrior:

> 'Over his head is shrieking
> A lean hag, quickly hopping
> Over the points of the weapons and shields;
> She is the grey-haired Morrígú.'[1]

With her, Fea and Nemain, Badb and Macha also hovered over the fighters, inspiring them with the madness of battle. All these were sometimes called by the name of 'Badb'. An account of the Battle of Clontarf, fought by Brian Boru in 1014 against the Norsemen, gives a gruesome picture of what the Gaels believed to happen in the spiritual world when battle lowered and men's blood was aflame. 'There arose a wild, impetuous, precipitate, mad, inexorable, furious, dark, lacerating, merciless, combative, contentious *badb*, which was shrieking and fluttering over their heads. And there arose also the satyrs, and sprites, and the maniacs of the valleys, and the witches and goblins and owls, and destroying demons of the air and firmament, and the demoniac phantom host; and they were inciting and sustaining valour and battle with them.' When the fight was over, they revelled among the bodies of the slain; the heads cut off as barbaric trophies were called 'Macha's acorn crop'. These grim creations of the savage mind had immense vitality. While Nuada, the supreme war god, vanished early out of the pantheon – killed by the Fomorii in the great battle fought between them and the gods – Badb and the Morrigan lived

---

[1]   It commemorates the battle of Magh Rath.

on as late as any of the Gaelic deities. Indeed, they may be said to survive still in the superstitious dislike and suspicion shown in all Celtic-speaking countries for their avatar, the hoodie crow.

After Nuada, the greatest of the gods was the Daghda, whose name seems to have meant the 'Good God' or 'Fire of God'. The old Irish tract called 'The Choice of Names' tells us that he was a god of the earth; he had a cauldron called 'The Undry' in which everyone found food in proportion to his merits and from which none went away unsatisfied. He also had a living harp called Uaithne. As he played on it, the seasons came in their order – spring following winter, and summer succeeding spring, autumn coming after summer and, in its turn, giving place to winter. He is represented as of venerable aspect and of simple mind and tastes, very fond of porridge and a valiant consumer of it. In an ancient tale of the Second Battle of Magh Tuireadh in the Harleian manuscript we have a description of his dress. He wore a brown, low-necked tunic that reached only down to his hips and over this a hooded cape that barely covered his shoulders. On his feet and legs were horsehide boots, the hairy side outwards. He carried, or rather drew after him on a wheel, an eight-pronged war club so huge that eight men would have been needed to carry it, and the wheel, as he towed the whole weapon along, made a track like a territorial boundary. Ancient and grey-headed as he was, and sturdy porridge-eater, it will be seen from this that he was a formidable fighter. He did great deeds in the battle between the gods and the Fomorii and on one occasion is even said to have captured single-handed a hundred-legged and four-headed monster called Mata, whom he dragged to the 'Stone of Benn' near the Boyne, killing him there.

Boann was the mother of Oenghus by the Daghda. Boann was connected in legend with the River Boyne, to which, according to the Book of Leinster, she gave its name and, indeed, its very existence. Formerly there was only a well, now called Trinity Well, shaded by nine magic hazel trees. These trees bore crimson nuts, and it was the property of the nuts that whoever ate of them immediately became possessed of the knowledge of everything that was in the world. The story is, in fact, a Gaelic version of the Hebrew myth of the Tree of the Knowledge of Good and Evil. One class of creatures alone had this privilege – divine salmon who lived in the well and swallowed the nuts as they dropped from the trees into the water and thus knew all things and appear in legend as the Salmons of Knowledge. All others, even the highest gods, were forbidden to approach the place. Only Boann, with the proverbial woman's curiosity, dared to disobey this fixed law. She came towards the sacred well, but as she did so its waters rose up at her and drove her away before them in a mighty, rushing flood. She escaped, but the waters never returned. They made the Boyne; and as for the all-knowing inhabitants of the well, they wandered disconsolately through the depths of the river, looking in vain for their lost nuts. One of these salmon was afterwards eaten by the famous Fionn Mac Cumhaill, upon whom all its omniscience descended (*see* Chapter 15, 'Fionn and the Fianna'). This way of accounting for the existence of a river is a favourite one in Irish legend and expresses the Celtic veneration for poetry and science, combined with the warning that they may not be approached without danger. It is told also of the Shannon, which according to the Book of Leinster burst, like the Boyne, from an inviolable well to pursue another presumptuous nymph called Sionan, daughter of Lodan, son of the sea god Lir. Sionan went to a certain well named Connla's Well, which is under the sea – that is, the Land of Youth. 'That is a well,' says the narrative, 'at which are the hazels of wisdom and inspirations, that is, the hazels of the science of poetry, and in the same hour their fruit and their blossom and their foliage break forth, and then fall upon the well in the same shower, which raises upon the water a royal surge of purple.' When Sionan came to the well we are not told what rites or preparation she had omitted, but the angry waters broke forth and overwhelmed her and washed her up on the Shannon shore, where she died, giving to the river its name. This myth of the hazels of inspiration and knowledge and their association with springing water runs through all Irish legend and was finely treated by the Irish poet Æ Russell in the following verses:

'A cabin on the mountain side hid in a grassy nook,
With door and window open wide, where friendly stars may look;
The rabbit shy may patter in, the winds may enter free
Who roam around the mountain throne in living ecstasy.

And when the sun sets dimmed in eve, and purple fills the air,
I think the sacred hazel tree is dropping berries there,
From starry fruitage, waved aloft where Connla's Well o'erflows;
For sure, the immortal waters run through every wind that blows.

I think when Night towers up aloft and shakes the trembling dew,
How every high and lonely thought that thrills my spirit through
Is but a shining berry dropped down through the purple air,
And from the magic tree of life the fruit falls everywhere.

The Daghda had several children, the most important of whom are Brigit,
Oenghus, Midhir, Oghma and Bodb Dearg (Bodb the Red). Of these, Brigit
will already be familiar to readers who know nothing of Celtic mythology.
Originally she was a goddess of fire and the hearth as well as of poetry, which
the Gaels deemed an immaterial, supersensual form of flame. But the early
Christianisers of Ireland adopted the pagan goddess into their roll of saint-
ship, and, thus canonised, she obtained immense popularity as St Bridget or
Bride (*see* Chapter 16, 'The Decline and Fall of the Gods').

Oenghus was called *Mac Oc*, which means the 'Son of the Young' or perhaps the 'Young God'. This most charming of the creations of Celtic mythology is represented as a Gaelic Eros, an eternally youthful exponent of love and
beauty. Like his father, he had a harp, but it was of gold, not oak, as the
Daghda's was, and so sweet was its music that no one could hear and not follow it. His kisses became birds that hovered invisibly over the young men and
maidens of Erin, whispering thoughts of love into their ears. He is chiefly connected with the banks of the Boyne, where he had a 'brugh' or fairy palace,
and many stories are told of his exploits and adventures.

Midhir, also the hero of legends, would seem to have been a god of the underworld, a Gaelic Pluto. As such, he was connected with the Isle of Falga – a
name for what was otherwise, and still is, called the Isle of Man – where he
had a stronghold in which he kept three wonderful cows and a magic cauldron. He was also the owner of the 'Three Cranes of Denial and Churlishness',
which might be described flippantly as personified 'gentle hints'. They stood
beside his door and when anyone approached to ask for hospitality, the first
one said: 'Do not come! do not come!' and the second added: 'Get away! get
away!' while the third chimed in with: 'Go past the house! go past the house!'
These three birds were, however, stolen from Midhir by Aitherne, an avari-
cious poet, to whom they would seem to have been more appropriate than to
their owner, who does not otherwise appear as a churlish and illiberal deity.
On the contrary, he is represented as the victim of others who plundered him
freely. The god Oenghus took away his wife, Etain (see Chapter 11, 'The Gods

in Exile'), while his cows, his cauldron and his beautiful daughter, Blathnad, were carried off as spoil by the heroes or demigods who surrounded King Conchobar in the golden age of Ulster.

Oghma, who appears to have been also called Cermait, that is, the 'honey-mouthed', was the god of literature and eloquence. He married another Etain, the daughter of Dian Cécht, the god of medicine, and had several children who play parts more or less prominent in the mythology of the Gaelic Celts. One of them was called Tuireann, whose three sons murdered the father of the sun god and were compelled as expiation to pay the greatest fine ever heard of – nothing less than the chief treasures of the world (*see* Chapter 8, 'The Gaelic Argonauts'). Another son, Cairbre, became the professional bard of the Tuatha Dé Danaan, while three others reigned for a short time over the divine race. As patron of literature, Oghma was naturally credited with having been the inventor of the famous ogham alphabet. This was an indigenous script of Ireland, which spread afterwards to Great Britain, inscriptions in oghamic characters having been found in Scotland, the Isle of Man, South Wales, Devonshire and at Silchester in Hampshire, the Roman city of Calleva Attrebatum. It was originally intended for inscriptions on upright pillar stones or on wands, the equivalents for letters being notches cut across or strokes made on one of the faces of the angle, the alphabet running as follows:

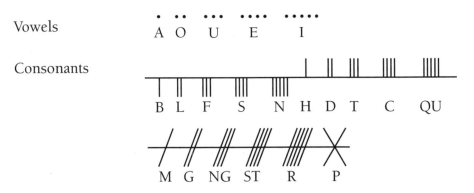

When afterwards written in manuscript, the strokes were placed over, under or through a horizontal line, in the manner above, and the vowels were represented by short lines instead of notches, as:

A good example of an oghamic inscription comes from a pillar on a small promontory near Dunmore Head in west Kerry and, read horizontally, reads:

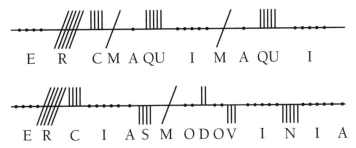

Erc, the son of the son or Erca (descendant of) Modovinia.

The origin of this alphabet is obscure. Some authorities consider it of great antiquity while others believe it entirely post-Christian. It seems, at any rate, to have been based upon, and consequently to presuppose a knowledge of, the Roman alphabet.

Oghma, besides being the patron of literature, was the champion or professional strong man of the Tuatha Dé Danaan. His epithet is *Grianainech*, that is, the 'Sunny-faced', from his radiant and shining countenance.

The last of the Daghda's more important children is Bodb Dearg, Bodb the Red, who plays a greater part in later than in earlier legend. He succeeded his father as king of the gods. He is chiefly connected with the south of Ireland, especially with the Galtee Mountains and with Lough Dearg, where he had a famous *sídh*, or underground palace.

The Poseidon of the Tuatha Dé Danaan pantheon was called Lir or Lêr, but we hear little of him in comparison with his famous son, Manannán, the greatest and most popular of his many children. Manannán Mac Lir was the special patron of sailors, who invoked him as 'God of Headlands' and of merchants, who claimed him as the first of their guild. His favourite haunts were the Isle of Man, to which he gave his name, and the Isle of Arran in the Firth of Clyde, where he had a palace called 'Emain of the Apple Trees'. He had many famous weapons – two spears called Yellow Shaft and Red Javelin, a sword called the Retaliator, which never failed to slay, as well as two others known as the Great Fury and the Little Fury. He had a boat called Wavesweeper, which propelled and guided itself wherever its owner wished, and a horse called Splendid Mane, which was swifter than the spring wind and travelled equally fast on land or over the waves of the sea. No weapon could hurt him through his magic mail and breastplate, and on his helmet there shone two magic jewels bright as the sun. He endowed the gods with the mantle that made them invisible at will, and he fed them from his pigs, which renewed themselves as soon as they had been eaten. Of these, no doubt, he made his Feast of Age, the banquet at which those who ate never grew old. Thus the people of the goddess Danu preserved their immortal youth while the ale of Goibhniu the smith god bestowed invulnerability upon them. It is fitting that Manannán himself should have been blessed beyond all the other gods with inexhaustible life. Up to the latest days of Irish heroic literature his luminous figure shines prominently, nor is it even yet wholly forgotten.

Goibhniu, the Gaelic Hephaestus, who made the people of the goddess Danu invulnerable with his magic drink, was also the forger of their weapons. It was he who, helped by Luchtaine, the divine carpenter, and Creidhne, the divine bronze-worker, made the armoury with which the Tuatha Dé Danaan conquered the Fomorii. Equally useful to them was Dian Cécht, the god of medicine, whose name is explained both in the 'Choice of Names' and in Cormac's *Glossary* as meaning 'God of Health'. It was he who once saved Ireland and was indirectly the cause of the name of the River Barrow. The Morrigan, the heaven god's fierce wife, had borne a son of such terrible aspect that the physician of the gods, foreseeing danger, counselled that he should be destroyed in his infancy. This was done; and Dian Cécht opened the infant's heart and found within it three serpents, capable, when they grew to full size, of depopulating Ireland. He lost no time in destroying these serpents also and burning them to ashes to avoid the evil that even their dead bodies might do. More than this, he flung the ashes into the nearest river, for he feared that there might be danger even in them; and, indeed, so venomous were they that the river boiled up and slew every living creature in it and therefore has been called 'Barrow' (boiling) ever since.

Dian Cécht had several children, of whom two followed their father's profession. These were Midach and his sister Airmid. There were also another daughter, Etain, who married Oghma, and three other sons called Cian, Cethé and Cú. Cian was the father by Ethlinn, the daughter of Balor the Fomor, of a son who was the crowning glory of the Gaelic pantheon – its Apollo, the sun god – Lugh, called Lamhfada, which means the 'Long-handed' or the 'Far-shooter'. It was not, however, with the bow, like the Apollo of the Greeks, but with the rod sling that Lugh performed his feats. His worshippers sometimes

Lugh's Magic Spear, from a drawing by H. R. Millar

saw the terrible weapon in the sky as a rainbow, and the Milky Way was called 'Lugh's Chain'. He also had a magic spear, which, unlike the rod sling, he had no need to wield himself, for it was alive and thirsted so for blood that only by steeping its head in a sleeping draught of pounded poppy leaves could it be kept at rest. When battle was near, it was drawn out and then it roared and struggled against its thongs, fire flashed from it, and, once slipped from the leash, it tore through and through the ranks of the enemy, never tiring of slaying. Another of his possessions was a magic hound that an ancient poem from the Book of Lismore, attributed to the Fiann hero, Caoilté, calls:

> 'That hound of mightiest deeds,
> Which was irresistible in hardness of combat,
> Was better than wealth ever known,
> A ball of fire every night.

> 'Other virtues had that beautiful hound
> (Better this property than any other property),
> Mead or wine would grow of it,
> Should it bathe in spring water.'

This marvellous hound, as well as the marvellous spear and the indestructible pigs of Manannán, were obtained for Lugh by the sons of Tuireann as part of the blood fine he exacted from them for the murder of his father, Cian (see Chapter 8, 'The Gaelic Argonauts'). A hardly less curious story is that which tells how Lugh got his name of the *Ioldanach*, or the 'Master of All Arts' (see Chapter 7, 'The Rise of the Sun God').

These are, of course, only the greater deities of the Gaelic pantheon, their gods and goddesses who answered to such Hellenic figures as Demeter, Zeus, Hera, Cronos, Athena, Eros, Hades, Hermes, Hephaestus, Aesculapius and Apollo. All of them had many descendants, some of whom play prominent parts in the heroic cycles of the 'Red Branch of Ulster' and of the 'Fianna'. In addition to these, there must have been a multitude of lesser gods who stood in much the same relation to the great gods as the rank and file of tribesmen did to their chiefs. Most of these were probably local deities of the various clans – the gods their heroes swore by. It is also possible that some may have been divinities of the aboriginal race, such Iberian gods as Nêt, Ri or Roi, Corb and Beth, but they play no recognisable part in the stories of the Gaelic gods.

Chapter 6

THE GODS ARRIVE

The people of the goddess Danu were not the first divine inhabitants of Ireland. Others had been before them, dwellers in 'the dark backward and abysm of time'. In this the Celtic mythology resembles those of other nations, in almost all of which we find an old, dim realm of gods standing behind the reigning pantheon. Such were Cronos and the Titans, dispossessed by Zeus who seemed, even to Hesiod, something of a *parvenu* deity. Gaelic tradition recognises two divine dynasties prior to the Tuatha Dé Danaan. The first of these was called 'The Race of Partholón'. Partholón, its head and leader, son of Sera, came – as all gods and men came, according to Celtic ideas – from the Otherworld and landed in Ireland with a retinue of twenty-four males and twenty-four females, including his queen, Dealgnaid, on the first of May, the day called 'Beltane', sacred to Bíle, the god of death. At this remote time, Ireland consisted of only one treeless, grassless plain, watered by three lakes and nine rivers. As the race of Partholón increased, however, the land stretched or widened under them – some said miraculously and others by the labours of Partholón's people. At any rate, during the three hundred years they dwelt there, it grew from one plain to four and acquired seven new lakes, which was fortunate, for the race of Partholón increased from forty-eight members to five thousand in spite of battles with the Fomorii.

These would seem to have been inevitable. Whatever gods ruled, they found themselves in eternal opposition to the not-gods – the powers of darkness, winter, evil and death. The race of Partholón warred against them with success. At the Plain of Ith, Partholón defeated their leader, a gigantic demon called Cichol the Footless, and dispersed his deformed and monstrous host. After this there was quiet for three hundred years. Then – on the same fatal first of May – there began a mysterious epidemic, which lasted a week and destroyed them all. In premonition of their end, they foregathered upon the original, first-created plain – then called *Sen Magh*, or the 'Old Plain' – so that those who survived might the more easily bury those who died. Their funeral place is still marked by a mound near Dublin, called Tallaght in maps but formerly known as *Tamlecht Muintre Partholain*, the 'Plague grave of Partholón's People'. This would seem to have been a development of the very oldest form of the legend – which knew nothing of a plague but merely represented the people of Partholón as having returned after their sojourn in Ireland to the Otherworld from which they had come – and is probably the result of the gradual euhemerisation, or transference, of the ancient gods into ancient men.

Following the race of Partholón came the race of Nemedh, which carried on the work and traditions of its forerunner. During its time, Ireland again enlarged herself to the extent of twelve new plains and four more lakes. Like the people of Partholón, the race of Nemedh struggled with the Fomorii and defeated them in four consecutive battles. Then Nemedh died, with two thousand of his people, from an epidemic, and the remnant, left without their leader, were terribly oppressed by the Fomorii. Two Fomorian kings – Morc, son of Dela, and Conan, son of Febar – had built a tower of glass on Tory Island, always their chief stronghold and where stories of them still linger, and from this vantage point they dictated a tax that recalls that paid, in Greek legend, to the Cretan Minotaur. Two-thirds of the children born to the race of Nemedh during the year were to be delivered up on each day of Samhain. Goaded by this to a last desperate effort, the survivors of Nemedh's people attacked the tower and took it, Conan perishing in the struggle. But their triumph was short-lived. Morc, the other king, collected his forces and inflicted such a slaughter on the people of Nemedh that, out of the sixteen thousand who had assembled for the storming of the tower, only thirty survived. And these returned whence they came or died – the two acts being, mythologically speaking, the same.

One cannot help seeing a good deal of similarity between the stories of these two mythical invasions of Ireland. Especially noticeable is the account of the epidemic that destroyed all Partholón's people and nearly all of Nemedh's. Hence it has been held that the two legends are duplicates and that there was at first only one, which has been adapted somewhat differently by two races, the Iberians and the Gaels. The account of Nemedh is thought by some to have been the original Celtic one and the Partholón story the version of it that the native races made to please themselves. The name 'Partholón', with its initial *p*, is entirely foreign to Gaelic speech. Moreover, the early chroniclers give Partholón ancestors whose decidedly non-Aryan names reappear afterwards as the names of Fir Bholg chiefs. Nemedh was later than Partholón in Ireland, as the Gaels, the 'Sons of Mil Espaine', or 'Milesians', were later than the Iberians or 'Fir Bholgs'.

These Fir Bholgs are found in myth as the next colonisers of Ireland. Varying traditions say that they came from Greece or from 'Spain' – which was a post-Christian euphemism for the Celtic Hades. They consisted of three tribes, called the 'Fir Dhomhnann' or 'Men of Domnu', the 'Fir Gailioin' or 'Men of Gailioin' and the 'Fir Bholg' or 'Men of Bolg', but in spite of the fact that the first-named tribe was the most important, they are usually called collectively after the last. Curious stories are told of their life in Greece and how they came to Ireland, but these are somewhat factitious and obviously do not belong to the earliest tradition.

During the time of their domination, we are told, they partitioned Ireland among them: the Fir Bholg held Ulster; the Fir Dhomhnann, divided into three kingdoms, occupied North Munster, South Munster and Connacht; while the Fir Gailioin owned Leinster. These five provinces met at a hill then called 'Balor's Hill' but afterwards the 'Hill of Uisneach'. It is near Rathconrath in the county of West Meath and was believed in early times to mark the exact centre of Ireland. They held the country from the departure of the people of Nemedh to the coming of the people of the goddess Danu, and during this period they had nine supreme kings. At the time of the arrival of the gods, their king's name was Eochaidh, son of Erc, surnamed 'The Proud'.

We have practically no other details regarding their life in Ireland. It is obvious, however, that they were not really gods but the pre-Aryan race that the Gaels, when they landed in Ireland, found already in occupation. There are many instances of peoples at a certain stage of culture regarding tribes in a somewhat lower one as semi-divine or, rather, half-diabolical. The suspicion and fear with which the early Celts must have regarded the savage aborigines made them seem 'larger than human'. They feared them for the weird magical rites that they practised in their inaccessible forts among the hills amid storms and mountain mists. The Gaels, who held themselves to be the children of light, deemed these 'dark Iberians' children of the dark. Their tribal names seem to have been, in several instances, founded on this idea. There were the *Corca-Oidce* ('People of Darkness') and the *Corca-Duibhne* ('People of the Night'). The territory of the western tribe of the *Hi Dorchaide* ('Sons of Dark') was called the 'Night Country'. The Celts, who held their own gods to have preceded them into Ireland, would not believe that even the Tuatha Dé Danaan could have wrested the land from these magic-skilled Iberians without battle.

They seem also to have been considered as in some way connected with the Fomorii. Just as the largest Iberian tribe was called the 'Men of Domnu', so the Fomorii were called the 'Gods of Domnu', and Indech, one of their kings, is a 'son of Domnu'. Thus eternal battle between the gods, children of Danu, and the giants, children of Domnu, would reflect, in the supernatural world, the perpetual warfare between invading Celt and resisting Iberian. It is shadowed, too, in the later heroic cycle. The champions of Ulster, Aryans and Gaels *par excellence*, have no such bitter enemies as the Fir Dhomhnann of Munster and the Fir Gailioin of Leinster. A few scholars would even see in the later death struggle between the High King of Ireland and his rebellious Fianna the last historic or mythological adumbration of racial war.

The enemies alike of Fir Bholg and Fomorii, the Tuatha Dé Danaan, gods of the Gaels, were the next to arrive. What is probably the earliest account tells us that they came from the sky. Later versions, however, give them a habitation on earth – some say in the north, others in the 'southern isles of the world'. They had dwelt in four mythical cities called Finias, Gorias, Murias and Falias, where they had learned poetry and magic – to the primitive mind two not very dissimilar things – and from where they had brought to Ireland their four chief treasures. From Finias came Nuada's sword, from whose stroke no one ever escaped or recovered; from Gorias, Lugh's terrible lance; from Murias, the Daghda's cauldron; and from Falias, the Stone of Fáil, better known as the Stone of Destiny, which afterwards fell into the hands of the early kings of Ireland. According to legend, it had the magic property of uttering a human cry when touched by the rightful King of Erin. Some have recognised in this miraculous stone the same rude block that Edward I brought from Scone in the year 1300 and placed in Westminster Abbey, where until

---

[1] It has been contended that the Fianna were originally the gods or heroes of an aboriginal people in Ireland, the myths about them representing the pre-Celtic and pre-Aryan ideal, as the sagas of the Red Branch of Ulster embodied that of the Celtic Aryans.

1996 it formed part of the Coronation Chair. It is a curious fact that, while Scottish legend asserts this stone to have come to Scotland from Ireland, Irish legend should also declare that it was taken from Ireland to Scotland. This would sound like conclusive evidence, but it was nonetheless held by leading archaeologists that the Stone of Scone and the Stone of Tara were never the same. The real *Lia Fáil* has been identified with a stone that has always remained in Ireland and was removed from its original position on Tara Hill in 1798 to mark the tomb of the rebels buried close by under a mound now known as 'the Croppies' grave'.

Whether the Tuatha Dé Danaan came from earth or heaven, they landed in a dense cloud on the coast of Ireland on the mystic first of May without having been opposed or even noticed by the people whom it will be convenient to follow the Harleian manuscript in calling the Fir Bholgs. In order that they might remain ignorant of the coming of the Tuatha Dé Danaan, the Morrigan, helped by Badb and Macha, made use of the magic they had learned in Finias, Gorias, Murias and Falias. They spread 'druidically formed showers and fog-sustaining shower clouds' over the country and caused the air to pour down fire and blood upon the Fir Bholgs, so that they were obliged to shelter themselves for three days and three nights. But the Fir Bholgs had druids of their own, and in the end they put a stop to these enchantments by counter-spells, and the air grew clear again.

The Tuatha Dé Danaan, advancing westward, had reached a place called the 'Plain of the Sea' in Leinster when the two armies met. Each sent out a warrior to parley. The two adversaries approached each other cautiously, their eyes peeping over the tops of their shields. Then, coming gradually nearer, they spoke to one another, and the desire to examine each other's weapons made them almost friends.

The envoy of the Fir Bholgs looked with wonder at the 'beautifully shaped, thin, slender, long, sharp-pointed spears' of the warrior of the Tuatha Dé Danaan, while the ambassador of the tribe of the goddess Danu was not less impressed by the lances of the Fir Bholgs, which were 'heavy, thick, pointless but sharply rounded'. They agreed to exchange weapons, so that each side might, by an examination of them, be able to come to some opinion as to its opponent's strength. Before parting, the envoy of the Tuatha Dé Danaan offered the Fir Bholgs, through their representative, peace, with a division of the country into two equal halves.

The Fir Bholg envoy advised his people to accept this offer, but their king, Eochaidh, son of Erc, would not. 'If we once give these people half,' he said, 'they will soon have the whole.'

The people of the goddess Danu were, on the other hand, very much impressed by the sight of the Fir Bholgs' weapons. They decided to secure a more advantageous position and, retreating farther west into Connacht, to a plain then called Nia but now Magh Tuireadh, near the present village of Cong, they drew up their line at its extreme end, in front of the pass of Balgatan, now called Benlevi, which offered a retreat in case of defeat.

The Fir Bholgs followed them and encamped on the nearer side of the plain. Then Nuada, King of the Tuatha Dé Danaan, sent an ambassador offering the same terms as before. Again the Fir Bholgs declined them.

'Then when,' asked the envoy, 'do you intend to give battle?'

'We must have a truce,' they said, 'for we want time to repair our armour, burnish our helmets and sharpen our swords. Besides, we must have spears like yours made for us, and you must have spears like ours made for you.'

The result of this chivalrous but, to modern ideas, amazing, parley was that a truce of one hundred and five days was agreed upon.

It was on Midsummer Day that the opposing armies at last met. The people of the goddess Danu appeared in 'a flaming line', wielding their 'red-bordered, speckled and firm shields'. Opposite to them were ranged the Fir Bholgs, 'sparkling, brilliant and flaming, with their swords, spears, blades and trowel spears'. The proceedings began with a kind of deadly hurley match, in which thrice nine of the Tuatha Dé Danaan played the same number of the Fir Bholgs and were defeated and killed. Then followed another parley to decide how the battle should be carried on, whether there should be fighting every day or only on every second day. Moreover, Nuada obtained from Eochaidh an assurance that the battles should always be fought with equal numbers, although this was, we are told, 'very disagreeable to the Fir Bholg king, because he had largely the advantage in the numbers of his army'. Then warfare recommenced with a series of single combats, like those of the Greeks and Trojans in the Iliad. At the end of each day the conquerors on both sides went back to their camps and were refreshed by being bathed in healing baths of medicinal herbs.

So the First Battle of Magh Tuireadh went on for four days, with terrible slaughter on each side. A Fir Bholg champion called Sreng fought in single combat with Nuada, the King of the Gods, and sheared off his hand and half his shield with one terrific blow. Eochaidh, the King of the Fir Bholgs, was even less fortunate than Nuada, for he lost his life. Suffering terribly from thirst, he went with a hundred of his men to look for water, and was followed and pursued as far as the strand of Ballysadare in Sligo. Here he turned to stand his ground but was killed, his grave being still marked by a tumulus. The Fir Bholgs, reduced at last to three hundred men, demanded single combat until all on one side were slain. Sooner than consent to this, however, the Tuatha Dé Danaan offered them a fifth part of Ireland, whichever province they might choose. They agreed and chose Connacht, ever afterwards their special home and where, until the middle of the seventeenth century, men were still to be found who traced their descent from Sreng.

The whole story has a singularly historical, curiously unmythological air about it, which contrasts strangely with the account of the other battle of the same name which the Tuatha Dé Danaan waged afterwards with the Fomorii. The neighbourhood of Cong still preserves both relics and traditions of the fight. On the plain of 'Southern Magh Tuireadh' (as it is called, to distinguish it from the 'Northern Magh Tuireadh' of the second battle) are many circles and tumuli. These circles are especially numerous near the village itself, and it is said that there were formerly others that have been used for making walls and dykes. Large cairns of stones, too, are scattered over what was certainly once the scene of a great battle. These various prehistoric monuments each have their still-told story. The Irish surgeon and antiquary Sir William Wilde, father of Oscar Wilde, relates in his book *Lough Corrib: Its Shores and Islands* that he was impressed by the unexpected agreement between the details of the legendary battle, as he read them in the ancient manuscript, and the traditions still attaching to the mounds, circles and cairns that he tells us he could not help coming to the conclusion that the account was absolutely historical. Certainly the coincidences are curious. His opinion was that the 'Fir Bholgs' were a colony of Belgae and that the 'Tuatha Dé Danaan' were Danes. But the people of the goddess Danu are too obviously mythical to make it worthwhile to seek any standing ground for them in the world of reality. In their superhuman attributes, they are quite different from the Fir Bholgs. In the epic cycle it is made as clear that the Tuatha Dé Danaan are divine beings as it is that the Fir Bholg, the Fir Dhomhnann and the Fir Gailioin stand on exactly the same footing as the men of Ulster. Later history records by which Milesian kings and on what terms of rack-rent the three tribes were allowed settlements in other parts of Ireland than their native Connacht. They appear in ancient, medieval and almost modern chronicles as the old race of the land. The truth seems to be that the whole story of the war between the gods and the Fir Bholgs is an invention of comparatively late times. In the earliest documents there is only one battle of Magh Tuireadh, fought between the people of the goddess Danu and the Fomorii. The idea of doubling it seems to date from after the eleventh century; and its inventor may very well have used the legends concerning this battlefield, where two unknown armies had fought in days gone by, in compiling his story. It never belonged to the same genuine mythological stratum as the legend of the original battle fought by the Tuatha Dé Danaan, the gods of the Gaels, against the Fomorii, the gods of the Iberians.

A very curious and interesting legend is found in the Book of the Dun Cow and is entitled 'The Legend of Tuan Mac Cairell'. It gives its own version of the invasions of Ireland.

St Finnen, an Irish abbot of the sixth century, is said to have gone to seek hospitality from a chief named Tuan Mac Cairell, who dwelt not far from Finnen's monastery at Moville, County Donegal. Tuan refused him admittance. The saint sat down on the doorstep of the chief and fasted for a whole Sunday, upon which the surly pagan warrior opened the door to him. Good relations were established between them, and the saint returned to his monks.

'Tuan is an excellent man,' said he to them. 'He will come to you and comfort you, and tell you the old stories of Ireland.'

This humane interest in the old myths and legends of the country is, it may here be observed, a feature as constant as it is pleasant in the literature of early Irish Christianity.

Tuan came shortly afterwards to return the visit of the saint, and invited him and his disciples to his fortress. They asked him for his name and lineage, and he gave an astounding reply. 'I am a man of Ulster,' he said. 'My name is Tuan son of Cairell. But once 1 was called Tuan son of Starn, son of Sera, and my father, Starn, was the brother of Partholón.'

'Tell us the history of Ireland,' then said Finnen, and Tuan began.

Partholón, he said, was the first of men to settle in Ireland. After the great pestilence he alone survived, 'for there is never a slaughter that one man does not come out of it to tell the tale.' Tuan was alone in the land, and he wandered about from one vacant fortress to another, from rock to rock, seeking shelter from the wolves. For twenty-two years he lived alone, dwelling in waste places, till at last he fell into extreme decrepitude and old age.

'Then Nemedh son of Agnoman took possession of Ireland. He [Agnoman] was my father's brother. I saw him from the cliffs and kept avoiding him. I was long-haired, clawed, decrepit, grey, naked, wretched, miserable. Then one evening I fell asleep, and when I woke again on the morrow I was changed into a stag. I was young again and glad of heart. Then I sang of the coming of Nemedh and of his race, and of my own transformation: "I have put on a new form, a skin rough and grey. Victory and joy are easy to me; a little while ago I was weak and defenceless."'

Tuan is then king of all the deer of Ireland, and so remained all the days of Nemedh and his race.

He tells how the Nemedians sailed for Ireland in a fleet of thirty-two barques, in each barque thirty persons. They went astray on the seas for a year and a half, and most of them perished of hunger and thirst or of shipwreck. Nine only escaped – Nemedh himself, with four men and four women. They landed in Ireland, and increased their number in the course of time till they were 8,060 men and women. Then all of them mysteriously died.

Again old age and decrepitude fell upon Tuan, but another transformation awaited him. 'Once I was standing at the mouth of my cave – I still remember it – and I knew that my body changed into another form. I was a wild boar. And I sang this song about it:

'"Today I am a boar – Time was when I sat in the assembly that gave the judgements of Partholón. It was sun, and all praised the melody. How pleasant was the strain of my brilliant judgement! How pleasant to the comely young women! My chariot went along in majesty and beauty. My voice was grave and sweet. My step was swift and firm in battle. My face was full of charm. Today, lo! I am changed into a black boar."

'That is what I said. Yea, of a surety I was a wild boar. Then I became young again, and I was glad. I was king of the boar herds in Ireland; and, faithful to my custom, I went the rounds of my abode when I returned into the lands of Ulster, at the times old age and wretchedness came upon me. For it was always there that my transformations took place, and that is why I went back thither to await the renewal of my body.'

Tuan then goes on to tell how Semion son of Stariat settled in Ireland, from whom descended the Fir Bholgs and two other tribes who persisted into historic times. Again old age comes on, his strength fails him, and he undergoes another transformation; he becomes 'a great eagle of the sea' and once more rejoices in renewed youth and vigour. He then tells how the Tuatha Dé Danaan, the People of Dana, came in, 'gods and false gods from whom everyone knows the Irish men of learning are sprung'. After these came the Sons of Mil Espaine, who conquered the Tuatha Dé Danaan. All this time Tuan kept the shape of the sea eagle, till one day, finding himself about to undergo another transformation, he fasted nine days, 'then sleep fell upon me, and I was changed into a salmon.' He rejoices in his new life, escaping for many years the snares of the fishermen, till at last he is captured by one of them and brought to the wife of Cairell, chief of the country. 'The woman desired me and ate me by herself, whole, so that I passed into her womb.' He is born again, and passes for Tuan son of Cairell, but the memory of his pre-existence and all his transformations and all the history of Ireland that he witnessed since the days of Partholón still abide with him, and he teaches all these things to the Christian monks, who carefully preserve them.

This wild tale, with its atmosphere of grey antiquity and of childlike wonder, reminds us of the transformations of the Welsh Taliesin, who also became an eagle, and points to that doctrine of the transmigration of the soul which haunted the imagination of the Celt.

Chapter 7

The Rise of the Sun God

The principal sources of information for this chapter are translations of the Harleian manuscript entitled *The Second Battle of Moytura.*.

It was as a result of the loss of his hand in this battle with the Fir Bholgs that Nuada got his name of Argetlámh, that is, the 'Silver-Handed'. For Dian Cécht, the physician of the Tuatha Dé Danaan, made him an artificial hand of silver so skilfully that it moved in all its joints and was as strong and supple as a real one. But, good as it was of its sort, it was a blemish, and, according to Celtic custom, no maimed person could sit on the throne. Nuada was deposed, and the Tuatha Dé Danaan went into council to appoint a new king.

They agreed that it would be a politic thing for them to conciliate the Fomorii, the giants of the sea, and make an alliance with them. So they sent a message to Bres, the son of the Fomorian king, Elathan, asking him to come and rule over them. Bres accepted this offer, and they made a marriage between him and Brigit, the daughter of the Daghda. At the same time, Cian, the son of Dian Cécht, the physician of the Tuatha Dé Danaan, had a son, Lugh, by Ethlinn, the daughter of the Fomor, Balor. Then Bres was made king and endowed with lands and a palace, and he, on his part, gave hostages that he would abdicate if his rule ever became unpleasing to those who had elected him.

But in spite of all his fair promises, Bres, who belonged in heart to his own fierce people, began to oppress his subjects with excessive taxes. He put a tax on every hearth, on every kneading trough and on every quern, as well as a poll tax of an ounce of gold on every member of the Tuatha Dé Danaan. By a crafty trick, too, he obtained the milk of all their cattle. He asked at first only for the produce of any cows that happened to be brown and hairless, and the people of the goddess Danu granted him this cheerfully, but Bres passed all the cattle in Ireland between two fires, so that their hair was singed off, and thus obtained the monopoly of the main source of food. To earn a livelihood, all the gods, even the greatest, were now forced to labour for him. Oghma, their champion, was sent out to collect firewood, while the Daghda was put to work building forts and castles.

One day, when the Daghda was at his task, his son Oenghus came to him. 'You have nearly finished that castle,' he said. 'What reward do you intend to ask from Bres when it is done?'

The Daghda replied that he had not yet thought of it.

'Let me give you some advice,' said Oenghus. 'Ask Bres to have all the cattle in Ireland gathered together upon a plain, so that you can pick out one for yourself. He will consent to that. Then choose the black-maned heifer called "Ocean".'

The Daghda finished building the fort and then went to Bres for his reward. 'What will you have?' asked Bres.

'I want all the cattle in Ireland gathered together upon a plain, so that I may choose one of them for myself.'

Bres did this, and the Daghda took the black-maned heifer Oenghus had told him of. The king, who had expected to be asked very much more, laughed at what he thought was the Daghda's simplicity. But Oenghus had been wise; as will be seen later.

Meanwhile Bres was infuriating the people of the goddess Danu by adding avarice to tyranny. It was for kings to be liberal to all-comers, but at the court of Bres no one ever greased his knife with fat or made his breath smell of ale. Nor were there ever any poets or musicians or jugglers or jesters there to give pleasure to the people, for Bres would distribute no largess. Next, he cut down the very subsistence of the gods. So scanty was his allowance of food that they began to grow weak with famine. Oghma, through feebleness, could carry only one-third of the wood needed for fuel, so that they suffered from cold as well as from hunger.

It was at this crisis that two physicians, Midach, the son, and Airmid, the daughter, of Dian Cécht, the god of medicine, came to the castle where the dispossessed King Nuada lived. Nuada's porter, blemished, like himself (for he had lost an eye), was sitting at the gate, and on his lap was a cat curled up asleep. The porter asked the strangers who they were.

'We are good doctors,' they said.

'If that is so,' he replied, 'perhaps you can give me a new eye.'

'Certainly,' they said. 'We could take one of the eyes of that cat and put it in the place where your lost eye used to be.'

'I should be very pleased if you would do that,' answered the porter, so Midach and Airmid removed one of the cat's eyes and put it in the hollow where the man's eye had been.

The story goes on to say that this was not wholly a benefit to him, for the eye retained its cat's nature and, when the man wished to sleep at nights, the cat's eye was always looking out for mice, while it could hardly be kept awake during the day. Nevertheless, he was pleased at the time, and went and told Nuada, who commanded that the doctors who had performed this marvellous cure should be brought to him.

As they came in, they heard the king groaning, for Nuada's wrist had festered where the silver hand joined the arm of flesh. Midach asked where Nuada's own hand was, and they told him that it had been buried long ago. But Midach dug it up, placed it to Nuada's stump and uttered an incantation over it, saying: 'Sinew to sinew, and nerve to nerve be joined!' and in three days and nights the hand had renewed itself and fixed itself to the arm, so that Nuada was whole again.

When Dian Cécht, Midach's father, heard of this he was very angry to think that his son should have excelled him in the art of medicine. He sent for him and struck him on the head with a sword, cutting the skin but not wounding the flesh. Midach easily healed this. So Dian Cécht hit him again, this time to the bone. Again Midach cured himself. The third time his father smote him, the sword went right through the skull to the membrane of the brain, but even this wound Midach was able to cure. At the fourth stroke, however, Dian Cécht cut the brain in two, and Midach could do nothing for that. He died, and Dian Cécht buried him. And on his grave there grew up three hundred and sixty-five stalks of grass, each one a cure for any illness of each of the three hundred and sixty-five nerves in a person's body. Airmid, Midach's sister, plucked all these very carefully and arranged them on her mantle according to their properties. But her angry and jealous father overturned the cloak and hopelessly confused them. If it had not been for that act, says the early writer, men would know how to cure every illness and so would be immortal.

The healing of Nuada's blemish happened just at the time when all the people of the goddess Danu had at last agreed that the exactions and tyranny of

Bres could no longer be borne. It was the insult he put upon Cairbre, son of Oghma, the god of literature, that caused things to come to this head. Poets were always held by the Celts in great honour, and when Cairbre, the bard of the Tuatha Dé Danaan, went to visit Bres, he expected to be treated with much consideration and fed at the king's own table. Instead of doing so, however, Bres lodged him in a small, dark room where there was no fire, no bed and no furniture except a mean table on which small cakes of dry bread were put on a little dish for his food. The next morning, Cairbre rose early and left the palace without having spoken to Bres. It was the custom of poets when they left a king's court to utter a panegyric on their host, but Cairbre treated Bres instead to a magical satire. It was the first satire ever made in Ireland and seems to us to bear upon it all the marks of an early effort. Roughly rendered, it said:

> 'No meat on the plates,
>   No milk of the cows;
> No shelter for the belated;
>   No money for the minstrels:
> May Bres's cheer be what he gives to others!'

This satire of Cairbre's was, we are assured, so virulent that it caused great red blotches to break out all over Bres's face. This in itself constituted a blemish such as should not be upon a king, and the Tuatha Dé Danaan called upon Bres to abdicate and let Nuada take the throne again.

Bres was obliged to do so. He went back to the country of the Fomorii, underneath the sea, and complained to his father, Elathan, its king, asking him to gather an army to reconquer his throne. The Fomorii assembled in council – Elathan, Tethra, Balor, Indech, and all the other warriors and chiefs – and they decided to come with a great host and take Ireland away and put it under the sea where the people of the goddess Danu would never be able to find it again.

At the same time, another assembly was also being held at Tara, the capital of the Tuatha Dé Danaan. Nuada was celebrating his return to the throne with a feast for his people. While it was at its height, a stranger clothed like a king came to the palace gate. The porter asked him his name and errand.

'I am called Lugh,' he said. 'I am the grandson of Dian Cécht by Cian, my father, and the grandson of Balor by Ethlinn, my mother.'

'But what is your profession?' asked the porter, 'for no one is admitted here unless he is a master of some craft.'

'I am a carpenter,' said Lugh.

'We have no need of a carpenter. We already have a very good one. His name is Luchtaine.'

'I am an excellent smith,' said Lugh.

'We do not want a smith. We have a very good one. His name is Goibhniu.'

'I am a professional warrior,' said Lugh.

'We have no need of one. Oghma is our champion.'

'I am a harpist,' said Lugh.

'We have an excellent harpist already.'

'I am a warrior renowned for skilfulness rather than for mere strength.'

'We already have a man like that.'

'I am a poet and tale-teller,' said Lugh.

'We have no need of such. We have a most accomplished poet and tale-teller.'

'I am a sorcerer,' said Lugh.

'We do not want one. We have numberless sorcerers and druids.'

'I am a physician,' said Lugh.

'Dian Cécht is our physician.'

'I am a cup-bearer,' said Lugh.

'We already have nine of them.'

'I am a worker in bronze.'

'We have no need of you. We already have a worker in bronze. His name is Creidhne.'

'Then ask the king,' said Lugh, 'if he has with him a man who is master of all these crafts at once, for, if he has, there is no need for me to come to Tara.'

So the doorkeeper went inside and told the king that a man had come who called himself Lugh the Ioldanach, or the 'Master of all Arts', and that he claimed to know everything.

The king sent out his best chess-player to play against the stranger. Lugh won, inventing a new move called 'Lugh's enclosure'.

Then Nuada invited him in. Lugh entered and sat down on the chair called the 'sage's seat', kept for the wisest man.

Oghma, the champion, was showing off his strength. Upon the floor was a flagstone so large that four score yokes of oxen would have been needed to move it. Oghma pushed it before him along the hall and out at the door. Then

Lugh's Enclosure, from a painting by E. Wallcousins

Lugh rose from his chair and pushed it back again. But this stone, huge as it was, was only a portion broken from a still greater rock outside the palace. Lugh picked it up and put it back into its place.

The Tuatha Dé Danaan asked him to play the harp for them. So he played the 'sleep tune', and the king and all his court fell asleep and did not wake until the same hour of the following day. Next he played a plaintive air, and they all wept. Lastly, he played a measure that sent them into transports of joy.

When Nuada had seen all these numerous talents of Lugh, he began to wonder whether one so gifted would not be of great help against the Fomorii. He took counsel with the others and, by their advice, lent his throne to Lugh for thirteen days, taking the 'sage's seat' at his side.

Lugh summoned all the Tuatha Dé Danaan to a council.

'The Fomorii are certainly going to make war on us,' he said. 'What can each of you do to help'?'

Dian Cécht the physician said: 'I will completely cure everyone who is wounded, provided his head is not cut off or his brain or spinal marrow hurt.'

'I,' said Goibhniu the smith, 'will replace every broken lance and sword with a new one, even though the war last seven years. And I will make the lances so well that they shall never miss their mark or fail to kill. Dulb, the smith of the Fomorii, cannot do as much as that. The fate of the fighting will be decided by my lances.'

'And I,' said Creidhne the bronze-worker, 'will furnish all the rivets for the lances, the hilts for the swords, and the rims and bosses for the shields.'

'And I,' said Luchtaine the carpenter, 'will provide all the shields and lance shafts.'

Oghma the champion promised to kill the King of the Fomorii, with thrice nine of his followers, and to capture one-third of his army.

'And you, O Daghda,' said Lugh, 'what will you do?'

'I will fight,' said the Daghda, 'both with force and craft. Wherever the two armies meet, I will crush the bones of the Fomorii with my club, till they are like hailstones under a horse's feet.'

'And you, O Morrigan?' said Lugh.

'I will pursue them when they flee,' she replied. 'And I always catch what I chase.'

'And you, O Cairbre, son of Etain?' said Lugh to the poet. 'What can you do?'

'I will pronounce an immediately effective curse upon them. By one of my satires I will take away all their honour, and, enchanted by me, they shall not be able to stand against our warriors.'

'And you, O sorcerers, what will you do?'

'We will hurl by our magic arts,' replied Mathgan, the head sorcerer, 'the twelve mountains of Ireland at the Fomorii. These mountains will be Slieve League, Denna Ulad, the Mourne Mountains, Bri Ruri, Slieve Bloom, Slieve Snechta, Slemish, Blai-Sliab, Nephin, Sliab Maccu Belgodon, Segais[1] and Cruachan Aigle.[2]'

Then Lugh asked the cup-bearers what they would do.

'We will hide away by magic,' they said, 'the twelve chief lakes and the twelve chief rivers of Ireland from the Fomorii, so that they shall not be able to find any water, however thirsty they may be. Those waters will conceal themselves from the Fomorii so that they shall not get a drop, while they will give drink to the people of the goddess Danu as long as the war lasts, even if it last seven years.' And they told Lugh that the twelve chief lakes were Lough Derg, Lough Luimnigh,[3] Lough Corrib, Lough Ree, Lough Mask, Strangford Lough, Lough Laeig, Lough Neagh, Lough Foyle, Lough Gara, Lough Reagh and Márloch, and that the twelve chief rivers were the Bush, the Boyne, the Bann, the Nem, the Lee, the Shannon, the Moy, the Sligo, the Erne, the Finn, the Liffey and the Suir.

Finally, the druid, Figol, son of Mamos, said: 'I will send three streams of fire into the faces of the Fomorii, and I will take away two-thirds of their valour and strength, but every breath drawn by the people of the goddess Danu will only make them more valorous and strong, so that even if the fighting lasts seven years, they will not be weary of it.'

All decided to make ready for a war, and to give the direction of it to Lugh.

---

[1]   The Curlieu Hills between Roscommon and Sligo.
[2]   Croagh Patrick.
[3]   The estuary of the Shannon.

Chapter 8

THE GAELIC ARGONAUTS

The preparations for this war are said to have lasted seven years. It was during this interval that there befell an episode that might almost be called the Argonautica of the Gaelic mythology, a story that is mentioned in the ninth-century 'Cormac's Glossary' and also in various Irish and Scottish manuscripts, including the Book of Lecan.

In spite of the dethronement of Bres, the Fomorii still claimed their annual tribute from the tribe of the goddess Danu and sent their tax-gatherers, nine times nine in number, to 'Balor's Hill' to collect it, but while they waited for the gods to come to tender their submission and their subsidy, they saw a young man approaching them. He was riding upon Splendid Mane, the horse of Manannán son of Lir, and was dressed in Manannán's breastplate and helmet, through which no weapon could wound their wearer, and he was armed with sword and shield and poisoned darts. 'Like to the setting sun,' says the story, 'was the splendour of his countenance and his forehead, and they were not able to look in his face for the greatness of his splendour.' And no wonder! for he was Lugh the Far-shooter, the new-come sun god of the Gaels. He fell upon the Fomorian tax-gatherers, killing all but nine of them, and these he spared only that they might go back to their kinsmen and tell how the gods had received them.

There was consternation in the undersea country.

'Who can this terrible warrior be?' asked Balor.

'I know,' said Balor's wife. 'He must be the son of our daughter Ethlinn, and I foretell that, since he has cast in his lot with his father's people, we shall never bear rule in Erin again.'

The chiefs of the Fomorii saw that this slaughter of their tax-gatherers signified that the Tuatha Dé Danaan meant fighting. They held a council to debate it. There came to it Elathan and Tethra and Indech, kings of the Fomorii; Bres himself, and Balor of the stout blows; Cethlenn the crooked tooth, Balor's wife; Balor's twelve white-mouthed sons; and all the chief Fomorian warriors and druids.

Meanwhile, upon earth, Lugh was sending messengers all over Erin to assemble the Tuatha Dé Danaan. Upon this errand went Lugh's father, Cian, who seems to have been a kind of lesser solar deity, son of Dian Cécht, the god of medicine. As Cian was going over the plain of Muirthemne,[1] he saw three armed warriors approaching him, and when they got nearer he recognised them as the three sons of Tuireann, son of Oghma, whose names were Brian, Iuchar and Iucharba. Between these three and Cian, with his brothers, Cethé and Cú, there was, for some reason, a private enmity. Cian saw that he was now at a disadvantage. 'If my brothers were with me,' he said to himself, 'what a fight we would make, but as I am alone it will be best for me to conceal myself.' Looking round, he saw a herd of pigs feeding on the plain. Like all the gods, he had the faculty of shape-shifting, so, striking himself with a magic wand, he changed himself into a pig, joined the herd and began feeding with them.

But he had been seen by the sons of Tuireann. 'What has become of the warrior who was walking on the plain a moment ago?' said Brian to his brothers.

'We saw him then,' they replied, 'but we do not know where he is now.'

'Then you have not used the proper vigilance which is needed in time of war,' said the elder brother. 'However, I know what has become of him. He has struck himself with a druidical wand and changed himself into a pig, and there he is, in that herd, rooting up the ground, just like all the other pigs. I can also tell you who he is. His name is Cian, and you know that he is no friend of ours.'

'It is a pity that he has taken refuge among the pigs,' they replied, 'for they belong to some one of the Tuatha Dé Danaan, and even if we were to kill them all Cian might still escape us.'

Again Brian reproached his brothers. 'You are very ignorant,' he said, 'if you cannot distinguish a magical beast from a natural beast. However, I will show you.' And he struck his two brothers with his own wand of shape-changing

---

[1] A part of County Louth between the Boyne and Dundalk. The heroic cycle connects it especially with Cúchulainn.

and turned them into two swift, slender hounds and set them upon the pigs.

The magic hounds soon found the magic pig and drove it out of the herd on to the open plain. Then Brian threw his spear and hit it. The wounded pig came to a stop. 'It was an evil deed of yours, casting that spear,' it cried in a human voice, 'for I am not a pig, but Cian, son of Dian Cécht. So give me quarter.'

Iuchar and Iucharba would have granted it and let him go, but their fiercer brother swore that Cian should be put an end to, even if he came back to life seven times. So Cian tried a fresh ruse. 'Give me leave,' he asked, 'only to re- turn to my own shape before you slay me.'

'Gladly,' replied Brian, 'for I would much rather kill a man than a pig.'

So Cian spoke the befitting spell, cast off his pig's disguise and stood before them in his own shape. 'You will be obliged to spare my life now,' he said.

'We will not,' replied Brian.

'Then it will be the worst day's work for all of you that you ever did in your lives,' he answered, 'for if you had killed me in the shape of a pig, you would only have had to pay the value of a pig, but if you kill me now, I tell you that there never has been, and there never will be, anyone killed in this world for whose death a greater blood fine will be exacted than for mine.'

But the sons of Tuireann would not listen to him. They slew him and pounded his body with stones until it was a crushed mass. Six times they tried to bury him, and the earth cast him back in horror, but the seventh time the mould held him, and they put stones upon him to keep him down. They left him buried there and went to Tara.

Meanwhile Lugh had been expecting his father's return. As he did not come, he determined to go and look for him. He traced him to the Plain of Muirthemne, and there he was at fault. But the indignant earth itself, which had witnessed the murder, spoke to Lugh and told him everything. So Lugh dug up his father's corpse and made certain how he had come to his death, then he mourned over him and laid him back in the earth, and heaped a bar- row over him and set up a pillar with his name on it in ogham.[1]

He went back to Tara and entered the great hall. It was filled with the peo- ple of the goddess Danu, and among them Lugh saw the three sons of Tuireann. So he shook the 'chiefs' chain', with which the Gaels used to ask for

---

[1] There is known to have been a hill called Ard Chein (Cian's Mound) in the district of Muirthemne, and it has been tentatively identified with one now called Dromslian.

a hearing in an assembly, and when all were silent, he said:

'People of the goddess Danu, I ask you a question. What would be the vengeance that any of you would take upon one who had murdered his father?'

A great astonishment fell upon them, and Nuada, their king, said: 'Surely it is not your father who has been murdered?'

'It is,' replied Lugh, 'and I am looking at those who murdered him, and they know how they did it better than I do.'

Then Nuada declared that nothing short of hewing the murderer of his father limb from limb would satisfy him, and all the others said the same, including the sons of Tuireann.

'The very ones who did the deed say that,' cried Lugh. 'Then let them not leave the hall till they have settled with me about the blood fine to be paid.'

'If it was I who had killed your father,' said the king, 'I should think myself lucky if you were willing to accept a fine instead of vengeance.'

The sons of Tuireann took counsel together in whispers. Iuchar and Iucharba were in favour of admitting their guilt, but Brian was afraid that if they confessed Lugh would withdraw his offer to accept a fine and would demand their deaths. So he stood out and said that although it was not they who had killed Cian yet sooner than remain under Lugh's anger, as he suspected them, they would pay the same fine as if they had.

'Certainly you shall pay the fine,' said Lugh, 'and I will tell you what it shall be. It is this: three apples and a pig's skin, and a spear and two horses and a chariot, and seven pigs and a hound whelp, and a cooking spit, and three shouts on a hill: that is the fine, and if you think it is too much I will remit some of it, but if you do not think it is too much then pay it.'

'If it were a hundred times that,' replied Brian, 'we should not think it too much. Indeed, it seems so little that I fear there must be some treachery concealed in it.'

'I do not think it too little,' replied Lugh. 'Give me your pledge before the people of the goddess Danu that you will pay it faithfully and I will give you mine that I will ask no more.'

So the sons of Tuireann bound themselves before the Tuatha Dé Danaan to pay the fine to Lugh.

When they had sworn and given sureties, Lugh turned to them again. 'I will now,' he said, 'explain to you the nature of the fine you have pledged yourselves to pay me, so that you may know whether it is too little or not'

And, with foreboding hearts, the sons of Tuireann set themselves to listen.

'The three apples that I have demanded,' he began, 'are three apples from the Garden of the Hesperides in the east of the world. You will know them by three signs. They are the size of the head of a month-old child, they are of the colour of burnished gold, and they taste of honey. Wounds are healed and diseases cured by eating them, and they do not diminish in any way by being eaten. Whoever casts one of them hits anything he wishes and then it comes back into his hand. I will accept no other apples instead of these. Their owners keep them perpetually guarded because of a prophecy that three young warriors from the west of the world will come to take them by force, and, brave as you may be, I do not think that you will ever get them.

'The pig's skin that I have demanded is the pig's skin of Tuis, King of Greece. It has two virtues: its touch perfectly cures all wounded or sick persons if only there is any life still left in them, and every stream of water through which it passes is turned into wine for nine days. I do not think that you will get it from the King of Greece, either with his consent or without it. And can you guess what spear it is that I have demanded?' asked Lugh.

'We cannot,' they said.

'It is the poisoned spear of Pisear, King of Persia. It is irresistible in battle; it is so fiery that its blade must always be held under water lest it destroy the city in which it is kept. You will find it very difficult to obtain.

'And the two horses and the chariot are the two wonderful horses of Dobhar, King of Sicily, which run equally well over land and sea. There are no other horses in the world like them, and no other vehicle equal to the chariot.

'And the seven pigs are the pigs of Easal, King of the Golden Pillars. Although they may be killed every night, they are found alive again the next day, and every person that eats part of them can never be afflicted with any disease.

'And the hound whelp I claim is the hound whelp of the King of Ioruaidhe. Her name is Failinis, and every wild beast she sees she catches at once. It will not be easy for you to secure her.

'The cooking spit that you must get for me is one of the cooking spits of the women of the Island of Fianchuivé, which is at the bottom of the sea between Erin and Alba.

'You have also pledged yourselves to give three shouts upon a hill. The hill

---

[1] The *Hill* (cnoc) of *Midkena*.

upon which they must be given is the hill called Cnoc Miodhchaoin,[1] in the north of Lochlann.[2] Miodhchaoin and his sons do not allow shouts to be given on that hill. Besides this, it was they who gave my father his military education, and even if I were to forgive you, they would not, so that, although you achieve all the other adventures, I think that you will fail in this one.

'Now you know what sort of a fine it is that you have bargained to pay me,' said Lugh.

And fear and astonishment fell upon the sons of Tuireann.

This tale is evidently the work of some ancient Irish storyteller who wished to compile from various sources a more or less complete account of how the Gaelic gods obtained their legendary possessions. The spear of Pisear, King of Persia, is obviously the same weapon as the lance of Lugh, which another tradition describes as having been brought by the Tuatha Dé Danaan from their original home in the city of Gorias; Failinis, the whelp of the King of Ioruaidhe, is Lugh's 'hound of mightiest deeds', which was irresistible in battle and turned any running water it bathed in into wine, a property here transferred to the magic pig's skin of King Tuis; and the seven swine of the King of the Golden Pillars must be the same undying porkers from whose flesh Manannán Mac Lir made the 'Feast of Age', which preserved the eternal youth of the gods (*see* Chapter 6, The Gods Arrive'). It was with horses and chariot that ran along the surface of the sea that Manannán used to journey to and fro between Erin and the Celtic Elysium in the West, and the apples that grew in the Garden of the Hesperides were surely of the same celestial growth as those that fed the inhabitants of that immortal country (*see* Chapter 11, 'The Gods in Exile), while the cooking spit reminds us of three such implements at Tara, made by Goibhniu and associated with the names of the Daghda and the Morrigan.

The burden of collecting all these treasures was placed upon the shoulders of the three sons of Tuireann.

They consulted together and agreed that they could never hope to succeed unless they had Manannán's magic horse, Splendid Mane, and Manannán's magic coracle, Wave-sweeper, but both these had been lent by Manannán to Lugh himself. So the sons of Tuireann were obliged to humble themselves to beg them from Lugh. The sun god would not lend them the horse for fear of making their task too easy, but he let them have the boat, because he knew

[2]   A mythical country inhabited by Fomorii.

how much the spear of Pisear and the horses of Dobhar would be needed in the coming war with the Fomorii. They bade farewell to their father and went down to the shore and put out to sea, taking their sister with them.

'Which portion of the fine shall we seek first?' said the others to Brian.

'We will seek them in the order in which they were demanded,' he replied, so they directed the magic boat to sail to the Garden of the Hesperides, and presently they arrived there.

They landed at a harbour and held a council of war. It was decided that their best chance of obtaining three of the apples would be by taking the shapes of hawks. Thus they would have strength enough in their claws to carry the apples away, together with sufficient quickness upon the wing to hope to escape the arrows, darts and sling stones that would be shot and hurled at them by the warders of the garden.

They swooped down upon the orchard from above. It was done so swiftly that they carried off the three apples, unhit either by shaft or stone. But their difficulties were not yet over. The king of the country had three daughters who were well skilled in witchcraft. By sorcery they changed themselves into three ospreys and pursued the three hawks. But the sons of Tuireann reached the shore first and, changing themselves into swans, dived into the sea. They came up close to their coracle and got into it and sailed swiftly away with the spoil.

Thus their first quest was finished, and they voyaged on to Greece to seek the pig's skin of King Tuis. No one could go without some excuse into a king's court, so they decided to disguise themselves as poets and to tell the door-keeper that they were professional bards from Erin, seeking largesse at the hands of kings. The porter let them into the great hall, where the poets of Greece were singing before the king.

When those had all finished, Brian rose and asked permission to show his art. This was accorded; and he sang:

> 'O Tuis, we conceal not thy fame.
> We praise thee as the oak above the kings;
> The skin of a pig, bounty without hardness!
> This is the reward which I ask for it.
>
> 'A stormy host and raging sea

81

> Are a dangerous power, should one oppose it.
> The skill of a pig, bounty without hardness!
> This is the reward I ask, O Tuis.'

'That is a good poem,' said the king, 'only I do not understand it.'

'I will explain it,' said Brian. '"We praise thee as the oak above the kings", this means that, as the oak excels all other trees, so do you excel all other kings in nobility and generosity. "The skin of a pig, bounty without hardness", that is a pig's skin which you have, O Tuis, and which I should like to receive as the reward of my poem. "A stormy host and raging sea are a dangerous power, should one oppose it", this means to say that we are not used to going without anything on which we have set our hearts, O Tuis.'

'I should have liked your poem better,' replied the king, 'if my pig's skin had not been mentioned in it. It was not a wise thing for you to have done, O poet. But I will measure three fills of red gold out of the skin, and you shall have those.'

'May all good be thine, O King!' answered Brian. 'I knew that I should get a noble reward.'

So the king sent for the pig's skin to measure out the gold with, but as soon as Brian saw it, he seized it with his left hand and slew the man who was holding it, and Iuchar and Iucharba also hacked about them, and they cut their way down to the boat, leaving the King of Greece among the dead behind them.

'And now we will go and get King Pisear's spear,' said Brian, so, leaving Greece, they sailed in their coracle to Persia.

Their plan of disguising themselves as poets had served them so well that they decided to make use of it again. So they went into the King of Persia's hall in the same way as they had entered that of the King of Greece. Brian first listened to the poets of Persia singing, then he sang his own song:

> 'Small the esteem of any spear with Pisear;
> The battles of foes are broken;
> No oppression to Pisear;
> Everyone whom he wounds.
>
> 'A yew tree, the finest of the wood,
> It is called King without opposition.
> May that splendid shaft drive on

Brian seizes the Pig's Skin, from a painting by J. H. F. Bacon ARA

Yon crowd into their wounds of death.'

'That is a good poem, O man of Erin,' said the king, 'but why is my spear mentioned in it?'

'The meaning is this,' replied Brian: 'I should like to receive that spear as a reward for my poem.'

'You make a rash request,' said the king. 'If I spare your life after having heard it, it will be a sufficient reward for your poem.'

Brian had one of the magic apples in his hand, and he remembered its boomerang-like quality. He hurled it full in the King of Persia's face, dashing out his brains. The Persians flew to arms, but the three sons of Tuireann conquered them and made them yield up the spear.

They had now to travel to Sicily to obtain the horses and chariot of King Dobhar, but they were afraid to go as poets this time for fear that the fame of their deeds might have got abroad. They therefore decided to pretend to be mercenary soldiers from Erin and offer the King of Sicily their service. This, they thought, would be the easiest way of finding out where the horses and the chariot were kept. So they went and stood on the green before the royal court.

When the King of Sicily heard that there had come mercenaries from Erin seeking wages from the kings of the world, he invited them to take service with him. They agreed; but although they stayed with him a fortnight and a month, they never saw the horses or even found out where they were kept. So they went to the king, and announced that they wished to leave him.

'Why?' he asked, for he did not want them to go.

'We will tell you, O King!' replied Brian. 'It is because we have not been honoured with your confidence, as we have been accustomed with other kings. You have two horses and a chariot, the best in the world, and we have not even been allowed to see them.'

'I would have shown them to you on the first day if you had asked me,' said the king, 'and you shall see them at once, for I have seldom had warriors with me so good as you are, and I do not wish you to leave me.'

So he sent for the steeds and had them yoked to the chariot, and the sons of Tuireann were witnesses of their marvellous speed and how they could run equally well over land or water.

Brian made a sign to his brothers, and they watched their opportunity carefully. As the chariot passed close beside them, Brian leaped into it, hurling its driver over the side. Then, turning the horses, he struck King Dobhar with Pisear's spear and killed him. He took his two brothers up into the chariot and they drove away.

By the time the sons of Tuireann reached the country of Easal, King of the Pillars of Gold, rumour had gone before them. The king came down to the harbour to meet them and asked them if it were really true that so many kings had fallen at their hands. They replied that it was true but that they had no quarrel with any of them, only they must obtain at all costs the fine demanded by Lugh. Then Easal asked them why they had come to his land, and they told him that they needed his seven pigs to add to the tribute. So Easal thought it better to give them up and to make friends with the three sons of Tuireann than to fight with such warriors. The sons of Tuireann were very glad at this, for they were growing weary of battles.

It happened that the King of Ioruaidhe, who had the hound whelp that Lugh had demanded, was the husband of King Easal's daughter. Therefore King Easal did not wish that there should be fighting between him and the three sons of Tuireann. He proposed to Brian and his brothers that he should sail with them to Ioruaidhe and try to persuade the king of the country to give up the hound whelp peacefully. They consented, and all set foot safely on the 'delightful, wonderful shores of Ioruaidhe',[1] as the manuscript calls them. But King Easal's son-in-law would not listen to reason. He assembled his warriors and fought, but the sons of Tuireann defeated them and compelled their king to yield up the hound whelp as the ransom for his life.

All these quests had been upon the earth, but the next was harder. No coracle, not even Manannán's Wave-sweeper, could penetrate to the Island of Fianchuivé, in the depths of the sea that severs Erin from Alba. So Brian left his brothers and put on his 'water dress, with his transparency of glass upon his head' – evidently an ancient Irish anticipation of a diver's outfit. Thus equipped, he explored the bottom of the sea for fourteen days before he found the island. But when at last he reached it and entered the hall of its queen, she and her sea maidens were so amazed at Brian's hardihood in having penetrated to their kingdom that they presented him with the cooking spit and sent him back safe.

---

[1] The country seems to have been identified with Norway or Iceland.

By this time, Lugh had found out by his magic arts that the sons of Tuireann had obtained all the treasures he had demanded as the blood fine. He desired to get them safely into his own custody before his victims went to give their three shouts upon Miodhchaoin's Hill. He therefore wove a druidical spell round them, so that they forgot the rest of their task altogether and sailed back to Erin. They searched for Lugh to give him the things, but he had gone away, leaving word that they were to be handed over to Nuada, the Tuatha Dé Danaan king. As soon as they were in safekeeping, Lugh came back to Tara and found the sons of Tuireann there. And he said to them:

'Do you not know that it is unlawful to keep back any part of a blood fine? So have you given those three shouts upon Miodhchaoin's Hill?'

Then the magic mist of forgetfulness fell from them and they remembered. Sorrowfully they went back to complete their task.

Miodhchaoin himself was watching for them, and when he saw them land, he came down to the beach. Brian attacked him, and they fought with the swiftness of two bears and the ferocity of two lions until Miodhchaoin fell.

Then Miodhchaoin's three sons – Corc, Conn and Aedh – came out to avenge their father, and they drove their spears through the bodies of the three sons of Tuireann, but the three sons of Tuireann also drove their spears through the bodies of the three sons of Miodhchaoin.

The three sons of Miodhchaoin were killed, and the three sons of Tuireann were so sorely wounded that birds might have flown through their bodies from one side to the other. Nevertheless Brian was still able to stand upright, and he held his two brothers, one in each hand, and kept them on their feet, and, all together, they gave three faint, feeble shouts.

Their coracle bore them, still living, to Erin. They sent their father, Tuireann, as a suppliant to Lugh, begging him to lend them the magic pig's skin to heal their wounds.

But Lugh would not, for he had counted upon their fight with the sons of Miodhchaoin to avenge his father Cian's death. So the children of Tuireann resigned themselves to die, and their father made a farewell song over them and over himself, and died with them.

Thus ends that famous tale – 'The Fate of the Sons of Tuireann', known as one of the 'Three Sorrowful Stories of Erin', the other two being 'The Fate of the Children of Lir', told in Chapter 11, and 'The Fate of the Sons of Usna', related in Chapter 14.

Chapter 9

THE WAR WITH THE GIANTS

By this time the seven years of preparation for war had come to an end. A week before the Day of Samhain, the Morrigan discovered that the Fomorii had landed upon Erin. She at once sent a messenger to tell the Daghda, who ordered his druids and sorcerers to go to the ford of the River Unius in Sligo and utter incantations against them.

The people of the goddess Danu, however, were not yet quite ready for battle. So the Daghda decided to visit the Fomorian camp as an ambassador and, by parleying with them, to gain a little more time. The Fomorii received him with apparent courtesy and, to celebrate his coming, prepared him a feast of porridge, for it was well known how fond he was of such food. They poured into their king's cauldron, which was as deep as five giants' fists, four score gallons of new milk, with meal and bacon in proportion. To this they added the whole carcasses of goats, sheep and pigs. They boiled the mixture together and poured it into a hole in the ground. 'Now,' said they, 'if you do not eat it all, we shall put you to death, for we will not have you go back to your own people and say that the Fomorii are inhospitable.' But they did not succeed in frightening the Daghda. He took his spoon, which was so large that two persons of our size might have reclined comfortably in the middle of it, dipped it into the porridge and fished up halves of salted pork and quarters of bacon.

'If it tastes as good as it smells,' he said, 'it is good fare.' And so it proved, for he ate it all and scraped up even what remained at the bottom of the hole. Then he went away to sleep it off, followed by the laughter of the Fomorii, for his stomach was so swollen that he could hardly walk. It was larger than the biggest cauldron in a large house and stood out like a sail before the wind.

But the little practical joke of the Fomorii upon the Daghda had given the Tuatha Dé Danaan time to collect their forces. It was on the eve of Samhain that the two armies came face to face. Even then the Fomorii could not believe that the people of the goddess Danu would offer them much resistance.

'Do you think they will really dare to give us battle?' said Bres to Indech, the son of Domnu.

'If they do not pay their tribute, we will pound their bones for them,' he replied.

The war of gods and giants naturally mirrored the warfare of the Gaels, in whose battles single combat figured largely. The main armies stood still while every day duels took place between ambitious combatants. But no great warriors either of the Tuatha Dé Danaan or of the Fomorii took part in them.

Sometimes a god, sometimes a giant, would be the victor, but there was a difference in the net results that astonished the Fomorii. If their own swords and lances were broken they were of no more use, and if their own champions were killed they never came back to life again, but it was quite otherwise with the people of the goddess Danu. Weapons shattered on one day reappeared upon the next in as good condition as though they had never been used, and warriors slain on one day came back on the morrow unhurt and ready, if necessary, to be killed again.

The Fomorii decided to send someone to discover the secret of these marvels. The spy they chose was Ruadan, the son of Bres and of Brigit, daughter of the Daghda, and therefore half-giant and half-god. He disguised himself as a Tuatha Dé Danaan warrior and went to look for Goibhniu. He found him at his forge, together with Luchtaine, the carpenter, and Creidhne, the bronze-worker. He saw how Goibhniu forged lance heads with three blows of his hammer, while Luchtaine cut shafts for them with three blows of his axe and Creidhne fixed the two parts together so adroitly that his bronze nails needed no hammering in. He went back and told the Fomorii, who sent him again, this time to try to kill Goibhniu.

He reappeared at the forge and asked for a javelin. Without suspicion, Goibhniu gave him one, and, as soon as he got it into his hand, he thrust it through the smith's body. But Goibhniu plucked it out and, hurling it back at his assailant, mortally wounded him. Ruadan went home to die, and his father, Bres, and his mother, Brigit, mourned for him, inventing for the purpose the Irish 'keening'. Goibhniu, on the other hand, took no harm. He went to the physician Dian Cécht, who, with his daughter Airmid, was always on duty at a miraculous well called the 'spring of health'. Whenever one of the Tuatha

Dé Danaan was killed or wounded, he was brought to the two doctors, who plunged him into the wonder-working water and brought him back to life and health again.

The mystic spring was not for long, however, allowed to help the people of the goddess. A young Fomorian chief, Octriallach, son of Indech, discovered it. He and some companions went to it by night, each carrying a large stone from the bed of the River Drowes. These they dropped into the spring until they had filled it, dispersed the healing water and formed a cairn above it. Legend has identified this place by the name of the 'Cairn of Octriallach'.

This success determined the Fomorii to fight a pitched battle. They drew out their army in line. There was not a warrior in it who had not a coat of mail and a helmet, a stout spear, a strong buckler and a heavy sword. 'Fighting the Fomors on that day,' says the old author, 'could only be compared to one of three things – beating one's head against a rock or plunging it into a fire or putting one's hand into a serpent's nest.'

All the great fighters of the Tuatha Dé Danaan were drawn out opposite to them, except Lugh. A council of the gods had decided that his varied accomplishments made his life too valuable to be risked in battle. They had therefore left him behind, guarded by nine warriors, but at the last moment Lugh escaped from his warders and appeared in his chariot before the army. He made them a patriotic speech. 'Fight bravely,' he said, 'that your servitude may last no longer. It is better to face death than to live in vassalage and pay tribute.' With these encouraging words, he drove round the ranks, standing on tiptoe so that all the Tuatha Dé Danaan might see him.

The Fomorii saw him too and marvelled. 'It seems wonderful to me,' said Bres to his druids, 'that the sun should rise in the west today and in the east every other day.'

'It would be better for us if it were so,' replied the druids.

'What else can it be, then?' asked Bres.

'It is the radiance of the face of Lugh of the Long Arms,' said they.

Then the two armies charged each other with a great shout. Spears and lances smote against shields, and so great was the shouting of the fighters, the shattering of shields, the clattering of swords, the rattling of quivers and the whistling of darts and javelins that it seemed as if thunder rolled everywhere.

They fought so closely that the heads, hands and feet of those on one side were touching the heads, hands and feet of those on the other side. They shed so much blood on to the ground that it became hard to stand on it without slipping, and the river of Unsenn was filled with dead bodies, so hard and swift and bloody and cruel was the battle.

Many great chiefs fell on each side. Oghma, the champion of the Tuatha Dé Danaan, killed Indech, the son of the goddess Domnu. But meanwhile Balor of the Mighty Blows raged among the gods, slaying their king, Nuada, as well as Macha, one of his warlike wives. At last he met with Lugh. The sun god shouted a challenge to his grandfather in the Fomorian speech. Balor heard it and prepared to use his death-dealing eye. 'Lift up my eyelid,' he said to his henchmen, 'that I may see this chatterer who talks to me.'

The attendants lifted Balor's eye with a hook, and if the glance of the eye beneath had rested upon Lugh, he would certainly have perished. But when it was half opened, Lugh flung a magic stone that struck Balor's eye out through the back of his head. The eye fell to the ground behind Balor and destroyed a whole rank of thrice nine Fomorii who were unlucky enough to be within sight of it.

An ancient poem has handed down the secret of this magic stone. It is there called a *tathlum*, meaning a 'brain-ball' such as the ancient Irish warriors used sometimes to make out of the brains of dead enemies hardened with lime.

'A tathlum, heavy, fiery, firm,
Which the Tuatha Dé Danaan had with them,
It was that broke the fierce Balor's eye,
Of old, in the battle of the great armies.

'The blood of toads and furious bears,
And the blood of the noble lion,
The blood of vipers and of Osmuinn's trunks –
It was of these the tathlum was composed.

'The sand of the swift Armorian sea,
And the sand of the teeming Red Sea –
All these, being first purified, were used
In the composition of the tathlum.

'Briun, the son of Bethar, no mean warrior,
Who on the ocean's eastern border reigned –

> It was he that fused, and smoothly formed,
> It was he that fashioned the tathlum.

> 'To the hero Lugh was given
> This concrete ball – no soft missile –
> In Magh Tuireadh of shrieking wails,
> From his hand he threw the tathlum.'

This blinding of the terrible Balor turned the fortunes of the fight, for the Fomorii wavered and the Morrigan came and encouraged the people of the goddess Danu with a song, beginning 'Kings arise to the battle', so that they took fresh heart and drove the Fomorii headlong back to their country underneath the sea.

Such was the battle that is called in Irish *Magh Tuireadh na bFomorach*, that is to say, the 'Plain of the Towers of the Fomorii', and, more popularly, the 'Battle of Magh Tuireadh the Northern', to distinguish it from the other Battle of Magh Tuireadh fought by the Tuatha Dé Danaan against the Fir Bholgs farther to the south. More of the Fomorii were killed in it, says the ancient manuscript, than there are stars in the sky, grains of sand on the seashore, snowflakes in winter, drops of dew upon the meadows in springtime, hailstones during a storm, blades of grass trodden under horses' feet or Manannán Mac Lir's white horses, the waves of the sea, when a tempest breaks. The 'towers' or pillars said to mark the graves of the combatants still stand upon the plain of Carrowmore near Sligo and form a fine collection of prehistoric monuments. Megalithic structures of almost every kind are found among them – stone cairns with dolmens in their interiors, dolmens standing open and alone, dolmens surrounded by one, two or three circles of stones and circles without dolmens – to the number of over a hundred. Some sixty such prehistoric remains stand together on an elevated plateau not more than a mile across and make the battlefield of Magh Tuireadh a most impressive ruin. What they really commemorated we may never know, but in all probability the place was the scene of some important and decisive early battle, the monuments marking the graves of the chieftains who were interred as the result of it. Those examined were found to contain burnt wood and the half-burnt bones of men and horses as well as implements of flint and bone. The actors, therefore, were still in the Neolithic Age. Whether the horses were domesticated ones buried with their riders or wild ones eaten at the funeral feasts, it would be hard to decide. The history of the real event must have been long lost even at the early date when its relics were pointed out as the records of a battle between the gods and the giants of Gaelic myth.

The Tuatha Dé Danaan, following the routed Fomorii, overtook and captured Bres. He begged Lugh to spare his life.

'What ransom will you pay for it?' asked Lugh.

'I will guarantee that the cows of Ireland shall always be in milk,' promised Bres.

But, before accepting, Lugh took counsel with his druids. 'What good will that be,' they decided, 'if Bres does not also lengthen the lives of the cows?'

This was beyond the power of Bres to do, so he made another offer. 'Tell your people,' he said to Lugh, 'that if they will spare my life they shall have a good wheat harvest every year.'

But they said: 'We already have the spring to plough and sow in, the summer to ripen the crops, the autumn for reaping, and the winter in which to eat the bread; and that is all we want.'

Lugh told this to Bres. But he also said: 'You shall have your life in return for a much less service to us than that.'

'The Kissing Stone', Carrowmore, Sligo

'What is it?' asked Bres.

'Tell us when we ought to plough, when we ought to sow and when we ought to harvest.'

Bres replied: 'You should plough on a Tuesday, sow on a Tuesday and harvest on a Tuesday.'

And this lying maxim (says the story) saved Bres's life.

Lugh, the Daghda and Oghma still pursued the Fomorii, who had carried off in their flight the Daghda's harp. They followed them into the submarine palace where Bres and Elathan lived, and there they saw the harp hanging on the wall. This harp of the Daghda's would not play without its owner's permission. The Daghda sang to it:

> 'Come, oak of the two cries!
> Come, hand of fourfold music!
> Come, summer! Come, winter!
> Voice of harps, bellows[1], and flutes!'

[1] ?Bagpipes.

For the Daghda's harp had these two names. It was called 'Oak of the two cries' and 'Hand of fourfold music'.

It leaped down from the wall, killing nine of the Fomorii as it passed, and came into the Dagdha's hand. The Daghda played to the Fomorii the three tunes known to all clever harpists – the weeping tune, the laughing tune and the sleeping tune. While he played the weeping tune, they were bowed with weeping. While he played the laughing tune, they rocked with laughter, and when he played the sleeping tune, tkey all fell asleep. And while they slept, Lugh, the Daghda and Oghma got away safely.

Next, the Daghda brought the black-maned heifer which he had, by the advice of Oenghus son of the Young, obtained from Bres. The wisdom of Oenghus had been shown in this advice, for it was this very heifer that the cattle of the people of the goddess Danu were accustomed to follow whenever it lowed, Now, when it lowed, all the cattle that the Fomorii had taken away from the Tuatha Dé Danaan came back again.

Yet the power of the Fomorii was not wholly broken. Four of them still carried on a desultory warfare by spoiling the corn, fruit and milk of their conquerors. But the Morrigan and Badb and Midhir and Oenghus pursued them and drove them out of Ireland for ever.

Last of all, the Morrigan and Badb went up on to the summits of all the high mountains of Ireland and proclaimed the victory. All the lesser gods who had not been in the battle came round and heard the news. And Badb sang a song which began:

> 'Peace mounts to the heavens,
> The heavens descend to earth,
> Earth lies under the heavens,
> Everyone is strong . . .'

but the rest of it has been lost and forgotten.

Then she added a prophecy in which she foretold the approaching end of the divine age and the beginning of a new one in which summers would be flowerless and cows milkless and women shameless and men strengthless, in which there would be trees without fruit and seas without fish, when old men; would give false judgments and legislators make unjust laws, when warriors would betray one another, and men would be thieves, and there would be no more virtue left in the world.

Chapter 10

The Conquest of the Gods by Mortals

Of what Badb had in mind when she uttered this prophecy we have no record. But it was true. The twilight of the Irish gods was at hand. A new race was coming across the sea to dispute the ownership of Ireland with the people of the goddess Danu. And these newcomers were not gods like themselves but men like ourselves, ancestors of the Gaels.

This story of the conquest of the gods by mortals – which seems such a strange one to us – is typically Celtic. The Gaelic mythology is the only one that has preserved it in any detail, but the doctrine would seem to have been common at one time to all the Celts. It was, however, of less shame to the gods than would otherwise have been, for men were of as divine descent as themselves. The dogma of the Celts was that men were descended from the god of death and first came from the Land of the Dead to take possession of the present world.[1] Caesar tells us in *De Bello Gallico*, his too short account of the Gauls, that they believed themselves to be sprung from Dis Pater or Pluto, the god of the underworld. In the Gaelic mythology Dis Pater was called Bíle, a name that has as its root the syllable *bel*, meaning 'to die'. The god Beli in British mythology was no doubt the same person, while the same idea is expressed by the same root in the name of Balor, the terrible Fomor whose glance was death.[3]

The post-Christian Irish chroniclers, seeking to reconcile Christian teachings with the still vital pagan mythology by changing the gods into ancient kings and incorporating them into the annals of the country, with appropriate dates, also disposed of the genuine early doctrine by substituting Spain for

---

[1] It may be noted that, according to Welsh legend, the ancestors of the Cymri came from Gwlâd yr Hâv, the 'Land of Summer', i.e. the Celtic Otherworld.

Hades and giving a highly fanciful account of the origin and wanderings of their ancestors. To use a Hibernicism, appropriate in this connection, the first Irishman was a Scythian called Fenius Farsa. Deprived of his own throne, he had settled in Egypt, where his son Niul married a daughter of the reigning pharaoh. Her name was Scota, and she had a son called Goidel, whose great-grandson was named Eber Scot, the whole genealogy probably being invented to explain the origin of the three names by which the Gaels called themselves – Finn, Scot and Goidel. Fenius and his family and clan were turned out of Egypt for refusing to join in the persecution of the children of Israel and so-journed in Africa for forty-two years. Their wanderings took them to 'the altars of the Philistines, by the Lake of Osiers', then, passing between Rusicada and the hilly country of Syria, they travelled through Mauretania as far as the Pillars of Hercules and from there landed in Spain where they lived many years, greatly increasing and multiplying. The same route is given by the twelfth-century British historian Geoffrey of Monmouth in his *Historia Brito-num* as that taken by Brutus and the Trojans when they came to colonise Britain. Its only connection with any kind of fact is that it corresponds fairly well with what ethnologists consider must have been the westward line of migration taken, not, curiously enough, by the Aryan Celts but by the pre-Aryan Iberians.

It is sufficient for us to find the first men in Spain, remembering that 'Spain' stood for the Celtic Hades or Elysium. In this country Bregon, the father of two sons, Bíle and Ith, had built a watchtower from which, one winter's evening, Ith saw, far off over the seas, a land he had never noticed before. 'It is on winter evenings, when the air is pure, that man's eyesight reaches farthest,' remarks the old tract called the 'Book of Invasions', contained in the Book of Leinster, and other ancient manuscripts, gravely accounting for the fact that Ith saw Ireland from Spain.

Wishing to examine it nearer, he set sail with thrice thirty warriors and landed without mishap at the mouth of the River Scêné, now called the Kenmare River. The country seemed to him to be uninhabited, and he marched with his men towards the north. At last he reached Aileach, near the present town of Londonderry.

Here he found the three reigning kings of the people of the goddess Danu, Mac Cuill, Mac Cecht and Mac Greine, the sons of Oghma and grandsons of the Daghda. These had succeeded Nuada the Silver-handed, who was killed in the battle with the Fomorii, and had met, after burying their predecessor in a barrow called Grianan of Aileach, which still stands on the base of the Inishowen Peninsula, between Lough Swilly and Lough Foyle, to divide his kingdom among them. Unable to arrive at any partition satisfactory to all, they appealed to the newcomer to arbitrate.

The advice of Ith was moral rather than practical. 'Act according to the laws of justice' was all that he would say to the claimants, and then he was indiscreet enough to burst into enthusiastic praises of Ireland for its temperate climate and its richness in fruit, honey, wheat and fish. Such sentiments from a foreigner seemed to the Tuatha Dé Danaan suggestive of a desire to take the country from them. They conspired together and treacherously killed Ith at a place since called 'Ith's Plain'. They, however, spared his followers, who returned to 'Spain', taking their dead leader's body with them. The indignation there was great, and Mil, Bile's son and Ith's nephew, determined to go to Ireland to get revenge.

Mil therefore sailed with his eight sons and their wives. Thirty-six chiefs, each with his shipful of warriors, accompanied him. By the magic arts of their druid, Amhairghin of the Fair Knee, they discovered the exact place at which Ith had landed before them and put in to shore there. Two alone failed to reach it alive. The wife of Amhairghin died during the voyage, and Aranon, a son of Mil, on approaching the land, climbed to the top of the mast to obtain a better view and, falling off, was drowned. The rest disembarked safely upon the first of May.

Amhairghin was the first to land. Planting his right foot on Irish soil, he burst into a poem preserved in both the Book of Lecan and the Book of Ballymote and, with the three following ones are said to be the oldest Irish literary records. It is a good example of the pantheistic philosophy of the Celtic races, and a very close parallel to it is contained in an early Welsh poem, called the 'Battle of the Trees' and attributed to the famous bard Taliesin. 'I am the wind that blows upon the sea,' sang Amhairghin. 'I am the ocean wave. I am the murmur of the surges. I am seven battalions. I am a strong bull. I am an eagle on a rock. I am a ray of the sun. I am the most beautiful of herbs. I am a courageous wild boar. I am a salmon in the water. I am a lake upon a plain. I am a cunning artist. I am a gigantic, sword-wielding champion. I can shift my shape like a god. In what direction shall we go? Shall we hold our council in the valley or on the mountain top? Where shall we make our home? What land is better than this island of the setting sun? Where shall we walk to and fro in peace and safety? Who can find you clear springs of water as I can? Who can tell you the age of the moon but I? Who can call the fish from the depths of the sea as I can? Who can cause them to come near the shore as I can? Who can change the shapes of the hills and headlands as I can? I am a bard who is called upon by seafarers to prophesy. Javelins shall be wielded to avenge our wrongs. I prophesy victory. I end my song by prophesying all other good things.'

The Welsh bard Taliesin sings in the same strain as the druid Amhairghin of his unity with, and therefore his power over, all nature, animate and inanimate. 'I have been in many shapes,' he says, 'before I attained a congenial form. I have been a narrow blade of a sword. I have been a drop in the air. I have been a shining star. I have been a word in a book. I have been a book in the beginning. I have been a light in a lantern a year and a half. I have been a bridge for passing over three score rivers. I have journeyed as an eagle. I have been a boat on the sea. I have been a director in battle. I have been a sword in the hand. I have been a shield in fight. I have been the string of a harp. I have been enchanted for a year in the foam of water. There is nothing in which I have not been.' It is strange to find Gael and Briton combining to voice almost in the same words this doctrine of the mystical Celts, who, while still in a state of semi-barbarism, saw, with some of the greatest of philosophers, the One in the Many, and a single Essence in all the manifold forms of life.

The Sons of Mil Espaine or Milesians (for so, following the Irish annalists, it will be convenient to call the first Gaelic settlers in Ireland) began their march on Tara, which was the capital of the Tuatha Dé Danaan, as it had been in earlier days the chief fortress of the Fir Bholgs and would in later days be the dwelling of the high kings of Ireland. On their way they met with a goddess called Banba, the wife of Mac Cuill. She greeted Amhairghin. 'If you have come to conquer Ireland,' she said, 'your cause is no just one.'

'Certainly it is to conquer it we have come,' replied Amhairghin, without condescending to argue upon the abstract morality of the matter.

'Then at least grant me one thing,' she asked.

'What is that?' replied Amhairghin.

'That this island shall be called by my name.'

'It shall be,' replied Amhairghin.

A little farther on, they met a second goddess, Fotla, the wife of Mac Cecht, who made the same request and received the same answer from Amhairghin.

Last of all, at Uisneach, the centre of Ireland, they came upon the third of the queens, Eriu, the wife of Mac Greine. 'Welcome, warriors,' she cried. 'To you who have come from afar this island shall henceforth belong, and from the setting to the rising sun there is no better land. And your race will be the most perfect the world has ever seen.'

'These are fair words and a good prophecy,' said Amhairghin.

'It will be no thanks to you,' broke in Donn, Mil's eldest son. 'Whatever success we have we shall owe to our own strength.'

'That which I prophesy has no concern with you,' retorted the goddess, 'and neither you nor your descendants will live to enjoy this island.' Then, turning to Amhairghin, she too asked that Ireland might be called after her.

'It shall be its principal name,' Amhairghin promised.

So it has happened. Of the three ancient names of Ireland – Banba, Fotla and Eriu – the last, in its genitive form of 'Erinn', is the one that has survived.

The invaders came to Tara, then called Drumcain, that is, the 'Beautiful Hill'. Mac Cuill, Mac Cecht and Mac Greine met them, with all the host of the Gaelic gods. As was usual, they held a parley. The people of the goddess Danu complained that they had been taken by surprise, and the Sons of Mil Espaine admitted that to invade a country without having first warned its inhabitants was not strictly according to the courtesies of chivalrous warfare. The Tuatha Dé Danaan proposed to the invaders that they should leave the island for three days, during which they themselves would decide whether to fight for their kingdom or to surrender it, but the Sons of Mil Espaine did not care for this, for they knew that as soon as they were out of the island the Tuatha Dé Danaan would oppose them with druidic enchantments, so that they would not be able to make a fresh landing. In the end, Mac Cuill, Mac Cecht and Mac Greine offered to submit the matter to the arbitration of Amhairghin, the Milesians' own lawgiver, with the express stipulation that if he gave an obviously partial judgment he was to suffer death at their hands. Donn asked his druid if he were prepared to accept this very delicate duty. Amhairghin replied that he was and at once delivered the first judgment pronounced by the Sons of Mil Espaine in Ireland.

'The men whom we found dwelling in the land, to them is possession
    due by right.
It is therefore your duty to set out to sea over nine green waves;

And if you shall be able to effect a landing again in spite of them,
You are to engage them in battle, and I adjudge to you the land in which
    you found them living.
I adjudge to you the land wherein you found them dwelling, by the right
    of battle.
But although you may desire the land which these people possess, yet
    yours is the duty to show them justice.
I forbid you from injustice to those you have found in the land, however
    you may desire to obtain it'

This judgment was considered fair by both parties. The Sons of Mil Espaine retired to their ships and waited at a distance of nine waves' length from the land until the signal was given to attack, while the Tuatha Dé Danaan, drawn up upon the beach, were ready with their druidic spells to oppose them.

The signal was given and the Sons of Mil Espaine bent to their oars, but they had hardly started before they discovered that a strong wind was blowing straight towards them from the shore, so that they could make no progress. At first they thought it might be a natural breeze, but Donn smelt magic in it. He sent a man to climb the mast of his ship to see if the wind blew as strong at that height as it did at the level of the sea. The man returned, reporting that the air was quite still 'up aloft'. Evidently it was a druidic wind. But Amhair-ghin soon coped with it. Lifting up his voice, he invoked the Land of Ireland itself, a power higher than the gods it sheltered.

'I invoke the land of Eriu!
The shining, shining sea!
The fertile, fertile hill!
The wooded vale!
The river abundant, abundant in water!
The fishful, fishful lake!'

In such strain runs the original incantation, one of those magic formulas whose power was held by ancient races to reside in their exact consecrated wording rather than in their meaning. To us it sounds nonsense, and so no doubt it did to those who put the old Irish mythical traditions into literary shape, for a later version expands and explains it as follows:

'I implore that we may regain the land of Erin,
 We who have come over the lofty waves,
This land whose mountains are great and extensive,
Whose streams are clear and numerous,
Whose woods abound with various fruit,
Its rivers and waterfalls are large and beautiful,
Its lakes are broad and widely spread,
It abounds with fountains on elevated grounds!
May we gain power and dominion over its tribes!
May we have kings of our own ruling at Tara!
May Tara be the regal residence of our many succeeding kings!
May the Milesians be the conquerors of its people!
May our ships anchor in its harbours!
May they trade along the coast of Erin!
May Eremon be its first ruling monarch!
May the descendants of Ir and Eber be mighty kings!
I implore that we may regain the land of Erin,
     I implore!'

The incantation proved effectual. The Land of Ireland was pleased to be propitious, and the druidic wind dropped down.

But success was not quite so easy as they had hoped. Manannán, son of the sea and lord of headlands, shook his magic mantle at them and hurled a fresh tempest out over the deep. The galleys of the Sons of Mil Espaine were tossed helplessly on the waves, many sinking with their crews. Donn was among the lost, thus fulfilling Eriu's prophecy, and three other sons of Mil also perished. In the end, a broken remnant, after long beating about the coasts, came to shore at the mouth of the River Boyne. They landed, and Amhairghin, from the shore, invoked the aid of the sea as he had already done that of the land.

'Sea full of fish!
Fertile land!
Fish swarming up!
Fish there!
Under-wave bird!
Great fish!

> Crab's hole!
> Fish swarming up!
> Sea full of fish!'

which, being interpreted like the preceding charm, seems to have meant:

> 'May the fishes of the sea crowd in shoals to the land for our use!
> May the waves of the sea drive forth to the shore abundance of fish!
> May the salmon swim abundantly into our nets!
> May all kinds of fish come plentifully to us from the sea!
> May its flatfishes also come in abundance!
> This poem I compose at the seashore that fishes may swim in shoals to
> our coast.'

Then, gathering their forces, they marched on the people of the goddess Danu.

Two battles were fought, the first in Glenn Faisi, a valley of the Slieve Mish Mountains south of Tralee, and the second at Tailtiu, now called Telltown. In both, the gods were beaten. Their three kings were killed by the three surviving sons of Mil – Mac Cuill by Eber, Mac Cecht by Eremon, and Mac Greine by the druid Amhairghin. Defeated and disheartened, they gave in and, retiring beneath the earth, left the surface of the land to their conquerors.

From this day begins the history of Ireland according to the annalists. Mil's eldest son, Donn, having perished, the kingdom fell by right to the second, Eremon. But Eber, the third son, backed by his followers, insisted upon a partition, and Ireland was divided into two equal parts. At the end of a year, however, war broke out between the brothers. Eber was killed in battle, and Eremon took the sole rule.

Chapter 11

THE GODS IN EXILE

But although mortals had conquered gods on a scale unparalleled in mythology, they had by no means entirely subdued them. Beaten in battle, the people of the goddess Danu had yet not lost their divine attributes and could use them either to help or hurt. 'Great was the power of the Daghda,' says a tract preserved in the Book of Leinster, 'over the sons of Mil, even after the conquest of Ireland; for his subjects destroyed their corn and milk, so that they must needs make a treaty of peace with the Daghda. Not until then, and thanks to his goodwill, were they able to harvest corn and drink the milk of their cows.' The basis of this lost treaty seems to have been that the Tuatha Dé Danaan, although driven from the soil, should receive homage and offerings from their successors. We are told in the verse Dinnsenchus of Magh Slecht that:

> 'Since the rule
> Of Eremon, the noble man of grace,
> There was worshipping of stones
> Until the coming of good Patrick of Macha.'[1]

Dispossessed of upper earth, the gods had, however, to seek for new homes. A council was convened, but its members were divided between two opinions. One section of them chose to shake the dust of Ireland off its disinherited feet and seek refuge in a paradise overseas, situated in some unknown and, except for favoured mortals, unknowable island of the west, the counterpart in Gaelic myth of the British

---

[1] See Chapter 4 – 'The Religion of the Ancient Britons and Druidism'.

> . . . 'island valley of Avilion;
> Where falls not hail, or rain, or any snow,
> Nor ever wind blows loudly; but it lies
> Deep-meadow'd, happy, fair with orchard lawns
> And bowery hollows crown'd with summer sea.'[1]

– a land of perpetual pleasure and feasting, described variously as the (Tír Tairnigirib ('Land of Promise'), Magh Mell (the 'Plain of Happiness'), Tír nam Beo (the 'Land of the Living'), Tír na Og (the 'Land of the Young') and Hy-Breasal ('Breasal's Island'). Celtic mythology is full of the beauties and wonders of this mystic country, and the tradition of it has never died out. Hy-Breasal has been set down on old maps as a reality again and again – some pioneers in the Spanish seas thought they had discovered it and called the land they found 'Brazil', and it is still said, by lovers of old lore, that a patient watcher, after long gazing westward from the westernmost shores of Ireland or Scotland, may sometimes be lucky enough to catch a glimpse against the sunset of its:

> 'summer isles of Eden lying in dark-purple spheres of sea'.

Of these divine emigrants the principal was Manannán Mac Lir. But although he had cast in his lot beyond the seas, he did not cease to visit Ireland. An old Irish king, Bran, the son of Febal, met him, according to a seventh-century poem, as Bran journeyed to, and Manannán from, the earthly paradise. Bran was in his boat and Manannán was driving a chariot over the tops of the waves, and he sang:

> 'Bran deems it a marvellous beauty
> In his coracle across the clear sea:
> While to me in my chariot from afar
> It is a flowery plain on which he rides about.
>
> 'What is a clear sea
> For the prowed skiff in which Bran is,

---

[1] Tennyson's: *Idylls of the King: The Passing of Arthur.*

That is a happy plain with profusion of flowers
To me from the chariot of two wheels.

'Bran sees
The number of waves beating across the clear sea:
I myself see in Magh Mon[1]
Red-headed flowers without fault.

'Sea-horses glisten in summer
As far as Bran has stretched his glance:
Rivers pour forth a stream of honey
In the land of Manannán son of Lir.

'The sheen of the main, on which thou art,
The white hue of the sea, on which thou rowest about,
Yellow and azure are spread out,
It is land, and is not rough.

'Speckled salmon leap from the womb
Of the white sea, on which thou lookest:
They are calves, they are coloured lambs
With friendliness, without mutual slaughter.

'Though but one chariot-rider is seen
In Magh Mell[2] of many flowers,
There are many steeds on its surface,
Though them thou seest not.

   .   .   .   .

'Along the top of a wood has swum
Thy coracle across ridges,
There is a wood of beautiful fruit
Under the prow of thy little skiff.

[1]   The Plain of Sports.
[2]   The Happy Plain.

'A wood with blossom and fruit,
On which is the vine's veritable fragrance;
A wood without decay, without defect,
On which are leaves of a golden hue.'

And, after this singularly poetic enunciation of the philosophical and mystical doctrine that all things are, under their diverse forms, essentially the same, he goes on to describe to Bran the beauties and pleasures of the Celtic Elysium.

But there were others – indeed, the most part – of the gods who refused to expatriate themselves. For these residences had to be found, and the Daghda, their new king, proceeded to assign to each of those who stayed in Ireland a *sídh*. These *sídhe* were barrows, or hillocks, each being the door to an underground realm of inexhaustible splendour and delight, according to the somewhat primitive ideas of the Celts. A description is given of one that the Daghda kept for himself and out of which his son Oenghus cheated him, which will serve as a fair example of all. There were apple trees there always in fruit, and one pig alive and another ready roasted, and the supply of ale never failed. One may still visit in Ireland the *sídhe* of many of the gods, for the spots are known, and the traditions have not died out. To Lir was given Sídh Fionnachaidh, now known as the 'Hill of the White Field', on the top of Slieve Fuad near Newtown Hamilton in County Armagh. Bodb Dearg received a *sídh* called by his own name, Sídh Bodb, just to the south of Portumna in Galway. Midhir was given the *sídh* of Bri Leith, now called Slieve Golry, near Ardagh in County Longford. Oghma's *sídh* was called Airceltrai. To Lugh was assigned Rodrubân. Manannán's son, Ilbhreach, received Sídh Eas Aedha Ruaidh, now the Mound of Mullachshee near Ballyshannon in Donegal. Fionnbharr had Sídh Meadha, now 'Knockma', about five miles west of Tuam, where, as present king of the fairies, he is said to live today, while the abodes of other gods of lesser fame are also recorded. For himself the Daghda retained two, both near the River Boyne in Meath, the best of them being the famous Brugh na Bóinne. None of the members of the Tuatha Dé Danaan was left unprovided for except one.

It was from this time that the Gaelic gods received the name by which they are known today – *Aes Sídhe*, the 'People of the Hills' or, more shortly, the Sídhe. Every god or fairy is a *Fer-Sídhe*, a 'Man of the Hill', and every goddess a *Bean-Sídhe*, a 'Woman of the Hill', the *banshee* of popular legend.

The most famous of such fairy hills are about five miles from Drogheda. They are still connected with the names of the Tuatha Dé Danaan, although they are now not called their dwelling places but their barrows or tombs. On the northern bank of the Boyne stand seventeen barrows, three of which – Knowth, Dowth and Newgrange – are of great size. The last named, the largest and best preserved, is over 300 feet in diameter and 70 feet high while its top makes a platform 120 feet across. It has been explored, and Roman coins, gold torcs, copper pins and iron rings and knives were found in it, but what else it may have once contained will never be known, for, like Knowth and Dowth, it was thoroughly ransacked by Danish spoilers in the ninth century. It is entered by a square doorway, the rims of which are elaborately ornamented with a kind of spiral pattern. This entrance leads to a stone passage, more than 60 feet long, which gradually widens and rises until it opens into a chamber with a conical dome 20 feet high. On each side of this central chamber is a recess, with a shallow oval stone basin in it. The huge slabs of which the whole is built are decorated on both the outer and the inner faces with the same spiral pattern as the doorway.

The origin of these astonishing prehistoric monuments is unknown, but they are generally attributed to the race that inhabited Ireland before the

Entrance to the Great Cairn of Newgrange, on the Boyne, near Drogheda

Celts. Gazing at marvellous Newgrange, one might very well echo the words of the old Irish poet Mac Nia, in the Book of Ballymote:

> 'Behold the *Sídh* before your eyes,
> It is manifest to you that it is a king's mansion,
> Which was built by the firm Daghda,
> It was a wonder, a court, an admirable hill.'

It is not, however, with Newgrange, or even with Knowth or Dowth, that the Daghda's name is now associated. It is a smaller barrow, nearer to the Boyne, which is known as the 'Tomb of the Daghda'. Verses as old as the eleventh century assert that the Tuatha Dé Danaan used the brughs for burial. It was about this period that the mythology of Ireland was being rewoven into spurious history. The poem, which is called the 'Chronicles of the Tombs', not only mentions the 'Monument of the Daghda' and the 'Monument of the Morrigan', but also records the last resting places of Oghma, Etain, Cairbre, Lugh, Boann and Oenghus.

We have for the present, however, to consider Oenghus in a far less sepulchral light. He is, indeed, very much alive in the following story contained in the Book of Leinster. The 'Son of the Young' was absent when the distribution of the *sídhe* was made. When he returned, he came to his father, the Daghda, and demanded one. The Daghda pointed out to him that they had all been given away. Oenghus protested, but what could be done? By fair means evidently nothing, but by craft a great deal. The wily Oenghus appeared to reconcile himself to fate and only begged his father to allow him to stay at the *sídh* of Brugh na Bóinne (Newgrange) for a day and a night. The Daghda agreed to this, no doubt congratulating himself on having got out of the difficulty so easily. But when he came to Oenghus to remind him that the time was up, Oenghus refused to go. He had been granted, he claimed, day and night, and it is of days and nights that time and eternity are composed; therefore there was no limit to his tenure of the *sídh*. The logic does not seem very convincing to modern minds, but the Daghda is said to have been satisfied with it. He abandoned the best of his two palaces to his son, who took peaceable possession of it. Thus it got a second name, that of the *Sídh* or *Brugh* of the 'Son of the Young'.

After this the Daghda does not play much active part in the history of the people of the goddess Danu. We next hear of a council of gods to elect a fresh ruler. There were five candidates for the vacant throne – Bodb Dearg, Midhir, Ilbhreach, son of Manannán, Lir and Oenghus himself, although the last-named, we are told, had little real desire to rule as he preferred a life of freedom to the dignities of kingship. The Tuatha Dé Danaan went into consultation, and the result of their deliberation was that their choice fell on Bodb Dearg for three reasons – firstly, for his own sake; secondly, for his father, the Daghda's sake; and thirdly, because he was the Daghda's eldest son. The other competitors approved this choice except two. Midhir refused to give hostages, as was the custom, to Bodb Dearg, and fled with his followers to 'a desert country round Mount Leinster' in County Carlow, while Lir retired in great anger to Sídh Fionnachaidh, declining to recognise or obey the new king.

Why Lir and Midhir should have so taken the matter to heart is difficult to understand unless it was because they were both among the oldest of the gods. The indifference of Oenghus is easier to explain. He was the Gaelic Eros and was busy living up to his character. At this time, the object of his love was a maiden who had visited him one night in a dream, only to vanish when he put out his arms to embrace her. All the next day, we are told in a story called 'The Dream of Oenghus' from an eighteenth-century manuscript, Oenghus took no food. Upon the following night, the unsubstantial lady again appeared and played and sang to him. That following day he also fasted. So things went on for a year, while Oenghus pined and wasted for love. At last the physicians of the Tuatha Dé Danaan guessed his complaint and told him how fatal it might be to him. Oenghus asked that his mother, Boann, might be sent for, and, when she came, he told her his trouble and implored her help. She went to the Daghda and begged him, if he did not wish to see his son die of unrequited love, a disease that all Dian Cécht's medicine and Goibhniu's magic could not heal, to find the dream maiden. The Daghda could do nothing himself, but he sent to Bodb Dearg, and the new king of the gods sent in turn to the lesser deities of Ireland, ordering all of them to search for her. For a year she could not be found, but at last the disconsolate lover received a message charging him to come and see if he could recognise the lady of his dreams. Oenghus came and knew her at once, even though she was surrounded by thrice fifty attendant nymphs. Her name was Caer, and she was the daughter of Ethal Anubal, who had a *sídh* at Uaman in Connacht. Bodb Dearg demanded her for Oenghus in marriage, but her father declared that he had no control over her. She was a swan maiden, he said, and every year, as soon as summer was over, she went with her companions to a lake called 'Dragon Mouth', and there all of them became swans. But refusing to be thus put off, Oenghus waited in patience until the day of the magical change and then went down to the shore of the lake. There, surrounded by thrice fifty swans, he saw Caer, herself a swan surpassing all the rest in beauty and whiteness. He called to her, proclaiming his passion and his name, and she promised to be his bride if he too would become a swan. He agreed, and with a word she changed him into swan shape and thus they flew side by side to his *sidh*, where they retook the human form and, no doubt, lived happily as long as could be expected of such changeable immortals as pagan deities.

Meanwhile, the people of the goddess Danu were justly incensed against both Lir and Midhir. Bodb Dearg made a yearly war upon Midhir in his *sidh*, and many of the divine race were killed on either side. But against Lir, the new king of the gods refused to move, for there had been a great affection between them. Many times Bodb Dearg tried to regain Lir's friendship by presents and compliments but for a long time without success.

At last Lir's wife died, to the sea god's great sorrow. When Bodb Dearg heard the news, he sent a messenger to Lir, offering him one of his own foster daughters, Aobh, Aoife and Ailbhe, the children of Ailioll of Arran. Lir, touched by this, came to visit Bodb Dearg at his *sidh* and chose Aobh for his wife. 'She is the eldest, so she must be the noblest of them,' he said. They were married and a great feast made, and Lir took her back with him to Sídh Fionnachaidh.

Aobh bore four children to Lir. The eldest was a daughter called Fionuala and the second was a son called Aed. The two others were twin boys called Fiachtra and Conn, but in giving birth to those Aobh died.

Bodb Dearg then offered Lir another of his foster children, and he chose the second, Aoife. Every year Lir and Aoife and the four children used to go to Manannán's 'Feast of Age', which was held at each of the *sidhe* in turn. The four children grew up to be great favourites among the people of the goddess Danu.

But Aoife was childless, and she became jealous of Lir's children, for she feared that he would love them more than he did her. She brooded over this until she began first to hope for and then to plot their deaths. She tried to persuade her servants to murder them, but they would not. So she took the four

The Dream Maiden visits Oenghus, from a painting by E. Wallcousins

children to Lake Darvra (now called Lough Derravargh in West Meath) and sent them into the water to bathe. Then she made an incantation over them and touched them each in turn with a druidic wand and changed them into swans.

But although she had magic enough to alter their shapes, she had not the power to take away their human speech and minds. Fionuala turned and threatened her with the anger of Lir and of Bodb Dearg when they came to hear of it. Aoife, however, hardened her heart and refused to undo what she had done. The children of Lir, finding their case a hopeless one, asked her how long she intended to keep them in that condition.

'You would be easier in mind,' she said, 'if you had not asked the question; but I will tell you. You shall be three hundred years here on Lake Darvra and three hundred years upon the Sea of Moyle,[1] which is between Erin and Alba, and three hundred years more at Irros Domnann[2] and the Isle of Glora in Erris.[3] Yet you shall have two consolations in your troubles. You shall keep your human minds and yet suffer no grief at knowing that you have been changed into swans, and you shall be able to sing the softest and sweetest songs that were ever heard in the world.'

Then Aoife went away and left them. She returned to Lir and told him that the children had fallen by accident into Lake Darvra and were drowned.

But Lir was not satisfied that she spoke the truth and went in haste to the lake to see if he could find traces of them. He saw four swans close to the shore and heard them talking to one another with human voices. As he approached, they came out of the water to meet him. They told him what Aoife had done and begged him to change them back into their own shapes. But Lir's magic was not as powerful as his wife's and he could not.

Nor even could Bodb Dearg – to whom Lir went for help – for all that he was king of the gods. What Aoife had done could not be undone. But she could be punished for it! Bodb ordered his foster daughter to appear before him, and when she came, he put an oath on her to tell him truly 'what shape of all others, on the earth, or above the earth, or beneath the earth, she most abhorred, and into which she most dreaded to be transformed'. Aoife was obliged to answer that she most feared to become a demon of the air. So Bodb Dearg struck her with his wand, and she fled from them, a shrieking demon.

[1] Now called North Channel.
[2] The peninsula of Erris in Mayo.
[3] A small island off Belmullet.

Lir and the Swans, from a painting by J. H. F. Bacon ARA

All the Tuatha Dé Danaan went to Lake Darvra to visit the four swans. The Sons of Mil Espaine heard of it and also went, for it was not until long after this that gods and mortals ceased to associate. The visit became a yearly feast, but at the end of three hundred years the children of Lir had to leave Lake Darvra and go to the Sea of Moyle to fulfil the second period of their exile.

They bade farewell to gods and men and went, and for fear lest they might be hurt by anyone, the Sons of Mil Espaine made it a law in Ireland that nobody should harm a swan from that time forth for ever.

The children of Lir suffered much from tempest and cold on the stormy Sea of Moyle, and they were very lonely. Once only during that long three hundred years did they see any of their friends. An embassy of the Tuatha Dé Danaan, led by two sons of Bodb Dearg, came to look for them and told them all that had happened in Erin during their exile.

At last that long penance came to an end, and they went to Irros Domnann and Innis Glora for their third stage. And while it was wearily dragging through, St Patrick came to Ireland and put an end to the power of the gods for ever. They had been banned and banished when the children of Lir found themselves free to return to their old home. Sídh Fionnechaidh was empty and deserted, for Lir had been killed by Caoilté, the cousin of Fionn Mac Cumhaill (*see* Chapter 15 – 'Fionn and the Fianna').

So, after long, vain searching for their lost relatives, they gave up hope and returned to the Innis Glora. They had a friend there, the Lonely Crane of Inniskea,[1] which has lived upon that island ever since the beginning of the world and will be still sitting there on the day of judgment. They saw no one else until one day a man came to the island. He told them that he was St Caemhoc[2] and that he had heard their story. He brought them to his church and preached the new faith to them, and they believed in Christ and consented to be baptised. This broke the pagan spell, and as soon as the holy water was sprinkled over them they returned to human shape. But they were very old and bowed – three aged men and an ancient woman. They did not live long after this, and St Caemhoc, who had baptised them, buried them all together in one grave.[2]

---

[1] An island off the coast of Mayo. Its lonely crane was one of the 'Wonders of Ireland' and was long an object of folk belief.

[2] This famous story of the *Fate of the Children of Lir* is not found in any manuscript earlier than the beginning of the seventeenth century.

But in telling this story we have leaped nine hundred years – a great space in the history even of gods. We must retrace our steps, if not quite to the days of Eremon and Eber, sons of Mil and first kings of Ireland, at any rate to the beginning of the Christian era.

At this time Eochaidh Airemh was high king of Ireland and reigned at Tara, while under him, as vassal monarchs, Conchobar Mac Nessa ruled over the Red Branch Champions of Ulster, Cú Roí Mac Daire, was king of Munster, Mesgedra was king of Leinster, and Ailill, with his famous queen, Medb, governed Connacht.

Shortly before, among the gods, Oenghus Son of the Young had stolen away Etain, the wife of Midhir. He kept her imprisoned in a bower of glass, which he carried everywhere with him, never allowing her to leave it for fear that Midhir might recapture her. The Gaelic Pluto, however, found out where she was and was laying plans to rescue her when a rival of Etain's herself decoyed Oenghus away from before the pleasant prison house and set his captive free. But instead of returning her to Midhir, she changed the luckless goddess into a fly and threw her into the air, where she was tossed about in great wretchedness at the mercy of every wind.

At the end of seven years, a gust blew her on to the roof of the house of Etair, one of the vassals of Conchobar, who was celebrating a feast. The unhappy fly, who was Etain, was blown down the chimney into the room below and fell, exhausted, into a golden cup full of beer, which the wife of the master of the house was just going to drink. And the woman drank Etain with the beer.

But, of course, this was not the end of her – for the gods cannot really die – but only the beginning of a new life. Etain was reborn as the daughter of Etair's wife, no one knowing that she was not of mortal lineage. She grew up to be the most beautiful woman in Ireland.

When she was twenty years old, her fame reached the high king, who sent messengers to see if she was as fair as people reported. They saw her and returned to the king full of her praises. So Eochaidh himself went to pay her a visit that is described in a fifteenth-century account, the Egerton manuscript, although, of course, the story is found in much more ancient authorities:

'A clear comb of silver was held in her hand, the comb was adorned with gold; and near her, as for washing, was a basin of silver whereon four birds had been chased, and there were little bright gems of carbuncles on the rims of the basin. A bright purple mantle waved round her; and beneath it was another mantle ornamented with silver fringes: the other mantle was clasped over her bosom with a golden brooch. A tunic she wore with a long hood that might cover her head attached to it; it was stiff and glossy with green silk beneath red embroidery of gold, and was clasped over her breasts with marvellously wrought clasps of silver and gold; so that men saw the bright gold and the green silk flashing against the sun. On her head were two tresses of golden hair,, and each tress had been plaited into four strands; at the end of each strand was a little ball of gold. And there was that maiden undoing her hair that she might wash it, her two arms out through the armholes of her smock. Each of her two arms was as white as the snow of a single night, and each of her cheeks was as rosy as the foxglove. Even and small were the teeth in her head, and they shone like pearls. Her eyes were as blue as a hyacinth, her lips delicate and crimson; very high, soft and white were her shoulders. Tender, polished and white were her writs; her fingers long and of great whiteness; her nails were beautiful and pink. White as snow, or the foam of a wave, was her neck; long was it, slender, and as soft as silk. Smooth and white were her thighs; her knees were round and firm and white; her ankles were as straight as the rule of a carpenter. Her feet were slim and as white as the ocean's foam; evenly set were her eyes; her eyebrows were of a bluish black, such as you see upon the shell of a beetle. Never a maid fairer than she, or more worthy of love, was till then seen by the eyes of men; and it seemed to them that she must be one of those that have come from the fairy mounds.'

The king wood her and made her his wife and brought her back to Tara.

Now it happened that the king had a brother named Ailill, who, on seeing Etain, was so smitten with her beauty that he fell sick of the intensity of his passion and wasted almost to death. While he was in this condition Eochaidh had to make a royal progress through Ireland. He left his brother – the cause of whose malady none suspected – in Etain's care, bidding her to do what she could for him and, if he died, to bury him with due ceremonies and erect an ogham stone above his grave. Etain visited the brother. She inquired the cause of his illness. He spoke to her in enigmas but at last, moved beyond control by her tenderness, he broke out in an avowal of his passion. His description of the yearning of hopeless love is a lyric of extraordinary intensity. 'It is closer than the skin,' he cries. 'It is like a battle with a spectre, it overwhelms like a flood. It is a weapon under the sea. It is a passion for an echo.' By ' a weapon under the sea' the poet meant that love is like one of the secret treasures of the gods in the kingdom of Mananan – as wonderful and as unattainable.

Etain was now in some perplexity, but she decided, with a kind of naive good nature, that although she was not in the least in love with Ailill, she cannot see a man die of longing for her, and she promised to be his. Possibly we are to understand here that she was prompted by the divine nature, ignorant of good and evil, and alive only to pleasure and to suffering. It must be said, however, that in the Celtic myths in general this, as we may call it, 'fairy' view of morality is the one generally prevalent both among Danaans and mortals – both alike strike one as morally irresponsible.

Etain now arranged a tryst with Ailill in a house outside Tara – for she will not do what she calls her 'glorious crime' in the king's palace. But Ailill on the eve of the appointed day fell into a profound slumber and missed his appointment. A being in his shape did, however, come to Etain but merely to speak coldly and sorrowfully of his malady and depart again. When the two meet once more, the situation was altogether changed. In Ailill's enchanted sleep his unholy passion for the queen had passed entirely away. Etain, on the other hand, became aware that behind the visible events there were mysteries that she did not understand.

The explanation soon followed. The being who came to her in the shape of Ailill was her Danaan husband, Midhir. He now came to woo her in his true shape, beautiful and nobly dressed, and told her who she really was and how she had been his wife among the people of the goddess Danu. He begged her to leave the king and come with him to his *sidh* at Bri Leith, but Etain refused with scorn.

'Do you think,' she said, 'that I would give up the high king of Ireland for a person whose name and kindred I do not know, except from his own lips?'

The god retired, baffled for the time. But one day, as King Eochaidh sat in his hall, a stranger entered. He was dressed in a purple tunic, his hair was like gold and his eyes shone like candles.

The king welcomed him.

'But who are you?' he asked, 'for I do not know you.'

'Yet I have known you a long time,' returned the stranger.

'Then what is your name?'

'Not a very famous one. I am Midhir of Bri Leith.'

'Why have you come here?'

'To challenge you to a game of chess.'

'I am a good chess-player,' replied the king, who was reputed to be the best in Ireland.

'I think I can beat you,' answered Midhir.

'But the chessboard is in the queen's room, and she is asleep,' objected the king.

'It does not matter,' replied Midhir. 'I have brought a board with me which can be in no way worse than yours.'

He showed it to the king, who admitted that the boast was true. The chessboard was made of silver set in precious stones, and the pieces were of gold.

'Play!' said Midhir to the king.

'I never play without a wager,' replied Eochaidh.

'What shall be the stake?' asked Midhir.

'I do not care,' replied Eochaidh.

'Good!' returned Midhir. 'Let it be that the loser pays whatever the winner demands.'

'That is a wager fit for a king,' said Eochaidh.

They played, and Midhir lost. The stake that Eochaidh claimed from him was that Midhir and his subjects should make a road through Ireland. The king watched the road being made and noticed how Midhir's followers yoked their oxen, not by the horns, as the Gaels did, but at the shoulders, which was better. He adopted the practice, and thus got his nickname, Airemh, that is, 'The Ploughman'.

After a year, Midhir returned and challenged the king again, the terms to be the same as before. Eochaidh agreed with joy, but this time he lost.

'I could have beaten you before if I had wished,' said Midhir, 'and now the stake I demand is Etain, your queen.'

The astonished king, who could not for shame go back on his word, asked for a year's delay. Midhir agreed to return upon that day in a year's time to claim Etain. Eochaidh consulted his warriors, and they decided to keep watch through the whole of the day fixed by Midhir and not to let anyone pass in or out of the royal palace until sunset. For Eochaidh held that if the fairy king could not get Etain upon that one day - his promise would be no longer binding on him.

So when the day came they barred the door and guarded it, but suddenly they saw Midhir among them in the hall. He stood beside Etain and sang this song to her, setting out the pleasures of the homes of the gods under the enchanted hills.

'O fair lady! will you come with me
To a wonderful country which is mine,
Where the people's hair is of golden hue,
And their bodies the colour of virgin snow?

'There no grief or care is known;
White are their teeth, black their eyelashes;
Delight of the eye is the rank of our hosts,
With the hue of the foxglove on every cheek.

'Crimson are the flowers of every mead,
Gracefully speckled as the blackbird's egg;
Though beautiful to see be the plains of Inisfail[1]
They are but commons compared to our great plains.

'Though intoxicating to you be the ale drink of Inisfail,
More intoxicating the ales of the great country;
The only land to praise is the land of which I speak,
Where no one ever dies of decrepit age.

'Soft sweet streams traverse the land;
The choicest of mead and of wine;
Beautiful people without and blemish;
Love without sin, without wickedness.

'We can see the people upon all sides,
But by no one can we be seen;
The cloud of Adam's transgression it is
That prevents them from seeing us.

'O lady, should you come to my brave land,
It is golden hair that will be on your head;

---

[1]   A poetic name for Ireland.

> Fresh pork, beer, new milk and ale,
> You there with me shall have, O fair lady!'

Then Midhir greeted Eochaidh and told him that he had come to take away Etain, according to the king's wager. And, while the king and his warriors looked on helplessly, he placed one arm round the now willing woman, and they both vanished. This broke the spell that hung over everyone in the hall – they rushed to the door but all they could see were two swans flying away.

The king would not, however, yield to the god. He sent to every part of Ireland for news of Etain, but his messengers all came back without having been able to find her. At last, a druid named Dalan learned, by means of oghams carved upon wands of yew, that she was hidden under Midhir's *sídh* of Bri Leith. So Eochaidh marched there with an army and began to dig deep into the abode of the gods of which the 'fairy hill' was the portal. Midhir, as terrified as was the Greek god Hades, according to the Iliad, when it seemed likely that the earth would be rent open and his domains laid bare to the sight, sent out fifty fairy maidens to Eochaidh, every one of them having the appearance of Etain, but the king would only be content with the real Etain, so that Midhir, to save his *sídh*, was at last obliged to give her up. And she lived with the King of Ireland after that until the death of both of them.

But Midhir never forgave the insult. He bided his time for three generations, until Eochaidh and Etain had a male descendant. For they had no son but only a daughter called Etain, like her mother, and this second Etain had a daughter called Mess Buachalla, who had a son called Conaire, surnamed Mór, 'the Great'. Midhir and the gods wove the web of fate round Conaire, so that he and all his men died violent deaths.

The tale in which the death of Conaire is related is one of the most antique and barbaric in conception of all Irish legends, but it has a magnificence of imagination that no other can rival. To this great story the tale of Etain and Midhir may be regarded as what the Irish called a *priomscel*, an 'introductory tale', showing the more remote origin of the events related.

The tale of Conaire introduces for the first time the law or institution of the *geis*, which plays henceforward a very important part in Irish legend, the violation or observance of a *geis* being frequently the turning point in a tragic narrative. The word *geis*, or alternatively *geas*, means a bond, a taboo, a magical injunction, the violation of which would lead to misfortune and death.

Every Irish chieftain or personage of note had certain *geise* peculiar to himself which he must not transgress. These *geise* had sometimes reference to a code of chivalry – thus Diarmaid, when appealed to by Grainne to take her away from Finn, is under *geise* not to refuse protection to a woman. Or they may be merely superstitious or fantastic – thus Conaire, as one of his *geise*, is forbidden to follow three red horsemen on a road, nor must he kill birds (this is because his totem was a bird). It is a *geis* to the Ulster champion Fergus that he must not refuse an invitation to a feast – on this turns the Tragedy of the Sons of Usna (see Chapter 14, 'Some Gaelic Love Stories'). It is not at all clear who imposed these *geise* or how anyone found out what his personal *geise* were – all that was doubtless an affair of the druids. But they were regarded as sacred obligations, and the worst misfortunes were to be apprehended from breaking them. Originally, no doubt, they were regarded as a means of keeping oneself in proper relations with the Otherworld.

Etain's daughter, Etain Oig, married Cormac, King of Ulster. She bore her husband only one daughter. Embittered by her barrenness and his lack of an heir, the king put Etain away and ordered that her infant be abandoned and thrown into a pit. 'Then his two thralls take her to a pit, and she smiles a laughing smile at them as they were putting her into it.' After that they cannot leave her to die, and so they took her to a cowherd of Eterscél, King of Tara, by whom she is fostered and taught 'till she became a good embroidress and there was not in Ireland a king's daughter dearer than she'. Hence the name she was given, Mess Buachalla, which means 'the cowherd's foster child'.

For fear of her being discovered, the cowherd kept her in a house of wickerwork having only a roof opening. But one of King Eterscél's folk had the curiosity to climb up and look in, and he saw there the fairest maiden in Ireland. He took word to the king, who ordered that an opening be made in the wall and the maiden fetched forth, because the king was childless, and it had been prophesied to him by his druid that a woman of unknown race would bear him a son. Then said the king: 'This is the woman that has been prophesied to me.'

Before her release, however, Mess Buachalla was visited by Nemglan, a bird god, who came down through her roof window. On the floor of the hut his bird plumage fell from him and revealed a glorious youth. Like Danaë, like Leda, like Ethlinn daughter of Balor, she gave her love to the god. Before they parted he told her that she will be taken to the king but that she will bear to her Danaan lover a son whose name shall be Conaire and that it shall be forbidden to him to go a hunting after birds.

So Conaire was born and grew up into a wise and noble youth, and he was fostered with a lord named Desa, whose three great-grandsons grew up with him from childhood. Their names were Ferlee and Fergar and Ferrogan, and Conaire, it is said, loved them well and taught them his wisdom.

Then King Eterscél died, and a successor had to be appointed. The oldest son did not succeed to the throne or chieftaincy as a matter of right, but the ablest and best of the family at the time was supposed to be selected by the clan. In this tale the selection is by means of divination. A bull feast was held – a bull was slain and the diviner would 'eat his fill and drink its broth', then he would go to bed, where a truth-compelling spell was chanted over him. Whoever he saw in his dream would be king. The dreamer cried in his sleep that he saw a naked man going towards Tara with a stone in his sling.

The bull feast was held at Tara, but Conaire was at that time with his three foster brothers playing a game on the Plains of Liffey. They separated, Conaire going towards Dublin, where he suddenly saw before him a flock of great birds, wonderful in colour and beauty. He drove after them in his chariot, but the birds would go a spear's cast in front and alight, and fly on again, never letting him come up with them until they reached the seashore. Then he alighted from his chariot and took out his sling to cast at them, whereupon they changed into armed men and turned on him with spears and swords. One of them, however, protected him and said: 'I am Nemglan, king of your father's birds; and you have been forbidden to cast at birds, for here there is no one but is your kin.'

'Till today,' said Conaire, 'I knew this not.'

'Go to Tara tonight,' said Nemglan. 'The bull feast is there, and through it you shall be made king. A man stark naked, who shall go at the end of the night along one of the roads to Tara, having a stone and a sling – 'tis he that shall be king.'

So Conaire stripped off his raiment and went naked through the night to Tara, where all the roads were being watched by chiefs having changes of royal raiment with them to clothe the man who should come according to the prophecy. When Conaire meets them they clothe him and bring him in, and he is proclaimed King of Erin.

A long list of Conaire's *geise* is here given, which are said to have been declared to him by Nemglan. 'The bird reign shall be noble,' said he, 'and these shall be your *geise*:

'You shall not go right-handwise round Tara, nor left-handwise round
    Bregia.[1]
You shall not hunt the evil beasts of Cerna,
You shall not go out every ninth night beyond Tara.
You shall not sleep in a house from which firelight shows after sunset, or
    in which light can be seen from without.
No three Reds shall go before you to the house of Red.
No rapine shall be wrought in your reign.
After sunset, no one woman alone or man alone shall enter the house in
    which you are.
You shall not interfere in a quarrel between two of your thralls.'

Conaire then entered upon his reign, which was marked by the fair seasons and bounteous harvests always associated with the reign of a good king. Foreign ships came to the ports. Oak mast for the swine was up to the knees every autumn; the rivers swarmed with fish. 'No one slew another in Erin during his reign, and to everyone in Erin his fellow's voice seemed as sweet as the strings of lutes. From mid-spring to mid-autumn no wind disturbed a cow's tail.'

Disturbance, however, came from another source. Conaire had put down all raiding and rapine, and his three foster brothers, who were born raiders, took it badly. They pursued their evil ways in pride and wilfulness, and were at last captured red-handed. Conaire would not condemn them to death, as the people begged him to do, but spared them for the sake of his kinship in fosterage. They were, however, banished from Erin and bidden to go raiding overseas, if raid they must. On the seas they met another exiled chief, Ingcél Cáech, the One-Eyed, son of the King of Britain, and joining forces with him they attacked the fortress in which Ingcél's father, mother and brothers were guests at the time, and all were destroyed in a single night. It was then the turn of Ingcél to ask their help in raiding the land of Erin, and gathering a host of other outlawed men, including the seven Manés, sons of Ailill and Medb of Connacht, besides Ferlee, Fergar, and Ferrogan, they made a descent upon Ireland, taking land on the Dublin coast near Howth.

[1] Bregia was the great plain lying eastwards of Tara between Boyne and Liffey.

Meantime Conaire had been lured by the machinations of the Tuatha Dé Danaan into breaking one after another of his *geise*. He settled a quarrel between two of his serfs in Munster, and travelling back to Tara they saw the country around it lit with the glare of fires and wrapped in clouds of smoke. An army from the north, they thought, must be raiding the country, and to escape it Conaire's company had to turn right-handwise round Tara and then left-handwise round the Plain of Bregia. But the smoke and flames were an illusion made by the gods, who were now drawing the toils closer round the doomed king. On his way past Bregia he chased 'the evil beasts of Cerna' – whatever they were – 'but he saw it not till the chase was ended.'

Conaire had now to find a resting place for the night, and he recollected that he was not far from the Hostel of the Leinster lord, Da Derga, which gives its name to this bardic tale, 'The Destruction of Da Derga's Hostel'. Conaire had been generous to him when Da Derga came visiting to Tara, and he determined to seek his hospitality for the night. Da Derga dwelt in a vast hall with seven doors near to the present town of Dublin, probably at Donnybrook, on the high road to the south. As the cavalcade are journeying there an ominous incident occurs – Conaire sees in front of them on the road three horsemen clad all in red and riding on red horses. He remembered his *geis* about the 'three Reds' and sent a messenger forward to bid them fall behind. But however the messenger lashed his horse he failed to get nearer than the length of a spear's throw to the three Red Riders. He shouted to them to turn back and follow the king, but one of them, looking over his shoulder, bade him ironically to look out for 'great news from a Hostel'. Again and again the messenger was sent to them with promises of great reward if they would fall behind instead of preceding Conaire. At last one of them chanted a mystic and terrible strain. 'Lo, my son, great the news. Weary are the steeds we ride – the steeds from the fairy mounds. Though we are living, we are dead. Great are the signs: destruction of life; sating of ravens; feeding of crows; strife of slaughter; wetting of sword edge; shields with broken bosses after sundown. Lo, my son!' Then they ride forward, and, alighting from their red steeds, fasten them at the portal of Da Derga's Hostel and sit down inside. 'Derga' means 'red'. Conaire had therefore been preceded by three red horsemen to the House of Red. 'All my *geise*,' he remarks forebodingly, 'have seized me tonight.'

From this point the story of Conaire Mór takes on a character of supernatural vastness and mystery, the imagination of the bardic narrator dilating, as it were, with the approach of the crisis. Night has fallen, and the pirate host of Ingcél is encamped on the shores of Dublin Bay. They hear the noise of the royal cavalcade, and a long-sighted messenger is sent out to discover what it is. He brings back word of the glittering and multitudinous host that has followed Conaire to the Hostel. A crashing noise is heard – Ingcél asks Ferrogan what it may be – it is the giant warrior Mac Cecht striking flint on steel to kindle fire for the king's feast. 'God send that Conaire be not there tonight,' cry the sons of Desa. 'Woe that he should be under the hurt of his foes.' But Ingcél reminds them of their compact – he had given them the plundering of his own father and brethren; they cannot refuse to stand by him in the attack he meditates on Conaire in the Hostel. A glare of the fire lit by Mac Cecht is now perceived by the pirate host, shining through the wheels of the chariots that are drawn up around the open doors of the Hostel. Another of the *geise* of Conaire has been broken.

Ingcél and his host now proceed to build a great cairn of stones, each man contributing one stone, so that there may be a memorial of the fight and also a record of the number slain when each survivor removes his stone again.

The scene now shifts to the Hostel, where the king's party has arrived and is preparing for the night. A solitary woman comes to the door and seeks admission. 'As long as a weaver's beam were each of her two shins, and they were as dark as the back of a stag beetle. A greyish, woolly mantle she wore. Her hair reached to her knee. Her mouth was twisted to one side of her head.' It was the Morrigan, the Danaan goddess of death and destruction. She leant against the doorpost of the house and looked evilly on the king and his company.

'Well, O woman,' said Conaire, 'if you are a witch, what see you for us?'

'Truly I see for you,' she answered, 'that neither fell nor flesh of yours shall escape from the place into which you have come, save what birds will bear away in their claws.'

She asks admission. Conaire declares that his *geis* forbids him to receive a solitary man or woman after sunset.

'If in sooth,' she says, 'it has befallen the king not to have room in his house for the meal and bed of a solitary woman, they will be gotten apart from him from someone possessing generosity.'

'Let her in, then,' says Conaire, 'though it is a *geis* of mine.'

A lengthy and brilliant passage now follows describing how Ingcél goes to spy out the state of affairs in the Hostel. Peeping through the chariot wheels, he takes note of all he sees, and describes to the sons of Desa the appearance and equipment of each prince and mighty man in Conaire's retinue, while Ferrogan and his brother declare who he is and what destruction he will work in the coming fight. There is Cormac, son of Conor, King of Ulster, the fair and good; there are three huge, black and black-robed warriors of the Picts; there is Conaire's steward, with bristling hair, who settles every dispute – a needle would be heard falling when he raises his voice to speak, and he bears a staff of office the size of a mill shaft; there is the warrior Mac Cecht, who lies supine with his knees drawn up – they resemble two bare hills, his eyes are like lakes, his nose a mountain peak, his sword shines like a river in the sun. Conaire's three sons are there, golden-haired, silk-robed, beloved of all the household, with 'manners of ripe maidens, and hearts of brothers, and valour of bears'. When Ferrogan hears of them he weeps and cannot proceed till hours of the night have passed. Three Fomorian hostages of horrible aspect are there also; and Conall Cearnach with his blood-red shield; and Duftach of Ulster with his magic spear, which, when there is a premonition of battle, must be kept in a brew of soporific herbs or it will flame on its haft and fly forth raging for massacre; and three giants from the Isle of Man with horses' manes reaching to their heels. A strange and unearthly touch is introduced by a description of three naked and bleeding forms hanging by ropes from the roof – they are the daughters of the Badb, another name for the Morrigan, or war goddess, 'three of awful boding,' says the tale enigmatically, 'those are the three that are slaughtered at every time.' We are probably to regard them as visionary beings, portending war and death, visible only to Ingcél. The hall with its separate chambers is full of warriors, cup-bearers, musicians playing and jugglers doing wonderful feats, and Da Derga with his attendants dispensing food and drink. Conaire himself is described: 'the ardour and energy of a king has he and the counsel of a sage; the mantle I saw round him is even as the mist of May Day – lovelier in each hue of it than the other.' His golden-hilted sword lies beside him – a forearm's length of it has escaped from the scabbard, shining like a beam of light. 'He is the mildest and gentlest and most perfect king that has come into the world, even Conaire son of Eterscél . . . great is the tenderness of the sleepy, simple man till he has chanced on a deed of valour. But if his fury and his courage are awakened when the champions of Erin and Alba are at him in the house, the Destruction will not be wrought so long as he is therein . . . sad were the quenching of that reign.'

Ingcél and the sons of Desa then march to the attack and surround the Hostel.

'Silence a while!' says Conaire. 'What is this?'

'Champions at the house,' says Conall Cearnach.

'There are warriors for them here,' answers Conaire.

'They will be needed tonight,' Conall rejoins.

One of Desa's sons rushes first into the Hostel. His head is struck off and cast out of it again. Then the great struggle begins. The Hostel is set on fire, but the fire is quenched with wine or any liquids that are in it. Conaire and his people sally forth – hundreds are slain, and the raiders, for the moment, are routed. But Conaire, who has done prodigies of fighting, is thirsty and can do no more until he gets water. The raiders by advice of their wizards have cut off the River Dodder, which flowed through the Hostel, and all the liquids in the house had been spilt on the fires.

The king, who is perishing of thirst, asks Mac Cecht to procure him a drink, and Mac Cecht turns to Conall and asks him whether he will get the drink for the king or stay to protect him while Mac Cecht does it.

'Leave the defence of the king to us,' says Conall, 'and go to seek the drink, for of you it is demanded.'

Mac Cecht then, taking Conaire's golden cup, rushes forth, bursting through the surrounding host, and goes to seek for water. Then Conall and Cormac of Ulster and the other champions issue forth in turn, slaying multitudes of the enemy. Some return wounded and weary to the little band in the Hostel, while others cut their way through the ring of foes. Conall, Sencha and Duftach stand by Conaire until the end, but Mac Cecht is long in returning. Conaire perishes of thirst, and the three heroes then fight their way out and escape, 'wounded, broken, and maimed'.

Meantime Mac Cecht has rushed over Ireland in frantic search for the water. But the Fairy Folk, who are here manifestly elemental powers controlling the forces of nature, have sealed all the sources against him. He tries the Well of Kesair in Wicklow in vain; he goes to the great rivers, Shannon and Slayney, Bann and Barrow – they all hide away at his approach; the lakes deny him also. At last he finds a lake, Lough Gara in Roscommon, which failed to hide itself in time, and there he fills his cup. In the morning he returned to the Hostel with the precious and hard-won draught, but found the defenders all dead or fled, and two of the raiders in the act of striking off the head of Conaire. Mac Cecht struck off the head of one of them, and hurled a huge pillar stone after the other, who was escaping with Conaire's head. The raiders fell dead on the spot, and Mac Cecht, taking up his master's head, poured the water into its mouth. Thereupon the head spoke, and praised and thanked him for the deed.

A woman then came by and saw Mac Cecht lying exhausted and wounded on the field.

'Come hither, O woman,' says Mac Cecht.

'I dare not go there,' says the woman, 'for horror and fear of you.'

But he persuades her to come and says: 'I know not whether it is a fly or gnat or an ant that nips me in the wound.'

The woman looked and saw a hairy wolf buried as far as the two shoulders in the wound. She seized it by the tail and dragged it forth, and it took 'the full of its jaws out of him.'.

'Truly,' says the woman, 'this is an ant of the Ancient Land.'

Mac Cecht took it by the throat and smote it on the forehead so that it died.

The tale ends in a truly heroic strain. Conall Cearnach, as we have seen, had cut his way out after the king's death, and made his way to Teltin, where he found his father, Amorgin, in the garth before his *dún*. Conall's shield arm had been wounded by thrice fifty spears, and he reached Teltin now with half a shield, and his sword, and the fragments of his two spears.

'Swift are the wolves that have hunted you, my son,' said his father.

''Tis this that has wounded us, old hero, an evil conflict with warriors,' Conall replied.

'Is your lord alive?' asked Amorgin.

'He is not alive,' says Conall.

'I swear to God what the great tribes of Ulster swear: he is a coward who goes out of a fight alive having left his lord with his foes in death.'

'My wounds are not white, old hero,' says Conall. He showed him his shield arm, whereon were thrice fifty spear wounds. The sword arm, which the shield had not guarded, was mangled and maimed and wounded and pierced, save that the sinews kept it to the body without separation.

'That arm fought tonight, my son,' says Amorgin.

'True is that, old hero,' says Conall of the Victories. 'Many are they to whom it gave drinks of death tonight in front of the hostel.'

So ends the story of Etain, and of the overthrow of Fairyland and the fairy vengeance wrought on the great-grandson of Eochaidh the High King.

Chapter 12

THE IRISH ILIAD

With Eber and Eremon, sons of Mil and conquerors of the gods, begins a fresh series of characters in Gaelic tradition – the early 'Milesian' kings of Ireland. Although monkish chroniclers have striven to find history in the legends handed down concerning them, they are nonetheless almost as mythical as the Tuatha Dé Danaan. The first of them who has the least appearance of reality is Tigernmas, who is recorded to have reigned a hundred years after the coming of the Sons of Mil Espaine. He seems to have been what is sometimes called a 'culture king', bearing much the same kind of relation to Ireland as Theseus bore to Athens or Minos to Crete. During his reign, nine new lakes and three new rivers broke forth from beneath the earth to give their waters to Erin. Under his auspices, gold was first smelted, ornaments of gold and silver were first made and clothes were first dyed. He is said to have perished mysteriously with three-quarters of the men of Erin while worshipping Cromm Cruach on the field of Magh Slecht. According to the Dinnsenchus of Magh Slecht:

> 'There came
> Tigernmas, the prince of Tara yonder,
> On Hallowe'en with many hosts,
> A cause of grief to them was the deed.

> 'Dead were the men
> Of Banba's host, without happy strength,
> Around Tigernmas, the destructive man in the North,
> From the worship of Cromm Cruach – 't was no luck for them.

129

'For I have learnt,
Except one-fourth of the keen Gaels
Not a man alive – lasting the snare!
Escaped without death in his mouth.'

In Tigernmas can be seen, perhaps, the great mythical king who, in almost all national histories, closes the strictly mythological age and inaugurates a new era of less obviously divine if hardly less apocryphal characters.

In spite, however, of the worship of the Tuatha Dé Danaan instituted by Eremon, we find the early kings and heroes of Ireland walking very familiarly with their gods. Eochaidh Airemh, high king of Ireland, was apparently reckoned a perfectly fit suitor for the goddess Etain and proved a far from unsuccessful rival of Midhir, the Gaelic Pluto (see Chapter 11, 'The Gods in Exile'). And adventures of love or war were carried quite as cheerfully among the *sídh* dwellers by Eochaidh's contemporaries – Conchobar Mac Nessa, King of Ulster, Cú Roí Mac Daire, King of Munster, Mesgedra, King of Leinster, and Ailill and Medb, King and Queen of Connacht.

All these figures of the second Gaelic cycle (that of the heroes of Ulster and especially of their great champion, Cúchulainn) lived, according to Irish tradition, at about the beginning of the Christian era. Conchobar, indeed, is said to have expired in a fit of rage on hearing of the death of Christ.

But this is a very transparent monkish interpolation into the original story. A quite different view is taken by most scholars, who would see gods and not men in all the legendary characters of the Celtic heroic cycles. On such a subject, however, one may legitimately take sides. Were King Conchobar and his Ulster champions, Fionn and his Fianna, Arthur and his Knights once living men round whom the attributes of gods have gathered or were they ancient deities renamed and stripped of some of their divinity to make them more akin to their human worshippers? History or mythology? A mingling, perhaps, of both. Cúchulainn may have been the name of a real Gaelic warrior, however suspiciously he may now resemble the sun god who is said to have been his father. King Conchobar may have been the real chief of a tribe of Irish Celts before he became an adumbration of the Gaelic sky god. It is the same problem that confronts us in dealing with the heroic legends of Greece and Rome. Were Achilles, Agamemnon, Odysseus, Paris, Aeneas gods, demigods or men? Let us call them all alike – whether they are Greek or Trojan heroes, Red Branch Champions or followers of the Gaelic Fionn or the British Arthur – demigods. Even so, they stand definitely apart from the older gods who were greater than they were.

We are stretching no point in calling them demigods, for the Red Branch Heroes were descended from the Tuatha Dé Dannan. Cúchulainn, the greatest hero of the Ulster cycle, was doubly so, for on his mother's side he was the grandson of the Daghda, while Lugh of the Long Hand is said to have been his father. His mother, Deichtire, daughter of Maga, the daughter of Oenghus 'Son of the Young', was half-sister to King Conchobar and termed a goddess in the Book of Leinster, and all the other principal heroes were of hardly less lofty descent. It is small wonder that they are described in ancient manuscripts as terrestrial gods and goddesses, Conchobar himself being called a terrestrial god of Ulster in the Book of the Dun Cow.

'Terrestrial' they may have been in form, but their acts were superhuman. Indeed, compared with the more modest exploits of the heroes of the Iliad, they were those of giants. Where Greek warriors slew their tens, these men of Ulster dispatched their hundreds. They came home after such exploits so heated that their cold baths boiled over. When they sat down to eat, they devoured whole oxen and drank their mead from vats. With one stroke of their favourite swords they beheaded hills for sport. The gods themselves hardly did more, and it is easy to understand that in those old days not only might the sons of gods look upon the daughters of men and find them fair, but immortal women also need not be too proud to form passing alliances with mortal men.

Some of the older deities seem to have already passed out of memory at the time of the compilation of the Ulster cycle. At any rate, they make no appearance in it. Dead Nuada rests in the Grianán of Aileach. Oghma lies low in Sídh Airceltrai, while the Daghda, thrust into the background by his son Oenghus, mixes himself very little in the affairs of Erin, being last heard of as chief cook to Conaire Mór, a mythical king of Ireland. But the Morrigan is no less eager in encouraging human or semi-divine heroes to war than she was when she revived the fainting spirits of the folk of the goddess Danu at the Battle of Magh Tuireadh. The gods who appear most often in the cycle of the Red Branch of Ulster are the same that have lived on throughout with the most persistent vitality. Lugh the Long-handed, Oenghus of the Brugh, Midhir, Bodb Dearg and Manannán son of Lir are the principal deities who move in the background of the stage where the chief parts are now played by mortals. But to make up for the loss of some of the greater divine figures, the ranks of the gods are being recruited from below. All manner of inferior divinities claim to be members of the tribe of the goddess Danu. The goblins and sprites and demons of the air who shrieked around battles are described collectively as Tuatha Dé Danaan in the Book of Leinster.

As for the Fomorii, they have lost their distinctive names, although they are still recognised as dwellers beneath the deep who at times raid the coast, and do battle with the heroes over whom Conchobar ruled at Emain Macha.

This seat of his government, the traditional site of which is still marked by an extensive prehistoric entrenchment, called Navan Fort, near Armagh, was the centre of an Ulster that stretched southwards as far as the Boyne, and round its ruler gathered such a galaxy of warriors as Ireland had never seen before or will again. They called themselves the 'Champions of the Red Branch', and there was not one of them who was not a hero, but they are all dwarfed by one splendid figure – Cúchulainn, whose name means 'Culann's Hound', described by one scholar as 'the Irish Achilles', while sees in him a Heracles of the Gaels. Like Achilles, he was the chosen hero of his people, in- vincible in battle and yet 'at once to early death and sorrows doomed beyond the lot of man', while, like Heracles, his life was a series of wonderful exploits and labours. It matters little enough, for the lives of all such mythical heroes must be of necessity somewhat alike.

The Irish romances relating to Cúchulainn and his cycle, number nearly a hundred and many of the tales exist in several slightly varying versions having been translated by different scholars.

If Achilles and Heracles were, as some think, personifications of the sun, Cúchulainn is not less so. Most of his attributes, as the old stories record them, are obviously solar symbols. He seemed generally small and insignifi- cant, yet when he was at his full strength, no one could look him in the face without blinking, while the heat of his constitution melted snow for thirty feet all round him. He turned red and hissed as he dipped his body into its bath – the sea. Terrible was his transformation when sorely oppressed by his enemies, as the sun is by mist, storm or eclipse. At such times, according to the *Táin Bó Cuailgne*, 'among the aerial clouds over his head were visible the virulent pouring showers and sparks of ruddy fire which the seething of his savage wrath caused to mount up above him. His hair became tangled about his head, as it had been branches of a red thorn bush stuffed into a strongly fenced gap. . . . Taller, thicker, more rigid, longer than mast of a great ship was the perpendicular jet of dusky blood which out of his scalp's very central point shot upwards and then was scattered to the four cardinal points; whereby was formed a magic mist of gloom resembling the smoky pall that drapes a regal dwelling, what time a king at nightfall of a winter's day draws near to it.'

So marvellous a being was, of course, of marvellous birth. His mother, Deichtire, was on the point of being married to an Ulster chieftain called Sualtam and was sitting at the wedding feast when a mayfly flew into her cup of wine and was unwittingly swallowed by her. That same afternoon she fell into a deep sleep, and in her dream the sun god Lugh appeared to her and told her that it was he whom she had swallowed and bore within her. He ordered her and her fifty attendant maidens to come with him at once, and he put upon them the shapes of birds, so that they were not seen to go. Nothing was heard of them again. But one day, months later, a flock of beautiful birds appeared before Emain Macha and drew out its warriors in their chariots to hunt them.

They followed the birds until nightfall when they found themselves at the Brugh na Bóinne, where the great gods had their homes. As they looked everywhere for shelter, they suddenly saw a splendid palace. A tall and handsome man, richly dressed, came out and welcomed them and led them in. Within the hall were a beautiful, noble-faced woman and fifty maidens, and on the tables were the richest meats and wines and everything fit for the needs of warriors. So they rested there the night, and during the night they heard the cry of a newborn child. The next morning, the man told them who he was and that the woman was Conchobar's half-sister, Deichtire, and he ordered them to take the child and bring it up among the warriors of Ulster. So they brought him back, together with his mother and the maidens, and Deichtire married Sualtam, and all the chiefs, champions, druids, poets and lawgivers of Ulster vied with one another in bringing up the mysterious infant.

At first they called him Sétanta, and this is how he came to change his name. While still a child he was the strongest of the boys of Emain Macha and the champion in their sports. One day he was playing hurley single-handed against all the others and beating them, when Conchobar, the king, rode by with his nobles on the way to a banquet given by Culann, the chief smith of the Ulster champions. Conchobar called to the boy, inviting him to go with them, and he replied that, when the game was finished, he would follow. As soon as the Ulster champions were in Culann's hall, the smith asked the king's permission to unloose his terrible watchdog, which was as strong and fierce as a hundred hounds, and Conchobar, forgetting that the boy was to follow them, gave his permission. Immediately the hound saw Sétanta coming, it rushed at him, open-mouthed. But the boy flung his playing ball into its mouth and then, seizing it by the hind legs, dashed it against a rock until he had killed it.

The smith Culann was very angry at the death of his dog, for there was no other hound in the world like him for guarding a house and flocks. So Sétanta promised to find and train up another one, not less good, for Culann, and, until it was trained, to guard the smith's house as though he were a dog himself. This is why he was called Cúchulainn, that is 'Culann's Hound'; and Cathbad the Druid prophesied that the time would come when the name would he in every man's mouth.

Not long after this, Cúchulainn overheard Cathbad giving druidic instruction and one of his pupils asking him what that day would be propitious for. Cathbad replied that, if any young man first took arms on that day, his name would be greater than that of any other hero's but his life would be short. At once, the boy went to King Conchobar and demanded arms and a chariot. Conchobar asked him who had put such a thought into his head, and he answered that it was Cathbad the Druid. So Conchobar gave him arms and armour and sent him out with a charioteer. That evening Cúchulainn brought back the heads of three champions who had killed many of the warriors of Ulster. He was then only seven years old.

The women of Ulster so loved Cúchulainn after this that the warriors grew jealous and insisted that a wife should be found for him. But Cúchulainn was very hard to please. He would have only one, Emer, the daughter of Forgall the Wily, the best maiden in Ireland for the six gifts – the gift of beauty, the gift of voice, the gift of sweet speech, the gift of needlework, the gift of wisdom and the gift of chastity. So he went to woo her, but she laughed at him for being a boy. Then Cúchulainn swore by the gods of his people that he would make his name known wherever the deeds of heroes were spoken of, and Emer promised to marry him if he could take her from her warlike family.

When Forgall, her father, came to know of this betrothal, he devised a plan to put an end to it. He went to visit King Conchobar at Emain Macha. There he pretended to have heard of Cúchulainn for the first time, and he saw him do all his feats. He said, loud enough to be overheard by all, that if so promising a youth dared to go to the Island of Scáthach the Amazon, in the east of Alba,[1] and learn all her warrior craft, no living man would be able to stand before him. It was hard to reach Scáthach's Isle, and still harder to return from it, and Forgall felt certain that, if Cúchulainn went, he would meet his death there.

Of course, nothing would now satisfy Cúchulainn but going. His two friends, Laoghaire Buadhach, 'the Battle-winner', and Conall Cearnach, Conall of the Victories, said that they would go with him. But before they had gone far, they lost heart and turned back. Cúchulainn went on alone at last he came to the Plain of Ill-luck, where he could not cross without being mired in its bottomless bogs or sticky clay, and while he was debating what he should do he saw coming towards him a young man with a face that shone like the sun,[2] and whose very look put cheerfulness and hope into his heart. The young man gave him a wheel and told him to roll it before him on the plain and to follow it wherever it went. So Cúchulainn set the wheel rolling, and as it went it blazed with light that shot like rays from its rim, and the heat of it made a firm path across the quagmire, where Cúchulainn followed safely.

When he had passed the Plain of Ill-luck and escaped the devouring beasts of the Perilous Glens, he came to the Bridge of the Cliff, beyond which was the country of Scáthach. Here he found on the other side many sons of the princes of Ireland who had come to learn feats of war from Scáthach, and they were playing at hurley on the green. Among them was his friend Ferdia, son of the Fir Bholg, Daman, and they all asked him for the news from Ireland. When he had told them all, he asked Ferdia how he should pass to the dun of Scáthach. Now the Bridge of the Cliff was very narrow and very high, and it crossed a gorge where far below swung the tides of a boiling sea in which ravenous monsters could be seen swimming.

'Not one of us has crossed that bridge,' said Ferdia, 'for there are two feats that Scáthach teaches last, and one is the leap across the bridge and the other the thrust of the Gae-Bholg.[1] For if a man steps upon one end of that bridge,

---

1 Owing to the similarity of the name the supernatural country of Scáthach, 'the Shadowy', was early identified with the islands of Skye, where the Cuillin Peaks still bear witness to the legend.
2 This, of course, was Cúchulainn's father, Lugh.

the middle straight away rises up and flings him back, and if he leaps upon it he may chance to miss his footing and fall into the gulf, where the sea monsters are waiting for him.'

But Cúchulainn waited until evening, when he had recovered his strength from his long journey, and then attempted the crossing of the bridge. Three times he ran towards it from a distance, gathering all his powers together, and strove to leap upon the middle, but three times it rose against him and flung him back, while his companions jeered at him because he would not wait for the help of Scáthach. But at the fourth leap he lit fairly on the centre of the bridge, and with one leap more he was across it and stood before the strong fortress of Scáthach, and she was amazed at his courage and vigour, and admitted him to be her pupil.

For a year and a day Cúchulainn stayed with Scáthach, and all the feats she had to teach he learned easily, and last of all she taught him the use of the Gae-Bholg, and gave him that dreadful weapon, which she had deemed no champion before him good enough to have. And the manner of using the Gae-Bholg was that it was thrown with the foot, and if it entered an enemy's body it filled every limb and crevice of him with its barbs. While Cúchulainn dwelt with Scáthach his friend above all friends and his rival in skill and valour was Ferdia, and before they parted they vowed to love and help one another as long as they should live.

Now while Cúchulainn was in the Land of the Shadows it chanced that Scáthach made war on the people of the Princess Aoife, who was the fiercest and strongest of the woman warriors of the world, so that even Scáthach feared to meet her in arms. On going forth to the war, therefore, Scáthach mixed with Cúchulainn's drink a sleepy herb so that he should not wake for four-and-twenty hours, by which time the army would be far on its way, for she feared that evil should come to him before he had got his full strength. But the potion that would have served another man for a day and a night only held Cúchulainn for one hour; and when he woke up he seized his arms and followed the army by its chariot tracks until he came up with them. Then it is said that Scáthach uttered a sigh, for she knew that he would not be restrained from the war.

When the armies met, Cúchulainn and the two sons of Scáthach wrought

---

[1] This means probably 'the belly spear'. With this terrible weapon Cúchulainn was fated in the end to slay his friend Ferdia.

great deeds on the enemy and slew six of the mightiest of Aoife's warriors. Then Aoife sent word to Scáthach and challenged her to single combat. But Cúchulainn declared that he would meet the fair Fury in place of Scáthach, and he asked first of all what were the things she most valued. 'What Aoife loves most,' said Scáthach, 'are her two horses, her chariot and her charioteer.' Then the pair met in single combat, and every champion's feat that they knew they tried on each other in vain, until at last a blow of Aoife's shattered the sword of Cúchulainn to the hilt.

At this Cúchulainn cried out: 'Ah me! behold the chariot and horses of Aoife, fallen into the glen!' Aoife glanced round, and Cúchulainn, rushing in, seized her round the waist and slung her over his shoulder and bore her back to the camp of Scáthach. There he flung her on the ground and put his knife to her throat. She begged for her life, and Cúchulainn granted it on condition that she made a lasting peace with Scáthach and gave hostages for her fulfilment of the pledge. To this she agreed, and Cúchulainn and she became not only friends but lovers.

Before Cúchulainn left the Land of Shadows he gave Aoife a golden ring, saying that if she should bear him a son he was to be sent to seek his father in Ireland as soon as he should have grown so that his finger would fit the ring. And Cúchulainn said, 'Charge him under *geise* that he shall not make himself known, that he never turn out of the way for any man, nor ever refuse a combat. And let his name be Connlai.'

Then Cúchulainn returned to Ireland and went in a scythed chariot to Forgall's palace. He leaped over its triple walls and slew everyone who came near him. Forgall met his death in trying to escape Cúchulainn's rage. He found Emer and placed her in his chariot and drove away, and, every time that Forgall's warriors came up to them, he turned and slew a hundred and put the rest to flight. He reached Emain Macha in safety, and he and Emer were married there.

And so great, after this, were the fame of Cúchulainn's prowess and Emer's beauty that the men and women of Ulster yielded them precedence – him among the warriors and her among the women – in every feast and banquet at Emain Macha.

But all that Cúchulainn had done up to this time was as nothing to the deeds he did in the great war which all the rest of Ireland, headed by Ailill and Medb, King and Queen of Connacht, made upon Ulster to get the Brown Bull of Cuailgne. This bull was one of two of fairy descent. They had originally been the swineherds of two of the gods, Bodb, King of the Sídhe of Munster, and Ochall Ochne, King of the Sídhe of Connacht. As swineherds they were in perpetual rivalry. The better to carry on their quarrel, they changed themselves into two ravens and fought for a year. Next they turned into water monsters that tore one another for a year in the Suir and a year in the Shannon. Then they became human again and fought as champions and ended by changing into eels. One of these eels went into the River Cruind in Cuailgne in Ulster, where it was swallowed by a cow belonging to Daire of Cuailgne, and the other into the spring of Uaran Garad in Connacht, where it passed into the belly of a cow of Queen Medb's. Thus were born those two famous beasts, Donn Cuailgne, the Brown Bull of Ulster, and Finnbhenach, the White-horned Bull of Connacht.

Now the White-horned Bull was so proud that he scorned to belong to a woman, and he went out of Medb's herds into those of her husband, Ailill, so that when Ailill and Medb one day, in their idleness, counted up their possessions to set them off one against the other, although they were equal in every other thing, in jewels and clothes and household vessels, in sheep and horses and swine and cattle, Medb had no one bull that was worthy to be set beside Ailill's White-horned. Refusing to be less in anything than her husband, the proud queen sent heralds, with gifts and compliments, to Daire, asking him to lend her the Brown Bull for a year. Daire would have done so gladly had not one of Medb's messengers been heard boasting in his cups that, if Daire had not lent the Brown Bull of his own free will, Medb would have taken it. This was reported to Daire, who at once swore that she should never have it. Medb's messenger returned, and the Queen of Connacht, furious at his refusal, vowed that she would take it by force.

She assembled the armies of all the rest of Ireland to go against Ulster and made Fergus Mac Roth, an Ulster champion who had quarrelled with King Conchobar, its leader. They expected to have an easy victory, for the warriors of Ulster were at that time lying under a magic weakness that fell upon them for many days in each year as the result of a curse laid upon them long before by a goddess who had been insulted by one of Conchobar's ancestors. Medb called up Gabalgline, a prophetess of her people, to foretell victory. 'How do you see our hosts?' asked the queen.

'I see crimson on them. I see red,' she replied.

'But the warriors of Ulster are lying in their sickness. Nay, how do you see our men?'

'I see them all crimson. I see them all red,' she repeated. And then she added to the astonished queen, who had expected a quite different foretelling: 'For I see a small man doing deeds of arms, though there are many wounds on his smooth skin. The hero light shines round his head, and there is victory on his forehead. He is richly clothed, and young and beautiful and modest, but he is a dragon in battle. His appearance and his valour are those of Cúchulainn of Muirthemne. Who that "Culann's hound" from Muirthemne may be, I do not know; but I know this, that all our army will be reddened by him. He is setting out for battle. He will hew down your hosts. The slaughter he shall make will be long remembered. There will be many women crying over the bodies mangled by the Hound of the Forge whom I see before me now.' For Cúchulainn was, for some reason unknown to us, the only man in Ulster who was not subject to the magic weakness and therefore it fell upon him to defend Ulster single-handed against the whole of Medb's army.

In spite of the injury done him by King Conchobar, Fergus still kept a love for his own country. He had not the heart to march upon the Ulster champions without first secretly sending a messenger to warn them, so that, although all the other champions of the Red Branch were helpless, Cúchulainn was watching the marches when the army came.

Now begins the story of the *aristeia* of the Gaelic hero. It is, after the manner of epics, the record of a series of single combats in each of which Cúchulainn slays his adversary. Man after man comes against him and not one goes back. In the intervals between the duels, Cúchulainn harasses the army with his sling, slaying a hundred men a day. He kills Medb's pet dog, bird and squirrel, and creates such terror that no one dares to stir out of the camp. Medb herself has a narrow escape, for one of her serving women, who puts on her mistress's golden headdress, is killed by a stone flung from Cúchulainn's sling.

The great queen determines to see with her own eyes this marvellous hero who is holding all her warriors at bay. She sends an envoy asking him to come and parley with her. Cúchulainn agrees, and at the meeting Medb is amazed at his boyish look. She finds it hard to believe that it is this beardless stripling of seventeen who is killing her champions, until the whole army seems as though it were melting away. She offers him her own friendship and great honours and possessions in Connacht if he will forsake Conchobar. He refuses, but she offers it again and again. At last Cúchulainn indignantly declares that the next man who comes with that message will do so at his peril. One bargain, however, he will make. He is willing to fight one of the men of Ireland every day, and while the duel lasts, the main army may march on; but, as soon as Cúchulainn has killed his man, it must halt until the next day. Medb agrees to this, thinking it better to lose one man a day than a hundred.

Medb makes the same offer to every famous warrior to induce him to go against Cúchulainn. The reward for the head of the champion will be the hand of her daughter, Findabair. In spite of this, not one of the aspirants to the princess can stand before Cúchulainn. All perish, and Findabair, when she finds out how she is being promised to a fresh suitor every day, dies of shame. But while Cúchulainn is engaged in these combats, Medb sends men who scour Ulster for the Brown Bull and find him and drive him, with fifty heifers, into her camp.

Meanwhile the Aes Sídhe, the fairy god clan, are watching the half-divine, half-mortal hero, amazed at his achievements. His exploits kindle love in the fierce heart of the Morrigan, the great war goddess. Cúchulainn is awoken from sleep by a terrible shout from the north. He orders his driver, Laeg, to yoke the horses to his chariot so that he may find out who raised it. They go in the direction from which the sound had come and meet with a woman in a chariot drawn by a red horse. She has red eyebrows and a red dress and a long, red cloak, and she carries a great, grey spear. He asks her who she is, and she tells him that she is a king's daughter and that she has fallen in love with him through hearing of his exploits. Cúchulainn says that he has other things to think of than love. She replies that she has been giving him her help in his battles and will still do so, and Cúchulainn answers that he does not need any woman's help. 'Then,' says she, 'if you will not have my love and help, you shall have my hatred and enmity. When you are fighting with a warrior as good as yourself, I will come against you in various shapes and hinder you, so that he shall have the advantage.' Cúchulainn draws his sword, but all he sees is a hoodie crow sitting on a branch. He knows from this that the red woman in the chariot was the great queen of the gods.

The next day, a warrior named Loch went to meet Cúchulainn. At first he refused to fight one who was beardless; so Cúchulainn smeared his chin with blackberry juice until it looked as though he had a beard. While Cúchulainn was fighting Loch, the Morrigan came against him three times – first as a heifer that tried to overthrow him, and next as an eel that got beneath his feet as he stood in running water, and then as a wolf that seized hold of his right arm. But Cúchulainn broke the heifer's leg, trampled upon the eel and put out one of the wolf's eyes, although every one of these three times Loch wounded him. In the end, Cúchulainn slew Loch with his invincible spear, the Gae-Bholg, a kind of harpoon made of a sea monster's bones, with thirty barbs. The Morrigan came back to Cúchulainn disguised as an old woman to have her wounds healed by him, for no one could cure them but he who had made them. She became his friend after this and helped him.

But the fighting was so continuous that Cúchulainn got no sleep except just for a while from time to time when he might rest a little with his head on his hand and his hand on his spear and his spear on his knee. So that his father, Lugh the Long-handed, took pity on him and came to him in the semblance of a tall, handsome man in a green cloak and a gold-embroidered silk shirt and carrying a black shield and a five-pronged spear. He put him into a sleep of three days and three nights, and while he rested, he laid druidic herbs on all his wounds, so that in the end he rose up again completely healed and as strong as at the very beginning of the war. While he was asleep, the boy troop of Emain Macha, Cúchulainn's old companions, came and fought instead of him and slew three times their own number but were all killed.

It was at this time that Medb asked Fergus Mac Roth, Cúchulainn's foster father to go and fight with Cúchulainn. Fergus answered that he would never fight against his own foster son. Medb asked him again and again, and at last he went but without his famous sword.

'Fergus, my guardian,' said Cúchulainn, 'it is not safe for you to come out against me without your sword.'

'If I had the sword,' replied Fergus, 'I would not use it on you.'

Then Fergus asked Cúchulainn, for the sake of all he had done for him in his boyhood, to pretend to fight with him and then give way before him and run away. Cúchulainn answered that he was very loth to be seen running from any man. But Fergus promised Cúchulainn that, if Cúchulainn would run away from Fergus then Fergus would run away from Cúchulainn at some future time, whenever Cúchulainn wished. Cúchulainn agreed to this, for he knew that it would be for the profit of Ulster. So they fought a little, and then Cúchulainn turned and fled in the sight of all Medb's army. Fergus went back; and Medb could not reproach him any more.

But she cast about to find some other way of vanquishing Cúchulainn. The agreement made had been that only one man a day should be sent against him. But now Medb sent the wizard Calatin with his twenty-seven sons and his grandson all at once, for she said 'they are really only one, for they are all from Calatin's body'. They never missed a throw with their poisoned spears, and every man they hit died, either on the spot or within the week. When Fergus heard of this, he was in great grief, and he sent a man called Fiacha, an exile, like himself, from Ulster, to watch the fight and report how it went. Now Fiacha did not mean to join in it, but when he saw Cúchulainn assailed by twenty-nine at a time and overpowered, he could not restrain himself. So he drew his sword and helped Cúchulainn, and between them they killed Calatin and his whole family.

As a last resource now, Medb sent for Ferdia, who was the great champion of the 'Men of Domnu', who had thrown in their lot with Medb in the war for the Brown Bull. Ferdia had been a companion and fellow pupil of Cúchulainn with Scáthach, and he did not wish to fight with him. But Medb told him that, if he refused, her satirists should make such lampoons on him that he would die of shame and his name would be a reproach for ever. She also offered him great rewards and honours and bound herself in six sureties to keep her promises. At last, reluctantly, he went.

Cúchulainn saw him coming and went out to welcome him, but Ferdia said that he had not come as a friend but to fight. Now Cúchulainn had been Ferdia's junior and serving boy in Scáthach's Island, and he begged him for the memory of those old times to go back, but Ferdia said he could not. They fought all day, and neither had gained any advantage by sunset. So they kissed one another and each went back to his camp. Ferdia sent half his food and drink to Cúchulainn, and Cúchulainn sent half his healing herbs and medicines to Ferdia, and their horses were put in the same stable, and their charioteers slept by the same fire. And so it happened on the second day. But at the end of the third day they parted gloomily, knowing that on the morrow one of them must fall, and their horses were not put in the same stall that night, neither did their charioteers sleep at the same fire. On the fourth day Cúchulainn succeeded in killing Ferdia by casting the Gae-Bholg at him from underneath. But when he saw that he was dying, the battle fury passed away, and he took his old companion up in his arms and carried him across the river on whose banks they had fought so that he might be with the men of Ulster in his death

Cúchulainn carries Ferdia across the river, from a painting by E. Wallcousins

and not with the men of Ireland. And he wept over him and said: 'It was all a game and a sport until Ferdia came. Oh, Ferdia! your death will hang over me like a cloud for ever. Yesterday he was greater than a mountain. Today he is less than a shadow.'

By this time, Cúchulainn was so covered with wounds that he could not bear his clothes to touch his skin but had to hold them off with hazel sticks and fill the spaces in between with grass. There was not a place on him the size of a needle point that had not a wound on it except his left hand, which held the shield.

But Sualtam, Cúchulainn's reputed father, had learned what a sore plight his son was in. 'Do I hear the heaven bursting, or the sea running away, or the earth breaking open,' he cried, 'or is it my son's groaning that I hear?'

He came to look for him and found him covered with wounds and blood. But Cúchulainn would not let his father either weep for him or try to avenge him. 'Go, rather,' he said to him, 'to Emain Macha and tell Conchobar that I can no longer defend Ulster against all the four provinces of Erin without help. Tell him that there is no part of my body on which there is not a wound and that, if he wishes to save his kingdom, he must make no delay.'

Sualtam mounted Cúchulainn's war horse, the Grey of Macha, and galloped to Emain Macha. Three times he shouted: 'Men are being killed, women carried off and cattle lifted in Ulster.' Twice he met with no response. The third time, Cathbad the Druid roused himself from his lethargy to denounce the man who was disturbing the king's sleep. In his indignation Sualtam turned away so sharply that the grey steed reared and struck its rider's shield against his neck with such force that he was decapitated. The startled horse then turned back into Conchobar's stronghold and dashed through it, Sualtam's severed head continuing to cry out: 'Men are being killed, women carried off and cattle lifted in Ulster.'

Such a portent was enough to rouse the most drowsy. Conchobar, himself again, swore a great oath. 'The heavens are over us, the earth is beneath us, and the sea circles us round, and unless the heavens fall, with all their stars or the earth gives way beneath us or the sea bursts over the land, I will restore every cow to her stable and every woman to her home.'

He sent messengers to rally Ulster, and they gathered and marched on the men of Erin. And then was fought such a battle as had never been seen before in Ireland. First one side, then the other, gave way and rallied again, until Cúchulainn heard the noise of the fight and rose up in spite of all his wounds and came to it.

He called out to Fergus Mac Roth, reminding him how he had bound himself with an oath to run from him when called upon to do so. So Fergus ran before Cúchulainn, and when Medb's army saw their leader running they broke and fled like one man.

But the Donn Cuailgne went with the army into Connacht, and there he met Ailill's bull, Finnbhenach. And he fought Finnbhenach and tore him limb from limb and carried off pieces of him on his horns, dropping the loins at Athlone and the liver at Trim. Then he went back to Cuailgne and turned mad, killing all who crossed his path, until his heart burst with bellowing, and he fell dead.

This was the end of the great war called Táin Bó Cuailgne, the 'Driving of the Cattle of Cooley'.

Yet, wondrous as it was, it was not the most marvellous of Cúchulainn's exploits. Like all the solar gods and heroes of Celtic myth, he carried his conquests into the dark region of Hades. On this occasion the mysterious realm is an island called Dún Scaith, that is, the 'Shadowy Town', and although its king is not mentioned by name, it seems likely that he was Midhir and that Dún Scaith is another name for the Isle of Falga or Man. The story, as a poem called 'The Phantom Chariot' in the Book of the Dun Cow relates it, is curiously sug-

Queen Medb's Cairn, Knocknarra, Sligo

gestive of a raid which the powers of light, and especially the sun gods, are represented as having made upon Hades in kindred British myth (*see* Chapter 22, 'The Victories of Light over Darkness'). The same loathsome combatants issue out of the underworld to repel its assailants. There was a pit in the centre of Dún Scaith, out of which swarmed a vast throng of serpents. No sooner had Cúchulainn and the heroes of Ulster disposed of these than 'a house full of toads' was loosed upon them – 'sharp, beaked monsters' (says the poem), which caught them by the noses, and these were in turn replaced by fierce dragons. Yet the heroes prevailed and carried off the spoil – three cows of magic qualities and a marvellous cauldron in which was always found an inexhaustible supply of meat with treasure of silver and gold to boot. They started back for Ireland in a coracle, the three cows being towed behind with the treasure in bags around their necks. But the gods of Hades raised a storm that wrecked their ship, and they had to swim home. Here Cúchulainn's more than mortal prowess came in useful. We are told that he floated nine men to shore on each of his hands and thirty on his head while eight more, clinging to his sides, used him as a kind of lifebelt.

After this came the tragedy of Cúchulainn's career, the unhappy duel in which he killed his only son, not knowing who he was. The story is one common, apparently, to the Aryan nations, for it is found not only in the Gaelic but in the Germanic and Persian mythic traditions. It will be remembered that Cúchulainn defeated a rival of Scáthach the Amazon, named Aoife, and compelled her to render submission. The hero also had a son by Aoife, and he asked that the boy should be called Connlai, and that, when he was of an age to travel, he should be sent to Ireland to find his father. Aoife promised this, but a little later news came to her that Cúchulainn had married Emer. Mad with jealousy, she determined to make the son avenge her slight upon the father. She taught him the craft of arms until there was no more that he could learn and sent him to Ireland. Before he started, she laid three *geise* upon him. The first was that he was not to turn back, the second that he was never to refuse a challenge, and the third that he was never to tell his name.

He arrived at Dundealgan, the modern Dundalk, Cúchulainn's home, and the warrior Conall came down to meet him and asked him his name and lineage. He refused to tell them, and this led to a duel in which Conall was disarmed and humiliated. Cúchulainn next approached him, asked the same question and received the same answer.

'Yet if I was not under a command,' said Connlai, who did not know he was speaking to his father, 'there is no man in the world to whom I would sooner tell it than to yourself, for I love your face.'

Even this compliment could not stave off the fight, for Cúchulainn felt it his duty to punish the insolence of this stripling who refused to declare who he was. The fight was a fierce one, and the invincible Cúchulainn found himself so pressed that the 'hero light' shone round him and transfigured his face. When Connlai saw this, he knew who his antagonist must be and purposely flung his spear slantways so that it might not hit his father. But before Cúchulainn understood, he had thrown the terrible Gae-Bholg. Connlai, dying, declared his name, and so passionate was Cúchulainn's grief that the men of Ulster were afraid that in his madness he might wreak his wrath upon them. They, therefore, called upon Cathbad the Druid to put him under a spell. Cathbad turned the waves of the sea into the appearance of armed men, and Cúchulainn smote them with his sword until he fell prone from weariness.

It would take too long to relate all the other adventures and exploits of Cúchulainn. Enough has been done if any reader of this chapter should be persuaded by it to study the wonderful saga of ancient Ireland for himself or herself. We must pass on quickly to its tragic close – the hero's death.

Medb, Queen of Connacht, had never forgiven him for keeping back her army from raiding Ulster and for slaying so many of her friends and allies, so she went secretly to all those whose relations Cúchulainn had killed (and they were many) and stirred them up to revenge.

Besides this, she had sent the three daughters of Calatin the Wizard, born after their father's death at the hands of Cúchulainn, to Alba and to Babylon to learn witchcraft. When they came back they were mistresses of every kind of sorcery and could make the illusion of battle with an incantation.

And lest she might fail even then, she waited with patience until the men of Ulster were again in their magic weakness, and there was no one to help Cúchulainn but himself.

Lugaid, son of the Cú Roí, King of Munster, whom Cúchulainn had killed for the sake of Blathnad, Midhir's daughter, gathered the Munster men. Erc, whose father had also fallen at Cúchulainn's hands, called the men of Meath. The King of Leinster brought out his army, and, with Ailill and Medb and all Connacht, they marched into Ulster again and began to ravage it.

Conchobar called his warriors and druids into council to see if they could find some means of putting off war until they were ready to meet it. He did not wish Cúchulainn to go out single-handed a second time against all the rest of Ireland, for he knew that if the champion perished the prosperity of Ulster would fall with him for ever. So when Cúchulainn came to Emain Macha, the king set all the ladies, singers and poets of the court to keep his thoughts from war until the men of Ulster had recovered from their weakness.

But while they sat feasting and talking in the 'sunny house', the three daughters of Calatin came fluttering down on to the lawn before it and began gathering grass and thistles and puffballs and withered leaves, and turning them into the semblance of armies. And, by the same magic, they caused shouts and shrieks and trumpet blasts and the clattering of arms to be heard all round the house, as though a battle were being fought.

Cúchulainn leaped up, red with shame to think that fighting should be going on without his help, and seized his sword, but Cathbad's son caught him by the arms. All the druids explained to him that what he saw was only an enchantment raised by the children of Calatin to draw him out to his death. But it was as much as all of them could do to keep him quiet while he saw the phantom armies and heard the magic sounds.

So they decided that it would be well to remove Cúchulainn from Emain Macha to Gleann-na-Bodhar, the 'Deaf Valley', until all the enchantments of the daughters of Calatin were spent. It was the quality of this valley that, if all the men of Ireland were to shout round it at once, no one within it would hear a sound.

But the daughters of Calatin went there too, and again they took thistles and puffballs and withered leaves and put on them the appearance of armed men, so that there seemed to be no place outside the whole valley that was not filled with shouting battalions. And they made the illusion of fires all around and the sound of women shrieking. Everyone who heard that outcry was frightened at it, not only the men and women but even the dogs.

Although the women and the druids shouted back with all the strength of their voices to drown it, they could not keep Cúchulainn from hearing. 'Alas!' he cried, 'I hear the men of Ireland shouting as they ravage the province. My triumph is at an end. My fame is gone. Ulster lies low for ever.'

'Let it pass,' said Cathbad. 'It is only the idle magic noises made by the children of Calatin who want to draw you out to put an end to you. Stay here with us and take no heed of them.'

Cúchulainn obeyed, and the daughters of Calatin went on for a long time filling the air with noises of battle, but they grew tired of it at last, for they saw that the druids and women had outwitted them.

They did not succeed until one of them took the form of a sweetheart of Cúchulainn's and came to him, crying out that Dundealgan was burnt and Muirthemne ruined and the whole province of Ulster ravaged. Then at last he was deceived and took his arms and armour and, in spite of all that was said to him, he ordered Laeg to yoke his chariot.

Signs and portents now began to gather as thickly round the doomed hero as they did round the wooers in the hall of Odysseus. His famous war horse, the Grey of Macha, refused to be bridled and shed large tears of blood. His mother, Deichtire, brought him a goblet full of wine, and three times the wine turned into blood as he put it to his lips. At the first ford he crossed, he saw a maiden of the *sídhe* washing clothes and armour, and she told him that it was the clothes and arms of Cúchulainn, who was soon to be dead. He met three ancient hags cooking a hound on spits of rowan, and they invited him to partake of it. He refused, for he was under a *geis* not eat the flesh of his namesake, but they shamed him it by telling him that he ate at rich men's tables and refused the hospitality of the poor. The forbidden meat paralysed half his body. Then he saw his enemies coming up against him in their chariots.

Cúchulainn had three spears, of which it was prophesied that each should kill a king. Three druids were charged in turn to ask for these spears, for it was not thought lucky to refuse anything to a druid. The first one came up to where Cúchulainn was making the plain red with slaughter. 'Give me one of those spears,' he said, 'or I will lampoon you.'

'Take it,' replied Cúchulainn. 'I have never yet been lampooned for refusing anyone a gift.' And he threw the spear at the druid and killed him. But Lugaid, son of Cú Roí, got the spear and killed Laeg with it. Laeg was the king of all chariot-drivers.

'Give me one of your spears, Cúchulainn,' said the second druid.

'I need it myself,' he replied.

'I will lampoon the province of Ulster because of you if you refuse.'

'I am not obliged to give more than one gift in a day,' said Cúchulainn, 'but Ulster shall never be lampooned because of me.' He threw the spear at the druid, and it went through his head. But Erc, King of Leinster, got it and mortally wounded the Grey of Macha, the king of all horses.

'Give me your spear,' said the third druid.

'I have paid all that is due from myself and Ulster,' replied Cúchulainn.

'I will satirise your kindred if you do not,' said the druid.

'I shall never go home, but I will be the cause of no lampoons there,' answered Cúchulainn, and he threw the spear at the asker and killed him. But Lugaid threw it back, and it went through Cúchulainn's body and wounded him to the death.

Then, in his agony, he greatly desired to drink. He asked his enemies to let him go to a lake that lay close by and quench his thirst and then come back again. 'If I cannot come back to you, come to fetch me,' he said, and they let him go.

Cúchulainn drank and bathed and came out of the water. But he found that he could not walk, so he called to his enemies to come to him. There was a pillar stone near, and he bound himself to it with his belt so that he might die standing up and not lying down. His dying horse, the Grey of Macha, came back to fight for him and killed fifty men with his teeth and thirty with each of his hoofs. But the 'hero light' had died out of Cúchulainn's face, leaving it as pale as 'a one-night's snow', and a crow came and perched upon his shoulder.

'Truly it was not upon that pillar that birds used to sit,' said Erc.

Now that they were certain that Cúchulainn was dead, they all gathered round him, and Lugaid cut off his head to take it to Medb. But vengeance came quickly, for Conall Cearnach was in pursuit, and he made a terrible slaughter of Cúchulainn's enemies.

Thus perished the great hero of the Gaels in the twenty-seventh year of his age, and with him fell the prosperity of Emain Macha and of the Red Branch of Ulster.

Chapter 13

THE LAND OF THE WEE FOLK

Of the stories of the men of Ulster that do not centre on the figure of Cúchulainn, one of the most interesting is that of Fergus Mac Leda and the King of the Wee Folk. In this tale Fergus appears as King of Ulster, but as he was contemporary with Conchobar and in the Táin Bó Cuailgne is represented as following him to war, he was probably really a sub-king, like Cúchulainn.

The tale is set in Faylinn, or the Land of the Wee Folk, a race of elves presenting an amusing parody of human institutions on a reduced scale but endowed (like dwarfish people generally in the literature of early races) with magical powers. Iubdan, the King of Faylinn, when flushed with wine at a feast, bragged of the greatness of his power and the invincibility of his armed forces – did they not have the strong man Glower, who with his axe had been known to hew down a thistle at a stroke? But the king's bard, Eisirt, had heard something of a giant race in a land called Ulster, one man of whom would annihilate a whole battalion of the Wee Folk, and he incautiously hinted as much to the boastful king. He was immediately clapped into prison for his audacity and allowed free only by promising to go immediately to the land of the mighty men and bring back evidence of the truth of his incredible story.

So off he went, and one fine day King Fergus and his lords found at the gate of their *dún* a tiny little fellow magnificently clad in the robes of a royal bard, who was demanding entrance. He was borne in upon the hand of Aeda, the king's dwarf and bard, and after charming the court by his wise and witty sayings, and receiving a noble largesse, which he at once distributed among the poets and other court attendants of Ulster, he left for home, taking with him as a guest the dwarf Aeda, before whom the Wee Folk fled as a 'Fomorian giant', although, as Eisirt explained, the average man of Ulster can carry him like a child. Iubdan was now convinced, but Eisirt put him under a *geis*, the bond of chivalry that no Irish chieftain can repudiate without being shamed, to go himself, as Eisirt had done, to the palace of Fergus and taste the king's porridge. Iubdan, after having seen Aeda, was much dismayed at the thought, but he prepared to go and bade Bebo, his wife, accompany him.

'You did an ill deed,' said she, 'when you condemned Eisirt to prison, but surely there is no man under the sun that can make you hear reason.'

So off they went, and Iubdan's fairy steed bore them over the sea until they reached Ulster, and by midnight they were standing before the king's palace.

'Let us taste the porridge as we are were bound,' said Bebo, 'and make off before daybreak.'

They stole in and found the porridge pot, to the rim of which Iubdan could reach only by standing on his horse's back. In straining downwards to get at the porridge he overbalanced and fell in. There in the thick porridge he was stuck fast, and there Fergus's scullions found him at the break of day, with the faithful Bebo lamenting. They bore him off to Fergus, who was amazed at finding another wee man, with a woman too, in his palace. He treated them hospitably but refused all appeals to let them go. The story now recounts in a spirit of broad humour several Rabelaisian adventures in which Bebo is concerned and gives a charming poem supposed to have been uttered by Iubdan in the form of advice to Fergus's fire steward as to the merits for burning of different kinds of timber. The following are extracts:

'Burn not the sweet apple tree of drooping branches, of the white blossoms, to whose gracious head each man puts forth his hand. . . . Burn not the noble willow, the unfailing ornament of poems; bees drink from its blossoms, all delight in the graceful tent. . . . The delicate, airy tree of the druids, the rowan with its berries, this burn; but avoid the weak tree, burn not the slender hazel. . . . The ash tree of the black buds burn not – timber that speeds the wheel, that yields the rider his switch; the ashen spear is the scale beam of battle.'

At last the Wee Folk came in a great multitude to beg the release of Iubdan. On the king's refusal, they visited the country with various plagues, snipping off the ears of corn, letting the calves suck all the cows dry, defiling the wells, and so forth, but Fergus was obdurate. In their quality as earth gods, dei terreni, they promised to make the plains before the palace of Fergus stand thick with corn every year without ploughing or sowing, but all was in vain. At last, however, Fergus agreed to ransom Iubdan against the best of his fairy treasures, so Iubdan recounted them – the cauldron that can never be emptied, the harp that plays by itself, and finally he mentioned a pair of water shoes, wearing which a man can go over or under water as freely as on dry land. Fergus accepted the shoes, and Iubdan was released.

But it was hard for a mortal to get the better of the gods – a touch of hidden malice lurked in magical gifts, and so it proved now. Fergus was never tired of exploring the lakes and rivers of Ireland, but one day, in Loch Rury, he met a hideous monster, the Muirdris, or river-horse, which inhabited that lake and from which he barely saved himself. With the terror of this encounter his face was twisted awry, but since a blemished man could not rule, his queen and nobles took pains to banish all mirrors from the palace and keep the knowledge of his condition from him. One day, however, he struck a servant for some negligence, and the maid, indignant, cried out: 'It were better for you, Fergus, to avenge yourself on the river-horse that has twisted your face than to do brave deeds on women!' Fergus demanded a mirror and looked in it. 'It is true,' he said, 'the river-horse of Loch Rury has done this thing.'

The conclusion is given in the words of a poem by Sir Samuel Ferguson. Fergus donned the magic shoes, took sword in hand, and went to Loch Rury:

> 'For a day and night
> Beneath the waves he rested out of sight,
> But all the Ultonians on the bank who stood
> Saw the loch boil and redden with his blood.
> When next at sunrise skies grew also red
> He rose – and in his hand the Muirdris' head.
> Gone was the blemish! On his goodly face
> Each trait symmetric had resumed its place;
> And they who saw him marked in all his mien
> A king's composure, ample and serene.
> He smiled; he cast his trophy to the bank,
> Said, "I, survivor, Ulstermen!" and sank.'

The humorous treatment of the fairy element in the story would mark it as belonging to a late period of Irish legend, but the tragic and noble conclusion unmistakably signs it as belonging to the Ulster bardic literature, and it falls within the same order of ideas, if it were not composed within the same period, as the tales of Cúchulainn.

Chapter 14

SOME GAELIC LOVE STORIES

The heroic age of Ireland was not, however, the mere orgy of battle that one might assume from Chapter 12. It had room for its Helen and its Andromache as well as for its Achilles and its Hector. Its champions could find time to make love as well as war. More than this, the legends of their courtships often have a romantic beauty found in no other early literature. The women have free scope of choice and claim the respect of their wooers. Indeed, it has been pointed out that the mythical stories of the Celts must have created the chivalrous romances of medieval Europe. In them, and in no other previous literature, do we find such knightly treatment of an enemy as we see in the story of Cúchulainn and Ferdia or such poetic delicacy towards a woman as is displayed in the wooing of Emer, which comes from a fragment of the Book of the Dun Cow. The talk between man and maid when Cúchulainn comes in his chariot to pay his suit to Emer at Forgall's *dún* might, save for its strangeness, almost have come out of some quite modern romance.

'Emer lifted up her lovely face and recognised Cúchulainn, and she said, "May God make smooth the path before you!"

'"And you,' he said, "may you be safe from every harm."'

She asks him where he has come from, and he tells her. Then he questions her about herself.

'I am a Tara of women,' she replies, 'the whitest of maidens, one who is gazed at but who gazes not back, a rush too far to be reached, an untrodden way. . . . I was brought up in ancient virtues, in lawful behaviour, in the keeping of chastity, in rank equal to a queen, in stateliness of form, so that to me is attributed every noble grace among the hosts of Erin's women.'

In more boastful strain Cúchulainn tells of his own birth and deeds. Not like the son of a peasant had he been reared at Conchobar's court but among heroes and champions, jesters and druids. When he is weakest his strength is that of twenty; alone he will fight against forty; a hundred men would feel safe under his protection.

One can imagine Emer's smile as she listens to these braggings. 'Truly,' she says, 'they are goodly feats for a tender boy, but they are not yet those of chariot chiefs.'

Modern, too, is the way in which she coyly reminds her wooer that she has an elder sister as yet unwed. But when at last he drives her to the point, she answers him with gentle but proud decision. Not by words but by deeds is she to be won. The man she will marry must have his name mentioned wherever the exploits of heroes are spoken of.

'Even as you have commanded, so shall all by me be done,' said Cúchulainn.

'And by me your offer is accepted, it is taken, it is granted,' replied Emer.

It seems a pity that after so fine a wooing Cúchulainn could not have kept faithful to the bride he had won. Yet such is not the way of heroes whom goddesses as well as mortal women conspire to tempt from their loyalty. It is told, in a story called 'The Sickbed of Cúchulainn', how Fand, the wife of Manannán Mac Lir, deserted by the sea god, sent her sister Lí Ban to Cúchulainn as an ambassador of love. At first he refused to visit her but ordered Laeg, his charioteer, to go with Lí Ban to Magh Mell, the Happy Plain, to spy out the land. Laeg returned enraptured. 'If all Ireland were mine,' he assured his master, 'with supreme rule over its fair inhabitants, I would give it up without regret to go and live in the place that I have seen.'

So Cúchulainn himself went and stayed a month in the Celtic Paradise with Fand, the fairest woman of the Sídhe. Returning to the land of mortals, he made a tryst with the goddess to meet him again in his own country by the yew tree at the head of Baile's strand.

But Emer came to hear of it and went to the meeting place herself with fifty of her maidens, each armed with a knife to kill her rival. There she found Cúchulainn, Laeg and Fand.

'What has led you, Cúchulainn,' said Emer, 'to shame me before the women of Erin and all honourable people? I came under your shelter, trusting in your faithfulness, and now you seek a cause of quarrel with me.'

But Cúchulainn, hero-like, could not understand why his wife should not be content to take her turn with this other woman – surely no unworthy rival,

155

Cúchulainn rebuked by Emer, from a drawing by H. R. Millar

for she was beautiful and came of the lofty race of gods. We see Emer yield at last with queenly pathos.

'I will not refuse this woman to you, if you long for her,' she said, 'for I know that everything that is new seems fair, and everything that is common seems bitter, and everything we have not seems desirable to us, and everything we have we think little of And yet, Cúchulainn, I was once pleasing to you, and I would wish to be so again.'

Her grief touched him. 'By my word,' he said, 'you are pleasing to me and will be as long as I live.'

'Then let me be given up,' said Fand.

'It is better that I should be,' replied Emer.

'No,' said Fand. 'It is I who must be given up in the end. It is I who will go, though I go with great sorrow. I would rather stay with Cúchulainn than live in the sunny home of the gods. O Emer, he is yours, and you are worthy of him! What my hand cannot have, my heart may yet wish well to. A sorrowful thing it is to love without return. Better to renounce than not to receive a love equal to one's own. It was not well of you, O fair-haired Emer, to come to kill Fand in her misery.'

It was while the goddess and the human woman were contending with one another in self-sacrifice that Manannán Mac Lir heard of Fand's trouble and was sorry that he had forsaken her. So he came, invisible to all but her alone. He asked her pardon, and she herself could not forget that she had once been happy with the 'horseman of the crested waves' and still might be happy with him again. The god asked her to make her choice between them, and, when she went to him, he shook his mantle between her and Cúchulainn. It was one of the magic properties of Manannán's mantle that those between whom it was shaken could never meet again. Then Fand returned with her divine husband to the country of the immortals, and the druids of Emain Macha gave Cúchulainn and Emer each a drink of oblivion so that Cúchulainn forgot his love and Emer her jealousy.

The scene of this story takes its name from another and hardly less beautiful love tale. The 'yew tree at the head of Baile's strand' had grown out of the grave of Baile of the Honeyed Speech, and it bore the appearance of Baile's love, Ailinn. This Gaelic Romeo and Juliet were of royal birth. Baile was heir to Ulster and Ailinn was daughter of the King of Leinster's son. Not by any feud of Montague and Capulet were they parted, however, but by the craft of a ghostly enemy. They had appointed to meet one another at Dundealgan, and Baile, who arrived there first, was greeted by a stranger. 'What news do you bring?' asked Baile.

'None,' replied the stranger, 'except that Ailinn of Leinster was setting out to meet her lover, but the men of Leinster kept her back, and her heart broke then and there from grief.' When Baile heard this, his own heart broke, and he fell dead on the strand, while the messenger went on the wings of the wind to the home of Ailinn, who had not yet started out.

'Whence come you?' she asked him.

'From Ulster, by the shore of Dundealgan, where I saw men raising a stone over one who had just died, and on the stone I read the name of Baile. He had come to meet some woman he was in love with, but it was destined that they should never see one another again in life.'

At this news Ailinn, too, fell dead and was buried, and we are told that an apple tree grew out of her grave, the apples of which bore the likeness of the face of Baile, while a yew tree sprang from Baile's grave and took the appearance of Ailinn. This legend, which is probably a part of the common heritage of the Aryans, is found in folklore over an area that stretches from Ireland to India. The Gaelic version has, however, an ending unknown to the others. The two trees, it relates, were cut down and made into wands upon which the poets of Ulster and of Leinster cut the songs of the love tragedies of their two provinces, in ogham. But even these mute memorials of Baile and Ailinn were destined not to be divided. After two hundred years, Airt the 'Lonely', High King of Ireland, ordered them to be brought to the hall of Tara, and as soon as the wands found themselves under the same roof, they all sprang together and no force or skill could part them again. So the king commanded them to be 'kept, like any other jewel, in the treasury of Tara.'

Neither of these stories, however, has as yet attained the fame of one now to be retold, which appears in many Gaelic versions, the oldest of which is in the Book of Leinster while the fullest are in two manuscripts in the Advocates' Library in Edinburgh. The version here is from one of these, the so-called Glenn Masain manuscript.

To many, no doubt, Gaelic romance is summed up in the one word Deirdre. It is the legend of this Gaelic Helen that the poets of the modern Celtic school most loved to elaborate, while for centuries storytellers told it round the peat fires of Ireland and the Highlands. Scholar and peasant alike combined to pre-

serve a tradition no one knows how many hundred years old, for it was written down in the twelfth-century Book of Leinster as one of the 'prime stories'
which every bard was bound to be able to recite. It ranks with the 'Fate of the
Sons of Tuireann' and with the 'Fate of the Children of Lir' as one of the 'Three
Sorrowful Stories of Erin'.

So favourite a tale has naturally been much altered and added to in its passage down the generations, but its essential story is as follows:

King Conchobar of Ulster was holding a festival in the house of one of his
bards, called Fedlimid, when Fedlimid's wife gave birth to a daughter, concerning whom Cathbad the Druid uttered a prophecy. He foretold that the
newborn child would grow up to be the most lovely woman the world had
ever seen but that her beauty would bring death to many heroes and much
peril and sorrow to Ulster. On hearing this, the Red Branch warriors demanded that she should be killed, but Conchobar refused and gave the infant
to a trusted serving woman to be hidden in a secret place in the solitude of the
mountains until she was of an age to be his own wife.

So Deirdre (as Cathbad named her) was taken away to a hut so remote from
the paths of people that none knew of it except Conchobar. Here she was
brought up by a nurse, a fosterer and a teacher, and saw no other living creatures except the beasts and birds of the hills. Nevertheless, she aspired to be
loved.

One day, her fosterer was killing a calf for their food, and its blood ran out
upon the snowy ground, which brought a black raven swooping to the spot. 'If
there were a man,' said Deirdre, 'who had hair of the blackness of that raven,
skin of the whiteness of the snow, and cheeks as red as the calf's blood, that is
the man whom I would wish to marry me.'

'Indeed there is such a man,' replied her teacher thoughtlessly. 'Naoise, one
of the sons of Usna, heroes of the same race as Conchobar the King.'

The curious Deirdre prevailed upon her teacher to bring Naoise to speak
with her. When they met she made good use of her time, for she offered
Naoise her love and begged him to take her away from King Conchobar.

Naoise, bewitched by her beauty, consented. Accompanied by his two
brothers, Ardan and Ainlé, and their followers, he fled with Deirdre to Alba,
where they made alliance with one of its kings and wandered over the land,
living by following the deer and by helping the king in his battles.

The revengeful Conchobar bided his time. One day, as the heroes of the

Red Branch feasted together at Emain Macha, he asked them if they had ever heard of a nobler company than their own. They replied that the world could not hold such another. 'Yet', said the king, 'we lack our full tale. The three sons of Usna could defend the province of Ulster against any other province of Ireland by themselves, and it is a pity that they should still be exiles for the sake of any woman in the world. Gladly would I welcome them back!'

'We ourselves,' replied the Ulster champions, 'would have counselled this long ago had we dared, O King!'

'Then I will send one of my three best champions to fetch them,' said Conchobar. 'Either Conall Cearnach or Cúchulainn, the son of Sualtam, or Fergus Mac Roth, and I will find out which of those three loves me best.'

First he called Conall to him secretly.

'What would you do, O Conall,' he asked, 'if you were sent to fetch the sons of Usna, and they were killed here in spite of your safe-conduct?'

'There is not a man in Ulster,' answered Conall, 'who had hand in it that would escape his own death from me.'

'I see that I am not dearest of all men to you,' replied Conchobar, and, dismissing Conall, he called Cúchulainn and put the same question to him.

'By my sworn word,' replied Cúchulainn, 'if such a thing happened with your consent, no bribe or blood fine would I accept in lieu of your own head, O Conchobar.'

'Truly,' said the king, 'it is not you I will send.'

The king then asked Fergus, and he replied that, if the sons of Usna were slain while under his protection, he would revenge the deed upon anyone who was party to it, save only the king himself.

'Then it is you who shall go,' said Conchobar. 'Set forth tomorrow and rest not by the way, and when you put foot again in Ireland at the *Dún* of Borrach, whatever may happen to you yourself, send the sons of Usna forward without delay.'

The next morning, Fergus, with his two sons, Illann the Fair and Buinne the Ruthless Red, set out for Alba in their galley and reached Loch Etive, by whose shores the sons of Usna were then living. Naoise, Ainlé and Ardan were sitting at chess when they heard Fergus's shout.

'That is the cry of a man of Erin,' said Naoise.

'Nay,' replied Deirdre, who had forebodings of trouble. 'Do not heed it; it is only the shout of a man of Alba.' But the sons of Usna knew better and sent

Ardan down to the seashore, where he found Fergus and his sons and gave them greeting and heard their message and brought them back with him.

That night Fergus persuaded the sons of Usna to return with him to Emain Macha. Deirdre, with her 'second sight', implored them to remain in Alba, but the exiles were weary for the sight of their own country and did not share their companion's fears. As they put out to sea, Deirdre uttered her beautiful 'Farewell to Alba', that land she was never to behold again.

> 'A lovable land is yon eastern land,
> Alba, with its marvels.
> I would not have come hither out of it,
> Had I not come with Naoise.
>
> 'Lovable are Dun-fidga and Dún-finn,
> Lovable the fortress over them;
> Dear to the heart Inis Draigende,
> And very dear is Dún Suibni.
>
> 'Caill Cuan!
> Unto which Ainlé would wend, alas!
> Short the time seemed to me,
> With Naoise in the region of Alba.
>
> 'Glenn Láid!
> Often I slept there under the cliff;
> Fish and venison and the fat of the badger
> Was my portion in Glenn Láid.
>
> 'Glenn Masáin!
> Its garlic was tall, its branches white;
> We slept a rocking sleep,
> Over the grassy estuary of Masáin.
>
> 'Glenn Etive!
> Where my first house I raised;
> Beauteous its wood – upon rising
> A cattle fold for the sun was Glenn Etive.

.   .   .   .   .

161

'Glenn Dá-Rúad!
My love to every man who hath it as an heritage!
Sweet the cuckoos' note on bending bough,
On the peak over Glenn Dá-Rúad.

'Beloved is Draigen,
Dear the white sand beneath its waves;
I would not have come from it, from the East,
Had I not come with my beloved.'

They crossed the sea and arrived at the *Dún* of Borrach, who bade them welcome to Ireland. Now King Conchobar had sent Borrach a secret command that he should offer a feast to Fergus on his landing. Strange taboos called *geasa* are laid upon the various heroes of ancient Ireland in the stories. There are certain things that each one of them may not do without forfeiting life or honour, and it was a *geis* upon Fergus to refuse a feast.

Fergus, we are told, 'reddened with anger from crown to sole' at the invitation. Yet he could not avoid the feast. He asked Naoise what he should do, and Deirdre broke in with: 'Do what is asked of you if you prefer to forsake the sons of Usna for a feast. Yet forsaking them is a good price to pay for it.'

Fergus, however, perceived a possible compromise. Although he himself could not refuse to stop to partake of Borrach's hospitality, he could send Deirdre and the sons of Usna on to Emain Macha at once, under the safeguard of his two sons, Illann the Fair and Buinne the Ruthless Red. So this was done, albeit to the annoyance of the sons of Usna and the terror of Deirdre. Visions came to the sorrowful woman. She saw the three sons of Usna and Illann, the son of Fergus, without their heads. She saw a cloud of blood always hanging over them. She begged them to wait in some safe place until Fergus had finished the feast. But Naoise, Ainlé and Ardan laughed at her fears. They arrived at Emain Macha, and Conchobar ordered the Red Branch palace to be placed at their disposal.

In the evening Conchobar called Levarcam, Deirdre's old teacher, to him. 'Go,' he said, 'to the Red Branch and see Deirdre, and bring me back news of her appearance, whether she still keeps her former beauty or whether it has left her.'

So Levarcam came to the Red Branch and kissed Deirdre and the three sons

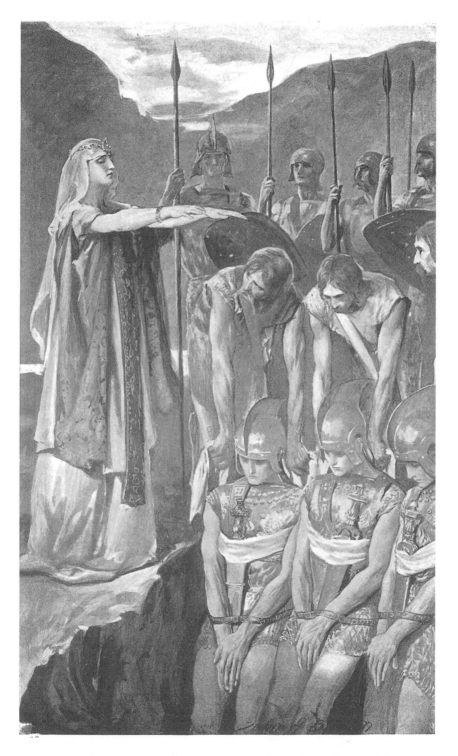

Deirdre's Lament, from a painting by J. H. F. Bacon ARA

of Usna, and warned them that Conchobar was preparing treachery. Then she went back to the king and reported to him that Deirdre's hard life upon the mountains of Alba had ruined her form and face so that she was no longer worthy of his regard.

At this, Conchobar's jealousy was partly allayed, and he began to doubt whether it would be wise to attack the sons of Usna. But later on, when he had drunk well of wine, he sent a second messenger to see if what Levarcam had reported about Deirdre was the truth.

The messenger, this time a man, went and looked in through a window. Deirdre saw him and pointed him out to Naoise, who flung a chessman at the peering face and put out one of its eyes. But the man went back to Conchobar and told him that, although one of his eyes had been struck out, he would gladly have stayed looking with the other, so great was Deirdre's loveliness.

Then Conchobar, in his wrath, ordered the men of Ulster to set fire to the Red Branch House and slay all within it except Deirdre. They flung firebrands upon it, but Buinne the Ruthless Red came out and quenched them and drove the assailants back with slaughter. But Conchobar called to him to parley and offered him a 'hundred' of land and his friendship to desert the sons of Usna. Buinne was tempted and fell, but the land given to him turned barren that very night in indignation at being owned by such a traitor.

The other of Fergus's sons was of a different make. He charged out, torch in hand, and cut down the Ulster champions, so that they hesitated to come near the house again. Conchobar dared not offer him a bribe, but he armed his own son, Fiacha, with his own magic weapons, including his shield, the Moaner, which roared when its owner was in danger, and sent him to fight Illann.

The duel was a fierce one, and Illann got the better of Fiacha, so that the son of Conchobar had to crouch down beneath his shield, which roared for help. Conall Cearnach heard the roar from far off and thought that his king must be in peril. He came to the place and, without asking questions, thrust his spear, Blue-green, through Illann. The dying son of Fergus explained the situation to Conall, who, by way of making some amends, at once killed Fiacha as well.

After this, the sons of Usna held their fort till dawn against all Conchobar's host. But, with day, they saw that they must either escape or resign themselves to perish. Putting Deirdre in their centre, protected by their shields, they opened the door suddenly and fled out.

They would have broken through and escaped had not Conchobar asked Cathbad the Druid to put a spell upon them, promising to spare their lives. So Cathbad raised the illusion of a stormy sea before and all around the sons of Usna. Naoise lifted Deirdre upon his shoulder, but the magic waves rose higher until they were all obliged to fling away their weapons and swim.

Then was seen the strange sight of men swimming upon dry land, and before the spell passed away the sons of Usna were seized from behind and brought to Conchobar.

In spite of his promise to the druid, the king condemned them to death. None of the men of Ulster would, however, deal the blow. In the end, a foreigner from Norway, whose father Naoise had slain, offered to behead them. Each of the brothers begged to die first, that he might not witness the deaths of the others. But Naoise ended this noble rivalry by lending their executioner the sword called the Retaliator, which had been given him by Manannán Mac Lir. They knelt down side by side, and one blow of the sword of the god shore off all their heads.

As for Deirdre, there are varying stories of her death but most of them agree that she did not survive the sons of Usna many hours. But before she died, she made an elegy over them. That it is of a singular pathos and beauty a few verses from the version in the Book of Leinster will show:

> 'Long the day without Usna's children!
> It was not mournful to be in their company!
> Sons of a king by whom sojourners were entertained,
> Three lions from the Hill of the Cave.
>
> .   .   .   .   .
>
> 'Three darlings of the women of Britain,
> Three hawks of Slieve Gullion,
> Sons of a king whom valour served,
> To whom soldiers used to give homage!
>
> .   .   .   .   .
>
> 'That I should remain after Naoise
> Let no one in the world suppose:
> After Ardan and Ainlé
> My time would not be long.

'Ulster's over-king, my first husband,
I forsook for Naoise's love.
Short my life after them:
I will perform their funeral game.

'After them I shall not be alive –
Three that would go into every conflict,
Three who liked to endure hardships,
Three heroes who refused not combats.

.   .   .   .   .

'O man, that diggest the tomb
And puttest my darling from me,
Make not the grave too narrow:
I shall be beside the noble ones.'

It was a poor triumph for Conchobar. Deirdre in all her beauty had escaped him by death. His own chief followers never forgave it. Fergus, when he returned from Borrach's feast and found out what had been done, gathered his own people, slew Conchobar's son and many of his warriors, and fled to Ulster's bitterest enemies, Ailill and Medb of Connacht. And Cathbad the Druid cursed both king and kingdom, praying that none of Conchobar's race might ever reign in Emain Macha again.

So it came to pass. The capital of Ulster was kept from ruin only by Cúchulainn's prowess. When he perished, it also fell and soon became what it is now – a grassy hill.

Chapter 15

Fionn and the Fianna

The epoch of Emain Macha is followed in the annals of ancient Ireland by a succession of monarchs who, although doubtless as mythical as King Conchobar and his court, seem to grow gradually more human. Their line lasts for about two centuries, culminating in a dynasty with which legend has occupied itself more than with its immediate predecessors. This is the one that began, according to the annalists, in AD 177 with the famous Conn 'the Hundred-Fighter', and, passing down to the reign of his even more famous grandson, Cormac 'the Magnificent', is connected with the third Gaelic cycle – that which relates the exploits of Fionn and the Fianna. All these kings had their dealings with the national gods. A story contained in a fifteenth-century Irish manuscript and called 'The Champion's Prophecy' tells how Lugh appeared to Conn, enveloped him in a magic mist, led him away to an enchanted palace and there prophesied to him the number of his descendants, the length of their reigns and the manner of their deaths. Another tradition relates how Conn's son, Connlai, was wooed by a goddess and borne away, like the British Arthur, in a boat of glass to the Earthly Paradise beyond the sea. Yet another relates Conn's own marriage with Bécuma of the Fair Skin, wife of that same Labraid of the Quick Hand on Sword who, in another legend, married Lí Ban, the sister of Fand, Cúchulainn's fairy love. Bécuma had been discovered in an intrigue with Gaiar, a son of Manannán, and, banished from the 'Land of Promise', crossed the sea that sunders mortals and immortals to offer her hand to Conn. The Irish king wedded her, but evil came of the marriage. She grew jealous of Conn's other son, Airt, and insisted upon his banishment, but they agreed to play chess to decide which should go, and Airt won. Airt, called 'the Lonely' because he had lost his brother Connlai, was king after Conn, but he is chiefly known to legend as the father of Cormac.

Many Irish stories occupy themselves with the fame of Cormac, who is pictured as a great legislator – a Gaelic Solomon. Certain traditions credit him with having been the first to believe in a purer doctrine than the Celtic polytheism and even with having attempted to put down druidism, in revenge for which a druid called Maelcen sent an evil spirit who placed a salmon bone crossways in the king's throat as he sat at table and so brought about his death. Another class of stories, however, makes him an especial favourite with those same heathen deities. Manannán Mac Lir was so anxious for his friendship that he decoyed him into fairyland and gave him a magic branch. It was of silver and bore golden apples, and when it was shaken, it made such sweet music that the wounded, the sick and the sorrowful forgot their pains and were lulled into deep sleep. Cormac kept this treasure all his life, but at his death it returned into the hands of the gods.

King Cormac was a contemporary of Fionn Mac Cumhaill, whom he appointed head of the *Fianna Eirinn*, more generally known as the Fianna. Around Fionn and his men have gathered a cycle of legends that were equally popular with the Gaels of both Scotland and Ireland. We read of their exploits in stories and poems preserved in the earliest Irish manuscripts, while in both Ireland and the West Highlands their names and the stories connected with them were current lore for centuries. The eighteenth-century Scottish poet James Macpherson used some of these floating traditions, as preserved in folk ballads, when he created his ancient bard Ossian.

How far Fionn and his followers may have been historical personages it is impossible to say. The Irish themselves have always held that the Fianna were a kind of native militia and that Fionn was their general. The early historical writers of Ireland supported this view. The chronicler Tierna of Clonmacnois, who died in 1088, believed in him, and the 'Annals of the Four Masters', compiled between the years 1632 and 1636 from older chronicles, while they ignore Conchobar and his Red Branch champions as unworthy of the serious consideration of historians, treat Fionn as a real person whose death took place in AD 283. One scholar, Eugene O'Curry, declared in the clearest language that Fionn, so far from being 'a merely imaginary or mythical character' was 'an undoubtedly historical personage; and that he existed about the time at which his appearance is recorded in the Annals is as certain as that Julius Caesar lived and ruled at the time stated on the authority of the Roman historians.'

The opinion of more recent Celtic scholars, however, is opposed to this view. Fionn's pedigree, preserved in the Book of Leinster, may seem at first to give some support to the theory of his real existence, but, on more careful examination of it, his own name and that of his father equally reveal him. Fionn, or Finn, meaning 'fair', is the name of one of the mythical ancestors of the Gaels, while his father's name, Cumhaill, signifies the 'sky' and is the same word as Camulus, the Gaulish heaven god identified by the Romans with Mars. His followers are as doubtfully human as himself. One may compare them with Cúchulainn and the rest of the heroes of Emain Macha. Their deeds are no less marvellous. Like the Ulster warriors, they move, too, on equal terms with the gods. 'The Fianna of Erin,' says a tract called *Agalamh na Senórach*, 'The Dialogue of the Elders', contained in thirteenth- and fourteenth-century manuscripts, 'had not more frequent and free intercourse with the men of settled habitation than with the Tuatha Dé Danaan.' Oenghus, Midhir, Lir, Manannán and Bodb Dearg, with their countless sons and daughters, loom as large in the Fiann or so-called 'Ossianic' stories as do the Fianna themselves. They fight for them or against them; they marry them and are given to them in marriage.

Another scholar, John Rhys, also hints that the Fianna inherited the conduct of that ancient war formerly waged between the Tuatha Dé Danaan and the Fomorii. The most common antagonists of Fionn and his heroes are tribes of invaders from overseas, called in the stories the *Lochlannach*. These 'Men of Lochlann' are usually identified by those who look for history in the stories of the Fiann cycle with the invading bands of Norsemen who harried the Irish coasts in the ninth century. But the nucleus of the Fiann tales antedates these Scandinavian raids, and mortal foes have probably merely stepped into the place of those immortal enemies of the gods whose 'Lochlann' was a country not over the sea but under it.

The earlier historians of Ireland were as ready with their dates and facts regarding the Fiann band as an institution as with the personality of Fionn. It was said to have been first organised by a king called Fiachadh in 300 BC and abolished, or rather exterminated, by Cairbre, the son of Cormac Mac Airt, in AD 284. We are told that it consisted of three regiments modelled on the Roman legion. Each of these bodies contained, on a peace footing, three thousand men but in time of war could be indefinitely strengthened. Its object was to defend the coasts of Ireland and the country generally, throwing its weight upon the side of any prince who happened to be assailed by foreign foes. During the six months of winter, its members were quartered upon the population, but during the summer they had to forage for themselves, which they did by hunting and fishing. Thus they lived in the woods and on the open moors, hardening themselves for battle by their adventurous life. The sites of their enormous campfires were long pointed out under the name of the 'Fianna cooking places'.

It was not easy to become a member of this famous band. A candidate had to be not only an expert warrior but a poet and a man of culture as well. He had practically to renounce his tribe – at any rate he made oath that he would neither avenge any of his relatives nor be avenged by them. He put himself under bonds, or *geasa*, never to refuse hospitality to anyone who asked, never to turn his back in battle, never to insult any woman and not to accept a dowry with his wife. In addition to all this, he had to pass successfully through the most stringent physical tests. Indeed, as these have come down to us, magnified by the enthusiastic Celtic imagination, they are of an altogether marvellous and impossible character. An aspirant to the *Fianna Eirinn*, we are told, had first to stand up to his knees in a pit dug for him, his only arms being his shield and a hazel wand, while nine warriors, each with a spear, standing within the distance of nine ridges of land, all hurled their weapons at him at once. If he failed to ward them all off, he was rejected. Should he succeed in this first test, he was given the distance of one tree-length's start and chased through a forest by armed men. If any of them came up to him and wounded him, he could not belong to the Fianna. If he escaped unhurt but had unloosed a single lock of his braided hair or had broken a single branch in his flight or if, at the end of the run, his weapons trembled in his hands, he was refused. As, besides these tests, he was obliged to jump over a branch as high as his forehead and stoop under one as low as his knee, while running at full speed, and to pluck a thorn out of his heel without hindrance to his flight, it is clear that even the rank and file of the Fianna must have been exceptional athletes.

But it is time to pass on to a more detailed description of these champions. They are a goodly company, no less heroic than the mighty men of Ulster. First comes Fionn himself, not the strongest in body of the Fianna but the truest, wisest and kindest, gentle to women, generous to men and trusted by all. If he could help it, he would never let anyone be in trouble or poverty. 'If the dead leaves of the forest had been gold, and the white foam of the water silver, Fionn would have given it all away.'

Fionn had two sons, Fergus and his more famous brother Oisín. Fergus of the sweet speech was the bard of the Fianna and also, because of his honeyed words, their diplomat and ambassador. Yet by the irony of fate, it is to Oisín, who is not mentioned as a poet in the earliest texts, that the poems concerning the Fianna, which James Macpherson wrote and made famous under the name of 'Ossianic Ballads', are attributed. Oisín's mother was Sadb, a daughter of Bodb Dearg. A rival goddess changed her into a deer – which explains how Oisín got his name, which means 'fawn'. With such advantages of birth, naturally he was speedy enough to run down a red deer hind and catch her by the ear, although far less swift-footed than his cousin Caoilté, the 'Thin Man'. Neither was he as strong as his own son Oscar, the mightiest of all the Fianna, yet, in his youth, so clumsy that the rest of the band refused to take him with them on their warlike expeditions. They changed their minds, however, when, one day, he followed them unawares, found them giving way before an enemy and, rushing to their help, armed only with a great log of wood which lay handy on the ground, turned the fortunes of the fight. After this, Oscar was hailed the best warrior of all the Fianna. In his first battle he slew three kings and in his fury he also slew by chance his own friend Linne. He was given command of a battalion, and its banner, called the Terrible Broom, was regarded as the centre of every battle, for it was never known to retreat a foot. Other prominent Fianna were Goll Mac Morna, at first Fionn's enemy but afterwards his follower, a man skilled alike in war and learning. Even although he was one-eyed, we are told that he was much loved by women but not as much as Fionn's cousin, Diarmaid ua Duibhne, whose fatal beauty ensnared even Fionn's betrothed bride, Grainne. Their comic character was Conan, who is represented as an old, bald, vain, irritable man, as great a braggart as Shakespeare's ancient Pistol and as foul-mouthed as Thersites, and yet, after he had once been shamed into activity, a true man of his hands. These are the prime Fiann heroes, the chief actors in its stories.

The Fiann epic begins, before the birth of its hero, with the struggle of two rival clans, each of whom claimed to be the real and only Fianna Eirinn. They were called the Clann Morna, of which Goll Mac Morna was head, and the Clann Baoisgne, commanded by Fionn's father, Cumhaill. A battle was fought at Cnucha (now Castleknock, near Dublin) in which Goll killed Cumhaill, and the Clann Baoisgne was scattered. Cumhal's wife, however, bore a posthumous son, who was brought up among the Slieve Bloom Mountains secretly for fear that his father's enemies should find and kill him. The boy, who was at first called Demna, grew up to be an expert hurler, swimmer, runner and hunter. Later, like Cúchulainn, he took a second, more personal name. Those who saw him asked who was the 'fair' youth. He accepted the omen and called himself Demna Fionn.

At length he wandered to the banks of the Boyne, where he found a soothsayer called Finegas living beside a deep pool near Slane, named Fec's Pool, in the hope of catching one of the 'salmons of knowledge' and, by eating it, obtaining universal wisdom. He had been there seven years without result, although success had been prophesied to one named Fionn. When the wandering son of Cumhaill appeared, Fionn the Seer engaged him as his servant. Shortly afterwards, he caught the coveted fish and handed it over to Fionn to cook, warning him to eat no portion of it.

'Have you eaten any of it?' he asked the boy as he brought it up ready boiled.

'No indeed,' replied Fionn; 'but while I was cooking it, a blister rose upon the skin and, laying my thumb down upon the blister, I scalded it, and so I put it into my mouth to ease the pain.'

The man was perplexed. 'You told me your name was Demna,' he said, 'but have you any other name?'

'Yes, I am also called Fionn.'

'It is enough,' replied his disappointed master. 'Eat the salmon yourself, for you must be the one of whom the prophecy told.'

Fionn ate the salmon of knowledge and thereafter he had only to put his thumb under his tooth, as he had done when he scalded it, to receive foreknowledge and magic counsel.[1]

Thus armed, Fionn was more than a match for the Clann Morna. Curious legends tell how he revealed himself to his father's old followers, confounded his enemies with his magic and turned them into faithful servants. Even Goll of the Blows had to submit to his sway. Gradually he welded the two opposing clans into one Fianna over which he ruled, taking tribute from the kings of Ireland, warring against the Fomorian 'Lochlannach', destroying every kind of giant, serpent or monster that infested the land and at last carrying his mythical conquests over all Europe.

Out of the numberless stories of the Fiann exploits it is hard to choose ex-

---

[1] This and other 'boy exploits' of Fionn Mac Cumhaill are contained in a little tract written upon a fragment of the ninth-century Psalter of Cashel.

Fionn finds the Salmon of Knowledge, from a drawing by H. R. Millar

amples. All are heroic, romantic, wild, fantastic. In many of them the Tuatha Dé Danaan play prominent parts. One such story connects itself with an earlier mythological episode already related in Chapter 11, 'The Gods in Exile'. The reader will remember how, when the Daghda gave up the kingship of the immortals, five aspirants appeared to claim it; how of these five – Oenghus, Midhir, Lir, Ilbhreach, son of Mannanán, and Bodb Dearg – the latter was chosen; how Lir refused to acknowledge him but was reconciled later; how Midhir, equally rebellious, fled to 'desert country round Mount Leinster' in County Carlow; and how a yearly war was waged upon him and his people by the rest of the gods to bring them to subjection. This war was still raging in the time of Fionn, and Midhir was not too proud to seek his help. One day that Fionn was hunting in Donegal with Oisín, Oscar, Caoilté and Diarmaid, their hounds roused a beautiful fawn, which, although at every moment apparently nearly overtaken, led them in full chase as far as Mount Leinster. Here it suddenly disappeared into a cleft in the hillside. Heavy snow, 'making the forest's branches as it were a withe-twist', now fell, forcing the Fianna to seek for some shelter, and they therefore explored the place into which the fawn had vanished. It led to a splendid *sídh* in the hollow of the hill. Entering it, they were greeted by a beautiful goddess maiden, who told them that it was she, Midhir's daughter, who had been the fawn and that she had taken that shape purposely to lead them there in the hope of getting their help against the army that was coming to attack the *sídh*. Fionn asked who the assailants would be and was told that they were Bodb Dearg with his seven sons, Oenghus 'Son of the Young' with his seven sons, Lir of Sídh Fionnechaidh with his twenty-seven sons and Fionnbharr of Sídh Meadha with his seventeen sons as well as numberless gods of lesser fame drawn from *sídhe* not only over all Ireland but from Scotland and the islands as well. Fionn promised his aid, and with the twilight of that same day, the attacking forces appeared and made their annual assault. They were beaten off after a battle that lasted all night with the loss of 'ten men, ten score, and ten hundred'. Fionn, Oscar and Diarmaid, as well as most of Midhir's many sons, were sorely wounded, but the leech Labhra healed all their wounds.

In fact, the Fianna did not always require the excuse of fairy alliance to start them making war on the race of the hills. One of the so-called 'Ossianic ballads' is entitled 'The Chase of the Enchanted Pigs of Oenghus of the Brugh'. This Oenghus is, of course, the 'Son of the Young', and the Brugh that famous *sidh* beside the Boyne out of which he cheated his father, the Daghda. After the friendly manner of gods towards heroes, he invited Fionn and a picked thousand of his followers to a banquet at the Brugh. They came to it in their finest clothes, 'goblets went from hand to hand, and waiters were kept in motion'. At last conversation fell upon the comparative merits of the pleasures of the table and of the chase, Oenghus stoutly contending that 'the gods' life of perpetual feasting' was better than all the Fiann huntings and Fionn as stoutly denying it. Fionn boasted of his hounds, and Oenghus said that the best of them could not kill one of his pigs. Fionn angrily replied that his two hounds, Bran and Sgeolan, would kill any pig that trod on dry land. Oenghus answered that he could show Fionn a pig that none of his hounds or huntsmen could catch or kill. Here were the makings of a pretty quarrel among such inflammable creatures as gods and heroes, but the steward of the feast interposed and sent everyone to bed. The next morning, Fionn left the Brugh, for he did not want to fight all Oenghus's fairies with his handful of a thousand men. A year passed before he heard more of it; then a messenger came from Oenghus, reminding Fionn of his promise to pit his men and hounds against Oenghus's pigs. The Fianna seated themselves on the tops of the hills, each with his favourite hound on a leash, and they had not been there long before there appeared on the eastern plain a hundred and one such pigs as no Fiann had ever seen before. Each was as tall as a deer and blacker than a smith's coals, having hair like a thicket and bristles like ships' masts. Yet such was the prowess of the Fianna that they killed them all, although each of the pigs slew ten men and many hounds. Then Oenghus complained that the Fianna had murdered his son and many others of the Tuatha Dé Danaan, who, indeed, were none other than the pigs whose forms they had taken. There were mighty recriminations on both sides, and in the end the enraged Fianna prepared to attack the Brugh na Boinne. Then only did Oenghus begin to yield, and, on the advice of Oisín, Fionn made peace with him and his fairy folk.

One day Fionn and his warriors, while resting from the chase for their midday meal, saw coming towards them a towering shape. It proved to be a young giant maiden, who gave her name as Bebhionn, daughter of Treon, from the Tír na mBan, the Land of Maidens. The gold rings on her fingers were as thick as an ox's yoke, and her beauty was dazzling. When she took off her gilded helmet, all bejewelled, her fair, curling golden hair broke out in seven score tresses, and Fionn cried: 'Great gods whom we adore, a huge marvel Cormac and Ethné and the women of the Fianna would esteem it to see Bebhionn, the blooming daughter of Treon.' The maiden explained that she had been betrothed against her will to a suitor named Aeda, son of a neighbouring king, and that hearing from a fisherman, who had been blown to her shores, of the power and nobleness of Fionn, she had come to seek his protection. While she was speaking, suddenly the Fianna were aware of another giant form close at hand. It was a young man, smooth-featured and of surpassing beauty, who bore a red shield and a huge spear. Without a word he drew near, and before the wondering Fianna could accost him he thrust his spear through the body of the maiden and passed away. Fionn, enraged at this violation of his protection, called on his chiefs to pursue and slay the murderer. Some of the Fianna chased him to the seashore and followed him into the surf, but he strode out to sea and was met by a great galley that bore him away to unknown regions. Returning, discomfited, to Fionn, they found the girl dying. She distributed her gold and jewels among them, and the Fianna buried her under a great mound and raised a pillar stone over her with her name in ogham letters in the place since called the Ridge of the Dead Woman.

In this tale we have, besides the element of mystery, that of beauty. It is an association of frequent occurrence in this period of Celtic literature, and to this, perhaps, is due the fact that although these tales seem to come from nowhere and to lead nowhere, but move in a dream world where there is no chase but seems to end in Fairyland and no combat that has any relation to earthly needs or objects, where all realities are apt to dissolve in a magic light and to change their shapes like morning mist, yet they linger in the memory with that haunting charm that has for many centuries kept them alive by the fireside.

Such are specimens of the tales that go to make up the Fiann cycle of sagas. Hunting is the most prominent feature of them, for the Fianna were essentially a race of mighty hunters, but the creatures of their chase were not always flesh and blood. Enchanters who wished the Fianna ill could always lure them into danger by taking the shape of boar or deer, and many a story begins with an innocent chase and ends with a murderous battle. But out of such struggles the Fianna always emerge successfully, as Oisín is represented proudly boasting, 'through truthfulness and the might of their hands'.

The most famous chase of all is, however, not that of deer or boar but of a woman and a man, Fionn's betrothed wife and his nephew Diarmaid. Ever fortunate in war, the Fiann leader found disaster in his love life. Wishing for a wife in his old age, he sent to seek Grainne, the daughter of Cormac, the High King of Ireland. Both King Cormac and his daughter consented, and Fionn's ambassadors returned with an invitation to the suitor to come in a fortnight's time to claim his bride. He arrived with his picked band and was received in state in the great banqueting hall of Tara. There they feasted, and there Grainne, the king's daughter, casting her eyes over the assembled Fiann heroes, saw Diarmaid ua Duibhne.

This Fiann Adonis had a beauty spot on his cheek which no woman could see without falling instantly in love with him. Grainne, for all her royal birth, was no exception to this rule. She asked a druid to point out to her the principal guests. The druid told her all their names and exploits. Then she called for a jewelled drinking horn and, filling it with a drugged wine, sent it round to each in turn except to Diarmaid. None could be so discourteous as to refuse wine from the hand of a princess. All drank and fell into deep sleep.

Then, rising, she came to Diarmaid, told him of her passion for him and asked for its return.

'I will not love the betrothed of my chief,' he replied, 'and, even if I wished, I dare not.' And he praised Fionn's virtues and decried his own fame. But Grainne merely answered that she put him under *geasa* (bonds that no hero could refuse to redeem) to flee with her and at once went back to her chair before the rest of the company awoke from their slumber.

After the feast, Diarmaid went round to his comrades, one by one, and told them of Grainne's love for him and of the *geasa* she had placed upon him to take her from Tara. He asked each of them what he ought to do. All answered that no hero could break a *geis* put upon him by a woman. He even asked Fionn, concealing Grainne's name, and Fionn gave him the same counsel as the others. That night, the lovers fled from Tara to the ford of the Shannon at Athlone, crossed it and came to a place called the Wood of the Two Tents, where Diarmaid wove a hut of branches for Grainne to shelter in.

Meanwhile Fionn had discovered their flight, and his rage knew no bounds. He sent his trackers, the Clann Neamhuain, to follow them. They tracked them to the wood, and one of them climbed a tree and, looking down, saw the hut, with a strong seven-doored fence built round it, and Diarmaid and Grainne inside. When the news came to the Fianna, they were sorry, for their sympathies were with Diarmaid and not with Fionn. They tried to warn him, but he took no heed for he had determined to fight and not to flee. Indeed, when Fionn himself came to the fence and called over it to Diarmaid, asking if he and Grainne were within, he replied that they were but that none should enter unless he gave permission.

So Diarmaid, like Cúchulainn in the war of Ulster against Ireland, found himself matched single-handed against a host, but, also like Cúchulainn, he had a divine helper. The favourite of the Tuatha Dé Danaan, he had been the pupil of Manannán Mac Lir in Tír Tairnigirib, the Land of Promise, and had been fostered by Oenghus of the Brugh. Manannán had given him his two spears, the Red Javelin and the Yellow Shaft, and his two swords, the Great Fury and the Little Fury. And now Oenghus came to look for his foster son and brought with him the magic mantle of invisibility used by the gods. He advised Diarmaid and Grainne to come out wrapped in the cloak and thus rendered invisible. Diarmaid still refused to flee but asked Oenghus to protect Grainne. Wrapping the magic mantle round her, the god led the princess away unseen by any of the Fianna.

By this time, Fionn had posted men outside all the seven doors in the fence. Diarmaid went to each of them in turn. At the first were Oisín and Oscar with the Clann Baoisgne. They offered him their protection. At the second were Caoilté and the Clann Ronan, who said they would fight to the death for him. At the third were Conan and the Clann Morna, also his friends. At the fourth stood Cuan with the Fianna of Munster, Diarmaid's native province. At the fifth were the Ulster Fianna, who also promised him protection against Fionn. But at the sixth were the Clann Neamhuain, who hated him, and at the seventh was Fionn himself.

'It is by your door that I will pass out, O Fionn,' cried Diarmaid. Fionn charged his men to surround Diarmaid as he came out and kill him. But he leaped the fence, passing clean over their heads, and fled away so swiftly that they could not follow him. He did not halt until he reached the place to which he knew Oenghus had taken Grainne. The friendly god left them with a little sage advice: never to hide in a tree with only one trunk; never to rest in a cave with only one entrance; never to land on an island with only one channel of approach; not to eat their supper where they had cooked it, nor to sleep where they had supped, and, where they had slept once, never to sleep again. With these guerrilla-like tactics, it was some time before Fionn discovered them.

However, he found out at last where they were and sent champions with venomous hounds to take or kill them. But Diarmaid conquered all who were sent against him.

Yet still Fionn pursued, until Diarmaid, as a last hope of escape, took refuge under a magic rowan tree, which bore scarlet fruit, the ambrosia of the gods. It had grown from a single berry dropped by one of the Tuatha Dé Danaan, who, when they found that they had carelessly endowed mortals with celestial and immortal food, had sent a huge, one-eyed Fomor called Searbhan to guard it, so that no man might eat its fruit. All day this Fomor sat at the foot of the tree, and all night he slept among its branches, and so terrible was his appearance that neither the Fianna nor any other people dared to come within several miles of him.

But Diarmaid was willing to brave the Fomor in the hope of getting a safe hiding place for Grainne. He came boldly up to him and asked leave to camp and hunt in his neighbourhood. The Fomor told him surlily that he might camp and hunt where he pleased so long as he refrained from taking any of the scarlet berries. So Diarmaid built a hut near a spring, and he and Grainne lived there, killing the wild animals for food.

But, unhappily, Grainne conceived so strong a desire to eat the rowan berries that she felt that she must die unless her wish could be gratified. At first she tried to hide this longing, but in the end she was forced to tell her companion. Diarmaid had no desire to quarrel with the Fomor, so he went to him and told him of the plight that Grainne was in and asked for a handful of the berries as a gift.

But the Fomor merely answered: 'I swear to you that if nothing would save the princess and her unborn child except my berries, and if she were the last woman upon the earth, she should not have any of them.' Whereupon Diarmaid fought Searbhan and, after much trouble, killed him.

It was reported to Fionn that the guardian of the magic rowan tree lived no longer, and he guessed that Diarmaid must have killed him, so he came down to the place with seven battalions of the Fianna to look for him. By this time Diarmaid had abandoned his own hut and taken possession of that built by Searbhan among the branches of the magic rowan tree. He was sitting in it with Grainne when Fionn and his men came and camped at the foot of the tree to wait until the heat of noon had passed before beginning their search.

To pass the time, Fionn called for his chessboard and challenged his son Oisín to a game. They played until Oisín had only one more move.

'One move would make you a winner,' said Fionn to him, 'but I challenge you and all the Fianna to guess it.'

Only Diarmaid, who had been looking down through the branches upon the players, knew the move. He could not resist dropping a berry on to the board so deftly that it hit the very chessman that Oisín ought to move in order to win. Oisín took the hint, moved it and won. A second and a third game were played, and in each case the same thing happened. Then Fionn felt sure that the berries that had prompted Oisín must have been thrown by Diarmaid.

He called out, asking Diarmaid if he were there, and the Fiann hero, who never spoke an untruth, answered that he was. So the rowan was surrounded by armed men, just as the hut in the woods had been. But, again, things happened in the same way, for Oenghus of the Brugh took away Grainne wrapped in the invisible magic cloak while Diarmaid, walking to the end of a thick branch, cleared the circle of Fianna at a bound and escaped untouched.

This was the end of the famous 'Pursuit', for Oenghus came as ambassador to Fionn, urging him to become reconciled to the fugitives, and all the best of the Fianna begged Fionn to consent. So Diarmaid and Grainne were allowed to return in peace.

But Fionn never really forgave, and soon afterwards he urged Diarmaid to go out to the chase of the wild boar of Beann Ghulban.[1] Diarmaid killed the boar without getting any hurt, for, like the Greek Achilles, he was invulnerable except in his heel alone. Fionn, who knew this, told him to measure out the length of the skin with his bare feet. Diarmaid did so. Then Fionn, declaring that he had measured it wrongly, ordered him to tread it again in the opposite direction. This was against the lie of the bristles, and one of them pierced Diarmaid's heel and inflicted a poisoned and mortal wound.

This 'Pursuit of Diarmaid and Grainne', which has been told at such length, marks in some degree the climax of the Fiann power, after which it began to decline towards its end. The friends of Diarmaid never forgave the treachery with which Fionn had arranged his death. The ever-slumbering rivalry between Goll and his Clann Morna and Fionn and his Clann Baoisgne began to show itself as open enmity. Quarrels arose, too, between the Fianna and the high kings of Ireland, which culminated at last in the annihilation of the Fianna at the Battle of Gabhra.

This is said to have been fought in AD 284. Fionn himself had perished a

---

[1] Now called Benbulbin. It is near Sligo.

year before it, in a skirmish with rebellious Fianna at the Ford of Brea on the Boyne. King Cormac Mac Airt, Grainne's father, was also dead. It was between Fionn's grandson, Oscar, and Cormac's son, Cairbre, that war broke out. This mythical battle was as fiercely waged as that of Arthur's last fight at Camluan. Oscar slew Cairbre and was slain by him. Aidin, Oscar's wife, died of grief after his death, and Oisín, Oscar's father, buried her on Ben Edar (Howth) and raised over her the great dolmen that is there to this day. Almost all the Fianna fell, as well as all Cairbre's forces.

Only two of the greater Fiann figures survived. One was Caoilté, whose swiftness of foot saved him at the end when all was lost. The famous story called the 'Dialogue of the Elders' represents him discoursing to St Patrick, centuries afterwards, of the Fianna' wonderful deeds. Having lost his friends of the heroic age, he is said to have cast in his lot with the Tuatha Dé Danaan. He fought in a battle with Ilbhreach, son of Manannán, against Lir himself and killed the ancient sea god with his own hand. The tale represents him taking possession of Lir's fairy palace of Sídh Fionnechaidh, after which we know no more of him except that he has taken rank in the minds of the Irish as one of, and a ruler among, the Sídhe.

The other was Oisín, who did not fight at Gabhra, for long before he had taken the great journey that most heroes of mythology take, to that bourne from which no ordinary mortal ever returns. Like Cúchulainn, it was on the invitation of a goddess that he went. The Fianna were hunting near Lake Killarney when a lady of more than human beauty came to them and told them that her name was Niamh, daughter of the Son of the Sea. The Gaelic poet, Michael Comyn, who, in the eighteenth century, rewove the ancient story into his own words, describes her in just the same way as one of the old bards would have done:[1]

> 'A royal crown was on her head;
> And a brown mantle of precious silk,
> Spangled with stars of red gold,
> Covering her shoes down to the grass.
>
> 'A gold ring was hanging down
> From each yellow curl of her golden hair;

---

[1]   W. B. Yeats wrote a poem on the same subject, *Wanderings of Oisín*.

Her eyes, blue, clear and cloudless,
Like a dewdrop on the top of the grass.

'Redder were her cheeks than the rose,
Fairer was her visage than the swan upon the wave,
And more sweet was the taste of her balsam lips
Than honey mingled thro' red wine.

'A garment, wide, long and smooth
Covered the white steed,
There was a comely saddle of red gold,
And her right hand held a bridle with a golden bit.

'Four shoes well-shaped were under him,
Of the yellow gold of the purest quality;
A silver wreath was on the back of his head,
And there was not in the world a steed better.'

Such was Niamh of the Golden Hair, Manannán's daughter, and it is small
wonder that, when she chose Oisín from among the sons of men to be her
lover, all Fionn's supplications could not keep him. He mounted behind her
on her fairy horse, and they rode across the land to the seashore and then over
the tops of the waves. As they went, she described the country of the gods to
him in just the same terms as Manannán himself had pictured it to Bran, son
of Febal, as Midhir had painted it to Etain, and as everyone that went there
described it to those who stayed at home on earth.

'It is the most delightful country to be found
Of greatest repute under the sun;
Trees drooping with fruit and blossom,
And foliage growing on the tops of boughs.

'Abundant, there, are honey and wine,
And everything that eye has beheld,
There will not come decline on thee with lapse of time.
Death or decay thou wilt not see.'

As they went they saw wonders. Fairy palaces with bright sun bowers and lime-white walls appeared on the surface of the sea. At one of these they halted, and Oisín, at Niamh's request, attacked a fierce Fomor who lived there and set free a damsel of the Tuatha Dé Danaan whom he kept imprisoned. He saw a hornless fawn leap from wave to wave, chased by one of those strange hounds of Celtic myth which are pure white with red ears. At last they reached Tír na Og, the Land of the Young, and there Oisín dwelt with Niamh for three hundred years before he remembered Erin and the Fianna. Then a great wish came upon him to see his own country and his own people again, and Niamh gave him leave to go and mounted him upon a fairy steed for the journey. One thing alone she made him swear – not to let his feet touch earthly soil. Oisín promised and reached Ireland on the wings of the wind. But, like the children of Lir at the end of their penance, he found all changed. He asked for Fionn and the Fianna and was told that they were the names of people who had lived long ago and whose deeds were written of in old books. The Battle of Gabhra had been fought, and St Patrick had come to Ireland and made all things new. The very forms of men had altered; they seemed dwarfs compared with the giants of his day. Seeing three hundred of them trying in vain to raise a marble slab, he rode up to them in contemptuous kindness and

Oisín's Cave, Glencoe

183

lifted it with one hand, but as he did so the golden saddle girth broke with the strain, and he touched the earth with his feet. The fairy horse vanished, and Oisín rose from the ground no longer divinely young and fair and strong but a blind, grey-haired, withered old man.

A number of spirited ballads, called the 'Dialogues of Oisín and Patrick', tell how Oisín, stranded in his old age on earthly soil, unable to help himself or find his own food, is taken by St Patrick into his house to be converted. The saint paints to him in the brightest colours the heaven that may be his own if he will but repent and in the darkest the hell in which he tells him his old comrades now lie in anguish. Oisín replies to the saint's arguments, entreaties and threats in language that is extraordinarily frank. He will not believe that heaven could be closed to the Fianna if they wished to enter it or that God himself would not be proud to claim friendship with Fionn. And if it be not so, what is the use to him of eternal life where there is no hunting or wooing fair women or listening to the songs and tales of bards? No, he will go to the Fianna, whether they sit at the feast or in the fire, and so he dies as he had lived.

Chapter 16

THE DECLINE AND FALL OF THE GODS

In spite, however, of the widespread popularity of the ballads that took the form of dialogues between Oisín and Patrick, certain traditions say that the saint succeeded in converting the hero. Caoilté, the other great surviving Fiann, was also represented as having gladly exchanged his pagan lore for the faith and salvation offered him. We see the same influence in the later legends concerning the Red Branch Champions. It was the policy of the first Christianisers of Ireland to describe the loved heroes of their still half-heathen flocks as having handed in their submission to the new creed. The tales about Conchobar and Cúchulainn were amended to prove that those very pagan personages had been miraculously brought to accept the gospel at the last. An entirely new story, called 'The Phantom Chariot', contained in the Book of the Dun Cow, told how the latter hero was raised from the dead by St Patrick so that he might bear witness of the truth of Christianity to Laoghaire the Second, King of Ireland, which he did with such fervour and eloquence that the sceptical monarch was convinced.

Daring attempts were also made to change the Tuatha Dé Danaan from pagan gods into Christian saints, but these were by no means so profitable as the policy pursued towards the more human-seeming heroes. With only one of them was there immediate success. Brigit, the goddess of fire, poetry and the hearth, is famous today as St Bridget or Bride. Most popular of all the Irish saints, she can still be easily recognised as the daughter of the Daghda. Her Christian attributes, almost all connected with fire, attest her pagan origin. She was born at sunrise; a house in which she dwelt blazed into a flame that reached to heaven; a pillar of fire rose from her head when she took the veil; and her breath gave new life to the dead. As with the British goddess Sulis, worshipped at Bath, who – the AD third-century Latin writer Polyhistor, tells us – 'ruled over the boiling springs, and at her altar there flamed a perpetual fire which never whitened into ashes but hardened into a stony mass', the sacred flame on her shrine at Kildare was never allowed to go out. It was extinguished once, in the thirteenth century, but was relighted and burnt with undying glow until the suppression of the monasteries by Henry VIII. This sacred fire might not be breathed on by impure human breath. For nineteen nights it was tended by her nuns, but on the twentieth night it was left untouched and kept itself alight miraculously. With so little of her essential character and ritual changed, it is small wonder that the half-pagan, half-Christian Irish gladly accepted the new saint in the stead of the old goddess.

A careful examination of Irish hagiology would probably result in the discovery of many other saints whose names and attributes might render them likely to have had previous careers as pagan gods. But their acceptance was not sufficiently general to do away with the need of other means of counteracting the still living influence of the pantheon of Gaelic gods. Therefore a fresh school of euhemerists arose to prove that the gods were never even saints but merely worldly men who had once lived and ruled in Erin. Learned monks worked hard to construct a history of Ireland from the Flood downwards. An amazing genealogy, compiled by Eugene O'Curry from the various pedigrees the monks elaborated and inserted into the Books of Ballymote, Lecan and Leinster, shows how not merely the Tuatha Dé Danaan but also the Fir Bholgs, the Fomorii, the Sons of Mil Espaine and the races of Partholón and Nemedh were descended from Noah. Japhet, the patriarch's son, was the father of Magog from whom came two lines, the first being the Sons of Mil Espaine, while the second branched out into all the other races.

Having once worked the gods first into universal history and then into the history of Ireland, it was an easy matter to supply them with dates of birth and death, local habitations and places of burial. We are told with precision exactly how long Nuada, the Daghda, Lugh and the others reigned at Tara. The barrows by the Boyne provided them with comfortable tombs. Their enemies, the Fomorii, became real invaders who were beaten in real battles. Thus it was thought to make plain prose of their gods.

It is only fair, however, to these early euhemerists to say that they have their modern disciples. There are many writers of recognised authority on their subjects who, in dealing with the history of Ireland or the composition of the British race, claim to find real peoples in the tribes mentioned in Gaelic mythology. Unfortunately, the only point they agree on is the accepted one – that the Sons of Mil Espaine were Aryan Celts. They are divided on the question of the Fir Bholgs, in whom some see the pre-Aryan tribes while others, led astray by the name, regard them as Belgic Gauls; and over the really mythological races they run wild. In the Tuatha Dé Danaan are variously found Gaels, Picts, Danes, Scandinavians, Ligurians and Finns, while the Fomorii rest under the suspicion of having been Iberians, Moors, Romans, Finns, Goths or Germans. As for the people of Partholón and Nemedh, they have even been explained as men of the Palaeolithic Age. This chaos of opinion was fortunately avoided by the native annalists, who had no particular views upon the question of race except that everybody came from 'Spain'.

Of course there were dissenters from this prevailing mania for making gods human. As late as the tenth century, a poet called Eochaidh O'Flynn, writing of the Tuatha Dé Danaan, at first seems to hesitate over whether to ascribe humanity or divinity to them and at last frankly avows their godhead. In his poem, preserved in the Book of Ballymote, he says:

> 'Though they came to learned Erinn
> Without buoyant, adventurous ships,
> No man in creation knew
> Whether they were of the earth or of the sky.
>
> 'If they were diabolical demons,
> They came from that woeful expulsion;[1]
> If they were of a race of tribes and nations,
> If they were human, they were of the race of Beothach.'

Then he enumerates them in due succession and ends by declaring:

> 'Though I have treated of these deities in their order,
> Yet I have not adored them.'

One may surmise with probability that lay people agreed rather with the poet than with the monk. Pious men in monasteries might write what they liked, but mere laymen would not be easily persuaded that their cherished gods had never been anything more than men like themselves. Probably they

---

[1] That is, from Heaven.

said little but acted in secret according to their inherited ideas. Let it be granted, for the sake of peace, that Goibhniu was only a man; nonetheless, his name was known to be uncommonly effective in an incantation. This applied equally to Dian Cécht, and invocations to both of them are contained in some verses that an eighth-century Irish monk wrote on the margin of a manuscript still preserved at St Gall in Switzerland. Some prescriptions of Dian Cécht's have come down to us, but it must be admitted that they hardly differ from those current among ordinary medieval physicians. Perhaps, after that unfortunate spilling of the herbs that grew out of Midach's body, he had to fall back upon empirical research. He invented a porridge for 'the relief of ailments of the body, as cold, phlegm, throat cats, and the presence of living things in the body, as worms'. It was compounded of hazel buds, dandelion, chickweed, sorrel and oatmeal, and was to be taken every morning and evening. He also prescribed against the effects of witchcraft and fourteen diseases of the stomach.

Goibhniu, in addition to his original character as the divine smith and sorcerer, gained a third reputation among the Irish as a great builder and bridge-maker. As such he is known as the Gobhan Saer, that is, Goibhniu the Architect, and marvellous tales, current all over Ireland attest to his prowess.

> 'Men call'd him Gobhan Saer, and many a tale
>   Yet lingers in the byways of the land
> Of how he cleft the rock, or down the vale
>   Led the bright river, childlike, in his hand:
> Of how on giant ships he spread great sail,
>   And many marvels else by him first plann'd.'

wrote Thomas D'Arcy M'Gee, an Irish poet. The round towers of Ireland were especially attributed to him, and the Christian clerics appropriated his popularity by describing him as having been the designer of their churches. He used, according to legend, to wander over the country clad like the Greek Hephaestus, whom he resembles, in working dress, seeking commissions and adventures. His works remain in the cathedrals and churches of Ireland, and, with regard to his adventures, many strange legends were current among people in remote parts of Ireland for many years.

Some of these are, as might have been expected, nothing more than half-

understood recollections of the ancient mythology. In them appear as characters others of the old, yet not quite forgotten gods – Lugh, Manannán and
Balor – names still remembered as those of long-past druids, heroes and kings
of Ireland in the misty olden time.

One or two of them are worth retelling. William Larminie, who in the nineteenth century was collecting folktales in Achill Island, took one from the lips
of an aged peasant which tells in its confused way what might almost be called
the central incident of Gaelic mythology, the mysterious birth of the sun god
from demoniac parentage and his eventual slaying of his grandfather when he
came to full age.

Gobhan the Architect and his son, young Gobhan, runs the tale, were sent
for by Balor of the Blows to build him a palace. They built it so well that Balor
decided never to let them leave his kingdom alive for fear that they should
build another one equally good for someone else. He therefore had all the
scaffolding removed from round the palace while they were still on the top,
with the intention of leaving them up there to die of hunger. But when they
discovered this they began to destroy the roof so that Balor was obliged to let
them come down.

He nonetheless refused to allow them to return to Ireland. The crafty
Gobhan, however, had his plan ready. He told Balor that the injury that had
been done to the palace roof could not be repaired without special tools,
which he had left behind him at home. Balor declined to let either old Gobhan
or young Gobhan go back to fetch them, but he offered to send his own son.
Gobhan gave Balor's son directions for the journey. He was to travel until he
came to a house with a stack of corn at the door. Entering it, he would find a
woman with one hand and a child with one eye.

Balor's son found the house and asked the woman for the tools. She expected
him, for it had been arranged between Gobhan and his wife what should be
done if Balor refused to let him return. She took Balor's son to a huge chest
and told him that the tools were at the bottom of it, so far down that she could
not reach them, and that he must get into the chest and pick them up himself.
But as soon as he was safely inside, she shut the lid on him, telling him that he
would have to stay there until his father allowed old Gobhan and young
Gobhan to come home with their pay. She sent the same message to Balor
himself, and there was an exchange of prisoners, Balor giving the two Gobh-
ans their pay and a ship to take them home and Gobhan's wife releasing Balor's

son. But before the two builders went, Balor asked them whom he should now employ to repair his palace. Old Gobhan told him that next to himself there was no workman in Ireland better than one Gavidjeen Go.

When Gobhan got back to Ireland, he sent Gavidjeen Go to Balor, but he gave him a piece of advice – to accept as pay only one thing: Balor's grey cow, which would fill twenty barrels at one milking. Balor agreed to this, but when he gave the cow to Gavidjeen Go to take back with him to Ireland, he omitted to include her byre rope, which was the only thing that would keep her from returning to her original owner.

The grey cow gave so much trouble to Gavidjeen Go by her straying that he was obliged to hire military champions to watch her during the day and bring her safely home at night. The bargain made was that Gavidjeen Go should forge the champion a sword for his pay but that if he lost the cow his life was to be forfeited.

At last, a certain warrior called Cian was unlucky enough to let the cow escape. He followed her tracks down to the seashore and right to the edge of the waves, and there he lost them altogether. He was tearing his hair in his perplexity when he saw a man rowing a coracle. The man, who was no other than Manannán Mac Lir, came in close to the shore and asked what was the matter.

Cian told him.

'What would you give to anyone who would take you to the place where the grey cow is?' asked Manannán.

'I have nothing to give,' replied Cian.

'All I ask,' said Manannán, 'is half of whatever you gain before you come back.'

Cian agreed to that willingly enough, and Manannán told him to get into the coracle. In the wink of an eye he had landed him in Balor's kingdom, the realm of the cold, where they roast no meat but eat their food raw. Cian was not used to this diet, so he lit himself a fire and began to cook some food. Balor saw the fire and came down to it, and he was so pleased that he appointed Cian to be his fire-maker and cook.

Now Balor had a daughter, Ethlinn, of whom a druid had prophesied that she would some day bear a son who would kill his grandfather. Therefore, like Acrisius in Greek legend, he shut her up in a tower, guarded by women, and allowed her to see no man but himself. One day Cian saw Balor go to the tower. He waited until he had come back and then went to explore. He had the gift of opening locked doors and shutting them again after him. When he got inside he lit a fire, and this novelty so delighted Balor's daughter that she invited him to visit her again. After this – in the Achill islander's quaint phrase – 'he was ever coming there, until a child happened to her.' Balor's daughter gave the baby to Cian to take away. She also gave him the byre rope that belonged to the grey cow.

Cian was in great danger now, for Balor had found out about the child. He led the grey cow away with the rope to the seashore and waited for Manannán. The son of Lir had told Cian that when he was in any difficulty he was to think of him and he would at once appear. Cian thought of him now, and in a moment Manannán appeared with his coracle. Cian got into the boat with the baby and the grey cow, just as Balor came down to the beach in hot pursuit.

Balor, by his incantations, raised a great storm to drown them, but Manannán, whose druidism was greater, stilled it. Then Balor turned the sea into fire to burn them, but Manannán put it out with a stone.

When they were safely back in Ireland, Manannán asked Cian for his promised reward.

'I have gained nothing but the boy, and I cannot cut him in two, so I will give him to you whole,' he replied.

'That is what I was wanting all the time,' said Manannán. 'When he grows up, there will be no champion equal to him.'

So Manannán baptised the boy, calling him the Dul-Dauna. This name, meaning 'Blind-Stubborn', is certainly a curious corruption of the original Ioldanach, 'Master of all Knowledge'. When the boy had grown up, he went one day to the seashore. A ship came past in which was a man. The traditions of Donnybrook Fair are evidently prehistoric, for the boy, without troubling to ask who the stranger was, took a dart 'out of his pocket', hurled it and hit him. The man in the boat happened to be Balor. Thus, in accordance with the prophecy, he was slain by his grandson, who, although the folktale does not name him, was obviously Lugh.

Another version of the same legend, collected by the Irish scholar O'Donovan on the coast of Donegal opposite Balor's favourite haunt, Tory Island, is interesting as completing the one just narrated. In this folktale, Goibhniu is called Gavida and is made one of three brothers, the other two being called Mac Kineely and Mac Samthainn. They were chiefs of Donegal, smiths and farmers, while Balor was a robber who harassed the mainland from his stronghold on Tory Island. The grey cow belonged to Mac Kineely, and Balor stole it. Its owner determined to be revenged and, knowing the prediction concerning Balor's death at the hands of an as yet unborn grandson, he persuaded a kindly fairy to spirit him in female disguise to Tor Mor, where Balor's daughter was kept imprisoned. The result of this expedition was not merely the one son necessary to fulfil the prophecy but three. This apparent superfluity was fortunate, for Balor drowned two of them, the other being picked out of the sea by the same fairy who had been incidentally responsible for his birth and handed over to his father, Mac Kineely, to be brought up. Shortly after this, Balor managed to capure Mac Kineely and, in retaliation for the wrong done him, chopped off his head upon a large white stone, still known locally as the 'Stone of Kineely'. Satisfied with this and quite unaware that one of his daughter's children had been saved from death and was now being brought up as a smith by Gavida, Balor went on with his career of robbery, varying it by visits to the forge to purchase arms. One day, being there during Gavida's absence, he began boasting to the young assistant of how he had achieved Mac Kineely's death. He never finished the story, for Lugh – which was the boy's name – snatched a red-hot iron from the fire and thrust it into Balor's eye and through his head.

Thus in these two folktales, gathered in different parts of Ireland at different times by different persons, survives quite a mass of mythological detail only to be found otherwise in ancient manuscripts containing still more ancient matter. Crystallised in them may be found the names of six members of the old Gaelic pantheon, each filling the same part as of old. Goibhniu has not lost his mastery of smithcraft; Balor is still the Fomorian king of the cold regions of the sea; his daughter Ethlinn becomes, by Cian, the mother of the sun god, Lugh, who still bears his old title of Ioldanach, although it is strangely corrupted into a name meaning almost the exact opposite, is still fostered by Manannán, Son of the Sea, and in the end grows up to destroy his grandfather by a blow in the one vulnerable place, his death-dealing eye. Perhaps, too, we may claim to see a genuine although jumbled tradition in the Fomor-like deformities of Gobhan's wife and child and in the story of the grey cow and her byre rope, which recalls that of the Daghda's black-maned heifer, Ocean.

Many stories still exist of Lugh as well as of Oenghus and others of the old gods. But next to the Gobhan Saer, the one whose fame is still greatest is that ever-potent and ever-popular figure, the great Manannán.

Cian finds Ethlinn, Balor's daughter, from a drawing by H. R. Millar

The last, perhaps, to receive open adoration, he is represented by kindly tradition as having been still content to help and watch over the people who had rejected and ceased to worship him. Up to the time of St Columba, he was the special guardian of Irishmen in foreign parts, assisting them in their dangers and bringing them home safe. For the peasantry, too, he caused favourable weather and good crops. His fairy subjects tilled the ground while men slept. But this is said to have come to an end at last. St Columba, having broken his golden chalice, gave it to a servant to get repaired. On his way the servant was met by a stranger who asked him where he was going. The man told him and showed him the chalice. The stranger breathed upon it, and at once the broken parts reunited. Then he begged him to return to his master, give him the chalice and tell him that Manannán son of Lir, who had mended it, desired to know in very truth whether he would ever attain paradise 'Alas,' said the ungrateful saint, 'there is no forgiveness for a man who does such works as this!' The servant went back with the answer, and Manannán, when he heard it, broke out into indignant lament. 'Woe is me, Manannán Mac Lir! For years I've helped the people of Ireland, but I'll do it no more, till they're as weak as water. I'll go to the grey waves in the Highlands of Scotland.' And there he remained.

He is not yet quite forgotten in his own island of Man, of which local tradition says he was the first inhabitant. He is also described as its king, who protected it from invasion by his magic. He would cause mists to rise at any moment and conceal the island, and by the same spell he could make one man seem like a hundred, and little chips of wood which he threw into the water to appear like ships of war. It is no wonder that he held his kingdom against all-comers until his sway was ended, like that of the other Gaelic gods, by the arrival of St Patrick. After this he seems to have declined into a traditional giant who used to leap from Peel Castle to Contrary Head for exercise or hurl huge rocks upon which the mark of his hand can still be seen. It is said that he took no tribute from his subjects or worshippers except bundles of green rushes, which were placed every Midsummer Eve upon two mountain peaks, one called Warrefield in olden days but now South Barrule, and the other called Man and not now to be identified. His grave, which is thirty yards long, is pointed out close to Peel Castle. The most curious legend connected with him, however, tells us that he had three legs on which he used to travel at a great pace. How this was done may be seen from the arms of the island on which are pictured his three limbs joined together and spread out like the spokes of a wheel.

An Irish tradition tells us that when Manannán left Ireland for Scotland, the vacant kingship of the gods or fairies was taken by one Mac Moincanta to the great grief of those who had known Manannán. Perhaps this great grief led to Mac Moincanta's being deposed, for the present king of the Irish fairies is the same Fionnbharr to whom the Daghda allotted the *sídh* of Meadha after the conquest of the Tuatha Dé Danaan by the Sons of Mil Espaine and who takes a prominent part in the Fiann stories. So great is the persistence of tradition in Ireland that this hill of Meadha, now spelt Knockma, is still considered to be the abode of him and his queen, Oonagh. Numberless stories are told about Fionnbharr, including, of course, that very favourite Celtic tale of the stolen bride and her recapture from the fairies by the siege and digging up of the *sídh* in which she was held prisoner. Fionnbharr, like Midhir of Bri Leith, carried away a human, Etain – the wife not of a high king but of an Irish lord. The modern Eochaidh Airemh, having heard an invisible voice tell him where he was to look for his lost bride, gathered all his workmen and labourers and proceeded to demolish Knockma. Every day they almost dug it up, but every night the breach was found to have been repaired by fairy workmen of Fionnbharr's. This went on for three days, when the Irish lord thought of the wellknown device of sanctifying the work of excavation by sprinkling the turnedup earth with salt. Needless to say, it succeeded. Fionnbharr gave back the bride, still in the trance into which he had thrown her, and the deep cut into the fairy hill still remains to furnish proof to the incredulous.

Fionnbharr does not always appear, however, in such an unfriendly guise. He was popularly reputed to have under his special care the family of the Kirwans of Castle Hacket on the northern slope of Knockma. Owing to his benevolent influence, the castle cellars never went dry nor did the quality of the wine deteriorate. He also looked after the stables, and it was owing to the exercise that he and his fairy followers gave the horses at night that John Kirwan's racing horses were so often successful on the Curragh. That such stories could have passed current as fact, which they undoubtedly did, is excellent proof of how late and how completely a mythology may survive.

Fionnbharr rules today over a wide realm of fairy folk. Many of these, again, have their own vassal chieftains forming a tribal hierarchy such as must have existed in the Celtic days of Ireland. Fionnbharr and Oonagh are high king and queen, but, under them, Cliodna is tributary queen of Munster and rules from a *sídh* near Mallow in County Cork, while, under her again, are Aoibhinn, queen of the fairies of North Munster, and Ainé, queen of the fairies of South Munster. These names form but a single instance. A map of fairy Ireland could without much difficulty be drawn, showing, with almost political exactness, the various kingdoms of the Sídhe.

Far less easy, however, would be the task of ascertaining the origin and lineage of these fabled beings. Some of them can still be traced as older gods and goddesses. In the eastern parts of Ireland, Badb and her sisters have become 'banshees' who wail over deaths not necessarily found in battle. Aynia, deemed the most powerful fairy in Ulster, and Ainé, queen of South Munster, are perhaps the same person, the mysterious and awful goddess once adored as Anu or Danu. Of the two, it is Ainé who especially seems to carry on the traditions of the older Anu, worshipped in Munster, according to the 'Choice of Names', as a goddess of prosperity and abundance. For many years she was propitiated by a magic ritual on every St John's Eve to ensure fertility during the coming year. The villagers round her *sídh* of Cnoc Ainé (Knockainy) carried burning bunches of hay or straw on poles to the top of the hill, and from there dispersed among the fields, waving these torches over the crops and cattle. This fairy or goddess was held to be friendly and, indeed, more than friendly to men. Whether or not she was the mother of the gods, she is claimed as first ancestress by half a dozen famous Irish families.

Among her children was the famous Earl Gerald, offspring of her alliance with the fourth Earl of Desmond, known as 'The Magician'. As in the well-known story of the Swan-maidens, the magician earl is said to have stolen Ainé's cloak while she was bathing and refused to return it unless she became his bride, but in the end he lost her. Ainé had warned her husband never to show surprise at anything done by their son, but a wonderful feat that he performed made the earl break this condition and Ainé was obliged by fairy law to leave him. Although she had lost her husband, however, she was not separated from her son, who was received into the fairy world after his death and now lives under the surface of Lough Gur in County Limerick, waiting, like the British Arthur, for the hour to strike in which he shall lead forth his warriors to drive the foreigners from Ireland. But this will not be until, by riding round the lake once in every seventh year, he shall have worn his horse's silver shoes as thin as a cat's ear.

Not only the tribe of Danu but heroes of the other mythical cycles swell the fairy host today. Donn, son of Mil, who was drowned before ever he set foot on Irish soil, lives at 'Donn's House', a line of sand hills in the Dingle Peninsula of Kerry, and as late as the eighteenth century we find him invoked by a local poet, half in jest, no doubt, but still perhaps also a little in earnest. The heroes of Ulster have no part in fairyland, but their enemy, Medb, is credited with queenly rule among the Sídhe and is held by some to have been the original of 'Queen Mab'. Caoilté, last of the Fianna, was in spite of his leanings towards Christianity enrolled among the Tuatha Dé Danaan, but none of his kin are known there, neither Oisín nor Oscar nor even Fionn himself. Yet not even to merely historical mortals are the gates of the gods necessarily closed. The Barry, chief of the barony of Barrymore, is said to inhabit an enchanted palace in Knockthierna, one of the Nagles Hills. The not less traditionally famous O'Donaghue, whose domain was near Killarney, now dwells beneath the waters of that lake and may still be seen, it is said, on May Day.

But besides these figures, which can be traced in mythology or history, and others who, although all written record of them has perished, are obviously of the same character, there are numerous beings who suggest a different origin from that of the Aryan-seeming fairies. They correspond to the elves and trolls of Scandinavian or the silenoi and satyrs of Greek myth. Such is the Leprechaun, who makes shoes for the fairies and knows where hidden treasures are; the Gan Ceanach or 'love-talker', who fills the ears of idle girls with pleasant fancies when, to merely mortal ideas, they should be busy with their work; the Pooka, who leads travellers astray or, taking the shape of an ass or mule, beguiles them to mount upon his back to their discomfiture; the Dulachan, who rides without a head; and other friendly or malicious sprites. From where do they come? A possible answer suggests itself. Preceding the Aryans and surviving the Aryan conquest all over Europe was a large non-Aryan population that must have had its own gods who would retain their worship, be revered by successive generations and remain rooted to the soil. May not these uncouth and half-developed Irish Leprechauns, Pookas and Dulachans, together with the Scotch Cluricanes, Brownies and their kin, be no 'creations of popular fancy' but the dwindling figures of those darker gods of 'the dark Iberians'?

197

Chapter 17

An Irish Odyssey: The Voyage of Mael Dúin

Besides the legends that cluster round great heroic names, and have, or at least pretend to have, the character of history, there are many others, great and small, that tell of adventures lying purely in regions of romance, and out of earthly space and time. As a specimen of these here is a summary of the 'Voyage of Mael Dúin', a most curious and brilliant piece of invention that is found in the Book of the Dun Cow and other early sources. It is only one of a number of such wonder voyages found in ancient Irish literature, but it is believed to have been the earliest of them all and model for the rest, and it had the distinction of having furnished the theme for the 'Voyage of Maeldune' to Tennyson, who made it into a wonderful creation of rhythm and colour, embodying kind of allegory of Irish history. It will be noticed at the end that we are in the unusual position of knowing the name of the author of this piece of primitive literature, though he does not claim to have composed but only to have 'put in order' the incidents of the 'Voyage'. Unfortunately we cannot tell when he lived, but the tale as we have it probably dates from the ninth century. Its atmosphere is entirely Christian, and it has no mythological significance except in so far as it teaches the lesson that the oracular injunctions of wizards should be obeyed. No adventure, or even detail, of importance is omitted in the following summary of the story, which is given thus fully because the reader may take it as representing a large and important section of Irish legendary romance.

The 'Voyage of Mael Dúin' begins, as Irish tales often do, by telling us of the conception of its hero.

There was a famous man of the sept of the Owens of Aran, named Ailill Edge-of-Battle, who went with his king on a foray into another territory. They encamped one night near a church and convent of nuns. At midnight Ailill, who was near the church, saw a certain nun come out to strike the bell for nocturns, and caught her by the hand. In ancient Ireland religious persons were not much respected in time of war, and Ailill did not respect her. When they parted, she said to him: 'Whence is your race, and what is your name?' Said the hero: 'Ailill of the Edge-of-Battle is my name, and I am of the Owenacht of Aran, in Thomond.'

Not long afterwards Ailill was slain by raiders from Leix, who burned the church of Doocloone over his head.

In due time a son was born to the woman, and she called his name Mael Dúin. He was taken secretly to her friend, the queen of the territory, and by her Mael Dúin was reared. 'Beautiful indeed was his form, and it is doubtful if there has been in flesh anyone so beautiful as he. So he grew up till he was a young warrior and fit to use weapons. Great, then, his brightness and his gaiety and his playfulness. In his play he outwent all his comrades in throwing balls, and in running and leaping and putting stones and racing horses.

One day a proud young warrior who had been defeated by him taunted him with his lack of knowledge of his kindred and descent. Mael Dúin went to his foster mother, the queen, and said: 'I will not eat nor drink till you tell me who are my mother and my father.'

'I am your mother,' said the queen, 'for none ever loved her son more than I love you.'

But Mael Dúin insisted on knowing all, and the queen at last took him to his own mother, the nun, who told him: 'Your father was Ailill of the Owens of Aran.'

Then Mael Dúin went to his own kindred and was well received by them, and with him he took as guests his three beloved foster-brothers, sons of the king and queen who had brought him up.

After a time Mael Dúin happened to be among a company of young warriors who were contending at putting the stone in the graveyard of the ruined church of Doocloone. Mael Dúin's foot was planted, as he heaved the stone, on a scorched and blackened flagstone, and one who was by, a monk, said to him: 'It were better for you to avenge the man who was burnt there than to cast stones over his burnt bones.'

'Who was that?' asked Mael Dúin.

'Ailill, your father,' the monk told him.

'Who slew him?' said he.

'Raiders from Leix;' the monk said, 'and they destroyed him on this spot.'

Then Mael Dúin threw down the stone he was about to cast and put his mantle round him and went home, and he asked the way to Leix. They told him he could only go there by sea.

At the advice of a druid he then built him a boat, or coracle, of skins lapped threefold one over the other, and the wizard also told him that seventeen men only must accompany him, and on what day he must begin the boat and on what day he must put out to sea.

So when his company was ready he put out and hoisted the sail, but had gone only a little way when his three foster brothers came down to the beach and entreated him to take them.

'Get you home,' said Mael Dúin, 'for none but the number I have may go with me.'

But the three youths would not be separated from Mael Dúin, and they flung themselves into the sea. He turned back, lest they should be drowned, and brought them into his boat. All, as we shall see, were punished for this transgression, and Mael Dúin condemned to wandering until expiation had been made.

Irish bardic tales excel in their openings. In this case, as usual, the *mise-en-scène* is admirably contrived. The narrative that follows tells how, after seeing his father's slayer on an island but being unable to land there, Mael Dúin and his party are blown out to sea, where they visit a great number of islands and have many strange adventures on them. The tale becomes, in fact, a *cento* of stories and incidents, some not very interesting, while in others, as in the adventure of the Island of the Silver Pillar, or the Island of the Flaming Rampart, or that where the episode of the eagle takes place, the Celtic sense of beauty, romance and mystery finds an expression unsurpassed, perhaps, in literature.

THE ISLAND OF THE SLAYER

Mael Dúin and his crew had rowed all day and half the night when they came to two small bare islands with two forts in them, and a noise was heard from them of armed men quarrelling. 'Stand off from me,' cried one of them, 'for I am a better man than you. 'Twas I slew Ailill of the Edge-of-Battle and burned the church of Doocloone over him, and no kinsman has avenged his death on me. And *you* have never done the like of that.'

Then Mael Dúin was about to land, and Germán and Diuran the Rhymer cried that God had guided them to the spot where they would be. But a great wind arose suddenly and blew them off into the boundless ocean, and Mael Dúin said to his foster brothers: 'You have caused this to be, casting yourselves on board in spite of the words of the druid.' And they had no answer, save only to be silent for a little space.

THE ISLAND OF THE ANTS

They drifted three days and three nights, not knowing whither to row, when at the dawn of the third day they heard the noise of breakers, and came to an island as soon as the sun was up. Here, before they could land, they met a swarm of ferocious ants, each the size of a foal, that came down the strand and into the sea to get at them, so they made off quickly and saw no land for three days more.

THE ISLAND OF THE GREAT BIRDS

This was a terraced island, with trees all round it, and great birds sitting on the trees. Mael Dúin landed first alone and carefully searched the island for any evil thing, but finding none, the rest followed him and killed and ate many of the birds, bringing others on board their boat.

THE ISLAND OF THE FIERCE BEAST

A great sandy island was this, and on it a beast like a horse but with clawed feet like a hound's. He flew at them to devour them, but they put off in time and were pelted by the beast with pebbles from the shore as they rowed away.

THE ISLAND OF THE GIANT HORSES

A great, flat island, which it fell by lot to Germán and Diuran to explore first. They found a vast green racecourse on which were the marks of horses' hoofs, each as big as the sail of a ship, and the shells of nuts of monstrous size were lying about, and much plunder. So they were afraid and took ship hastily again, and from the sea they saw a horse race in progress and heard the shouting of a great multitude cheering on the white horse or the brown, and saw the giant horses running swifter than the wind.[1] So they rowed away with all their might, thinking they had come upon an assembly of demons.

---

1 Horse racing was a particular delight to the ancient Irish, and is mentioned in a ninth-century poem in praise of May as one of the attractions of that month. The name of the month of May given in an ancient Gaulish calendar means 'the month of horse racing'.

THE ISLAND OF THE STONE DOOR

A full week passed, and then they found a great, high island with a house standing on the shore. A door with a valve of stone opened into the sea, and through it the sea waves kept hurling salmon into the house. Mael Dúin and his party entered, and found the house empty of folk, but a great bed lay ready for the chief to whom it belonged, and a bed for each three of his company, and meat and drink beside each bed. Mael Dúin and his party ate and drank their fill, and then sailed off again.

THE ISLAND OF THE APPLES

By the time they had come here they had been a long time voyaging, and food had failed them, and they were hungry. This island had precipitous sides from which a wood hung down, and as they passed along the cliffs Mael Dúin broke off a twig and held it in his hand. Three days and nights they coasted the cliff and found no entrance to the island, but by that time a cluster of three apples had grown on the end of Mael Dúin's rod, and each apple sufficed the crew for forty days.

THE ISLAND OF THE WONDROUS BEAST

This island had a fence of stone round it, and within the fence a huge beast that raced round and round the island. And anon it went to the top of the island, and then performed a marvellous feat, namely, it turned its body round and round inside its skin, the skin remaining unmoved, while again it would revolve its skin round and round the body. When it saw the party it rushed at them, but they escaped, pelted with stones as they rowed away. One of the stones pierced through Mael Dúin's shield and lodged in the keel of the boat.

THE ISLAND OF THE BITING HORSES

Here were many great beasts resembling horses, that tore continually pieces of flesh from each other's sides, so that all the island ran with blood. They rowed hastily away, and were now disheartened and full of complaints, for they knew not where they were nor how to find guidance or aid in their quest.

THE ISLAND OF THE FIERY SWINE

With great weariness, hunger and thirst they arrived at the tenth island, which was full of trees loaded with golden apples. Under the trees went red beasts, like fiery swine, that kicked the trees with their legs, so the apples fell and the beasts consumed them. The beasts came out at morning only, when a multitude of birds left the island, and swam out to sea till nones, when they turned and swam inward again till vespers, and ate the apples all night.

Mael Dúin and his comrades landed at night and felt the soil hot under their feet from the fiery swine in their caverns underground. They collected all the apples they could, which were good both against hunger and thirst, and loaded their boat with them and put to sea once more, refreshed.

THE ISLAND OF THE LITTLE CAT

The apples had failed them when they came hungry and thirsting to the eleventh island. This was, as it were, a tall white tower of chalk reaching up to the clouds, and on the rampart about it were great houses white as snow. They entered the largest of them and found no man in it but a small cat playing on four stone pillars that were in the midst of the house, leaping from one to the other. It looked a little on the Irish warriors but did not cease from its play. On the walls of the houses there were three rows of objects hanging up, one row of brooches of gold and silver, and one of neck torks of gold and silver, each as big as the hoop of a cask, and one of great swords with gold and silver hilts. Quilts and shining garments lay in the room, and there, also, were a roasted ox and a flitch of bacon and abundance of liquor.

'Has this been left for us?' said Mael Dúin to the cat. It looked at him a moment and then continued its play. So there they ate and drank and slept, and stored up what remained of the food. Next day, as they made to leave the house, the youngest of Mael Dúin's foster brothers took a necklace from the wall, and was bearing it out when the cat suddenly 'leaped through him like a fiery arrow', and he fell, a heap of ashes, on the floor. Thereupon Mael Dúin, who had forbidden the theft of the jewel, soothed the cat and replaced the necklace, and they strewed the ashes of the dead youth on the seashore and put to sea again.

THE ISLAND OF THE BLACK AND WHITE SHEEP

This had a brazen palisade dividing it in two, and a flock of black sheep on one side and of white sheep on the other. Between them was a big man who tended the flocks, and sometimes he put a white sheep among the black, when it became black at once, or a black sheep among the white, when it immediately turned white. By way of an experiment Mael Dúin flung a peeled white wand on the side of the black sheep. It at once turned black, whereat they left the place in terror and without landing.

THE ISLAND OF THE GIANT CATTLE

A great and wide island with a herd of huge swine on it. They killed a small pig and roasted it on the spot, as it was too great to carry on board. The island rose up into a very high mountain, and Diuran and Germán went to view the country from the top of it. On their way they met a broad river. To try the depth of the water Germán dipped in the haft of his spear, which at once was consumed as with liquid fire. On the other bank was a huge man guarding what seemed a herd of oxen. He called to them not to disturb the calves, so they went no farther and speedily sailed away.

THE ISLAND OF THE MILL

Here they found a great and grim-looking mill, and a giant miller grinding corn in it. 'Half the corn of your country,' he said, 'is ground here. Here comes to be ground all that men begrudge to each other.' Heavy and many were the loads they saw going to it, and all that was ground in it was carried away westwards. So they crossed themselves and sailed away.

THE ISLAND OF THE BLACK MOURNERS

An island full of black people continually weeping and lamenting. One of the two remaining foster brothers landed on it, and immediately turned black and fell to weeping like the rest. Two others went to fetch him, and the same fate befell them. Four others then went with their heads wrapped in cloths that they should not look on the land or breathe the air of the place, and they seized two of the lost ones and brought them away perforce, but not the foster brother. The two rescued ones could not explain their conduct except by saying that they had to do as they saw others doing about them.

THE ISLAND OF THE FOUR FENCES

Four fences of gold, silver, brass and crystal divided this island into four parts, kings in one, queens in another, warriors in a third, maidens in the fourth. On landing, a maiden gave them food like cheese that tasted to each man as he wished it to be, and an intoxicating liquor that put them asleep for three days.

When they awoke they were at sea in their boat, and of the island and its inhabitants nothing was to be seen.

THE ISLAND OF THE GLASS BRIDGE

Here we come to one of the most elaborately wrought and picturesque of all the incidents of the voyage. The island they now reached had on it a fortress with a brazen door and a bridge of glass leading to it. When they sought to cross the bridge it threw them backwards.[1] A woman came out of the fortress with a pail in her hand, and lifting from the bridge a slab of glass she let down her pail into the water beneath and returned to the fortress. They struck on the brazen portcullis before them to gain admittance, but the melody given forth by the smitten metal plunged them in slumber till the morrow morn. Thrice over this happened, the woman each time making an ironical speech about Mael Dúin. On the fourth day, however, she came out to them over the bridge, wearing a white mantle with a circlet of gold on her hair, two silver sandals on her rosy feet, and a filmy silken smock next her skin.

'My welcome to you, O Mael Dúin,' she said, and she welcomed each man of the crew by his own name. Then she took them into the great house and allotted a couch to the chief and one for each three of his men. She gave them abundance of food and drink, all out of her one pail, each man finding in it what he most desired. When she had departed they asked Mael Dúin if they should woo the maiden for him.

'How would it hurt you to speak with her?' said Mael Dúin.

They do so, and she replies: 'I know not, nor have ever known, what sin is.'

Twice over this is repeated. 'Tomorrow,' she says at last, 'you shall have your answer.'

When the morning broke, however, they found themselves once more at sea, with no sign of the island or fortress or lady.

THE ISLAND OF THE SHOUTING BIRDS

They heard from afar a great cry and chanting, as it were a singing of psalms, and rowing for a day and night they came at last to an island full of birds, black, brown and speckled, all shouting and speaking. They sailed away without landing.

---

[1] Like the bridge to Scáthach's *dún*, see Chapter 12.

THE ISLAND OF THE ANCHORITE

Here they found a wooded island full of birds, and on it a solitary man whose only clothing was his hair. They asked of him his country and kin. He tells them that he was a man of Ireland who had put to sea with a sod of his native country under his feet.[1] God had turned the sod into an island, adding a foot's breadth to it and one tree for every year. The birds are his kith and kin, and they all wait there till Doomsday miraculously nourished by angels. He entertained them for three nights and then they sailed away.

THE ISLAND OF THE MIRACULOUS FOUNTAIN

This island had a golden rampart and a soft white soil like down. In it they found another anchorite clothed only in his hair. There was a fountain in it that yielded whey or water on Fridays and Wednesdays, milk on Sundays and feasts of martyrs, and ale and wine on the feasts of Apostles, of Mary, of John the Baptist, and on the high tides of the year.

THE ISLAND OF THE SMITHY

As they approached this they heard from afar a sound as if it were the clanging of a tremendous smithy, and heard men talking of themselves. 'Little boys they seem,' said one, 'in a little trough yonder.' They rowed hastily away but did not turn their boat, so as not to seem to be fleeing; but after a while a giant smith came out of the forge holding in his tongs a huge mass of glowing iron, which he cast after them, and all the sea boiled round it, as it fell astern of their boat.

THE SEA OF CLEAR GLASS

After that they voyaged until they entered a sea that resembled green glass. Such was its purity that the gravel and the sand of the sea were clearly visible through it; and they saw no monsters or beasts therein among the crags but only the pure gravel and the green sand. For a long space of the day they were voyaging in that sea, and great was its splendour and its beauty.[2]

---

[1] Probably we are to understand that he was a hermit seeking for an islet on which to dwell in solitude and contemplation. The western islands of Ireland abound in the ruins of huts and oratories built by single monks or little communities.

[2] Tennyson is particularly happy in his description of these undersea islands.

THE UNDERSEA ISLAND

They next found themselves in a sea, thin like mist, that seemed as if it would not support their boat. In the depths they saw roofed fortresses and a fair land around them. A monstrous beast lodged in a tree there, with droves of cattle about it, and beneath it an armed warrior. In spite of the warrior, the beast ever and anon stretched down a long neck and seized one of the cattle and devoured it. Much dreading lest they should sink through the mist-like sea, they sailed over it and away.

THE ISLAND OF THE PROPHECY

When they arrived here they found the water rising in high cliffs round the island, and, looking down, saw on it a crowd of people, who screamed at them, 'It is they, it is they,' till they were out of breath. Then came a woman and pelted them from below with large nuts, which they gathered and took with them. As they went they heard the folk crying to each other: 'Where are they now?'

'They are gone away.'

'They are not.'

'It is likely,' says the tale, 'that there was someone concerning whom the islanders had a prophecy that he would ruin their country and expel them from their land.'

THE ISLAND OF THE SPOUTING WATER

Here a great stream spouted out of one side of the island and arched over it like a rainbow, falling on the strand at the farther side. And when they thrust their spears into the stream above them they brought out salmon from it as much as they would, and the island was filled with the stench of those they could not carry away.

THE ISLAND OF THE SILVER COLUMN

The next wonder to which they came forms one of the most striking and imaginative episodes of the voyage. It was a great silver column, four-square, rising from the sea. Each of its four sides was as wide as two oar strokes of the boat. Not a sod of earth was at its foot, but it rose from the boundless ocean and its summit was lost in the sky. From that summit a huge silver net was flung far away into the sea and through a mesh of that net they sailed. As they did so Diuran hacked away a piece of the net.

'Destroy it not,' said Mael Dúin, 'for what we see is the work of mighty men.'

Diuran said: 'For the praise of God's name I do this, that our tale may be believed, and if I reach Ireland again this piece of silver shall be offered by me on the high altar of Armagh.' Two ounces and a half it weighed when it was measured afterwards in Armagh.

'And then they heard a voice from the summit of yonder pillar, mighty, clear and distinct. But they knew not the tongue it spoke, or the words it uttered.'

THE ISLAND OF THE PEDESTAL

The next island stood on a foot, or pedestal, that rose from the sea, and they could find no way of access to it. In the base of the pedestal was a door, closed and locked, which they could not open, so they sailed away, having seen and spoken with no one.

THE ISLAND OF THE WOMEN

Here they found the rampart of a mighty dún, enclosing a mansion. They landed to look on it and sat on a hillock nearby. Within the dún they saw seventeen maidens busy at preparing a great bath. In a little while a rider, richly clad, came up swiftly on a racehorse and lighted down and went inside, one of the girls taking the horse. The rider then went into the bath, when they saw that it was a woman. Shortly after that one of the maidens came out and invited them to enter, saying: 'The Queen invites you.' They went into the fort and bathed, and then sat down to meat, each man with a maiden over against him and Mael Dúin opposite to the queen. And Mael Dúin was wedded to the queen, and each of the maidens to one of his men, and at nightfall canopied chambers were allotted to each of them. On the morrow morn they made ready to depart, but the queen would not have them go and said: 'Stay here, and old age will never fall on you, but you shall remain as you are now for ever and ever, and what you had last night you shall have always. And be no longer a-wandering from island to island on the ocean.'

She then told Mael Dúin that she was the mother of the seventeen girls they had seen, and her husband had been king of the island. He was now dead, and she reigned in his place. Each day she went into the great plain in the interior of the island to judge the folk and returned to the dún at night.

So they remained there for three months of winter but at the end of that time it seemed they had been there three years, and the men wearied of it and longed to set forth for their own country.

'What shall we find there,' said Mael Dúin, 'that is better than this?'

But still the people murmured and complained, and at last they said: 'Great is the love that Mael Dúin has for his woman. Let him stay with her alone if he will, but we will go to our own country.' But Mael Dúin would not be left after them, and at last one day, when the queen was away judging the folk, they went on board their bark and put out to sea. Before they had gone far, however, the queen came riding up with a clew of twine in her hand, and she flung it after them. Mael Dúin caught it in his hand, and it clung to his hand so that he could not free himself, and the queen, holding the other end, drew them back to land. And they stayed on the island another three months.

Twice again the same thing happened, and at last the people averred that Mael Dúin held the clew on purpose, so great was his love for the woman. So the next time another man caught the clew, but it clung to his hand as before, so Diuran smote off his hand, and it fell with the clew into the sea. 'When she saw that she at once began to wail and shriek, so that all the land was one cry, wailing and shrieking.' And thus they escaped from the Island of the Women.

THE ISLAND OF THE RED BERRIES
On this island were trees with great red berries that yielded an intoxicating and slumbrous juice. They mingled it with water to moderate its power, and filled their casks with it, and sailed away.

THE ISLAND OF THE EAGLE
A large island, with woods of oak and yew on one side of it, and on the other a plain, whereon were herds of sheep, and a little lake in it; and there also they found a small church and a fort, and an ancient grey cleric, clad only in his hair. Mael Dúin asked him who he was.

'I am the fifteenth man of the monks of St Brennan of Birr,' he said. 'We went on our pilgrimage into the ocean, and they have all died save me alone.' He showed them the tablet (?calendar) of the Holy Brennan, and they prostrated themselves before it, and Mael Dúin kissed it. They stayed there for a season, feeding on the sheep of the island.

One day they saw what seemed to be a cloud coming up from the southwest. As it drew near, however, they saw the waving of pinions, and perceived that it was an enormous bird. It came into the island, and, alighting very wearily on a hill near the: lake, it began eating the red berries, like grapes, which grew on a huge tree branch as big as a full-grown oak, that it had brought with it, and the juice and fragments of the berries fell into the lake, reddening all the water. Fearful that it would seize them in its talons and bear them out to sea, they lay hidden in the woods and watched it. After a while, however, Mael Dúin went out to the foot of the hill, but the bird did him no harm, and then the rest followed cautiously behind their shields, and one of them gathered the berries off the branch which the bird held in its talons, but it did them no evil and regarded them not at all. And they saw that it was very old, and its plumage dull and decayed.

At the hour of noon two eagles came up from the southwest and alit in front of the great bird, and after resting awhile they set to work picking off the insects that infested its jaws and eyes and ears. This they continued till vespers, when all three ate of the berries again. At last, on the following day, when the great bird had been completely cleansed, it plunged into the lake, and again the two eagles picked and cleansed it. Till the third day the great bird remained preening and shaking its pinions, and its feathers became glossy and abundant, and then, soaring upwards, it flew thrice round the island and away to the quarter whence it had come, and its flight was now swift and strong, whence it was manifest to them that this had been its renewal from old age to youth, according as the prophet said, *Thy youth is renewed like the eagle's.*

Then Diuran said: 'Let us bathe in that lake and renew ourselves where the bird has been renewed.'

'Nay,' said another, 'for the bird has left his venom in it.'

But Diuran plunged in and drank of the water. From that time so long as he lived his eyes were strong and keen, and not a tooth fell from his jaw nor a hair from his head, and he never knew illness or infirmity.

Thereafter they bade farewell to the anchorite and fared forth on the ocean once more.

THE ISLAND OF THE LAUGHING FOLK

Here they found a great company of men laughing and playing incessantly. They drew lots as to who should enter and explore it, and it fell to Mael Dúin's foster brother. But when he set foot on it he at once began to laugh and play with the others, and could not leave off, nor would he come back to his comrades, so they left him and sailed away.[1]

THE ISLAND OF THE FLAMING RAMPART

They now came in sight of an island that was not large, and it had about it a rampart of flame that circled round and round it continually. In one part of the rampart there was an opening, and when this opening came opposite to them they saw through it the whole island, and saw those who dwelt therein, even men and women, beautiful, many, and wearing adorned garments, with vessels of gold in their hands. And the festal music which they made came to the ears of the wanderers. For a long time they lingered there, watching this marvel, 'and they deemed it delightful to behold'.

THE ISLAND OF THE MONK OF TORY

Far off among the waves they saw what they took to be a white bird on the water. Drawing near to it they found it to be an aged man clad only in the white hair of his body, and he was throwing himself in prostrations on a broad rock.

'From Torach[2] I have come hither,' he said, 'and there I was reared. I was cook in the monastery there, and the food of the Church I used to sell for myself, so that I had at last much treasure of raiment and brazen vessels and goldbound books and all that man desires. Great was my pride and arrogance.

'One day as I dug a grave in which to bury a churl who had been brought on to the island, a voice came from below where a holy man lay buried, and he said: "Put not the corpse of a sinner on me, a holy, pious person!"'

After a dispute the monk buried the corpse elsewhere and was promised an eternal reward for doing so. Not long thereafter he put to sea in a boat with all his accumulated treasures, meaning apparently to escape from the island with his plunder. A great wind blew him far out to sea, and when he was out of sight of land the boat stood still in one place. He saw near him a man (angel) sitting on the wave.

'Whither go you?' said the man.

'On a pleasant way whither I am now looking,' said the monk.

---

[1]   This disposes of the last of the foster brothers who should not have joined the party.
[2]   Tory Island, off the Donegal coast. There was there a monastery and a church dedicated to St Columba.

'It would not be pleasant to you if you knew what is around you,' said the man. 'So far as eye can see there is one crowd of demons all gathered around you, because of your covetousness and pride, and theft, and other evil deeds. Your boat has stopped, nor will it move until you do my will, and the fires of hell shall get hold of you.'

He came near to the boat and laid his hand on the arm of the fugitive, who promised to do his will.

'Fling into the sea,' he said, 'all the wealth that is in your boat.'

'It is a pity, ' said the monk, 'that it should go to loss.'

'It shall in nowise go to loss. There will be one man whom you will profit.'

The monk thereupon flung everything into the sea save one little wooden cup, and he cast away oars and rudder. The man gave him a provision of whey and seven cakes, and bade him abide wherever his boat should stop. The wind and waves carried him hither and thither till at last the boat came to rest upon the rock where the wanderers found him. There was nothing there but the bare rock, but remembering what he was bidden he stepped out upon a little ledge over which the waves washed, and the boat immediately left him, and the rock was enlarged for him. There he remained seven years, nourished by otters which brought him salmon out of the sea, and even flaming firewood on which to cook them, and his cup was filled with good liquor every day. 'And neither wet nor heat nor cold affects me in this place.'

At the noon hour miraculous nourishment was brought for the whole crew, and thereafter the ancient man said to them:

'You will all reach your country, and the man that slew your father, O Mael Dúin, you will find him in a fortress before you. And slay him not, but forgive him, because God has saved you from manifold great perils, and you too are men deserving of death.'

Then they bade him farewell and went on their accustomed way.

THE ISLAND OF THE FALCON

This was uninhabited save for herds of sheep and oxen. They landed on it and ate their fill, and one of them saw there a large falcon. 'This falcon,' he said, 'is like the falcons of Ireland.'

'Watch it,' said Mael Dúin, 'and see how it will go from us.'

It flew off to the southeast, and they rowed after it all day till vespers.

THE HOMECOMING

At nightfall they sighted a land like Ireland and soon came to a small island where they ran their prow ashore. It was the island where dwelt the man who had slain Ailill.

They went up to the dún that was on the island and heard men talking within it as they sat at meat. One man said: 'It would be ill for us if we saw Mael Dúin now.'

'That Mael Dúin has been drowned,' said another.

'Maybe it is he who shall waken you from sleep tonight,' said a third.

"If he should come now,' said a fourth, 'what should we do?'

'Not hard to answer that,' said the chief of them. 'Great welcome should he have if he were to come, for he has been a long space in great tribulation.'

Then Mael Dúin smote with the wooden clapper against the door.

'Who is there?' asked the doorkeeper.

'Mael Dúin is here,' said he.

They entered the house in peace, and great welcome was made for them, and they were arrayed in new garments. And then they told the story of all the marvels that God had shown them, according to the words of the 'sacred poet', who said, *Haec olim meminisse juvabit*.[1]

Then Mael Dúin went to his own home and kindred, and Diuran the Rhymer took with him the piece of silver that he had hewn from the net of the pillar and laid it on the high altar of Armagh in triumph and exultation at the miracles that God had wrought for them. And they told again the story of all that had befallen them, and all the marvels they had seen by sea and land, and the perils they had endured.

The story ends with the following words:

'Now Aed the Fair [Aed Finn[2]], chief sage of Ireland, arranged this story as it standeth here; and he did so for a delight to the mind, and for the folks of Ireland after him.'

---

[1] 'One day we shall delight in the remembrance of these things.' The quotation is from Virgil's Aeneid. 'Sacred poet' is a translation of the *vates sacer* of Horace.

[2] The sage and poet has not been identified from any other record. Praise and thanks to him, whoever he may have been.

213

Part 3

The Gods of Britain and their Stories

Chapter 18

THE GODS OF THE BRITISH CELTS

The descriptions and the stories of the British gods have hardly come down to us in so ample or so compact a form as those of the deities of the Gaels as they are preserved in the Irish and Scottish manuscripts. They have also suffered far more from the euhemerists who tried to prove them to be human. Only in the 'Four Branches of the Mabinogi' do the gods of the Britons appear in anything like their real character of supernatural beings, masters of magic, and untrammelled by the limitations that hedge in mortals. Apart from those four fragments of mythology and from a very few scattered references in the early Welsh poems, one must search for them under strange disguises. Some masquerade as kings in Geoffrey of Monmouth's more than apocryphal *Historia Regum Britanniae*. Others have received an undeserved canonisation that must be stripped from them before they can be seen in their true colours. Others, again, were adopted by the Norman-French romancers and turned into the champions of chivalry now known as Arthur's Knights of the Round Table. But however disguised, their real nature can still be discerned. The Gaels and the Britons were only two branches of one race – the Celtic. In many of the gods of the Britons we will recognise, with names alike and attributes the same, the familiar features of the Gaelic Tuatha Dé Danaan.

The British gods are sometimes described as divided into three families – the 'Children of Don', the 'Children of Nudd' and the 'Children of Llyr'. But these three families are really only two, for Nudd, or Lludd as he is variously called, is himself described as a son of Beli, who was the husband of the goddess Don. There can be no doubt that Don herself is the same divine personage as Danu, the mother of the Tuatha Dé Danaan, and that Beli is the British equivalent of the Gaelic Bíle, the universal Dis Pater or Pluto who sent out the first Gaels from Hades to take possession of Ireland. With the other family, the 'Children of Llyr', we are equally on familiar ground, for the British Llyr can be none other than the Gaelic sea god Lir. These two families or tribes are usually regarded as in opposition, and their struggles seem to symbolise in British myth that same conflict between the powers of heaven, light and life and of the sea, darkness and death, which are shadowed in Gaelic mythology in the battles between the Tuatha Dé Danaan and the Fomorii.

For the children of Don were certainly gods of the sky. Their names are writ large in heaven. The glittering W that we call Cassiopeia's Chair was to our British ancestors *Llys Don*, or 'Don's Court'; our Northern Crown was *Caer Aranrhod*, the 'Castle of Aranrhod', Don's daughter; while the Milky Way was the 'Castle of Gwydion', Don's son. More than this, the greatest of her children, the Nudd or Lludd whom some make the head of a dynasty of his own, was the Zeus alike of the Britons and of the Gaels. His epithet of *Llaw Ereint*, that is, 'of the Hand of Silver', proves him the same personage as Nuada the 'Silver-handed'. The legend that must have existed to explain this peculiarity has been lost in British ground, but it was doubtless the same as that told of the Irish god. With it, and, no doubt, much else, has disappeared any direct account of battles fought by him as sky god against Fomor-like enemies. But under the faint disguise of a king of Britain, an ancient Welsh tale records how he put an end to three supernatural 'plagues' that oppressed his country (*see* Chapter 26, 'The Decline and Fall of the Gods'). In addition to this, we find him under his name of Nudd described in a Welsh triad as one of 'the three generous heroes of the Isle of Britain', while another makes him the owner of twenty-one thousand milch cows – an expression that must to the primitive mind have implied inexhaustible wealth. Both help us to the concept of a god of heaven and battle, triumphant, and therefore rich and liberal.

More tangible evidence is, however, not lacking to prove the widespread nature of his worship. A temple dedicated to him in Roman times under the name of Nodens or Nudens has been discovered at Lydney on the banks of the Severn. The god is pictured on a plaque of bronze as a youthful deity, haloed like the sun and driving a four-horsed chariot. Flying spirits, typifying the winds, accompany him; while his power over the sea is symbolised by attendant Tritons. This was in the west of Britain, while in the east there is good reason to believe that he had a shrine overlooking the Thames. Tradition declares that St Paul's Cathedral occupies the site of an ancient pagan temple; while the spot on which it stands was called, we know from Geoffrey of Monmouth, 'Parth Lludd' by the Britons and 'Ludes Geat' by the Saxons (*see* Chapter 26 – 'The Decline and Fall of the Gods').

Great, however, as he probably was, Lludd or Nudd occupies less space in Welsh story, as we have it now, than his son. Gwyn ap Nudd has outlived in tradition almost all his supernatural kin. It is tempting to see in him the British equivalent of the Gaelic Fionn Mac Cumhaill. The name of both alike means 'white', both are sons of the heaven god, both are famed as hunters. Gwyn, however, is more than that, for his game is man. In the early Welsh poems he is a god of battle and of the dead, and as such fills the part of a psychopomp, the god who conducted the slain into Hades and there ruled over them. In later semi-Christianised story he is described as 'Gwyn ap Nudd, whom God has placed over the brood of devils in Annwn, lest they should destroy the present race'. Later again, as paganism still further degenerated, he came to be considered as king of the *Tylwyth Teg*, the Welsh fairies, and his name as such has hardly yet died out of his last haunt, the romantic vale of Neath. He is the wild huntsman of Wales and the West of England, and it is his pack that is sometimes heard hunting in waste places at night.

In his earliest guise, as a god of war and death, he is the subject of a poem in dialogue contained in the Black Book of Caermarthen. Obscure, like most of the ancient Welsh poems, it is yet a spirited production and may be quoted here as a favourable specimen of the poetry of the early Cymri. In it we shall see mirrored perhaps the clearest figure of the British pantheon, the 'mighty hunter', not of deer but of men's souls, riding his demon horse and cheering on his demon hound to the fearful chase. He knows when and where all the great warriors fell, for he gathered their souls upon the field of battle and now rules over them in Hades or upon some 'misty mountain top' (Gwyn was said specially to frequent the summits of hills). It describes a mythical prince, named Gwyddneu Garanhir, known to Welsh legend as the ruler of a lost country now covered by the waters of Cardigan Bay, asking protection of the god, who accords it and then relates the story of his exploits:

> Gwyddneu
> A bull of conflict was he, active in dispersing an arrayed army,
> The ruler of hosts, indisposed to anger,
> Blameless and pure his conduct in protecting life.

Gwyn

Against a hero stout was his advance,
The ruler of hosts, disposer of wrath,
There will be protection for thee since thou askest it.

Gwyddneu

For thou hast given me protection
How warmly wert thou welcomed!
The hero of hosts, from what region thou comest?

Gwyn

I come from battle and conflict
With a shield in my hand;
Broken is the helmet by the pushing of spears.

Gwyddneu

I will address thee, exalted man,
With his shield in distress.
Brave man, what is thy descent?

Gwyn

Round-hoofed is my horse, the torment of battle,
Fairy am I called, Gwyn the son of Nudd,
The lover of Creurdilad, the daughter of Lludd.

Gwyddneu

Since it is thou, Gwyn, an upright man,
From thee there is no concealing:
I am Gwyddneu Garanhir.

Gwyn

Hasten to my ridge, the Tawë abode;
Not the nearest Tawë name I to thee,
But that Tawë which is the farthest.

Polished is my ring, golden my saddle and bright:
To my sadness
I saw a conflict before Caer Vandwy.[1]

[1] A name for Hades, of unknown meaning.

Before Caer Vandwy a host I saw,
Shields were shattered and ribs broken;
Renowned and splendid was he who made the assault.

Gwyddneu
Gwyn, son of Nudd, the hope of armies,
Quicker would legions fall before the hoofs
Of thy horse than broken rushes to the ground.

Gwyn
Handsome my dog, and round-bodied,
And truly the best of dogs;
Dormarth[1] was he, which belonged to Maelgwyn.

Gwyddneu
Dormarth with the ruddy nose! what a gazer
Thou art upon me because I notice
Thy wanderings on Gwibir Vynyd.[2]

Gwyn
I have been in the place where was killed Gwendoleu,
The son of Ceidaw, the pillar of songs,
When the ravens screamed over blood

I have been in the place where Bran was killed,
The son of Iweriadd, of far extending fame,
When the ravens of the battlefield screamed.

I have been where Llacheu was slain,
The son of Arthur, extolled in songs,
When the ravens screamed over blood.

---

[1] Dormarth means 'Death's Door'.
[2] An alternative is:
    'Dormarth, red-nosed, ground-grazing –
    On him we perceived the speed
    Of thy wandering on Cloud Mount.'

I have been where Meurig was killed,
The son of Carreian, of honourable fame,
When the ravens screamed over flesh.

I have been where Gwallawg was killed,
The son of Goholeth, the accomplished,
The resister of Lloegyr, the son of Lleynawg.

I have been where the soldiers of Britain were slain,
From the east to the north:
I am the escort of the grave.[1]

I have been where the soldiers of Britain were slain,
From the east to the south:
I am alive, they in death!

A line in this poem allows us to see Gwyn in another and less sinister role. 'The lover of Creurdilad, the daughter of Lludd,' he calls himself, and an episode in the mythical romance of 'Culhwch and Olwen', preserved in the Red Book of Hergest, gives the details of his courtship. Gwyn had as rival a deity called Gwythyr ap Gwreidawl, that is 'Victor, son of Scorcher'. These two waged perpetual war for Creurdilad, or Creiddylad, each in turn stealing her from the other until the matter was referred to Arthur, who decided that Creiddylad should be sent back to her father and that Gwyn and Gwythyr 'should fight for her every first of May, from henceforth until the day of doom, and that whichever of them should then be conqueror should have the maiden'. What satisfaction this would be to the survivor of what might be somewhat flippantly described as, in two senses, the longest engagement on record, is not very clear, but its mythological interpretation appears fairly obvious. In Gwyn, god of death and the underworld, and in the solar deity, Gwythyr, we may see the powers of darkness and sunshine, of winter and summer, in contest, each alternately winning and losing a bride who would seem to represent the spring with its grain and flowers. Creiddylad, whom the story of 'Culhwch and Olwen' calls 'the most splendid maiden in the three islands of the mighty and in the three islands adjacent', is, in fact, the British

---

[1] Or: 'I am alive, they in their graves!'

Persephone. As the daughter of Lludd, she is child of the shining sky. But a different tradition must have made her a daughter of Llyr, the sea god, for her name as such passed through Geoffrey of Monmouth to Shakespeare, in whose hands she became that pathetic figure Cordelia in *King Lear*. It may not be altogether unworthy of notice, although perhaps it is only a coincidence, that in some myths the Greek Persephone is made a daughter of Zeus and in others of Poseidon.

Gwyn ap Nudd had a brother, Edeyrn, of whom so little has come down to us that he finds his most suitable place in a footnote. Unmentioned in the earliest Welsh legends, he first appears as a knight of Arthur's court in the Red Book stories of 'Culhwch and Olwen', the 'Dream of Rhonabwy' and 'Geraint, the Son of Erbin'. He accompanied Arthur on his expedition to Rome and is said also to have slain 'three most atrocious giants' at Brentenol (Brent Knoll) near Glastonbury. His name occurs in a catalogue of Welsh saints, where he is described as a bard, and the chapel of Bodedern near Holyhead still stands to his honour. He is best known from Tennyson's Idyll of 'Geraint and Enid', which follows very closely the Welsh romance of 'Geraint, the Son of Erbin'.

Turning from the sky god and his son, we find others of Don's children to have been the exponents of those arts of life that early races held to have been taught directly by the gods to men. Don herself had a brother, Math fab Mathonwy, son of a mysterious Mathonwy and recognisable as a benevolent ruler of the underworld akin to Beli, or perhaps that god himself under another title, for the name Math, which means 'coin, money, treasure', recalls that of Plouton, the Greek god of Hades, in his guise of possessor and giver of metals. It was a belief common to the Aryan races that wisdom as well as wealth came originally from the underworld, and we find Math represented, in the Mabinogi bearing his name, as handing on his magic lore to his nephew and pupil Gwydion, who, there is good reason to believe, was the same divine personage whom the Germanic tribes worshipped as Woden and Odin. Thus equipped, Gwydion fab Don became the druid of the gods, the 'master of illusion and phantasy', and, not only that, but the teacher of all that is useful and good, the friend and helper of mankind, and the perpetual fighter against niggardly underworld powers for the good gifts that they refused to allow out of their keeping. Shoulder to shoulder with him in this 'holy war' of culture against ignorance and light against darkness, stood his brothers Amaethon, god of agriculture, and Gofannon, a god of smithcraft identical with the Gaelic

223

Goibhniu. He also had a sister called Aranrhod, or 'Silver Circle', who, as is common in mythologies, was not only his sister but also his wife. So Zeus wedded Hera, and indeed it is difficult to say where otherwise the partners of gods are to come from. Of this connection two sons were born at one birth – Dylan and Lleu, who are considered as representing the twin powers of darkness and light. The sea was inseparably connected with darkness by the Celts, and as soon as the dark twin was born and named he plunged headlong into his native element. 'And immediately when he was in the sea,' says the Mabinogi of Math fab Mathonwy, 'he took its nature and swam as well as the best fish that was therein. And for that reason was he called Dylan, the Son of the Wave. Beneath him no wave ever broke.' He was killed with a spear at last by his uncle, Gofannon, and, according to the bard Taliesin, the waves of Britain, Ireland, Scotland and the Isle of Man wept for him. Beautiful legends grew up around his death. The clamour of the waves dashing upon the beach is the expression of their longing to avenge their son. The sound of the sea rushing up the mouth of the River Conway is still known as 'Dylan's death groan'. A small promontory on the Caernarfon side of the Menai Straits, called *Pwynt Maen Tylen* or *Pwynt Maen Dulan* preserves his name.

The other child of Gwydion and Aranrhod grew up to become the British sun god Lleu Llaw Gyffes, the exact counterpart of the Gaelic Lugh Lamhfada, 'Light the Long-handed'. Like all solar deities, his growth was rapid. When he was a year old he seemed to be two years, at the age of two he travelled by himself, and when he was four years old he was as tall as a boy of eight and was his father's constant companion.

One day, Gwydion took him to the castle of Aranrhod – not her castle in the sky but her abode on earth, the still-remembered site of which is marked by a patch of rocks in the Menai Straits, accessible without a boat only during the lowest spring and autumn tides. Aranrhod had disowned her son and did not recognise him when she saw him with Gwydion. She asked who he was and was much displeased when told. She demanded to know his name and when Gwydion replied that he had as yet received none, she 'laid a destiny upon' him, after the fashion of the Celts, that he should be without a name until she chose to bestow one on him herself.

To be without a name was a very serious thing to the Celts, who seem to have held the primitive theory that the name and the soul are the same. So Gwydion cast about to think by what craft he might extort from Aranrhod some remark from which he could name their son. The next day he went down to the seashore with the boy, both of them disguised as cobblers. He made a boat out of seaweed by magic and some beautifully coloured leather out of some dry sticks and sedges. Then they sailed the boat to the port of Aranrhod's castle and, anchoring it where it could be seen, began ostentatiously to stitch away at the leather. Naturally, they were soon noticed, and Aranrhod sent someone out to see who they were and what they were doing. When she found that they were shoemakers, she remembered that she wanted some shoes. Gwydion, although he had her measure, purposely made them first too large and then too small. This brought Aranrhod herself down to the boat to be fitted.

While Gwydion was measuring Aranrhod's foot for the shoes, a wren came and stood on the deck. The boy took his bow and arrow and hit the wren in the leg – a favourite shot of Celtic 'crack' archers, at any rate in romance. The goddess was pleased to be amiable and complimentary. 'Truly,' said she, 'the lion aimed at it with a steady hand.' It is from such incidents that primitive people take their names all the world over. The boy had got his.

'It is no thanks to you,' said Gwydion to Aranrhod, 'but now he has a name. And a good name it is. He shall be called Llew Llaw Gyffes', that is 'the Lion with the Steady Hand'. This name of the sun god is a good example of how obsolete the ancient pagan tradition had become before it was put into writing. The old word *Lleu*, meaning 'light', had passed out of use, and the scribe substituted for a name that was unintelligible to him one like it which he knew, namely *Llew*, meaning 'lion'. The word *Gyffes* seems also to have suffered change and to have meant originally not 'steady', but 'long'.

At any rate, Aranrhod was defeated in her design to keep her son nameless. Neither did she even get her shoes, for as soon as he had gained his object Gwydion allowed the boat to change back into seaweed and the leather to return to sedge and sticks. So, in her anger, she put a fresh destiny on the boy, that he should not take arms till she herself gave them to him.

Gwydion, however, took Lleu to Dinas Dinllev, his castle, which still stands at the edge of the Menai Straits, and brought him up as a warrior. As soon as he thought him old enough to have arms, he took him with him again to Caer Aranrhod. This time they were disguised as bards. Aranrhod received them gladly, heard Gwydion's songs and tales, feasted them and prepared a room for them to sleep in.

The next morning Gwydion got up very early and prepared his most powerful incantations. By his druidic arts he made it seem as if the whole country rang with the shouts and trumpets of an army, and he put a spell over everyone so that they saw the bay filled with ships. Aranrhod came to him in terror, asking what could be done to protect the castle. 'Give us arms,' he replied, 'and we will do the best we can.' So Aranrhod's maidens armed Gwydion, while Aranrhod herself put arms on Lleu. By the time she had finished, all the noises had ceased and the ships had vanished. 'Let us take our arms off again,' said Gwydion. 'We shall not need them now.'

'But the army is all round the castle!' cried Aranrhod.

'There was no army,' answered Gwydion. 'It was only an illusion of mine to cause you to break your prophecy and give our son arms. And now he has got them, without thanks to you.'

'Then I will lay a worse destiny on him,' cried the infuriated goddess. 'He shall never have a wife of the people of this earth.'

'He shall have a wife in spite of you,' said Gwydion.

So Gwydion went to Math, his uncle and tutor in magic, and between them they made a woman out of flowers by charms and illusion. 'They took the blossoms of the oak and the blossoms of the broom and the blossoms of the meadowsweet, and produced from them a maiden, the fairest and most graceful that man ever saw.' They called her Blodeuwedd (Flower-face) and gave her to Lleu as his wife. And they gave Lleu a palace called Mur y Castell near Bala Lake.

All went well until one day, Gronwy Pebyr, one of the gods of darkness, came by, hunting, and killed the stag at nightfall near Lleu's castle. The sun god was away upon a visit to Math, but Blodeuwedd asked the stranger to take shelter with her. That night they fell in love with one another and conspired together how Lleu might be put away. When Lleu came back from Math's court, Blodeuwedd, like a Celtic Delilah, wormed out of him the secret of how his life was preserved. He told her that he could die in only one way – he could not be killed either inside or outside a house, either on horseback or on foot, but that if a spear that had been a year in the making and which was never worked upon except during the sacrifice on Sunday were to be cast at him as he stood beneath a roof of thatch, after having just bathed, with one foot upon the edge of the bath and the other upon a buck goat's back, it would cause his death. Blodeuwedd piously thanked Heaven that he was so well protected and sent a messenger to her lover, telling him what she had learned. Gronwy set to work on the spear and in a year it was ready. When she knew this, Blodeuwedd asked Lleu to show her exactly how it was he could be killed.

Lleu agreed, and Blodeuwedd prepared the bath under the thatched roof and tethered the goat by it. Lleu bathed and then stood with one foot upon the edge of the bath and the other upon the goat's back. At this moment, Gronwy, from an ambush, flung the spear and hit Lleu, who, with a terrible cry, changed into an eagle and flew away. He never came back, and Gronwy Pebyr took possession of both his wife and his palace.

But Gwydion set out to search everywhere for his son. At last, one day, he came to a house in North Wales where the man was in great anxiety about his sow, for as soon as the sty was opened every morning, she rushed out and did not return again until late in the evening. Gwydion offered to follow her, and at dawn the man took him to the sty and opened the door. The sow leaped forth and ran, and Gwydion ran after her. He tracked her to a brook between Snowdon and the sea, still called Nant y Llew, and saw her feeding underneath an oak. On the top of the tree there was an eagle, and, every time it shook itself, there fell off it lumps of putrid meat that the sow ate greedily. Gwydion suspected that the eagle must be Lleu. So he sang this verse:

> 'Oak that grows between the two banks;
> Darkened is the sky and hill!
> Shall I not tell him by his wounds,
> That this is Lleu?'

The eagle, on hearing this, came halfway down the tree. So Gwydion sang:

> 'Oak that grows in upland ground,
> Is it not wetted by the rain? Has it not been drenched
> By nine score tempests?
> It bears in its branches Lleu Llaw Gyffes.'

The eagle came slowly down until it was on the lowest branch. Gwydion sang:

> 'Oak that grows beneath the steep;
> Stately and majestic is its aspect!
> Shall I not speak it?
> That Lleu will come to my lap?'

Blodeuwedd's invitation to Gronwy Pebyr, from a painting by E. Wallcousins

Then the eagle came down and sat on Gwydion's knee. Gwydion struck it with his magic wand, and it became Lleu again, wasted to skin and bone by the poison on the spear.

Gwydion took him to Math to be healed and left him there while he went to Mur y Castell, where Blodeuwedd was. When she heard that he was coming, she fled, but Gwydion overtook her and changed her into an owl, the bird that hates the day.

A still older form of this probably extremely ancient myth of the sun god – the savage and repulsive details of which speak of a hoary antiquity – makes the chase of Blodeuwedd by Gwydion to have taken place in the sky, the stars scattered over the Milky Way being the traces of it. As for her accomplice, the Mabinogi of Math fab Mathonwy tells us that Lleu would accept no satisfaction short of Gronwy's submitting to stand exactly where Lleu had stood, to be shot at in his turn. To this he was obliged to agree, and Lleu killed him.

There are two other sons of Beli and Don of whom so little is recorded that it would hardly be worthwhile mentioning them were it not for the wild poetry of the legend connected with them in the Iolo Manuscripts, 'The Tale of Rhitta Gawr'. The tale, put into writing at a time when all the gods were being transfigured into simple mortals, tells us that they were two kings of Britain, brothers. One starlight night they were walking together.

'See,' said Nynniaw to Peibaw, 'what a fine, widespreading field I have.'

'Where is it?' asked Peibaw.

'There,' replied Nynniaw. 'The whole stretch of the sky, as far as the eye sees.'

'Look then,' returned Peibaw, 'what a number of cattle I have grazing on your field.'

'Where are they?' asked Nynniaw.

'All the stars that you can see,' replied Peibaw, 'every one of them of fiery-coloured gold, with the moon for a shepherd over them.'

'They shall not feed on my field,' cried Nynniaw.

'They shall,' exclaimed Peibaw.

'They shall not,' cried Nynniaw.

'They shall,' said Peibaw.

'They shall not,' Nynniaw answered, and so they went on, from contradiction to quarrel, and from private quarrel to civil war, until the armies of both of them were destroyed and the two authors of the evil were turned by God into oxen for their sins.

Last of the children of Don, we find a goddess called Penardun, of whom little is known except that she was married to the sea god Llyr. This incident is curious as forming a parallel to the Gaelic story that tells of intermarriage between the Tuatha Dé Danaan and the Fomorii (*see* Chapter 7, 'The Rise of the Sun God'). Brigit, the Daghda's daughter, was married to Bres, son of Elathan, while Cian, the son of Dian Cécht, was the father of Lugh by Ethlinn, the daughter of Balor. So, in this kindred mythology, a slender tie of relationship binds the gods of the sky to the gods of the sea.

The name Llyr is supposed, like its Irish equivalent Lir, to have meant 'the Sea'. The British sea god is undoubtedly the same as the Gaelic. Indeed, the two facts that he is described in Welsh literature as Llyr Llediath, that is, 'Llyr of the Foreign Dialect' and is given a wife called Iweriadd (Ireland) suggest that he may have been borrowed by the Britons from the Gaels later than any mythology common to both. As a British god, he was the far-off original of Shakespeare's King Lear. The chief city of his worship is still called after him, Leicester, that is, Llyr-cestre, in still earlier days, Caer Llyr.

Llyr, we have noticed, married two wives, Penardun and Iweriadd. By the daughter of Don he had a son called Manawydan fab Lyr, who is identical with the Gaelic Manannán Mac Lir.[1] We know less of his character and attributes than we do of the Irish god, but we find him equally a ruler in that Hades or Elysium which the Celtic mind always connected with the sea. Like all the inhabitants of that Otherworld, he is at once a master of magic and of the useful arts, which he taught willingly to his friends. To his enemies, however, he could show a different side of his character. A triad in the Iolo manuscript, composed by the Azure Bard of the Chair, tells us that:

> 'The achievement of Manawydan the Wise,
> After lamentation and fiery wrath,
> Was the constructing of the bone fortress of Oeth and Anoeth',

which is described as a prison made, in the shape of a beehive, entirely of human bones mortared together and divided into innumerable cells, forming a kind of labyrinth. In this ghastly place he immured those whom he found trespassing in Hades, and among his captives was no less a person than the famous Arthur (*see* Chapter 24, 'The Treasures of Britain').

[1] The old Irish tract called *Coir Anmann* ('Choice of Names') says – 'Manannán Mac Lir . . . the Britons and the men of Erin deemed that he was the god of the sea'.

'Ireland' bore two children to Llyr: a daughter called Branwen and a son called Bran. The little we know of Branwen of the 'Fair Bosom' shows her as a goddess of love – child, like the Greek Aphrodite, of the sea. Bran, on the other hand, is, even more clearly than Manawydan, a dark deity of Hades. He is represented as of colossal size, so huge, in fact, the Mabinogi of Branwen, Daughter of Llyr tells us, that no house or ship was big enough to hold him. He delighted in battle and carnage, like the hoodie crow or raven from which he probably took his name, but he was also the special patron of bards, minstrels and musicians, and we find him in one of the poems ascribed to Taliesin claiming to be himself a bard, a harper, a player on the crowth, and seven score other musicians all at once. His son was called Caradawc the Strong-armed, who, as the British mythology crumbled, became confounded with the historical Caratacus, known popularly as 'Caractacus'.

Both Bran and Manawydan were especially connected with the Swansea peninsula. The bone fortress of Oeth and Anoeth was placed by tradition in Gower. That Bran was equally at home there may be proved from the *Morte D'Arthur*, in which storehouse of forgotten and misunderstood mythology Bran of Gower survives as 'King Brandegore'.

Such identification of a mere mortal country with the Otherworld seems strange enough to us but to our Celtic ancestors it was a quite natural thought. All islands – and peninsulas, which, viewed from an opposite coast, probably seemed to them islands – were deemed to be pre-eminently homes of the dark Powers of Hades. Difficult of access, protected by the turbulent and dangerous sea, sometimes rendered quite invisible by fogs and mists and, at other times, looming up ghostlily on the horizon, often held by the remnant of a hostile lower race, they gained a mystery and a sanctity from the law of the human mind that has always held the unknown to be the terrible. The Cornish Britons, gazing from the shore, saw Gower and Lundy, and deemed them outposts of the oversea Otherworld. To the Britons of Wales, Ireland was. no human realm, a view reciprocated by the Gaels, who saw Hades in Britain, while the Isle of Man was a little Hades common to them both. Nor even was the sea always necessary to sunder the world of ghosts from that of 'shadow-casting men'. Glastonbury Tor, surrounded by almost impassable swamps, was one of the special haunts of Gwyn ap Nudd. The Britons of the north held that beyond the Roman wall and the vast Caledonian wood lived ghosts and not men. Even the Roman province of Demetia – called by the

Welsh Dyfed and corresponding roughly to the modern county of Pembroke-shire – was, as a last stronghold of the aborigines, identified with the mythic underworld.

As such, ancient Dyfed was ruled by a local tribe of gods whose greatest figures were Pwyll, 'Head of Annwn' (the Welsh name for Hades), with his wife, Rhiannon, and their son, Pryderi. These beings are described as hostile to the children of Don but friendly to the race of Llyr. According to the Mabinogi of Manawydan fab Llyr, after Pwyll's death or disappearance, his widow, Rhiannon, becomes the wife of Manawydan. In a poem of Taliesin's we find Manawydan and Pryderi joint rulers of Hades and warders of that magic cauldron of inspiration which the gods of light attempted to steal or capture and which became famous afterwards as the 'Holy Grail'. Another of their treasures were the 'Three Birds of Rhiannon', which, we are told in an ancient book, could sing the dead to life and the living into the sleep of death. Fortunately they sang seldom. 'There are three things,' says a Welsh triad, 'which are not often heard: the song of the birds of Rhiannon, a song of wisdom from the mouth of a Saxon, and an invitation to a feast from a miser.'

Nor is the list of British gods complete without mention of Arthur, al-though most readers will be surprised to find him in such company. The genius of Tennyson, who drew his materials mostly from the Norman-French romances, has stereotyped the popular conception of Arthur as a king of early Britain who fought for his fatherland and the Christian faith against invading Saxons. Possibly there may, indeed, have been a powerful British chieftain bearing that typically Celtic name, which is found in Irish legend as Artur, one of the sons of Nemedh, who fought against the Fomorii, and on the Continent as Artaius, a Gaulish deity whom the Romans identified with Mercury and who seems to have been a patron of agriculture. But the original Arthur stands upon the same ground as Cúchulainn and Fionn. His deeds are mythic, because superhuman. His companions can be shown to have been divine. Some we know were worshipped in Gaul. Others are children of Don, of Llyr and of Pwyll, dynasties of older gods to whose head Arthur seems to have risen as his cult waxed and theirs waned. Stripped of their godhead, and strangely trans-formed, they fill the pages of romance as Knights of the Table Round.

These deities were the native gods of Britain. Many others are, however, mentioned on inscriptions found in our island, but these were almost all ex-otic and imported. Imperial Rome brought people of diverse races among her legions, and these people brought their gods. Scattered over Britain, but especially in the north, near Hadrian's Wall, we find evidence that deities of many nations – from Germany to Africa, and from Gaul to Persia – were sporadically worshipped. Most of these foreign gods were Roman, but a temple at Eboracum (now York) was dedicated to Serapis, and Mithras, the Persian sun god, was also adored there, while at Corbridge in Northumberland (the ancient Corspitium) there have been found altars to the Tyrian Hercules and to Astarte. The war god was also invoked under many strange names – as Cocidius by a colony of Dacians in Cumberland, as Toutates, Camulus, Coriticus, Belatucador, Alator, Loucetius, Condates and Rigisamos by men of different countries. A goddess of war was worshipped at Bath under the name of Nemetona. The sulphur springs of that town were under the patronage of a divinity called Sulis, identified by the Romans with Minerva, and she was helped by a god of medicine described on a dedicatory tablet as 'Sol Apollo Anicetus'. Few of these 'strange gods', however, seem to have taken hold of the imagination of the native Britons. Their worshippers did not proselytise, and their general influence was probably about equal to that of an evangelical Christian church in a Turkish town. The sole exceptions to this rule are where the foreign gods are Gaulish, but in several instances it can be proved that they were not so much of Roman as of original Celtic importation. The warlike heaven god Camulus appears in Gaelic heroic myth as Cumhaill, the father of Fionn, and in British mythical history as Coel, a duke of Caer Coelvin (known earlier as Camulodunum and now as Colchester), who seized the crown of Britain and spent his short reign in a series of battles. It is said that the 'Old King Cole' of the old ballad, who 'was a merry old soul', represents the last faint tradition of the Celtic god.

The name of the sun god Maponos is found on altars in both Gaul and Britain and in Welsh literature as Mabon, a follower of Arthur, while another Gaulish sun god, Belenus, who had a splendid temple at Bajocassos (the modern Bayeux), although not mentioned in the earliest British mythology, as its scattered records have come down to us, must have been connected with Bran, for we find in Geoffrey of Monmouth's history 'King Belenus' as brother of 'King Brennius', and in the *Morte D'Arthur* 'Balin' as brother of 'Balan'. A second-century Greek writer gives an account of a god of eloquence worshipped in Gaul under the name of Ogmios and represented as equipped like Heracles, a description that exactly corresponds to the concept of the Gaelic

Oghma, at once patron of literature and writing and professional strong man of the Tuatha Dé Danaan. Nemetona, the war goddess worshipped at Bath, was probably the same as Nemain, one of Nuada's Valkyr wives, while a broken inscription to *athubodva*, which probably stood, when intact, for *Cathubodva*, may well have been addressed to the Gaulish equivalent of Badb Catha, the 'War-fury'. Lugh or Lleu was also widely known on the Continent as Lugus. Three important towns – Laon, Leyden and Lyons – were all anciently called after him *Lugudunum* (Lugus' town), and at the last and greatest of these a festival was still held in Roman times upon the sun god's day – the first of August – which corresponded to the Lughnasadh (Lugh's commemoration) held in ancient Ireland. Brigit, the Gaelic Minerva, is also found in Britain as Brigantia, tutelary goddess of the Brigantes, a northern tribe, and in eastern France as Brigindo, to whom Iccavos, son of Oppianos, made a dedicatory offering of which there is still record.

Other less striking agreements between the mythical divine names of the insular and continental Celts might be cited. These recorded should, however, prove sufficiently that Gaul, Gael and Briton shared in a common heritage of mythological names and ideas, which they separately developed into three superficially different but essentially similar cults.

Chapter 19

THE ADVENTURES OF THE GODS OF ANNWN

It is with the family of Pwyll, deities connected with the southwest corner of Wales, called by the Romans Demetia and by the Britons Dyfed, that the earliest consecutive accounts of the British gods begin. The first of the Four Branches of the Mabinogi tells us how 'Pwyll, Prince of Dyfed', gained the right to be called *Pen Annwn*, the 'Head of Hades'. Indeed, it almost seems as if it had been deliberately written to explain how the same person could be at once a mere mortal prince, however legendary, and a ruler in the mystic Otherworld, so reconciling two conflicting traditions. But to an earlier age than that in which the legend was put into a literary shape, such forced reconciliation would not have been needed, for the two legends would not have been considered to conflict. When Pwyll, head of Annwn, was a mythic person whose tradition was still alive, the unexplored, rugged and savage country of Dyfed, populated by the aboriginal Iberians whom the Celts had driven into such remote districts, appeared to those who dwelt on the eastern side of its dividing river, the Tywi, at least a dependency of Annwn if not that weird realm itself. As men grew bolder, however, the frontier was crossed, and Dyfed, entered and traversed, was found to be not so unlike other countries. Its inhabitants, if not of Celtic race, were still of flesh and blood. So that, although the province still continued to bear to a late date the names of the 'Land of Illusion' and the 'Realm of Glamour', particularly by the fourteenth-century Welsh poet Darydd ab Gwilym, it was no longer deemed to be Hades itself. That fitful and shadowy country had folded its tents and departed over or under seas.

The story of 'Pwyll, Prince of Dyfed', as translated from the Mabinogi of Pwyll, Prince of Dyfed, tells us how there was war in Annwn between its two

235

kings – or between two, perhaps, of its many chieftains. Arawn ('Silver-tongue') and Hafgan ('Summer-white') each coveted the dominions of the other. In the continual contests between them, Arawn was worsted, and in despair he visited the upper earth to seek for a mortal ally.

At this time Pwyll, Prince of Dyfed, held his court at Arbeth. He had, however, left his capital on a hunting expedition to Glyn Cûch, known today as a valley on the borders of the two counties of Pembrokeshire and Carmarthenshire. Like so many kings of European and Oriental romance when an adventure is at hand, he became separated from his party and was lost. He could, however, still hear the cry of his hounds and was listening to them when he also distinguished the cry of another pack coming towards him. As he watched and listened, a stag came into view and the strange hounds pulled it down almost at his feet. At first Pwyll hardly looked at the stag, he was so taken up with gazing at the hounds, for 'of all the hounds that he had seen in the world, he had never seen any that were like unto these. For their hair was of a brilliant shining white, and their ears were red; and as the whiteness of their bodies shone, so did the redness of their ears glisten.' They were, indeed, although Pwyll does not seem to have known it, of the true Hades breed – the snow-white, red-eared hounds that we meet in Gaelic legends and that are still said to be sometimes heard and seen scouring the hills of Wales by night. Seeing no rider with the hounds, Pwyll drove them away from the dead stag and called up his own pack to it.

While he was doing this, a man 'upon a large, light-grey steed, with a hunting horn round his neck and clad in garments of grey woollen in the fashion of a hunting garb' appeared and berated Pwyll for his unsportsmanlike conduct. 'Greater discourtesy,' said he, 'I never saw than your driving away my dogs after they had killed the stag and calling your own to it. And though I may not be revenged upon you for this, I swear that I will do you more damage than the value of a hundred stags.'

Pwyll expressed his contrition and, asking the newcomer's name and rank, offered to atone for his fault. The stranger told his name – Arawn, a king of Annwn – and said that Pwyll could gain his forgiveness only in one way, by going to Annwn instead of him and fighting for him with Hafgan. Pwyll agreed to do this, and Arawn put his own appearance on the mortal prince so that not a person in Annwn – not even Arawn's own wife – would know that he was not that king. He led him by a secret path into Annwn and left him before his castle, charging him to return to the place where they had first met at the end of a year from that day. On the other hand, Arawn took on Pwyll's shape and went to Arbeth.

No one in Annwn suspected Pwyll of being anyone else than their king. He spent the year in ruling the realm, in hunting, minstrelsy and feasting. Both by day and night, he had the company of Arawn's wife, the most beautiful woman he had ever yet seen, but he refrained from taking advantage of the trust placed in him. At last the day came when he was to meet Hafgan in single combat. One blow settled it, for Pwyll, Hafgan's destined conqueror, thrust his antagonist an arm's and a spear's length over the crupper of his horse, breaking his shield and armour and mortally wounding him. Hafgan was carried away to die, and Pwyll, in the guise of Arawn, received the submission of the dead king's subjects and annexed his realm. Then he went back to Glyn Cûch to keep his tryst with Arawn.

They retook their own shapes, and each returned to his own kingdom. Pwyll learned that Dyfed had never been ruled so well or been so prosperous as during the year just passed. As for Arawn, he found his enemy gone and his domains extended. And when he caressed his wife, she asked him why he did so now, after the lapse of a whole year. So he told her the truth, and they both agreed that they had indeed got a true friend in Pwyll.

After this, the kings of Annwn and Dyfed cemented the friendship between them. From that time forward, says the story, Pwyll was no longer called Prince of Dyfed but *Pen Annwn*, 'the Head of Annwn'.

The second mythological incident in the Mabinogi of Pwyll, Prince of Dyfed, tells how Pwyll won his wife, Rhiannon, thought to have been a goddess either of the dawn or of the moon. There was a mound outside Pwyll's palace at Arbeth that had a magical quality. To anyone who sat on it there happened one of two things: either he received wounds and blows or else he saw a wonder. One day, it occurred to Pwyll that he would like to try the experience of the mound. So he went and sat on it.

No unseen blows assailed Pwyll, but he had not been sitting long upon the mound before he saw, coming towards him, 'a lady on a pure-white horse of large size, with a garment of shining gold around her', riding very quietly. He sent a man on foot to ask her who she was, but, although she seemed to be moving so slowly, the man could not catch up with her. He failed utterly to overtake her, and she passed on out of sight.

The next day Pwyll went again to the mound. The woman appeared, and this time Pwyll sent a horseman. At first the horseman only ambled along at about the same pace at which the woman seemed to be going, then, failing to get near her, he urged his horse into a gallop. But whether he rode slow or fast, he could come no closer to the woman than before, although she seemed to the eyes of those who watched to have been going only at a foot's pace.

The day after that Pwyll determined to accost the woman himself. She came at the same gentle walk, and Pwyll at first rode easily, and then at his horse's topmost speed, but with the same result, or lack of it. At last, in despair, he called to the mysterious woman to stop.

'I will stop gladly,' said she, 'and it would have been better for your horse if you had asked me before.' She told him that her name was Rhiannon, daughter of Hefeydd Hen. The nobles of her realm had determined to give her in marriage against her will, so she had come to seek out Pwyll, who was the man of her choice. Pwyll was delighted to hear this, for he thought that she was the most beautiful woman he had ever seen. Before they parted, they had plighted troth and Pwyll had promised to appear on that day twelvemonth at the palace of her father. Then she vanished, and Pwyll returned to Arbeth.

At the appointed time Pwyll went to visit Hefeydd Hen with a hundred followers. He was received with much welcome and the disposition of the feast put under his command, as the Celts seem to have done to especially honoured guests. As they sat at table, with Pwyll between Rhiannon and her father, a tall auburn-haired youth came into the hall, greeted Pwyll and asked a boon of him.

'Whatever boon you may ask of me,' said Pwyll thoughtlessly, 'if it is in my power, you shall have it.'

Then the suitor threw off all disguise, called the guests to witness Pwyll's promise and claimed Rhiannon as his bride. Pwyll was dumb.

'Be silent as long as you will,' said the masterful Rhiannon. 'Never did a man make worse use of his wits than you have done.'

'Lady,' replied the amazed Pwyll, 'I knew not who he was.'

'He is the man to whom they would have given me against my will,' she answered, 'Gwawl, the son of Clud.[1] You must bestow me upon him now, lest shame befall you.'

---

[1] Clud was probably the goddess of the River Clyde.

'Never will I do that,' said Pwyll.

'Bestow me upon him,' she insisted, 'and I will cause that I shall never be his.'

So Pwyll promised Gwawl that he would make a feast that day year at which he would resign Rhiannon to him.

The next year the feast was made, and Rhiannon sat by the side of her unwelcome bridegroom. But Pwyll was waiting outside the palace with a hundred men in ambush. When the banquet was at its height, he came into the hall, dressed in coarse, ragged garments, shod with clumsy old shoes and carrying a leather bag. But the bag was a magic one, which Rhiannon had given to her lover with directions as to its use. Its quality was that, however much was put into it, it could never be filled.

'I crave a boon,' Pwyll said to Gwawl.

'What is it?' Gwawl replied.

'I am a poor man, and all I ask is to have this bag filled with meat.'

Gwawl granted what he said was 'a request within reason' and ordered his followers to fill the bag, but the more they put into it, the more room in it there seemed to be. Gwawl was astonished and asked why this was. Pwyll replied that it was a bag that could never be filled until someone possessed of lands and riches should tread the food down with both his feet.

'Do this for the man,' said Rhiannon to Gwawl.

'Gladly I will,' replied he, and he put both his feet into the bag, but no sooner had he done so than Pwyll slipped the bag over Gwawl's head and tied it up at the mouth. He blew his horn, and all his followers came in.

'What have you got in the bag?' asked each one in turn.

'A badger,' replied Pwyll.

Then each, as he received Pwyll's answer, kicked the bag or hit it with a stick. 'Then,' says the story, 'was the game of "Badger in the Bag" first played.'

Gwawl, however, fared better than we suspect that the badger usually did, for Hefeydd Hen interceded for him. Pwyll willingly released him on condition that he promised to give up all claim to Rhiannon and renounced all projects of revenge. Gwawl consented and gave sureties, and went away to his own country to have his bruises healed.

This country of Gwawl's was, no doubt, the sky, for he was evidently a sun god. His name reveals him, for the meaning of 'Gwawl' is 'light'. It was one of the hours of victory for the dark powers, such as were celebrated in the Celtic calendar by the Feast of Samhain, or Summer End.

There was no hindrance now to the marriage of Pwyll and Rhiannon. She became his bride and returned with him to Dyfed.

For three years they were without an heir, and the nobles of Dyfed became discontented. They petitioned Pwyll to take another wife instead of Rhiannon. He asked for a year's delay. This was granted, and before the end of the year a son was born. On the night of his birth, however, the six women set to keep watch over Rhiannon all fell asleep at once, and when they woke up the boy had vanished. Fearful lest their lives should be forfeited for their neglect, they agreed to swear that Rhiannon had eaten her child. They killed a litter of puppies and smeared some of the blood on Rhiannon's face and hands and put some of the bones by her side. Then they awoke her with a great outcry and accused her. She swore that she knew nothing of the death of her son, but the women persisted that they had seen her devour him and had been unable to prevent it. The druids of that day were not sufficiently practical anatomists to be able to tell the bones of a child from those of a dog, so they condemned Rhiannon on the evidence of the women, but even now Pwyll would not put her away, so she was assigned a penance. For seven years she was to sit by a horse block outside the gate and offer to carry visitors into the palace upon her back. 'But it rarely happened,' says the Mabinogi, 'that any would permit her to do so.'

Exactly what had become of Rhiannon's child seems to have been a mystery even to the writer of the Mabinogi. It was, at any rate, in some way connected with the equally mysterious disappearance on every night of the first of May – Beltane, the Celtic sun festival – of the colts foaled by a beautiful mare belonging to Ternyon Twryv Vliant, one of Pwyll's vassals. Every May-Day night the mare foaled, but no one knew what became of the colt. Ternyon decided to find out. He caused the mare to be taken into a house, and there he watched it, fully armed. Early in the night the colt was born. Then there was a great noise, and an arm with claws came through the window and gripped the colt's mane. Ternyon hacked at the arm with his sword and cut it off. Then he heard wailing, and he opened the door and found a baby in swaddling clothes wrapped in a satin mantle. He took it up and brought it to his wife, and they decided to adopt it. They called the boy Gwri Wallt Euryn, that is 'Gwri of the Golden Hair'.

The older the boy grew, the more it seemed to Ternyon that he became like Pwyll. Then he remembered that he had found him on the very night that

Rhiannon lost her child. So he consulted with his wife, and they both agreed that the baby they had so mysteriously found must be the same that Rhiannon had so mysteriously lost. And they decided that it would not be right for them to keep the son of another while so good a woman as Rhiannon was being punished wrongfully.

So the very next day Ternyon set out for Arbeth, taking the boy with him. They found Rhiannon sitting as usual by the gate, but they would not allow her to carry them into the palace on her back. Pwyll welcomed them, and that evening, as they sat at supper, Ternyon told his hosts the story from beginning to end, and he presented her son to Rhiannon.

As soon as everyone in the palace saw the boy, they admitted that he must be Pwyll's son, so they adopted him with delight, and Pendaran Dyfed, the head druid of the kingdom, gave him a new name. He called him 'Pryderi', meaning 'trouble', from the first word that his mother had uttered when he was restored to her. For she had said: '*Trouble* is indeed at an end for me if this be true.'

Chapter 20

The Wooing of Branwen and the Beheading of Bran

In the Mabinogi of Branwen, the Daughter of Llyr, in the second of the 'Four Branches', Pryderi, having reached man's estate and married to a wife called Cigfa, appears as a guest or vassal at the court of a greater god of Hades than himself – Bran, the son of the sea god Llyr. The children of Llyr – Bran, with his sister Branwen of the 'Fair Bosom' and his half-brother Manawydan, as well as two sons of Manawydan's mother, Penardun, by an earlier marriage, were holding court at *Twr Branwen*, 'Branwen's Tower', now called Harlech. As they sat on a cliff looking over the sea, they saw thirteen ships coming from Ireland. The fleet sailed close under the land, and Bran sent messengers to ask who they were and why they had come. It was replied that they were the vessels of Matholwch, King of Ireland, and that he had come to ask Bran for his sister Branwen in marriage. Bran consented, and they fixed upon Aberffraw in Anglesey as the place at which to hold the wedding feast. Matholwch and his fleet went there by sea, and Bran and his host by land. When they arrived and met, they set up pavilions; for 'no house could ever hold the blessed Bran'. And there Branwen became the King of Ireland's bride.[1]

These relations were not long, however, allowed to be friendly. Of the two other sons of Llyr's wife, Penardun, the mother of Manawydan, one was called Nisien and the other Efnisien. Nisien was a lover of peace and would always 'cause his family to be friends when their wrath was at the highest', but Efnisien 'would cause strife between his two brothers when they were most at peace'. Now Efnisien was enraged because his consent had not been asked to

---

[1] Matholwch can perhaps be compared with Math and the story generally with the Greek myth of Persephone.

242

Branwen's marriage. Out of spite at this, he cut off the lips, ears, eyebrows and tails of all Matholwch's horses.

When the King of Ireland found this out, he was very indignant at the insult, but Bran sent an embassy to him twice, explaining that it had not been done by his consent or with his knowledge. He appeased Matholwch by giving him a sound horse in place of every one that Efnisien had mutilated, as well as a staff of silver as large and tall as Matholwch himself and a plate of gold as broad as Matholwch's face. To these gifts he added a magic cauldron brought from Ireland. Its property was that any slain man who was put into it was brought to life again except if he had he lost the use of speech. The King of Ireland accepted this recompense for the insult done to him, renewed his friendship with the children of Llyr and sailed away with Branwen to Ireland.

Before a year was over, Branwen bore a son. They called him Gwern and put him out to be foster-nursed among the best men of Ireland. But during the second year news came to Ireland of the insult that Matholwch had received in Britain. The King of Ireland's foster brothers and near relations insisted that he should revenge himself upon Branwen. So the queen was compelled to serve in the kitchen, and every day the butcher gave her a box upon the ear. That this should not become known to Bran, all traffic was forbidden between Ireland and Britain. This went on for three years.

In the meantime Branwen had reared a tame starling, and she taught it to speak and tied a letter of complaint to the root of its wing and sent it off to Britain. At last it found Bran, whom its mistress had described, and settled on his shoulder, ruffling its wings. This exposed the letter, and Bran read it. He sent messengers to one hundred and forty-four countries to raise an army to go to Ireland. Leaving his son Caradawc with six others in charge of Britain, he started out – himself wading through the sea while his men went by ship.

No one in Ireland knew that they were coming until the royal swineherds, tending their pigs near the seashore, beheld a marvel. They saw a forest on the surface of the sea – a place where certainly no forest had been before – and near it a mountain with a lofty ridge on its top and a lake on each side of the ridge. Both the forest and the mountain were swiftly moving towards Ireland. They informd Matholwch, who could not understand it and sent messengers to ask Branwen what she thought it might be. 'It is the men of the Island of the Mighty,'[1] said she, 'who are coming here because they have heard of my ill-

---

[1]   A bardic name for Britain.

treatment. The forest that is seen on the sea is made of the masts of ships. The mountain is my brother Bran, wading into shoal water, the lofty ridge is his nose and the two lakes, one on each side of it, are his eyes.'

The men of Ireland were terrified. They fled beyond the Shannon and broke down the bridge over it. But Bran lay down across the river, and his army walked over him to the opposite side.

Matholwch now sent messengers suing for peace. He offered to resign the throne of Ireland to Gwern, Branwen's son and Bran's nephew.

'Shall I not have the kingdom myself?' said Bran and would not hear of anything else.

So the counsellors of Matholwch advised him to conciliate Bran by building him a house so large that it would be the first house that had ever held him and in it to hand over the kingdom to his will. Bran consented to accept this, and the vast house was built.

It concealed treachery. Upon each side of the hundred pillars of the house was hung a bag, and in the bag was an armed man, who was to cut himself out at a given signal. But Efnisien came into the house and, seeing the bags there, suspected the plot.

'What is in this bag?' he said to one of the Irish as he came up to the first one.

'Meal,' replied the Irishman.

Then Efnisien kneaded the bag in his hands, as though it really contained meal, until he had killed the man inside; and he treated all of them in turn in the same way.

A little later the two armies met in the house. The men of Ireland came in on one side and the men of Britain on the other, and they met at the hearth in the middle and sat down. The Irish court did homage to Bran, and they crowned Gwern, Branwen's son, King of Ireland in place of Matholwch. When the ceremonies were over, the boy went to each of his uncles to make acquaintance with them. Bran fondled and caressed him and so did Manawydan and Nisien. But when he came to Efnisien, the wicked son of Penardun seized the child by the feet and dropped him head-first into the great fire.

When Branwen saw her son killed, she tried to leap into the flames after him, but Bran held her back. Then every man armed himself, and such a tumult was never heard in one house before. Day after day they fought, but the Irish had the advantage, for they had only to plunge their dead men into the magic cauldron to bring them back to life. When Efnisien knew this, he saw a way of atoning for the misfortunes his evil nature had brought upon Britain. He disguised himself as an Irishman and lay upon the floor as if dead until they put him into the cauldron. Then he stretched himself and, with one desperate effort, burst both the cauldron and his own heart.

Thus things were made equal again, and in the next battle the men of Britain killed all the Irish. But of themselves there were only seven left unhurt – Pryderi, Manawydan, Gluneu, the son of Taran,[1] Taliesin the Bard, Ynawag, Grudyen, the son of Muryel, and Heilyn, the son of Gwinn the Ancient.

Bran himself was wounded in the foot with a poisoned dart and was in agony, so he ordered his seven surviving followers to cut off his head and to take it to the White Mount in London,[2] and to bury it there with the face towards France. He prophesied how they would perform the journey. At Harlech they would be feasting seven years, the birds of Rhiannon singing to them all the time and Bran's own head conversing with them as agreeably as when it was on his body. Then they would be fourscore years at Gwales.[3] All this while Bran's head would remain uncorrupted and would talk so pleasantly that they would forget the flight of time. But at the destined hour someone would open a door that looked towards Cornwall, and after that they could stay no longer but must hurry to London to bury the head.

So the seven survivors beheaded Bran and set off, taking Branwen also with them. They landed at the mouth of the River Alaw in Anglesey. Branwen first looked back towards Ireland and then forward towards Britain. 'Alas,' she cried, 'that I was ever born! Two islands have been destroyed because of me.' Her heart broke with sorrow, and she died. An old Welsh poem, 'The Gododin of Anuerin', says with a touch of real pathos:

> 'Softened were the voices in the brakes
> Of the wondering birds
> On seeing the fair body.
> Will there not be relating again
> Of that which befell the paragon
> At the stream of Amlwch?'

[1] This personage may have been the same as the Gaulish god Taranis. Mention, too, is made in an ancient Irish glossary of 'Etirun, an idol of the Britons'.
[2] This spot, called by a twelfth-century Welsh poet 'The White Eminence of London, a place of splendid fame', was probably the hill on which the Tower of London now stands.
[3] The island of Grassholm, off the coast of Pembrokeshire.

'They made her a four-sided grave,' says the Mabinogi, 'and buried her upon the banks of the Alaw.' The traditional spot has always borne the name of *Ynys Branwen.*

The seven went on towards Harlech, and as they journeyed they met men and women who gave them the latest news. Caswallawn, a son of Beli, the husband of Don, had destroyed the ministers left behind by Bran to take care of Britain. He had made himself invisible by the help of a magic veil and thus had killed all of them except Pendaran Dyfed, foster father of Pryderi, who had escaped into the woods, and Caradawc, son of Bran, whose heart had broken from grief. Thus he had made himself king of the whole island in place of Manawydan, its rightful heir now that Bran was dead.

However, the destiny was upon the seven that they should go on with their leader's head. They went to Harlech and feasted for seven years, the three birds of Rhiannon singing them songs compared with which all other songs seemed unmelodious. Then they spent four score years in the Isle of Gwales, eating and drinking and listening to the pleasant conversation of Bran's head. The 'Entertaining of the Noble Head' this eighty years' feast was called. Bran's head, indeed, is almost more notable in British mythology than Bran before he was decapitated. Taliesin and the other bards invoke it repeatedly as *Urddawl Ben* (the 'Venerable Head') and *Uther Ben* (the 'Wonderful Head').

But all pleasure came to an end when Heilyn, the son of Gwinn, opened the forbidden door, like Bluebeard's wife, 'to know if that was true which was said concerning it'. As soon as they looked towards Cornwall, the spell that had kept them merry for eighty-seven years failed and left them as grieved about the death of their lord as though it had happened that very day. They could not rest for sorrow but went at once to London and laid the now dumb and corrupting head in its grave on Tower Hill with its face turned towards France to watch that no foe came from foreign lands to Britain. There it reposed until, ages afterwards, Arthur, in his pride of heart, dug it up 'as he thought it beneath his dignity to hold the island otherwise than by valour'. In the words of Tennyson in *Idylls of the King,* disaster in the shape of

> 'the godless hosts
> Of heathen swarming o'er the Northern sea'[1]

came of this disinterment, and therefore it is called in a triad one of the 'Three Wicked Uncoverings of Britain'.

Chapter 21

THE WAR OF ENCHANTMENTS

According to the Mabinogi of Manawydan, the Son of Llyr, Manawydan was now the sole survivor of the family of Llyr. He was homeless and landless, but Pryderi offered to give him a realm in Dyfed and his mother, Rhiannon, for a wife. The lady, her son explained, was still not uncomely and her conversation was pleasing. Manawydan seems to have found her attractive, while Rhiannon was not less taken with the son of Llyr. They were wedded, and so great became the friendship of Pryderi and Cigfa, Manawydan and Rhiannon, that the four were seldom apart.

One day, after holding a feast at Arbeth, they went up to the same magic mound where Rhiannon had first met Pwyll. As they sat there, thunder pealed, and immediately a thick mist sprang up so that not one of them could see the other. When it cleared, they found themselves alone in an uninhabited country. Except for their own castle, the land was desert and untilled, without sign of dwelling, man or beast. One touch of some unknown magic had utterly changed the face of Dyfed from a rich realm to a wilderness.

Manawydan and Pryderi, Rhiannon and Cigfa traversed the country on all sides but found nothing except desolation and wild beasts. For two years they lived in the open upon game and honey.

During the third year they grew weary of this wild life and decided to go into Lloegyr[1] and support themselves by some handicraft. Manawydan could make saddles, and he made them so well that soon no one in Hereford, where they had settled, would buy from any saddler but himself. This aroused the enmity of all the other saddlers, and they conspired to kill the strangers. So the four went to another city.

Here they made shields, and soon no one would purchase a shield unless it

[1] Saxon Britain – England.

had been made by Manawydan and Pryderi. The shield-makers became jealous, and again a move had to be made.

But they fared no better at the next town, where they practised the craft of cobblers, Manawydan shaping the shoes and Pryderi stitching them. So they went back to Dyfed again and occupied themselves in hunting.

One day, the hounds of Manawydan and Pryderi roused a white wild boar. They chased it until they came to a castle at a place where both the huntsmen were certain that no castle had been before. Into this castle went the boar and the hounds after it. For some time, Manawydan and Pryderi waited in vain for their return. Pryderi then proposed that he should go into the castle and see what had become of them. Manawydan tried to dissuade him, declaring that whoever their enemy was who had laid Dyfed waste had also caused the appearance of this castle. But Pryderi insisted upon entering.

In the castle he found neither the boar nor his hounds nor any trace of man or beast. There was nothing but a fountain in the centre of the castle floor and, on the brink of the fountain, a beautiful golden bowl fastened to a marble slab by chains.

Pryderi was so pleased with the beauty of the bowl that he put out his hands and took hold of it. Whereupon his hands stuck to the bowl, so that he could not move from where he stood.

Manawydan waited for him until the evening and then returned to the palace and told Rhiannon. She, more daring than her husband, rebuked him for cowardice and went straight to the magic castle. In the court she found Pryderi, his hands still glued to the bowl and his feet to the slab. She tried to free him but became fixed herself, and with a clap of thunder and a fall of mist the castle vanished with its two prisoners.

Manawydan was now left alone with Cigfa, Pryderi's wife. He calmed her fears and assured her of his protection. But they had lost their dogs and could not hunt any more, so they set out together to Lloegyr to practise again Manawydan's old trade of cobbling. A second time, the envious shoemakers conspired to kill them, so they were obliged to return to Dyfed.

But Manawydan took back a burden of wheat with him to Arbeth and sowed three crofts, all of which sprang up abundantly.

When harvest time came, he went to look at his first croft and found it ripe. 'I will reap this tomorrow,' he said, but in the morning he found nothing but the bare straw. Every ear had been taken away.

So he went to the next croft, which was also ripe. But when he came to cut it, he found it had been stripped like the first. Then he knew that whoever had wasted Dyfed and carried off Rhiannon and Pryderi was also at work upon his wheat.

The third croft was also ripe, and over this one he determined to keep watch. In the evening he armed himself and waited. At midnight he heard a great tumult and, looking out, saw a host of mice coming. Each mouse bit off an ear of wheat and ran off with it. He rushed among them but could catch only one, which was more sluggish than the rest. This one he put into his glove and took it back and showed it to Cigfa.

'Tomorrow I will hang it,' he said.

'It is not a fit thing for a man of your dignity to hang a mouse,' she replied.

'Nevertheless will I do so,' said he.

'Do so then,' said Cigfa.

The next morning Manawydan went to the magic mound and set up two forks on it to make a gallows. He had just finished when a man dressed like a poor scholar came towards him and greeted him.

'What are you doing, Lord?' he said.

'I am going to hang a thief,' replied Manawydan.

'What sort of a thief? I see an animal like a mouse in your hand, but a man of rank like yours should not touch so mean a creature. Let it go free.'

'I caught it robbing me,' replied Manawydan, 'and it shall die a thief's death.'

'I do not care to see a man like you doing such a thing,' said the scholar. 'I will give you a pound to let it go.'

'I will not let it go,' replied Manawydan, 'nor will I sell it.'

'As you will, Lord. It is nothing to me,' returned the scholar. And he went away.

Manawydan laid a crossbar along the forks. As he did so, another man came by, a priest riding on a horse. He asked Manawydan what he was doing and was told.

'My lord,' he said, 'such a reptile is worth nothing to buy, but rather than see you degrade yourself by touching it, I will give you three pounds to let it go.'

'I will take no money for it,' replied Manawydan. 'It shall be hanged.'

'Let it be hanged,' said the priest and went his way.

Manawydan put the noose round the mouse's neck and was just going to draw it up when he saw a bishop coming, with his whole retinue.

'Thy blessing, Lord Bishop,' he said.

'Heaven's blessing upon you,' said the bishop. 'What are you doing?'

'I am hanging a thief,' replied Manawydan. 'This mouse has robbed me.'

'Since I happen to have come at its doom, I will ransom it,' said the bishop. 'Here are seven pounds. Take them and let it go.'

'I will not let it go,' replied Manawydan.

'I will give you twenty-four pounds of ready money if you will let it go,' said the bishop.

'I would not, for as much again,' replied Manawydan.

'If you will not free it for that,' said the bishop, 'I will give you all my horses and their baggage to let it go.'

'I will not,' replied Manawydan.

'Then name your own price,' said the bishop.

'That offer I accept,' replied Manawydan. 'My price is that Rhiannon and Pryderi be set free.'

'They shall be set free,' replied the bishop.

'Still I will not let the mouse go,' said Manawydan.

'What more do you ask?' exclaimed the bishop.

'That the charm be removed from Dyfed,' replied Manawydan.

'It shall be removed,' promised the bishop. 'So set the mouse free.'

'I will not,' said Manawydan, 'till I know who the mouse is.'

'She is my wife,' replied the bishop, 'and I am called Llwyd, the son of Kil-coed, and I cast the charm over Dyfed and upon Rhiannon and Pryderi to avenge Gwawl fab Clud, for the game of "badger in the bag" which was played on him by Pwyll, Head of Annwn. It was my household that came in the guise of mice and took away your corn. But since my wife has been caught, I will restore Rhiannon and Pryderi and take the charm off Dyfed if you will let her go.'

'I will not let her go,' said Manawydan, 'until you have promised that there shall be no charm put upon Dyfed again.'

'I will promise that also,' replied Llwyd. 'So let her go.'

'I will not let her go,' said Manawydan, 'unless you swear to take no revenge for this hereafter.'

'You have done wisely to claim that,' replied Llwyd. 'Much trouble would else have come upon your head because of this. Now I swear it. So set my wife free.'

'I will not,' said Manawydan, 'until I see Rhiannon and Pryderi.

Then he saw them coming towards him, and they greeted one another.

'Now set my wife free,' said the bishop.

'I will, gladly,' replied :. So he released the mouse, and Llwyd struck her with a wand and turned her into 'a young woman, the fairest ever seen'.

And when Manawydan looked round him, he saw Dyfed tilled and cultivated again, as it had formerly been.

The powers of light had, this time, the victory. Little by little, they increased their mastery over the dominion of darkness until we find the survivors of the families of Llyr and Pwyll mere vassals of Arthur.

Chapter 22

THE VICTORIES OF LIGHT
OVER DARKNESS

The powers of light were, however, by no means invariably successful in their struggles with the powers of darkness. Even Gwydion fab Don had to serve his apprenticeship to misfortune. Assailing Caer Sidi – the Otherworld under one of its many titles – he was caught by Pwyll and Pryderi and endured a long imprisonment (*see* the Spoiling of Annwn, quoted in Chapter 23, 'The Mythological Arrival of Arthur'). The sufferings he underwent made him a bard – an ancient Celtic idea that one can still see surviving in the popular tradition that whoever dares to spend a night alone either upon the chair of the Giant Idris (the summit of Cadair Idris in Gwynedd) or under the haunted Black Stone of Arddu upon the Llanberis side of Snowdon will be found in the morning either inspired or mad. How he escaped we are not told, but the episode does not seem to have quenched his ardour against the natural enemies of his kind.

Helped by his brother, Amaethon, god of agriculture, and his son, Lleu, he fought the Battle of Godeu or 'the Trees', an exploit that is not the least curious of Celtic myths. It is known also as the Battle of Achren or Ochren, a name for Hades of unknown meaning but appearing again in the remarkable Welsh poem that describes the 'Spoiling of Annwn' by Arthur. The King of Achren was Arawn, and he was helped by Bran, who apparently had not then made his fatal journey to Ireland. The war was made to secure three boons for man – the dog, the deer and the lapwing, all of them creatures for some reason sacred to the gods of the nether world.

Gwydion was this time not alone, as he apparently was when he made his first unfortunate reconnaissance of Hades. Besides his brother and his son, he had an army that he raised for the purpose. For a leader of Gwydion's magical attainments there was no need of standing troops. He could call battalions into being with a charm and dismiss them when they were no longer needed. The name of the battle shows what he did on this occasion, and the bard Taliesin adds his testimony:

'I have been in the battle of Godeu, with Lleu and Gwydion,
They changed the forms of the elementary trees and sedges'.

In a poem devoted to it he describes in detail what happened. The trees and grasses, he tells us, hurried to the fight. The alders led the van, but the willows and the quickens came late, and the birch, although courageous, took long in arraying himself. The elm stood firm in the centre of the battle and would not yield a foot. Heaven and earth trembled before the advance of the oak tree, that stout door-keeper against an enemy. The heroic holly and the hawthorn defended themselves with their spikes. The heather kept off the enemy on every side, and the broom was well to the front, but the fern was plundered and the furze did not do well. The stout, lofty pine, the intruding pear tree, the gloomy ash, the bashful chestnut tree, the prosperous beech, the long-en-during poplar, the scarce plum tree, the shelter-seeking privet and woodbine, the wild, foreign laburnum, 'the bean, bearing in its shade an army of phan-toms', rose bush, raspberry, ivy, cherry tree and medlar – all took their parts.

In the ranks of Hades there were equally strange fighters. We are told of a hundred-headed beast carrying a formidable battalion under the root of its tongue and another in the back of its head. There was a gaping black toad with a hundred claws, and a crested snake of many colours within whose flesh a hundred souls were tormented for their sins – in fact, it would need a Doré or a Dante to do justice to this weird battle between the arrayed magics of heaven and hell.

It was magic that decided its fate. There was a fighter in the ranks of Hades who could not be overcome unless his antagonist guessed his name – a pecu-liarity of the earth gods that has been preserved in fairytales. Gwydion guessed the name and sang these two verses:

'Sure-hoofed is my steed impelled by the spur;
The high sprigs of alder are on thy shield;
Bran art thou called, of the glittering branches!

'Sure-hoofed is my steed in the day of battle:
The high sprigs of alder are on thy hand:
Bran . . . by the branch thou bearest
Has Amaethon the Good prevailed!'[1]

Thus the power of the dark gods was broken, and the sons of Don retained for the use of men the deer, the dog and the lapwing, stolen from that underworld whence all good gifts came.

It was always to obtain some practical benefit that the gods of light fought against the gods of darkness. The last and greatest of Gwydion's raids upon Hades was undertaken to procure – pork!

According to the Mabinogi of Math fab Mathonwy, Gwydion had heard that there had come to Dyfed some strange beasts such as had never been seen before. They were called 'pigs' or 'swine', and Arawn, King of Annwn, had sent them as a gift to Pryderi, son of Pwyll. They were small animals, and their flesh was said to be better than the flesh of oxen. He thought it would be a good thing to get them, either by force or fraud, from the dark powers. Math fab Mathonwy, who ruled the children of Don from his Olympus of Caer Dathyl,[1] gave his consent, and Gwydion set off with eleven others to Pryderi's palace.[2] They disguised themselves as bards so as to be received by Pryderi, and Gwydion, who was 'the best teller of tales in the world', entertained the Prince of Dyfed and his court more than they had ever been entertained by any storyteller before. Then he asked Pryderi to grant him a boon – the animals that had come from Annwn. But Pryderi had pledged his word to Arawn that he would neither sell nor give away any of the new creatures until they had increased to double their number, and he told the disguised Gwydion so.

'Lord,' said Gwydion, 'I can set you free from your promise. Neither give me the swine at once nor yet refuse them to me altogether, and tomorrow I will show you how.'

He went to the lodging Pryderi had assigned him and began to work his charms and illusions. Out of fungus he made twelve gilded shields and twelve horses with gold harness and twelve black greyhounds with white breasts, each wearing a golden collar and leash. And these he showed to Pryderi.

'Lord,' said he, 'there is a release from the word you spoke last evening con-

---

[1] Now called Pen y Gaer. It is on the summit of a hill halfway between Llanrwst and Conwy.
[2] Said to have been at Rhuddlan Teivi, which is perhaps Glan Teivy near Cardigan Bridge.

Gwydion conquers Pryderi, from a drawing by E. Wallcousins

cerning the swine – that you may neither give them nor sell them. You may exchange them for something that is better. I will give you these twelve horses with their gold harness, and these twelve greyhounds with their gold collars and leashes, and these twelve gilded shields for them.'

Pryderi took counsel with his men and agreed to the bargain. So Gwydion and his followers took the swine and went away with them, hurrying as fast as they could, for Gwydion knew that the illusion would not last longer than a day. The memory of their journey was long kept up. Every place where they rested between Dyfed and Caer Dathyl is remembered by a name connecting it with pigs. There is a Mochdre ('Swine's Town') in the counties of Powys and Conwy, and a Castell y Moch ('Swine's Castle') near Mochnant ('Swine's Brook'). They shut up the pigs in safety and then assembled all Math's army, for the horses and hounds and shields had returned to fungus, and Pryderi, who guessed Gwydion's part in it, was coming northward in hot haste.

There were two battles – one at Maenor Penardd near Conwy and the other at Maenor Alun near Caernarfon. Beaten in both, Pryderi fell back upon Nant Call, about nine miles from Caernarfon. Here he was again defeated with great slaughter and sent hostages asking for peace and a safe retreat.

This was granted by Math, but nonetheless the army of the sons of Don insisted on following the retreating host and harassing it. So Pryderi sent a complaint to Math, demanding that if there must still be war Gwydion, who had caused all the trouble, should fight with him in single combat.

Gwydion agreed, and the champions of light and darkness met face to face. But Pryderi was the waning power, and he fell before the strength and magic of Gwydion. 'And at Maen Tyriawc, above Melenryd, was he buried, and there is his grave,' says the Mabinogi, although the ancient Welsh poem called the 'Verses of the Graves of the Warriors' in the Black Book of Carmarthen assigns him a different resting place:

> 'In Aber Gwenoli is the grave of Pryderi,
> Where the waves beat against the land.'

This decisive victory over Hades and its kings was the end of the struggle until it was renewed with still more complete success by one greater than Gwydion – the invincible Arthur.

Chapter 23

THE MYTHOLOGICAL ARRIVAL OF ARTHUR

The 'Coming of Arthur', his sudden rise into prominence, is one of the many problems of Celtic mythology. He is not mentioned in any of the Four Branches of the Mabinogi, which deal with the races of British gods equivalent to the Tuatha Dé Danaan. The earliest references to him in Welsh literature seem to treat him as merely a warrior chieftain, no better, if no worse, than several others, such as 'Geraint, a tributary prince of Devon', immortalised both by the bards[1] and by Tennyson. Then, following upon this, we find him lifted to the extraordinary position of a king of gods, to whom the old divine families of Don, of Llyr and of Pwyll pay unquestioned homage. Triads tell us that Lludd – the Zeus of the older pantheon – was one of Arthur's 'Three Chief War Knights' and Arawn, King of Annwn, one of his 'Three Chief Counselling Knights'. In the story called the 'Dream of Rhonabwy', in the Red Book of Hergest, he is shown as a leader to whom are subject those we know to have been gods – sons of Nudd, of Llyr, of Bran, of Gofannon and of Aranrhod. In another 'Red Book' tale, that of 'Culhwch and Olwen', even greater gods are his vassals. Amaethon, son of Don, ploughs for him, and Gofannon, son of Don, rids the iron, while two other sons of Beli, Nynniaw and Peibaw, 'turned into oxen on account of their sins', toil at the yoke that a mountain may be cleared and tilled and the harvest reaped in one day. He assembles his champions to seek the 'treasures of Britain', and Manawydan son of Llyr, Gwyn, son of Nudd, and Pryderi ,son of Pwyll rally round him at his call.

---

[1] A poem in praise of Geraint, 'the brave man from the region of Dyvnaint [Devon] . . . the enemy of tyranny and oppression', is contained in both the Black Book of Carmarthen and the Red Book of Hergest. 'When Geraint was born, open were the gates of heaven', begins its last verse.

The most probable explanation is that the fames of two separate Arthurs have been accidentally confused to the exceeding renown of a composite, half-real, half-mythical personage into whom the two blended. One of these was a divine Arthur, a god more or less widely worshipped in the Celtic world – the same, no doubt, whom an *ex voto* inscription found in southeastern France calls *Mercurius Artaius*. The other was a human Arthur, who held among the Britons the post that, under Roman domination, had been called *Comes Britannae*. This 'Count of Britain' was the supreme military authority. He had a roving commission to defend the country against foreign invasion, and under his orders were two slightly subordinate officers, the *Dux Britanniarum* (Duke of the Britains), who had charge of Hadrian's Wall, and the *Comes Littoris Saxonici* (Count of the Saxon Shore), who guarded the southeastern coasts. The Britons, after the departure of the Romans, long kept intact the organisation their conquerors had built up, and it seems reasonable to believe that this post of leader in war was as that which early Welsh literature describes as 'emperor', a title given to Arthur alone among the British heroes. The fame of Arthur the Emperor blended with that of Arthur the God, so that it became conterminous with the area over which we have traced Brythonic settlement in Great Britain. Hence the many disputes, ably if unprofitably, conducted over 'Arthurian localities' and the sites of such cities as Camelot and of Arthur's twelve great battles. Historical elements doubtless coloured the tales of Arthur and his companions, but they are nonetheless as essentially mythic as those told of their Gaelic analogues – the Red Branch Heroes of Ulster and the Fianna.

Of those two cycles, it is with the latter that the Arthurian legend shows most affinity. Arthur's position as supreme war leader of Britain curiously parallels that of Fionn's as general of a 'native Irish militia'. His 'Round Table' of warriors also reminds one of Fionn's Fianna sworn to adventure. Both alike battle with human and superhuman foes. Both alike harry Europe, even to the walls of Rome. The love story of Arthur, his wife Gwenhwyvar (Guinevere), and his nephew Medrawd (Mordred), resembles in several ways that of Fionn, his wife Grainne, and his nephew Diarmaid. In the stories of the last battles of Arthur and of the Fianna, the essence of the kindred myth still subsists, although the actual exponents of it slightly differ. At the fight of Camluan, it was Arthur and Medrawd themselves who fought the final duel, but in the last stand of the Fianna at Gabhra, the original protagonists have given place to their descendants and representatives. Both Fionn and Cormac were already dead. It is Oscar, Fionn's grandson, and Cairbre, Cormac's son, who fight and slay each other. And again, just as Arthur was thought by many not to have really died but to have passed to 'the island valley of Avilion', so a Scottish legend tells us how, ages after the Fianna, a man, landing by chance upon a mysterious western island, met and spoke with Fionn Mac Cumhaill. Even the alternative legend, which makes Arthur and his warriors wait under the earth in a magic sleep for the return of their triumph, is also told of the Fianna.

But these parallels, although they illustrate Arthur's pre-eminence, do not show his real place among the gods. To determine this, we must examine the ranks of the older dynasties carefully to see if any are missing whose attributes this newcomer may have inherited. We find Lludd and Gwyn, Arawn, Pryderi and Manawydan side by side with him under their own names. Among the children of Don are Amaethon and Gofannon. But here the list stops with a notable omission. There is no mention in later myth of Gwydion. That greatest of the sons of Don has fallen out and vanished without a sign.

Singularly enough, too, the same stories that were once told of Gwydion are now attached to the name of Arthur. So that we may assume that Arthur, the prominent god of a new pantheon, has taken the place of Gwydion in the old. A comparison of Gwydion myths and Arthur myths shows an almost exact correspondence in everything but name.

Like Gwydion, Arthur is the exponent of culture and of arts. Therefore we see him carrying on the same war against the underworld for wealth and wisdom that Gwydion and the sons of Don waged against the sons of Llyr, the Sea, and of Pwyll, the Head of Hades.

Like Gwydion too, Arthur suffered early reverses. He failed, indeed, even where his prototype had succeeded. Gwydion, we know from the Mabinogi of Math, successfully stole Pryderi's pigs, but Arthur was utterly baffled in his attempt to capture the swine of a similar prince of the underworld, called March ap Meirchion.[1] Also as with Gwydion, his earliest reconnaissance of Hades was disastrous and led to his capture and imprisonment. Manawydan fab Llyr, confined him in the mysterious and gruesome bone fortress of Oeth and Anoeth, and there he languished for three days and three nights before a

---

[1] A triad in the Hengwrt manuscript. It was Trystan who was watching the swine for his uncle, while the swineherd went with a message to Essylt (Iseult), 'and Arthur desired one pig by deceit or by theft, and could not get it'.

rescuer came in the person of Goreu, his cousin (*see* note to Chapter 24, 'The Treasures of Britain'), but in the end he triumphed. A Welsh poem ascribed to the bard Taliesin relates, under the title 'The Spoiling of Annwn', an expedition of Arthur and his followers into the very heart of that country from which he appears to have returned (for the verses are somewhat obscure) with the loss of almost all his men but in possession of the object of his quest – the magic cauldron of inspiration and poetry.

Taliesin tells the story as an eyewitness. He may well have done so, for it was his boast that from the creation of the world he had allowed himself to miss no event of importance. He was in Heaven, he tells us, when Lucifer fell, and in the court of Don before Gwydion was born. He had been among the constellations both with Mary Magdalene and with the pagan goddess Aranrhod. He carried a banner before Alexander and was chief director of the building of the Tower of Babel. He saw the fall of Troy and the founding of Rome. He was with Noah in the Ark, and he witnessed the destruction of Sodom and Gomorrah, and he was present both at the Manger of Bethlehem and at the Cross of Calvary.

Taliesin's presence in Welsh Celtic mythology is of a late date, taken from a manuscript of the late sixteenth or seventeenth century and never appears to have enjoyed much popularity in Wales. He is to be the son of Cerridwen, born under strange, supernatural circumstances. Cerridwen had two, or perhaps three, children born before the birth of Taliesin. One was Crearwy, an extremely beautiful daughter, and one was Afagddu, a very ugly son. To compensate her son for his unfortunate physical appearance, Cerridwen decided to try to endow him with other virtues, specifically special powers relating to inspiration and knowledge. To do this, she brewed a potion of various herbs in a large cauldron. This had to boil for a year and a day in order to have the required result, which was three drops of magical fluid that would endow Afagddu with the desired talents. Gwion Bach was appointed to stir the potion regularly, and towards the end of the year he accidentally splashed his finger with three drops of the potion from the cauldron. Without thinking, he put his fingers in his mouth to cool them and so partook of the magical brew. Fearing for his life, he fled, and the cauldron, having been deprived of its three magical drops of fluid, cracked, the remainder of the potion running into a stream. Cerridwen set off in pursuit of Gwion, he frequently changing shape to avoid her and she frequently changing shape in order to catch him.

After a great deal of shape-changing, Gwion changed himself into a grain of wheat on the threshing floor of a barn and was eaten by Cerridwen, who had turned into a hen. Having swallowed the grain of wheat, Cerridwen discovered that she was pregnant and gave birth to a beautiful baby boy. She did not want the child but was unwilling to kill him. She therefore put the child in a bag and threw him into the river. The bag and child were retrieved by Elffin, who is said to have been so impressed by the beauty of the baby's brow that he called out 'Taliesin', meaning 'radiant brow', and so the child was named. Taliesin inherited the inspirational powers originally intended for Afagddu and became famous for his poetic prowess and was also said to have had the gift of prophecy.

But, unfortunately, Taliesin, as a credible personage, rests under exactly the same disabilities as Arthur himself. It is not denied by scholars that there was a real Taliesin, a sixth-century bard to whom were attributed and who may have actually composed some of the poems in the Book of Taliesin,[1] but there was also another Taliesin, whom, as a mythical poet of the British Celts, has been equated with the Gaelic Oisín. The traditions of the two mingled, endowing the historic Taliesin with the god-like attributes of his predecessor and clothing the mythical Taliesin with some of the actuality of his successor.

It is regrettable that our bard did not at times sing a little less incoherently, for his poem contains the fullest description that has come down to us of the Otherworld as the Britons conceived it. Apparently the numerous names, all different and some now untranslatable, refer to the same place, and they must be collated to form a right idea of what Annwn was like. With the exception of an obviously spurious last verse, here omitted, the poem is magnificently pagan and quite a storehouse of British mythology.

> 'I will praise the Sovereign, supreme Lord of the land,
> Who hath extended his dominion over the shore of the world.
> Stout was the prison of Gweir,[2] in Caer Sidi,

---

[1] The existence of a sixth-century bard of this name, a contemporary of the heroic stage of British resistance to the Germanic invaders, is well attested. A number of poems are found in medieval Welsh manuscripts, chief among them the so-called *Book of Taliesin*, ascribed to this sixth-century poet. Some of these are almost as old as any remains of Welsh poetry and may go back to the early tenth or the ninth century. Others are productions of the tw_eventh, twelfth and even thirteenth centuries.

[2] A form of the name Gwydion.

Through the spite of Pwyll and Pryderi:
No one before him went into it.
The heavy blue chain firmly held the youth,
And before the spoils of Annwn woefully he sang,
And thenceforth till doom he shall remain a bard.
Thrice enough to fill Prydwen[1] we went into it;
Except seven, none returned from Caer Sidi.[2]

'Am I not a candidate for fame, to be heard in song
In Caer Pedryvan,[3] four times revolving?
The first word from the cauldron, when was it spoken?
By the breath of nine maidens it was gently warmed.
Is it not the cauldron of the chief of Annwn? What is its fashion?
A rim of pearls is round its edge.
It will not cook the food of a coward or one forsworn.
A sword flashing bright will be raised to him,
And left in the hand of Lleminawg.
And before the door of the gate of Uffern[4] the lamp was burning.
When we went with Arthur – a splendid labour! –
Except seven, none returned from Caer Vedwyd.[5]

'Am I not a candidate for fame, to be heard in song
In Caer Pedryvan, in the Isle of the Strong Door,
Where twilight and pitchy darkness meet together,
And bright wine is the drink of the host?
Thrice enough to fill Prydwen we went on the sea.
Except seven, none returned from Caer Rigor.[6]

'I will not allow much praise to the leaders of literature.
Beyond Caer Wydyr[7] they saw not the prowess of Arthur;
Three score hundreds stood on the walls;
It was hard to converse with their watchman.

[1] The name of Arthur's ship.
[2] Revolving Castle.
[3] Four-cornered Castle.
[4] The Cold Place.
[5] Castle or Revelry.
[6] Kingly Castle.
[7] Glass Castle.

Thrice enough to fill Prydwen we went with Arthur;
Except seven, none returned from Caer Golud.[2]

'I will not allow much praise to the spiritless.
They know not on what day, or who caused it,
Or in what hour of the serene day Cwy was born,
Or who caused that he should not go to the dales of Devwy.
They know not the brindled ox with the broad headband,
Whose yoke is seven score handbreadths.
When we went with Arthur, of mournful memory,
Except seven, none returned from Caer Vandwy.[1]

'I will not allow much praise to those of drooping courage,
They know not on what day the chief arose,
Nor in what hour of the serene day the owner was born,
Nor what animal they keep, with its head of silver.
When we went with Arthur, of anxious striving,
Except seven, none returned from Caer Ochren.'[3]

Many of the allusions of this poem will perhaps never be explained. We know no better than the 'leaders of literature' whom the vainglorious Taliesin taunted with their ignorance and lack of spirit in what hour Cwy was born or even who he was, much less who prevented him from going to the dales of Devwy, wherever they may have been. We are in the dark as much as they were with regard to the significance of the brindled ox with the broad headband and of the other animal with the silver head, unless they should be 'the yellow and the brindled bull' mentioned in the story of Culhwch and Olwen (*see* Chapter 24, "The Treasures of Britain'). But the earlier portion of the poem is, fortunately, clearer, and it gives glimpses of a grandeur of savage imagination. The strong-doored, four-square fortress of glass, manned by its dumb, ghostly sentinels, spun round in never-ceasing revolution, so that few could find its entrance; it was pitch-dark save for the twilight made by the lamp burning before its circling gate. Feasting went on there and revelry, and in its centre, choicest of its many riches, was the pearl-rimmed cauldron of

---

[1] Castle of Riches.
[2] Meaning is unknown. See Chapter 16 – 'The Gods of the Britons'.
[3] Meaning is unknown. See Chapter 20 – 'The Victories of Light over Darkness'.

poetry and inspiration kept bubbling by the breaths of nine British pythons, so that it might give forth its oracles. To this scanty information we may add a few lines, also by Taliesin and contained in a poem called 'A Song Concerning the Sons of Llyr ab Brochwel Powys':

> 'Perfect is my chair in Caer Sidi:
> Plague and age hurt not him who's in it –
> They know, Manawydan and Pryderi.
> Three organs round a fire sing before it,
> And about its points are ocean's streams
> And the abundant well above it –
> Sweeter than white wine the drink in it.'

Little is, however, added by it to our knowiedge. It reminds us that Annwn was surrounded by the sea – 'the heavy blue chain' which held Gweir so firmly – it informs us that the 'bright wine' that was 'the drink of the host' was kept in a well; it adds to the revelry the singing of the three organs; it makes a point that its inhabitants were freed from age and death, and, last of all, it shows us, as we might have expected, the ubiquitous Taliesin as a privileged resident of this delightful region. We have two clues as to where the country may have been situated. Lundy Island, off the coast of Devon, was anciently called Ynys Wair, the 'Island of Gweir' or Gwydion. The Welsh translation of the *Seint Greal*, an Anglo-Norman romance embodying much of the old mythology, lo-cates its 'Turning Castle' – evidently the same as Caer Sidi – in the district around and comprising Puffin Island off the coast of Anglesey, but these are slender threads by which to tether to firm ground a realm of the imagination.

With Gwydion, too, have disappeared the whole of the characters con-nected with him in that portion of the Mabinogi of Math fab Mathonwy, which recounts the myth of the birth of the sun god. Neither Math himself, nor Lleu Llaw Gyffes, nor Dylan, nor their mother, Aranrhod, play any more part; they have vanished as completely as Gwydion. But the essence of the myth of which they were the figures remains intact. Gwydion was the father by his sister Aranrhod, wife of a waning heaven god called Nwyvre (Space), of twin sons, Lleu, a god of light, and Dylan, a god of darkness, and we find this same story woven into the very innermost texture of the legend of Arthur. The new Aranrhod, although called 'Morgawse' by Sir Thomas Malory in the *Morte*

D'Arthur and 'Anna' by Geoffrey of Monmouth, is known to earlier Welsh myth as 'Gwyar'. She was the sister of Arthur and the wife of the sky god Lludd, and her name, which means 'shed blood' or 'gore', reminds us of the relationship of the Morrigan, the war goddess of Ireland, to the heaven god Nuada. The new Lleu Llaw Gyffes is called Gwalchmei, that is, the 'Falcon of May', and the new Dylan is Medrawd, at once Arthur's son and Gwalchmei's brother and the bitterest enemy of both.

Besides these 'old friends with new faces', Arthur brings with him into prominence a fresh pantheon, most of whom also replace the older gods of the heavens and earth and the regions under the earth. The Zeus of Arthur's cycle is called Myrddin, who passed into the Norman-French romances as 'Merlin'. All the myths told of him bear witness to his high estate. The first name of Britain, before it was inhabited, was, we learn from a triad, *Clas Myrddin*, that is, 'Myrddin's Enclosure'. He is given a wife whose attributes recall those of the consorts of Nuada and Lludd. She is described as the only daughter of Coel – the British name of the Gaulish Camulus, a god of war and the sky – and was called Elen Lwyddawg, that is, 'Elen, Leader of Hosts'. Her memory is still preserved in Wales in connection with ancient roadways, such names as *Ffordd Elen* ('Elen's Road') and *Sarn Elen* ('Elen's Causeway') seeming to show that the paths on which armies marched were ascribed or dedicated to her. As Myrddin's wife, she is credited with having founded the town of Carmarthen (*Caer Myrddin*) as well as the 'highest fortress in Arvon', which must have been the site near Beddgelert still called *Dinas Emrys*, the 'Town of Emrys', one of Myrddin's epithets or names.

Myrddin, or rather the British Zeus under whatever name, has been credited as having been the god especially worshipped at Stonehenge. Certainly this impressive temple, always unroofed and open to the sun and wind and rain of heaven, would seem peculiarly appropriate to a British supreme god of light and sky. Neither are we quite without documentary evidence that will allow us to connect it with him. Geoffrey of Monmouth, whose historical fictions usually conceal mythological facts, relates that the stones that compose it were erected by Merlin. Before that they had stood in Ireland, on a hill that Geoffrey calls 'Mount Killaraus' and which can be identified as the same spot known to Irish legend as the 'Hill of Uisneach' and still earlier connected with Balor. According to British tradition, the primeval giants who first colonised Ireland had brought them from their original home on 'the farthest coast of

Africa' on account of their miraculous virtues, for any water in which they were bathed became a sovereign remedy either for sickness or for wounds. By the order of Aurelius, a half-real, half-mythical king of Britain, Merlin brought them to England to be set up on Salisbury Plain as a monument to the British chieftains treacherously slain by Hengist and his Saxons. With this scrap of native information about Stonehenge we may compare the only other piece we have – the account of the classical Diodorus, who called it a temple of Apollo. At first these two statements seem to conflict, but it is far from unlikely that the earlier Celtic settlers in Britain made little or no religious distinction between sky and sun. The sun god, as a separate personage, seems to have been the concept of a comparatively late age. Celtic mythology allows us to be present, as it were, at the births both of the Gaelic Lugh Lamhfada and the British Lleu Llaw Gyffes.

Even the well-known story of Myrddin's or Merlin's final imprisonment in a tomb of airy enchantment – 'a tour withouten walles, or withoute eny closure' – reads marvellously like a myth of the sun 'with all his fires and travelling glories round him'. Encircled, shielded and made splendid by his atmosphere of living light, the Lord of Heaven moves slowly towards the west to disappear at last into the sea (as one local version of the myth puts it), or on to a far-off island (as another says) or into a dark forest (the choice of a third). When the myth became finally fixed, it was Bardsey Island, off the extreme westernmost point of Gwynedd, that was selected as his last abode. Onto it he went with nine attendant bards, taking with him the 'Thirteen Treasures of Britain', thenceforth lost to men. Bardsey Island no doubt derives its name from this story, and what is probably an allusion to it is found in a work of the first-century Greek writer Plutarch, who describes a grammarian called Demetrius as having visited Britain and brought home an account of his travels. He mentioned several uninhabited and sacred islands off our coasts, which he said were named after gods and heroes, but there was one especially in which Cronos was imprisoned with his attendant deities and Briareus keeping watch over him as he slept, 'for sleep was the bond forged for him'. Doubtless this disinherited deity, whom the Greek, after his fashion, called 'Cronos', was the British heaven and sun god after he had descended into the prison of the west.

Among other newcomers is Kai, who, as Sir Kay the Seneschal, fills so large a part in the later romances. In the *Seint Greal*, purged of his worst offences and reduced to a surly butler to Arthur, he is only a shadow of the earlier Kai who murdered Arthur's son Llacheu and can only be acquitted, through the obscurity of the poem that relates the incident, of having also carried off, or having tried to carry off, Arthur's wife, Gwenhwyvar. He is thought to have been a personification of fire on the strength of a description given of him in the mythical romance of 'Culhwch and Olwen'. 'Very subtle', it says, 'was Kai. When it pleased him he could render himself as tall as the highest tree in the forest. And he had another peculiarity – so great was the heat of his nature, that, when it rained hardest, whatever he carried remained dry for a hand's-breadth above and a hand's-breadth below his hand, and when his companions were coldest, it was to them as fuel with which to light their fire.'

Another personage who owes his prominence in the Arthurian story to his importance in Celtic myth was March ap Meirchion, whose swine Arthur attempted to steal, as Gwydion had done those of Pryderi. In the romances he has become the cowardly and treacherous Mark, king, according to some stories, of Cornwall but, according to others, of the whole of Britain, and known to all as the husband of the Fair Iseult and the uncle of Sir Tristrem. But as a deformed deity of the underworld he can be found in Gaelic as well as in British myth. He cannot be considered as originally different from Morc, a king of the Fomorii at the time when from their Glass Castle they so fatally oppressed the Children of Nemedh. The Fomorii were distinguished by their animal features, and March, whose name means 'horse', had the same peculiarity. When Sir Thomas Malory in the *Morte D'Arthur* relates how, to please Arthur and Sir Launcelot, Sir Dinadan made a song about Mark, 'which was the worst lay that ever harper sang with harp or any other instruments', he does not tell us wherein the sting of the lampoon lay. It no doubt reminded King Mark of the unpleasant fact that he had – not like his Phrygian counterpart, ass's but – horse's ears. He was, in fact, a Celtic Midas, a distinction that he shared with one of the mythical kings of early Ireland, called Labhraidh Loingsech.

Neither can we pass over Urien, a deity of the underworld akin to, or perhaps the same as, Bran. Like that son of Llyr, he was at once a god of battle and of minstrelsy. He was adored by the bards as their patron; his badge was the raven (*bran* in Welsh), while, to make his identification complete, there is a poem in the Red Book of Hergest that tells how Urien, wounded, ordered his own head to be cut off by his attendants. His wife was Modron, known as the mother of Mabon, the sun god to whom inscriptions exist as Maponos. Another of the children of Urien and Modron is Owain, which was perhaps only another name for Mabon. In 'The Death-song of Owain' Taliesin calls him 'chief of the glittering west', and he is as certainly a sun god as his father, Urien, 'lord of the evening' or 'lord of the cultivated plain', was a ruler of the dark underworld.

It is by reason of the pre-eminence of Arthur that we find gathered round him so many gods, all probably various tribal personifications of the same few mythological ideas. The Celts, both of the Gaelic and the British branches, were split up into numerous petty tribes, each with its own local deities embodying the same essential concepts under different names. There was the god of the underworld, gigantic in figure, patron alike of warrior and minstrel, teacher of the arts of eloquence and literature, and owner of boundless wealth, whom some of the British tribes worshipped as Bran, others as Urien, others as Pwyll, or March, or Math, or Arawn, or Ogyrvran. There was the lord of an Elysium – Hades in its aspect of a paradise of the departed rather than of the primeval subterranean realm where all things originated – whom the Britons of Wales called Gwyn or Gwynwas, the Britons of Cornwall Melwas, and the Britons of Somerset Avallon or Avallach. Under this last title, his realm is called *Ynys Avallon*, 'Avallon's Island' or, as we know the word, Avilion. It was said to be in the 'Land of Summer', which, in the earliest myth, signified Hades, and it was only in later days that the mystic Isle of Avilion became fixed to earth as Glastonbury and the Elysian 'Land of Summer' as Somerset. There was a mighty ruler of heaven, a 'god of battles' worshipped on high places, in whose hands was 'the stern arbitrament of war'. Some knew him as Lludd, others as Myrddin or as Emrys. There was a gentler deity, friendly to humans, to help whom he fought or cajoled the powers of the underworld. Gwydion he was called, and Arthur. Last, perhaps, to be imagined in concrete shape, there was a long-armed, sharp-speared sun god who aided the culture god in his work and was known as Lleu, or Gwalchmei, or Mabon, or Owain, or Peredur, and no doubt by many another name, and with him is usually found a brother representing not light but darkness. This expression of a single idea by different names may also be observed in Gaelic myth although not quite so clearly. In the hurtling of clan against clan, many such divinities disappeared altogether or survived only as names to make up, in Ireland, the vast, shadowy population claiming to be Tuatha Dé Danaan and, in Britain, the long list of Arthur's followers. Others – gods of stronger communities – would increase their fame as their worshippers increased their territory, until, as happened in Greece, the chief deities of many tribes came together to form a national pantheon.

We have already tried to explain the 'Coming of Arthur' historically. Mythologically he came, as, according to Celtic ideas, all things came originally, from the underworld. His father is called Uther Pendragon both by Malory and Geoffrey of Monmouth, but Uther Pendragon is *Uther Ben*, that is, Bran under his name of the 'Wonderful Head' (for the word 'dragon' is not part of the name but a title signifying 'war leader'), so that in spite of the legend that describes Arthur as having disinterred Bran's head on Tower Hill, where it watched against invasion, because he thought it beneath his dignity to keep Britain in any other way than by valour (*see* Chapter 20 – 'The Wooing of Branwen and the Beheading of Bran'), we must recognise the King of Hades as his father. This being so, it would only be natural that he should take a wife from the same eternal country, and we need not be surprised to find in Gwenhwyvar's father, Ogyrvran, a personage corresponding in all respects to the Celtic concept of the ruler of the underworld. He was of gigantic size (he is called Ogynran the Giant); he was the owner of a cauldron out of which three Muses had been born; and he was the patron of the bards, who deemed him to

*King Arthur's Castle, Tintagel, where Arthur's parents are said to
have first come together*

have been the originator of their art. More than this, his very name, analysed into its original *ocur vran*, means the evil *bran*, or raven, the bird of death.

But Welsh tradition credits Arthur with three wives, each of them called Gwenhwyvar. This peculiar arrangement is probably the result of the Celtic love of triads, and one may compare them with the three Etains who pass through the mythico-heroic story of Eochaidh Airemh, Etain and Midhir. Of these three Gwenhwyvars,[1] besides the Gwenhwyvar, daughter of Ogyrvran, one was the daughter of Gwyrd Gwent, of whom we know nothing but the name, and the other of Gwythyr ap Gwreidawl, the same 'Victor, son of Scorcher,' with whom Gwyn ap Nudd fought in earlier myth perpetual battle for the possession of Creiddylad, daughter of the sky god Lludd. This same eternal strife between the powers of light and darkness for the possession of a symbolic damsel is waged again in the Arthurian cycle, but it is no longer for Creiddylad that Gwyn contends but for Gwenhwyvar, and no longer with Gwythyr but with Arthur. It would seem to have been a Cornish form of the myth, for the dark god is called Melwas and not Gwynwas or Gwyn, his name in Welsh. Melwas lay in ambush for a whole year and finally succeeded in carrying off Gwenhwyvar to his palace in Avilion. But Arthur pursued and besieged that stronghold, just as Eochaidh Airemh had, in the Gaelic version of the universal story, mined and sapped at Midhir's *sídh* of Bri Leith (*see* Chapter 11, 'The Gods in Exile'). Mythology, as well as history, repeats itself, and Melwas was obliged to restore Gwenhwyvar to her rightful lord.

It is not Melwas, however, who in the best-known versions of the story contends with Arthur for the love of Gwenhwyvar. The most widespread early tradition makes Arthur's rival his nephew Medrawd. Here a striking parallel can be traced between the British legend of Arthur, Gwenhwyvar and Medrawd, and the Gaelic story of Airemh, Etain and Midhir. The two myths are practically counterparts, for the names of all the three pairs agree in their essential meaning. 'Airemh', like 'Arthur', signifies the 'Ploughman', the divine institutor of agriculture; 'Etain', the 'Shining One', is a fit parallel to 'Gwenhwyvar', the 'White Apparition'; while 'Midhir' and 'Medrawd' both come from the same root, a word meaning 'to hit', either literally, or else metaphorically, with the mind, in the sense of coming to a decision. To attempt to explain this myth is to raise the vexed question of the meaning of mythology. Is

---

[1] The enumeration of Arthur's three Gwenhwyvars forms one of the Welsh triads.

it day and dark that strive for dawn, or summer and winter for the lovely spring, or does it shadow forth the rescue of the grain that makes man's life from the devouring underworld by the farmer's wit? When this can be finally resolved, a multitude of Celtic myths will be explained. Everywhere arise the same combatants for the stolen bride; one has the attributes of light, the other is a champion of darkness.

Even in Sir Thomas Malory's version of the Arthurian story, taken by him from French romances far removed from the original tradition, we find the myth subsisting. Medrawd's original place as the lover of Arthur's queen had been taken in the romances by Sir Launcelot, who, if he was not some now undiscoverable Celtic god,[1] must have been an invention of the Norman adapters. But the story that makes Medrawd Arthur's rival has been preserved in the account in the *Morte D'Arthur* of how Sir Mordred would have wedded Guinevere by force as part of the rebellion that he made against his king and uncle. This strife was Celtic myth long before it became part of the pseudo-history of early Britain. The triads tell us how Arthur and Medrawd raided each other's courts during the owner's absence. Medrawd went to Kelli Wic in Cornwall, ate and drank everything he could find there and insulted Queen Gwenhwyvar, in revenge for which Arthur went to Medrawd's court and killed man and beast. Their struggle only ended with the Battle of Camluan, and that mythical combat, which chroniclers have striven to make historical, is full of legendary detail. Tradition tells how Arthur and his antagonist shared their forces three times during the fight, which caused it to be known as one of the 'Three Frivolous Battles of Britain', the idea of doing so being one of 'Britain's Three Criminal Resolutions'. Four alone survived the fray: one because he was so ugly that all shrank from him, believing him to be a devil; another whom no one touched because he was so beautiful that they took him for an angel; a third whose great strength no one could resist; and Arthur himself, who, after revenging the death of Gwalchmei upon Medrawd, went to the island of Avilion to heal himself of his grievous wounds.

And thence – from the Elysium of the Celts – popular belief has always been that he will some day return. But just as the gods of the Gaels are said to

---

[1] In the mysterious Lancelot, not found in Arthurian story before the Norman adaptations of it, can be seen perhaps a British sun god or solar hero. A number of interesting comparisons can be drawn between him and the Peredur and Owain of the later 'Mabinogion' tales as well as with the Gaelic Cúchulainn.

dwell sometimes in the 'Land of the Living', beyond the western wave, and sometimes in the palace of a hollow hill, so Arthur is sometimes thought to be in Avilion and sometimes to be sitting with his champions in a charmed sleep in some secret place, waiting for the trumpet to be blown that shall call him forth to reconquer Britain. The legend is found in the Eildon Hills, in the Snowdon district, at Cadbury in Somerset, the best authenticated Camelot, in the Vale of Neath in South Wales, as well as in other places. He slumbers, but he has not died. The ancient Welsh poem called 'The Verses of the Graves of the Warriors' in the Black Book of Carmarthen enumerates the last resting places of most of the British gods and demigods. 'The grave of Gwydion is in the marsh of Dinlleu', the grave of Lleu Llaw Gyffes is 'under the protection of the sea with which he was familiar', and 'where the wave makes a sullen sound is the grave of Dylan'. We know the graves of Pryderi, of Gwalchmei, of March, of Mabon, even of the great Beli, but

'Not wise the thought – a grave for Arthur'.[1]

---

[1] A translation of the Welsh line more correct than the famous rendering: 'Unknown is the grave of Arthur'.

Chapter 24

THE TREASURES OF BRITAIN

It is in keeping with the mythological character of Arthur that the early Welsh tales recorded of him are of a different nature from those that swell the pseudo-histories of Nennius and Geoffrey of Monmouth. We hear nothing of that subjugation of the countries of Western Europe, which fills so large a part in the two books that Geoffrey has devoted to him. Conqueror he is, but his conquests are not in any land known to geographers. It is against Hades, and not against Rome, that he achieves his highest triumphs. This is the true history of King Arthur, and we may read more fragments and snatches of it in two prose tales preserved in the Red Book of Hergest. Both these tales date, in the actual form in which they have come down to us, from the twelfth century, but in each of them the writer seems to be stretching out his hands to gather in the dying traditions of a very remote past.

When a Welsh man-at-arms named Rhonabwy lay down one night to sleep upon a yellow calfskin, the only furniture in the noisome hut in which he had taken shelter, which was comparatively free from vermin, he had the vision that is related in the tale called 'The Dream of Rhonabwy'. He thought that he was travelling with his companions towards the Severn, when they heard a rushing noise behind them and, looking back, saw a gigantic rider upon a monstrous horse. So terrible was the horseman's appearance that they all started to run from him. But their running was of no avail, for every time the horse drew in its breath, it sucked them back to its very chest, only, however, to fling them forward as it breathed out again. In despair they fell down and sought their pursuer's mercy. He granted it, asked their names and told them, in return, his own. He was known as Iddawc the Agitator of Britain, for it was he who, in his love of war, had purposely precipitated the Battle of Camluan. Arthur had sent him to reason with Medrawd, but although Arthur had charged him with the fairest sayings he could think of, Iddawc translated them into the harshest he could devise. But he had done seven years' penance and had been forgiven, and was now riding to Arthur's camp. Thither he insisted upon taking Rhonabwy and his companions.

Arthur's army was encamped for a mile around the ford of Rhyd y Groes, on both sides of the road, and on a small flat island in the middle of the river was the emperor himself, in conversation with Bedwini the Bishop and Gwarthegyd, the son of Kaw. Like Oisín, when he came back to Ireland after his three hundred years' sojourn in Tír Tairnigirib, the 'Land of Promise' (*see* Chapter 15, 'Fionn and the Fianna'), Arthur marvelled at the puny size of the people whom Iddawc had brought for him to look at. 'And where, Iddawc, did you find these little men?'

'I found them, Lord, up yonder on the road.'

Then the Emperor smiled.

'Lord,' said Iddawc, 'why do you laugh?'

'Iddawc,' replied Arthur, 'I laugh not, but it pitieth me that men of such stature as these should have this island in their keeping, after the men that guarded it of yore.' Then he turned away, and Iddawc told Rhonabwy and his companions to keep silent and they would see what they would see.

The scope of this book allows no space to describe the persons and equipments of the warriors who came riding down with their companies to join Arthur as he made his great march to fight the Battle of Mount Badon, thought by some to be historical and located at Bath. The reader who turns to the tale itself will see what Rhonabwy saw. Many of Arthur's warriors he will know by name: Caradawc the Strong-armed, who is here called a son not of Bran but of Llyr; March ap Meirchion, the underworld king; Kai, described as 'the fairest horseman in all Arthur's court'; Gwalchmei, the son of Gwyar and of Arthur himself; Mabon, the son of Modron; Tristan, son of Tallwch, the lover of 'The Fair Iseult'; Goreu, Arthur's cousin and his rescuer from Manawydan's bone prison of Oeth and Anoeth. These and many more will pass before him, as they passed before Rhonabwy during the three days and three nights that he slept and dreamed upon the calfskin.

This story of the 'Dream of Rhonabwy', elaborate as it is in all its details, is in substance little more than a catalogue. The intention of its unknown author seems to have been to draw a series of pictures of what he considered to be the principal among Arthur's followers. The other story – that of 'Culhwch and

Olwen' – also takes this catalogue form, but the matters enumerated are of a different kind. It is not so much a record of men as of things. Not the heroes of Britain, but the treasures of Britain are its subject. One might compare it with the Gaelic story of the adventures of the three sons of Tuireann (*see* Chapter 8, 'The Gaelic Argonauts').

The 'Thirteen Treasures of Britain' were famous in early legend. They belonged to gods and heroes and were current in our island until the end of the divine age when Merlin, fading out of the world, took them with him into his airy tomb, never to be seen by mortal eyes again. According to tradition, they consisted of a sword, a basket, a drinking horn, a chariot, a halter, a knife, a cauldron, a whetstone, a garment, a pan, a platter, a chessboard and a mantle, all possessed of not less marvellous qualities than the apples, the pigskin, the spear, the horses and chariot, the pigs, the hound whelp and the cooking spit that the sons of Tuireann obtained for Lugh (*see* Chapter 8, 'The Gaelic Argonauts'). It is these same legendary treasures that reappear, no doubt, in the story of 'Culhwch and Olwen'. The number tallies, for there are thirteen of them. Some are certainly, and others probably, identical with those of the other tradition. That there should be discrepancies need cause no surprise, for it is not unlikely that there were several different versions of their legend. Everyone had heard of the Thirteen Treasures of Britain. Many, no doubt, disputed as to what they were. Others might ask whence they came. The story of 'Culhwch and Olwen' was composed to tell them. They were won by Arthur and his mighty men.

Culhwch is the hero of the story and Olwen is its heroine, but only, as it were, by courtesy. The pair provide a love interest that, as in the tales of all primitive people, is kept in the background. The woman in such romances takes the place of the gold and gems in more modern 'treasure hunt' stories. She is won by overcoming external obstacles and not by any difficulty in obtaining her own consent. In this romance, Culhwch was the son of a king who afterwards married a widow with a grown-up daughter whom his stepmother urged Culhwch to marry. On his modestly replying that he was not yet of an age to wed, she laid the destiny on him that he should never have a wife at all unless he could win Olwen, the daughter of a terrible father called 'Hawthorn, Chief of Giants', in Welsh, *Yspaddaden Penkawr*.

The 'Chief of Giants' was as hostile to suitors as he was monstrous in shape, and no wonder! for he knew that on his daughter's marriage his own life would come to an end. Both in this peculiarity and in the description of his ponderous eyebrows, which fell so heavily over his eyes that he could not see until they had been lifted up with forks, he reminds one of the Fomor, Balor. Of his daughter, on the other hand, the Welsh tale gives a description as beautiful as Olwen was herself. 'More yellow was her head than the flower of the broom, and her skin was whiter than the foam of the wave, and fairer were her hands and her fingers than the blossoms of the wood anemone amidst the spray of the meadow fountain. The eye of the trained hawk, the glance of the three-mewed falcon was not brighter than hers. Her bosom was more snowy than the breast of the white swan, her cheek was redder than the reddest roses. Whoso beheld her was filled with her love. Four white trefoils sprung up wherever she trod. And therefore was she called Olwen.'[1]

Culhwch had no need to see her to fall in love with her. He blushed at her very name and asked his father how he could obtain her in marriage. His father reminded him that he was Arthur's cousin and advised him to claim Olwen from him as a boon.

So Culhwch 'pricked forth upon a steed with head dappled grey, of four winters old, firm of limb, with shell-formed hoofs, having a bridle of linked gold on his head, and upon him a saddle of costly gold. And in the youth's hand were two spears of silver, sharp, well-tempered, headed with steel, three ells in length, of an edge to wound the wind and cause blood to flow, and swifter than the fall of the dewdrop from the blade of reed grass upon the earth when the dew of June is at the heaviest. A gold-hilted sword was upon his thigh, the blade of which was of gold, bearing a cross of inlaid gold of the hue of the lightning of heaven. His war horn was of ivory. Before him were two brindled white-breasted greyhounds, having strong collars of rubies about their necks, reaching from the shoulder to the ear. And the one that was on the left side bounded across to the right side, and the one on the right to the left, and like two sea swallows sported around him. And his courser cast up four sods with his four hoofs, like four swallows in the air, about his head, now above, now below. About him was a four-cornered cloth of purple, and an apple of gold was at each corner, and every one of the apples was of the value of an hundred kine. And there was precious gold of the value of three hundred kine upon his shoes, and upon his stirrups, from his knee to the tip of his toe. And the blade of grass bent not beneath him, so light was his courser's tread as he journeyed towards the gate of Arthur's palace.'

Nor did this bold suitor stand greatly upon ceremony. He arrived after the portal of the palace had been closed for the night and, contrary to all precedent, sent to Arthur demanding instant entry. Although, too, it was the custom for visitors to dismount at the horse block at the gate, he did not do so but rode his charger into the hall. After greetings had passed between him and Arthur, and he had announced his name, he demanded Olwen for his bride at the hands of the emperor and his warriors.

Neither Arthur nor any of his court had ever heard of Olwen. However, he promised his cousin either to find her for him or to prove that there was no such person. He ordered his most skilful warriors to accompany Culhwch: Kai, with his companion Bedwyr, the swiftest of men; Kynddelig, who was as good a guide in a strange country as in his own; Gwrhyr, who knew all the languages of men as well as of all other creatures; Gwalchmei, who never left an adventure unachieved; and Menw, who could render himself and his companions invisible at will.

They travelled until they came to a castle on an open plain. Feeding on the plain was a countless herd of sheep and on a mound close by a monstrous shepherd with a monstrous dog. Menw cast a spell over the dog, and they approached the shepherd. He was called Custennin, a brother of Yspaddaden, while his wife was a sister of Culhwch's own mother. The evil chief of giants had reduced his brother to servitude and murdered all his twenty-four sons except one, who was kept hidden in a stone chest. Therefore he welcomed Culhwch and the embassy from Arthur and promised to help them secretly, the more readily since Kai offered to take the one surviving son under his protection. Custennin's wife procured Culhwch a secret meeting with Olwen, and the damsel did not altogether discourage her wooer's suit.

The party started for Yspaddaden's castle. Without raising any alarm, they slew the nine porters and the nine watchdogs, and came unhindered into the hall. They greeted the ponderous giant and announced the reason for their coming.

'Where are my pages and my servants?' he said. 'Raise up the forks beneath my two eyebrows, which have fallen over my eyes, so that I may see the fashion of my son-in-law.' He glared at them and told them to come again upon the next day.

---

[1] That is, 'She of the White Track'. The beauty of Olwen was proverbial in medieval Welsh poetry.

They turned to go, and as they did so Yspaddaden seized a poisoned dart and threw it after them. But Bedwyr caught it and cast it back, wounding the giant's knee. They left him grumbling, slept at the house of Custennin and returned the next morning.

Again they demanded Olwen from her father, threatening him with death if he refused. 'Her four great-grandmothers and her four great-grandsires are yet alive,' replied Yspaddaden. 'It is needful that I take counsel of them.' So they turned away, and as they went he flung a second dart, which Menw caught and hurled back, piercing the giant's body.

The next time they came, Yspaddaden warned them not to shoot at him again unless they desired death. Then he ordered his eyebrows to be lifted up, and as soon as he could see he flung a poisoned dart straight at Culhwch. But the suitor himself caught it and flung it back so that it pierced Yspaddaden's eyeball and came out through the back of his head. Here again we are reminded of the myth of Lugh and Balor. Yspaddaden, however, was not killed, although he was very much discomforted. 'A cursed ungentle son-in-law, truly!' he complained. 'As long as I remain alive my eyesight will be the worse. Whenever I go against the wind, my eyes will water; and peradventure my head will burn, and I shall have a giddiness every new moon. Cursed be the fire in which it was forged! Like the bite of a mad dog is the stroke of this poisoned iron.'

It was now the turn of Culhwch and his party to warn the giant that there must be no more dart-throwing. He appeared, indeed, more amenable to reason and allowed himself to be placed opposite to Culhwch, in a chair, to discuss the amount of his daughter's bride price.

Its terms, as he gradually unfolded them, were terrific. The blood fine paid for Cian to Lugh seems, indeed, a trifle beside it (*see* Chapter 7, 'The Rise of the Sun God'). To obtain grain for food and liquor at his daughter's wedding a vast hill that he showed to Culhwch must be rooted up, levelled, ploughed, sown and harvested in one day. No one could do this except Amaethon, son of Don, the divine husbandman, and Gofannon, son of Don, the divine smith, and they must have the service of three pairs of magic oxen. He must also have returned to him the same nine bushels of flax that he had sown in his youth and had never come up, for only out of this very flax should be made the white wimple for Olwen's head. For mead, too, he must have honey 'nine times sweeter than the honey of the virgin swarm'.

Then followed the enumeration of the thirteen treasures to be paid to him as a dowry. Such a list of wedding presents was surely never known! No pot could hold such honey as he demanded but the magic vessel of Llwyr, the son of Llwyryon. There would not be enough food for all the wedding guests, unless he had the basket of Gwyddneu Garanhir from which all the men in the world could be fed, thrice nine at a time. No cauldron could cook the meat except that of Diwrnach the Gael. The mystic drinking horn of Gwlgawd Gododin must be there, to give them drink. The harp of Teirtu, which, like the Daghda's, played of itself, must make music for them. The giant father-in-law's hair could only be shorn with one instrument – the tusk of Twrch Trwyth, White-tooth, King of the Boars, and not even by that unless it was plucked alive out of its owner's mouth. Also, before the hair could be cut, it must be spread out, and this could not be done until it had been first softened with the blood of the Hag of Hell, the perfectly black sorceress, daughter of the perfectly white sorceress from the Source of the Stream of Sorrow on the borders of hell. Nor could the sorceress's blood be kept warm enough unless it was placed in the bottles of Gwyddolwyn Gorr, which preserved the heat of any liquor put into them, although it was carried from the east of the world to the west. Another set of bottles he must also have to keep milk for his guests in – those bottles of Rhinnon Rhin Barnawd in which no drink ever turned sour. For himself, he required the sword of Gwrnach the Giant, which that personage would never allow out of his own keeping because it was destined that he himself should fall by it. Last of all, he must be given the comb, the razor and the scissors that lay between the ears of Twrch Trwyth, a king changed into the most terrible of wild boars.

It is the chase of this boar that gives the story of 'Culhwch and Olwen' its alternative title – 'The Twrch Trwyth'. The task was one worthy of gods and demigods. Its contemplation might well have appalled Culhwch, who, however, was not so easily frightened. To every fresh demand, every new obstacle put in his way, he gave the same answer:

'It will be easy for me to achieve this, although you may think that it will not be easy.'

Whether it was easy or not will be seen from the conditions under which alone the hunt could be brought to a successful end. No ordinary hounds or huntsmen would do. The chief of the pack must be Drudwyn, the whelp of Greid, led in the one leash that would hold him, fastened by the one chain strong enough to the one collar that would contain his neck. No huntsman could hunt with this dog except Mabon, son of Modron, and he had, ages before, been taken from between his mother and the wall when he was three nights old, and it was not known where he was or even whether he were living or dead. There was only one steed that could carry Mabon, namely Gwynn Mygdwn, the horse of Gweddw. Two other marvellous hounds, the cubs of Gast Rhymhi, must also be obtained; they must be held in the only leash they would not break, for it would be made out of the beard of the giant Dissull, plucked from him while he was still alive. Even with this, no huntsman could lead them except Kynedyr Wyllt, who was himself nine times more wild than the wildest beast upon the mountains. All Arthur's mighty men must come to help, even Gwyn ap Nudd, upon his black horse, and how could he be spared from his terrible duty of restraining the devils in hell from breaking loose and destroying the world?

Here is material for romance indeed! But, unhappily, we shall never know the full story of how all these magic treasures were obtained, all these magic hounds captured and compelled to hunt, all these magic huntsmen brought to help. The story – which has been described as 'saving the finest tales of the "Arabian Nights", the greatest romantic fairy tale the world has ever known' – is not, as we have it now, complete. It reads fully enough, but on casting backwards and forwards between the list of feats to be performed and the body of the tale that is supposed to relate them all, we find many of them lacking. 'The host of Arthur,' we are told, 'dispersed themselves into parties of one and two,' each intent upon some separate quest. The adventures of some of them have come down but those of others have not. We are told how Kai slew Gwrnach the Giant with his own sword; how Gwythyr ap Gwreidawl, Gwyn's rival for the love of Creiddylad, saved an anthill from fire, and how the grateful ants searched for and found the very flax seeds sown by Yspaddaden in his youth; how Arthur's host surrounded and took Gast Rhymhi's cubs, and how Kai and Bedwyr overcame Dissull and plucked out his beard with wooden tweezers to make a leash for them. We learn how Arthur went to Ireland and brought back the cauldron of Diwrnach the Gael full of Irish money; how Twrch Trwyth was chased and killed; and how Arthur condescended to slay the Hag of Hell with his own hand. That others of the treasures were acquired is hinted rather than said. Most important of all (for so much depended on him), we find out where the stolen Mabon was and learn how he was rescued.

The Treasures of Britain, from a drawing by E. W. Wallcousins

So many ages had elapsed since Mabon had disappeared that there seemed little hope of ever finding news of him. Nevertheless Gwrhryr, who spoke the languages of all creatures, went to enquire of that ancient bird, the Ousel of Cilgwri, but the Ousel, although in her time she had pecked a smith's anvil down to the size of a nut, was yet too young to have heard of Mabon. She sent Gwrhryr to a creature formed before her, the Stag of Redynvre. But although the Stag had lived to see an oak sapling slowly grow to be a tree with a thousand branches and as slowly decay again until it was a withered stump, he had never heard of Mabon.

Therefore he sent him on to a creature still older than himself – the Owl of Cwm Cawlwyd. The wood she lived in had been thrice rooted up and had thrice re-sown itself and yet in all that immense time she had never heard of Mabon. There was only one who might have, she told Gwrhryr, and he was the Eagle of Gwern Abwy.

Here at last they struck Mabon's trail. 'The Eagle said: "I have been here for a great space of time, and when I first came hither there was a rock here, from the top of which I pecked at the stars every evening; and now it is not so much as a span high. From that day to this I have been here, and I have never heard of the man for whom you inquire, except once when I went in search of food as far as Llyn Llyw. And when I came there, I struck my talons into a salmon, thinking he would serve me as food for a long time. But he drew me into the deep, and I was scarcely able to escape from him. After that I went with my whole kindred to attack him and to try to destroy him, but he sent messengers and made peace with me; and came and sought me to take fifty fish spears out of his back. Unless he know something of him whom you seek, I cannot tell who may. However, I will guide you to the place where he is."'

It happened that the Salmon did know. With every tide he went up the Severn as far as the walls of Gloucester, and there, he said, he had found such wrong as he had never found anywhere else. So he took Kai and Gwrhryr upon his shoulders and carried them to the wall of the prison where a captive was heard lamenting. This was Mabon, son of Modron, who was suffering such imprisonment as not even Lludd or Greid, the other two of the 'Three Paramount Prisoners of Britain',[1] had endured before him. But it came to an

---

[1]   So says the text, but a triad gives the 'Three Paramount Prisoners of Britain' differently. 'The three supreme prisoners of the Island of Britain, Llyr Llediath in the prison of Euroswydd Wledig, and Madoc, or Mabon, and Gweir, son of Gweiryoth, and one more

end now, for Kai sent to Arthur, and he and his warriors stormed Gloucester and brought Mabon away.

All was at last ready for the final achievement – the hunting of Twrch Trwyth, who was now, with his seven young pigs, in Ireland. Before he was roused, it was thought wise to send the wizard Menw to find out by ocular inspection whether the comb, the scissors and the razor were still between his ears. Menw took the form of a bird and settled upon the boar's head. He saw the coveted treasures and tried to take one of them, but Twrch Trwyth shook himself so violently that some of the venom from his bristles spurted over Menw, who was never quite well again from that day.

Then the hunt was up, the men surrounded him, and the dogs were loosed at him from every side. On the first day, the Irish attacked him. On the second day, Arthur's household encountered him and were worsted. Then Arthur himself fought with him for nine days and nine nights without even killing one of the little pigs.

A truce was now called so that Gwrhryr, who spoke all languages, might go and parley with him. Gwrhryr begged him to give up in peace the comb, the scissors and the razor, which were all that Arthur wanted. But the Boar Trwyth, indignant at having been so annoyed, would not. On the contrary, he promised to go on the morrow into Arthur's country and do all the harm he could there.

So Twrch Trwyth with his seven pigs crossed the sea into Wales, and Arthur followed with his warriors in the ship *Prydwen*. Here the story becomes wonderfully realistic and circumstantial. We are told of every place they passed through on the long chase through South Wales and can trace the course of the hunt over the map. We know of every check the huntsmen had and what happened every time the boars turned to bay. The 'casualty list' of Arthur's men is completely given; and we can also follow the shrinking of Twrch Trwyth's herd, as his little pigs fell one by one. None was left but Trwyth the boar king himself by the time the Severn estuary was reached, at the mouth of the River Wye.

Here the hunt came with him and drove him into the water, and in this un-

---

exalted than the three, and that was Arthur, who was for three nights in the Castle of Oeth and Anoeth, and three nights in the prison of Wen Pendragon, and three nights in the dark prison under the stone. And one youth released him from these three prisons; that youth was Goreu, the son of Custennin, his cousin.'

familiar element he was outmatched. Osla Big Knife,[1] Manawydan fab Llyr, Kacmwri, the servant of Arthur, and Gwyngelli caught him by his four feet and plunged his head under water, while the two chief huntsmen, Mabon, son of Modron, and Kynedyr Wyllt, came, one on each side of him, and took the scissors and the razor. Before they could get the comb, however, he shook himself free and struck out for Cornwall, leaving Osla and Kacmwri half-drowned in the Severn.

And all this trouble, we are told, was mere play compared with the trouble they had with him in Cornwall before they could get the comb. But at last they secured it and drove the boar out over the deep sea. He passed out of sight, with two of the magic hounds in pursuit of him, and none of them has ever been heard of since.

The sight of these treasures, paraded before Yspaddaden, chief of giants, was of course his death warrant. All who wished him ill came to gloat over his downfall. But they should have been put to shame by the giant, whose end had, at least, a certain dignity. 'My daughter,' he said to Culhwch, 'is yours, but you need not thank me for it, but Arthur, who has accomplished all this. By my free will you should never have had her, for with her I lose my life.'

Thereupon they cut off his head and put it upon a pole, and that night the undutiful Olwen became Culhwch's bride.

---

[1] The 'big knife' was, we are told in the story, 'a short broad dagger. When Arthur and his hosts came before a torrent they would seek for a narrow place where they might pass the water, and would lay the sheathed dagger across the torrent, and it would form a bridge sufficient for the armies of the three islands of Britain, and of the three islands adjacent, with their spoil.'

Chapter 25

THE GODS AS KING ARTHUR'S KNIGHTS

It is not, however, by such fragments of legend that Arthur is best known to English readers. Not Arthur the god but Arthur the 'blameless king', who founded the Table Round, from which he sent forth his knights 'to ride abroad redressing human wrongs' as described in Tennyson's *Idylls of the King*, is the figure whom the name conjures up. Nor is it even from Sir Thomas Malory's *Morte D'Arthur* that this concept comes to most of us but from Tennyson's *Idylls of the King*, but Tennyson so modernised the ancient tradition that it retains little of the old Arthur but the name. He tells us himself that his poem had but very slight relation to:

> . . . 'that grey king, whose name, a ghost,
> Streams like a cloud, man-shaped, from mountain peak,
> And cleaves to cairn and cromlech still; or him
> Of Geoffrey's book, or him of Malleor's . . .'

but that he merely used the legend to give a substantial form to his ideal figure of the perfect English gentleman – a title to which the original Arthur could scarcely have laid claim. Still less does there remain in it the least trace of anything that could suggest mythology.

As much as this, however, might be said of Malory's book. We may be fairly certain that the good Sir Thomas had no idea that the personages of whom he wrote had ever been anything different from the Christian knights that they had become in the late French romances from which he compiled his own fifteenth-century work. The old gods had been, from time to time, very completely euhemerised. The characters of the 'Four Branches of the Mabinogi' are still recognisable as divine beings. In the later Welsh stories, however, their divinity merely hangs about them in shreds and tatters, and the first Norman adapters of these stories made them still more definitely human. By the time Malory came to build up his *Morte D'Arthur* from the foreign romances, they had altered so much that the shapes and deeds of gods could only be recognised under their medieval knightly disguises by those who had known them in their ancient forms.

We have chosen Malory's *Morte D'Arthur* as almost the sole representative of Arthurian literature later than the Welsh poems and prose stories, for three reasons. Firstly, because it is the English Arthurian romance *par excellence* from which all later English authors, including Tennyson, drew their material. Secondly, because the mass of foreign literature dealing with the subject of Arthur is in itself a life study and could not by any possibility be compressed within the limits of a chapter. Thirdly, because Malory's fine judgment caused him to choose the best and most typical foreign tales to weave into his own romance, and hence it is that we find most of our old British gods – both those of the earlier cycle and those of the system connected with Arthur – striding disguised through his pages.

Curiously enough, Sir Edward Strachey, in his preface to the 'Globe' edition of Caxton's *Morte D'Arthur*, uses almost the same image to describe Malory's prose poem that Matthew Arnold handled with such effect in his *Study of Celtic Literature* to point out the real nature of the Mabinogion. 'Malory,' he says, 'has built a great, rambling, medieval castle, the walls of which enclose rude and even ruinous work of earlier times.' How rude and how ruinous these relics were Malory doubtless had not the least idea, for he has completely jumbled the ancient mythology. Not only do gods of the older and newer order appear together, but the same deities, under very often only slightly varying names, come up again and again as totally different characters.

Take, for example, the ancient deity of death and Hades. As King Brandegore or Brandegoris (Bran of Gower), he brings five thousand mounted men to oppose King Arthur, but as Sir Brandel or Brandiles (Bran of Gwales[1]), he is a valiant Knight of the Round Table, who dies fighting in Arthur's service. Again, under his name of Uther Pendragon (Uther Ben), he is Arthur's father, although as King Ban of Benwyck (the 'Square Enclosure', doubtless the same as Taliesin's *Caer Pedryvan* and Malory's *Carbonek*), he is a foreign monarch who is Arthur's ally. Yet again, as the father of Guinevere, Ogyrvran has be-

---

[1] Grassholm Island, the scene of 'The Entertaining of the Noble Head'.

come Leodegrance. As King Uriens or Urience of Gore (Gower), he marries one of Arthur's sisters, fights against him but finally tenders his submission and is enrolled among his knights. Urien may also be identified in the *Morte D'Arthur* as King Rience or Ryons of North Wales and as King Nentres of Garloth, while, to crown the varied disguises of this Proteus of British gods, he appears in an isolated episode as Balan, who fights with his brother Balin until they kill one another.

One may generally tell the divinities of the underworld in these romances by their connection not with the settled and civilised parts of England but with the wild and remote north and west and the still wilder and remoter islands. Just as Bran and Urien are kings of Gower, so Arawn, under the corruptions of his name into 'Anguish' and 'Anguissance', is made King of Scotland or Ireland, both countries having been probably confounded as the same land of the Scotti or Gaels. Pwyll, Head of Annwn, we likewise discover under two disguises. As Pelles, 'King of the Foreign Country'[2] and Keeper of the Holy Grail, he is a personage of great mythological significance, albeit the real nature of him and his surroundings has been overlaid with a Christian veneer as foreign to the original of Pelles as his own kingdom was to Arthur's knights. The Chief of Hades figures as a 'cousin nigh unto Joseph of Arimathie', who, 'while he might ride supported much Christendom and holy church'. He is represented as the father of Elayne (Elen), whom he gives in marriage to Sir Launcelot, bestowing upon the couple a residence called 'Castle Bliant', the name of which, there is good evidence to show, is connected with that of Pwyll's vassal called Ternyon in the first of the Mabinogi. Under his other name of Sir Pelleas – the hero of Tennyson's Idyll of *Pelleas and Ettarre* – the primitive myth of Pwyll is touched at a different point. After his unfortunate love passage with Ettarre (or Ettard, as Malory calls her), Pelleas is represented as marrying Nimue, whose original name, Rhiannon, reached this form as well as that of 'Vivien' through a series of miscopyings of successive scribes.

With Pelles or Pelleas is associated a King Pellean or Pellam, his son, and equally with him the Keeper of the Grail, who can be no other than Pryderi. Like that deity in the Mabinogi of Math, he is defeated by one of the gods of light. The dealer of the blow, however, is not Arthur, as successor to Gwydion, but Balin, the Gallo-British sun god Belenus.

Another dark deity, Gwyn ap Nudd, we discover under all of his three titles. Called variously Sir Gwinas, Sir Guynas and Sir Gwenbaus by Malory in the *Morte D'Arthur*, the Welsh Gwynwas (or Gwyn) is altogether on Arthur's side. The Cornish Melwas, split into two different knights, divides his allegiance. As Sir Melias or Meleaus de Lile ('of the Isle'), he is a Knight of the Round Table, although, on the quarrel between Arthur and Launcelot, he sides with the knight against the king. But as Sir Meliagraunce or Meliagaunce it is he who, as in the older myth, captures Queen Guinevere and carries her off to his castle. Under his Somerset name of Avallon or Avallach, he is connected with the episode of the Grail. King Evelake is a Saracen ruler who was converted by Joseph of Arimathea and brought by him to Britain. In his convert's enthusiasm, he attempted the quest of the holy vessel but was not allowed to succeed. As a consolation, however, it was divinely promised him that he should not die until he had seen a knight of his blood in the ninth degree who should achieve it. This was done by Sir Percival, King Evelake being then three hundred years old.

Turning from deities of darkness to deities of light, we find the sky god figuring largely in the *Morte D'Arthur*. The Lludd of the earlier mythology is Malory's King Loth or Lot of Orkney, through an intrigue with whose wife Arthur becomes the father of Sir Mordred. Lot's wife was the mother also of Sir Gawain or Gauvain, whose birth Malory does not, however, attribute to Arthur, although such must have been the original form of the myth. Sir Gawain of the Arthurian legend is the Gwalchmei of the Welsh stories, the successor of the still earlier Lleu Llaw Gyffes, just as Sir Mordred – the Welsh Medrawd – corresponds to Lleu's brother Dylan. As Sir Mordred retains the dark character of Medrawd, so Sir Gawain, even in Malory, shows the attributes of a solar deity. We are told that his strength increased gradually from dawn until high noon, and then as gradually decreased again – a piece of pagan symbolism that forms a good example of the appositeness of Sir Edward Strachey's figure, for it stands out of the medieval narrative like an ancient brick in some more modern building.

The Zeus of the later cycle, Emrys or Myrddin, appears in the *Morte D'Arthur* under both his names. The word 'Emrys' becomes 'Bors', and King Bors of Gaul is made a brother of King Ban of Benwyck – that is, Bran of the Square Enclosure, the ubiquitous underworld god. Myrddin we meet under no such disguise. The ever popular Merlin still retains intact the attributes of the sky god. He remains above and apart from all the knights, higher even in some respects than King Arthur to whom he stands in much the same position as

The beguiling of Merlin

Math does to Gwydion in the Mabinogi. Like Math, he is an enchanter, and, like Math, too, who could hear everything said in the world in however low a tone if only the wind met it, he is practically omniscient. The account of his final disappearance, as told in the *Morte D'Arthur*, is only a re-embellishment of the original story, the nature myth giving place to what novelists call 'a feminine interest'. Everyone knows how the great magician fell into a dotage upon the 'lady of the lake', whom Malory calls Nimue and Tennyson Vivien – both names being that of Rhiannon in disguise. As the *Morte D'Arthur* has it, 'Merlin would let her have no rest, but always he would be with her . . . and she was ever passing weary of him, and fain would have been delivered of him, for she was afeard of him because he was a devil's son, and she could not put him away by no means. And so on a time it happed that Merlin showed to her in a rock whereas was a great wonder, and wrought by enchantment, that went under a great stone. So, by her subtle working, she made Merlin to go under that stone to let her wit of the marvels there, but she wrought so there for him that he never came out for all the craft that he could do. And so she departed and left Merlin.'

Merlin's living grave is still to be seen at the end of the *Val des Fées* in the forest of Brecilien in Brittany. The tomb of stone is certainly only a prosaic equivalent for the tower of woven air in which the heaven god went to his rest. Still, it is not quite so unpoetic as the leather sack in which Rhiannon, the original of Nimue, caught and imprisoned Gwawl, the earlier Merlin, like a badger in a bag (*see* Chapter 19, 'The Adventures of the Gods of Annwn').

Elen, Myrddin's consort, appears in Malory as five different Elaines. Two of them are wives of the dark god under his names of King Ban and King Nentres. A third is called the daughter of King Pellinore, a character of uncertain origin. But the two most famous are the ladies who loved Sir Launcelot – Elaine the Fair, Elaine the Lovable, Elaine the Lily Maid of Astolat,[1] and the luckier and less scrupulous Elaine, daughter of King Pelles and mother of Sir Launcelot's son, Galahad.

But it is time, now that the most important figures of British mythology have been shown under their knightly disguises and their place in Arthurian legend indicated, to pass on to some account of the real subject matter of Sir Thomas Malory's romance. Externally, it is the history of an Arthur, King of Britain, whom most people of Malory's time considered as eminently a histori-

---

[1] Whose story is told by Tennyson in the *Idylls* and by Malory in the *Morte D'Arthur*.

Sir Galahad, from a painting by G. F. Watts RA

cal character. Around this central narrative of Arthur's reign and deeds are grouped in the form of episodes the personal exploits of the knights believed to have supported him by forming a kind of household guard. But with the exception of a little magnified and distorted legendary history, the whole cycle of romance may be ultimately resolved into a few myths, not only retold but recombined in several forms by their various tellers. The Norman adapters of the *Matière de Bretagne* found the British mythology already in the process of transformation, some of the gods having dwindled into human warriors and others into hardly less human druids and magicians. Under their hands the British warriors became Norman knights who did their deeds of prowess in the tilt yard and found their inspiration in the fantastic chivalry popularised by the *Trouvères*, while the druids put off their still somewhat barbaric druidism for the more conventional magic of the Latin races. More than this, as soon as the real sequence and *raison d'être* of the tales had been lost sight of, their adapters used a free hand in reweaving them. Most of the romancers had their favourite characters whom they made the central figure in their stories. Sir Gawain, Sir Percival, Sir Tristan and Sir Owain (all of them probably once local British sun gods) appear as the most important personages of the romances called after their names, stories of the doughty deeds of christened knights who had little left about them either of Briton or of pagan.

It is only the labours of scholars that can bring back to us at this late date things long forgotten when Malory's book was issued from Caxton's press. But oblivion is not annihilation, and the old myths lying embedded in their later setting can be pointed out with almost the same certainty with which the geologist can show us the fossils in rock. Thus treated, they resolve themselves into three principal motifs, prominent everywhere in Celtic mythology: the birth of the sun god, the struggle between light and darkness, and the raiding of the underworld by friendly gods for the good of mankind.

The first has been already dealt with in Chapter 23, 'The Mythological Arrival of Arthur'. It is the retelling of the story of the origin of the sun god in the Mabinogi of Math fab Mathonwy. For Gwydion we now have Arthur. Instead of Aranrhod, the wife of the superannuated sky god Nwyvre, we find the wife of King Lot, the superannuated sky god Lludd. Lleu Llaw Gyffes rises again as Sir Gawain (Gwalchmei) and Dylan as Sir Mordred (Medrawd), while the wise Merlin, the Jupiter of the new system, takes the place of his wise prototype, Math. Connected with this first myth is the second – the struggle between light and darkness of which there are several versions in the *Morte D'Arthur*. The leading one is the rebellion of the evilly disposed Sir Mordred against Arthur and Sir Gawain, while on other stages Balan – the dark god Bran – fights with Balin – the sun god Belenus; and the same Balin or Belenus gives an almost mortal stroke to Pellam, the Pryderi of the older mythology.

The same myth has also a wider form, in which the battle is waged for possession of a maiden. Thus (to seek no other instances) Gwenhwyvar was contended for by Arthur and Medrawd, or, in an earlier form of the myth, by Arthur and Gwyn. In the *Morte D'Arthur*, Gwyn, under the corruption of his Cornish name Melwas into 'Sir Meliagraunce', still captures Guinevere, but it is no longer Arthur who rescues her. That task, or privilege, has fallen to a new champion. It is Sir Launcelot who follows Sir Meliagraunce, defeats and slays him, and rescues the fair captive. But Sir Launcelot, it must be stated – probably to the surprise of those to whom the Arthurian story without Launcelot and Queen Guinevere must seem almost like the play of 'Hamlet with Hamlet left out' – is unknown to the original tradition. Welsh song and story are silent with regard to him, and he is not improbably a creation of some Norman romancer who calmly appropriated to his hero's credit deeds earlier told of other 'knights'.

But the romantic treatment of these two myths by the adapters of the *Matière de Bretagne* are of smaller interest to us now than that of the third. The attraction of the Arthurian story lies no less in the battles of Arthur or the loves of Guinevere than in the legend that has given it its lasting popularity – the Christian romance of the Quest of the Holy Grail. So great and various has been the inspiration of this legend to works of art, literature and music that it seems almost a kind of sacrilege to trace it back, like the rest of Arthur's story, to a paganism that could not have even understood, much less created, its mystic beauty. Nonetheless the whole story is directly evolved from primitive pagan myths concerning a miraculous cauldron of fertility and inspiration.

In the later romances, the Holy Grail is a Christian relic of marvellous potency. In the *Morte D'Arthur* It held the Paschal lamb eaten at the Last Supper, and after the death of Christ, Joseph of Arimathea had filled it with the Saviour's blood. But before it received this tradition, it had been the magic cauldron of all the Celtic mythologies – the Daghda's 'Undry', which fed all who came to it and from which none went away unsatisfied (*see* Chapter 5, 'The Gods of the Gaels'), Bran's cauldron of Renovation, which brought the dead back to life (*see* Chapter 20, 'The Wooing of Branwen and the Beheading of Bran), the cauldron of Ogyrvran the Giant from which the Muses ascended (*see* Chapter 23, 'The Mythological Arrival of Arthur'), the cauldrons captured by Cúchulainn from the King of the Shadowy City (*see* Chapter 12, 'The Irish Iliad') and by Arthur from the chief of Hades (*see* Chapter 23 – 'The Mythological Arrival of Arthur') as well as several other mythical vessels of less note.

In its transition from pagan to Christian form, hardly one of the features of the ancient myth has been really obscured. We may recount the chief attributes, as Taliesin tells them in his 'Spoiling of Annwn', of the cauldron captured by Arthur. It was the property of Pwyll and of his son Pryderi, who lived in a kingdom of the Otherworld called, among other titles, the Revolving Castle, the Four-cornered Castle, the Castle of Revelry, the Kingly Castle, the Glass Castle and the Castle of Riches. This place was surrounded by the sea and in other ways made difficult of access. There was no lack of wine there, and its happy inhabitants spent, with music and feasting, an existence that neither disease nor old age could assail. As for the cauldron, it had a rim of pearls around its edge; the fire beneath it was kept fanned by the breaths of nine maidens; it spoke, doubtless in words of prophetic wisdom; and it would not cook the food of a liar or coward (*see* Chapter 23, 'The Mythological Arrival of Arthur). Here we have considerable data on which to base a parallel between the pagan cauldron and the Christian Grail.

Nor have we far to go in search of correspondences, for they are nearly all preserved in Malory's romance. The mystic vessel was kept by King Pelles, who is Pwyll, in a castle called Carbonek, a name that resolves itself in the hands of the philologist into *Caer bannawg*, the 'square' or 'four-cornered castle' – in other words, the *Caer Pedryvan* of Taliesin's poem. Of the character of the place as a Castle of Riches and a Castle of Revelry, where 'bright wine was the drink of the host', we have more than a hint in the account in the *Morte D'Arthur*, twice given, of how, upon the appearance of the Grail – borne, it should be noticed, by a maiden or angel – the hall was filled with good odours and every knight found on the table all the kinds of meat and drink he could imagine as most desirable. It could not be seen by sinners, a Christian refinement of the savage idea of a pot that would not cook a coward's food, but the sight of it alone would cure the wounds and sickness of those who approached it faithfully and humbly, and in its presence neither old age nor sickness could oppress them, this last attribute not being mentioned by Malory

The Cauldron of Inspiration, from a drawing by E. Wallcousins

but stated in the romance called *Seint Greal*. And although in Malory we find no reference either to the spot having been surrounded by water or to the castle as a 'revolving' one, we have only to turn from the *Morte D'Arthur* to the *Seint Greal* to discover both. Gwalchmei, going to the castle of King Peleur (Pryderi), finds it encircled by a great water, while Peredur, approaching the same place, sees it turning with greater speed than the swiftest wind. Moreover, archers on the walls shoot so vigorously that no armour can resist their shafts, which explains how it happened that, of those who went with Arthur, 'except seven, none returned from Caer Sidi'.

It is noticeable that Arthur himself never attempts the quest of the Grail, although it was he who had achieved its pagan original. We find in Malory four competitors for the mantle of Arthur – Sir Pelleas, Sir Bors, Sir Percival and Sir Galahad. The first of these may be put out of court at once. Sir Pelleas, who, being himself Pelles or Pwyll, the keeper of it, could have had no reason for such exertions. At the second we may look doubtfully, for Sir Bors is no other than Emrys or Myrddin, and, casting back to the earlier British mythology, we do not find the sky god personally active in securing boons by force or craft from the underworld. The other two have better claims – Sir Percival and Sir Galahad. 'Sir Percival' is the Norman-French name for Peredur, the hero of a story in the Red Book of Hergest, which gives the oldest form of a Grail quest we have. It dates from before the Norman romances and forms almost a connecting link between tales of mythology and of chivalry. Peredur or Sir Percival, therefore, is the oldest, most primitive of Grail seekers. On the other hand, Sir Galahad is the latest and youngest. But there is reason to believe that Galahad, in Welsh 'Gwalchaved', the 'Falcon of Summer', is the same solar hero as Gawain, in Welsh 'Gwalchmei', the 'Falcon of May'. Both are made, in the story of 'Culhwch and Olwen', sons of the same mother, Gwyar. Sir Gawain himself is in one Arthurian romance the achiever of the Grail. It is needless to attempt to choose between these two. Both have the attributes of sun gods. Gwalchmei, the successor of Lleu Llaw Gyffes, and Peredur Paladrhir, that is to say, the 'Spearman with the Long Shaft', may be allowed to claim equal honours. What is important is that the quest of the Grail, once the chief treasure of Hades, is still accomplished by one who takes, in later legend, the place of Lleu Llaw Gyffes and Lugh Lamhfada in the earlier British and Gaelic myths as a long-armed solar deity victorious in his strife against the Powers of Darkness.

Chapter 26

THE DECLINE AND FALL OF THE GODS

If there be love of fame in celestial minds, those gods might count themselves fortunate who shared in the transformation of Arthur. Their divinity had fallen from them, but in their new roles as heroes of romance they entered upon vivid reincarnations. The names of Arthur's Knights of the Round Table might almost be described as household names, while the gods who were allocated no part in the Table Round are known only to those who busy themselves with antiquarian lore. It is true that a few folktales survived into the early twentieth century in the remoter parts of Wales in which the names of such ancient British deities as Gwydion, Gwyn, Aranrhod and Dylan appear, but it was in such a chaos of jumbled and distorted legend that it was hard to pick out even the slenderest thread of story. They had none of the definite coherence of the contemporary Gaelic folktales quoted in a previous chapter as still preserving the myths about Goibhniu, Lugh, Cian, Manannán, Ethlinn and Balor.

There have been, however, other paths by which the fame of a god might descend to a posterity that would no longer credit his divinity. The rolls of early British history were open to welcome any number of mythical personages provided that their legends were attractive. Geoffrey of Monmouth's famous work is, under its grave pretence of exact history, as mythological as the *Morte D'Arthur* or even the Mabinogion. The annals of early British saintship were not less accommodating. A god whose tradition was too potent to be ignored or extinguished was canonised as a matter of course by clerics who held as an axiom that 'the toleration of the cromlech facilitated the reception of the Gospel.' Only the most irreconcilable escaped them – such a one as Gwyn ap Nudd, who, found almost useless by Geoffrey and intractable by the monkish writers, remains the last survivor of the old gods – dwindled to the proportions of a fairy but unsubdued.

This part of resistance is perhaps the most dignified, for deities can be sadly changed by the caprices of their euhemerisers. Don, whom we knew as the mother of the heaven gods, seems strangely described as a *king* of Lochlin and Dublin who led the Irish into north Wales in AD 267, as described in the Iolo manuscript. More recognisable is *his* son Gwydion, who introduced the knowledge of letters into the country of his adoption. The dynasty of 'King' Don, according to the Iolo manuscript, held north Wales for a hundred and twenty-nine years, when the North British king, Cunedda, invaded the country, defeated the Irish in a great battle and drove them across the sea to the Isle of Man. This battle is historical, and, putting Don and Gwydion out of the question, probably represented the last stand of the Gael in the extreme west of Britain against the second and stronger wave of Celtic invasion. In the same collection of Iolo manuscripts is found a curious and even comic euhemeristic version of the strange myth of the bone prison of Oeth and Anoeth, which Manawydan fab Llyr, built in Gower. The new reading makes that ghastly abode a real building, constructed out of the bones of the 'Caesarians' (Romans) killed in battle with the Cymri. It consisted of numerous chambers, some of large bones and some of small, some above ground and some under. Prisoners of war were placed in the more comfortable cells, the underground dungeons being kept for traitors to their country. Several times the 'Caesarians' demolished the prison, but each time the Cymri rebuilt it stronger than before. At last, however, the bones decayed and, being spread upon the ground, made an excellent manure! 'From that time forth' the people of the neighbourhood 'had astonishing crops of wheat and barley and of every other grain for many years'.

It is not, however, in these, so to speak, unauthorised narratives that we can best refind our British deities but in the compact, coherent and at times almost convincing *Historia Regum Britanniae* of Geoffrey of Monmouth, published in the first half of the twelfth century and for hundreds of years gravely quoted as the leading authority on the early history of our islands. The more modern critical spirit, of course, relegated it to the region of fable. We can no longer accept the pleasant tradition of the descent of the Britons from the survivors of Troy led westward in search of a new home by Brutus, the great-grandson of the pious Aeneas. Nor indeed does any portion of the History, from Aeneas to Athelstan, quite persuade the latter-day reader. Its kings succeed one another in plausible sequence, but they themselves are too obviously the heroes of popular legend.

A large part of Geoffrey's chronicle – two books out of twelve – is, of course, devoted to Arthur. In it he tells the story of that paladin's conquests not only in his own country against the Saxons, the Irish, the Scots and the Picts but over all western Europe. We see the British champion, after annexing Ireland, Iceland, Gothland and Orkney, following up these minor victories by subduing Norway, Dacia (by which Denmark seems to have been meant), Aquitaine and Gaul. After such triumphs there was clearly nothing left for him but the overthrow of the Roman empire, and this he had practically achieved when the rebellion of Mordred brought him home to his death, or rather (for even Geoffrey does not quite lose hold of the belief in the undying Arthur) to be carried to the island of Avallon to be healed of his wounds, the crown of Britain falling to 'his kinsman Constantine, the son of Cador, Duke of Cornwall, in the five hundred and forty-second year of our Lord's incarnation'. On the more personal incidents connected with Arthur, Geoffrey openly professes to keep silence, possibly regarding them as not falling within the province of his History, but we are told shortly how Mordred took advantage of Arthur's absence on the Continent to seize the throne, marry Guanhamara (Guinevere) and ally himself with the Saxons, only to be defeated at that fatal battle, called by Geoffrey 'Cambula', in which Mordred, Arthur and Walgan – the 'Sir Gawain' of Malory and the Gwalchmei of the earlier legends – all met their dooms.

We find the gods of the older generation standing in the same position with regard to Arthur in Geoffrey's History as they do in the later Welsh triads and tales. Alhough rulers, they are still his vassals. In 'three brothers of royal blood', called Lot, Urian and Augusel, who are represented as having been chiefs in the north, we may discern Lludd, Urien and Arawn. To these three Arthur restored 'the rights of their ancestors', handing over the semi-sovereignty of Scotland to Augusel, giving Urian the government of Murief (Moray) and re-establishing Lot 'in the consulship of Loudonesia [Lothian], and the other provinces belonging to him'. Two other rulers subject to him are Gunvasius, King of Orkney, and Malvasius, King of Iceland, in whom we recognise Gwyn under Latinised forms of his Welsh name Gwynwas and his Cornish name Melwas. But it is characteristic of Geoffrey of Monmouth's loose hold on his materials that, not content with having connected several of these gods with Arthur's period he further endows them with reigns of their own. Urien was Arthur's vassal, but Urianus was himself King of Britain centuries before Arthur was born. Lud (that is, Lludd) succeeded his father, Beli. We hear nothing of his silver hand, but we learn that he was 'famous for the building of cities and for rebuilding the walls of Trinovantum,[1] which he also surrounded with innumerable towers . . . and though he had many other cities, yet he loved this above them all, and resided in it the greater part of the year, for which reason it was afterwards called Kaerlud, and by the corruption of the word, Caerlondon, and again by change of languages, in process of time, London, as also by foreigners who arrived here, and reduced this country under their subjection, it was called Londres. At last, when he was dead, his body was buried by the gate which to this time is called in the British tongue after his name Parthlud, and in the Saxon, Ludesgata.' He was succeeded by his brother, Cassibellawn (Cassivelaunus) during whose reign Julius Caesar first invaded Britain.

Lludd, however, is not entirely dependent upon Geoffrey of Monmouth for his reputation as a king of Britain. One of the old Welsh romances, 'The Story of Lludd and Llefelys' in the Mabinogion, relates the rebuilding of London by Lludd in almost the same words as Geoffrey. The story that these pseudo-historical details introduce is, however, an obviously mythological one. It tells us how, in the days of Lludd, Britain was oppressed by three plagues. The first was the arrival of a strange race of sorcerers called the Coranaid (the name means 'dwarfs'), who had three qualities that made them unpopular: they paid their way in 'fairy money', which, although apparently real, returned afterwards – like the shields, horses and hounds made by Gwydion, son of Don, to deceive Pryderi – into the fungus out of which it had been charmed by magic; they could hear everything that was said over the whole of Britain in however low a tone provided only that the wind met it; and they could not be injured by any weapon. The second was 'a shriek that came on every May eve over every hearth in the island of Britain, and went through people's hearts and so scared them that the men lost their hue and their strength, and the women their children, and the young men and the maidens their senses, and all the animals and trees and the earth and the waters were left barren'. The third was a disappearance of the food hoarded in the king's palace, which was so com-

[1] That is, London, under its traditional earlier name, Troja Nova, given it by Brutus.

plete that a year's provisions vanished in a single night and so mysterious that no one could ever find out its cause.

By the advice of his nobles, Lludd went to France to obtain the help of its king, his brother Llefelys, who was 'a man great of counsel and wisdom'. In order to be able to consult with his brother without being overheard by the Coranaid, Llefelys caused a long tube of brass to be made through which they talked to one another. The sorcerer tribe, however, got to know of it, and although they could not hear what was being said inside the speaking tube, they sent a demon into it who whispered insulting messages up and down it, as though from one brother to the other. But Lludd and Llefelys knew one another too well to be deceived by this stratagem, and they drove the demon out of the tube by flooding it with wine. Then Llefelys told Lludd to take certain insects, which he would give him, and pound them in water. When the water was sufficiently permeated with their essence, he was to call both his own people and the Coranaid together, as though for a conference, and in the midst of the meeting to cast it over all of them alike. The water, although harmless to his own people, would nevertheless prove a deadly poison to the Coranaid.

As for the shriek, Llefelys explained it to be raised by a dragon. This monster was the Red Dragon of Britain, and it raised the shriek because it was being attacked by the White Dragon of the Saxons, which was trying to overcome and destroy it. The French king told his brother to measure the length and breadth of Britain and, when he had found the exact centre of the island, to cause a pit to be dug there. In this pit was to be placed a vessel containing the best mead that could be made, with a covering of satin over it to hide it. Lludd was then to watch from some safe place. The dragons would appear and fight in the air until they were exhausted, then they would fall together on to the top of the satin cloth and so draw it down with them into the vessel full of mead. Naturally they would drink the mead, and, equally naturally, they would then sleep. As soon as Lludd was sure that they were helpless, he was to go to the pit, wrap the satin cloth round both of them and bury them together in a stone coffin in the strongest place in Britain. If this were safely done, there would be no more heard of the shriek.

And the disappearance of the food was caused by 'a mighty man of magic', who put everyone to sleep by charms before he removed the king's provisions. Lludd was to watch for him, sitting by the side of a cauldron full of cold water.

As often as he felt the approach of drowsiness, he was to plunge into the cauldron. Thus he would be able to keep awake and frustrate the thief.

So Lludd came back to Britain. He pounded the insects in the water and then summoned both the men of Britain and the Coranaid to a meeting. In the midst of it, he sprinkled the water over everyone alike. The natives took no harm from this mythological 'beetle powder', but all the Coranaid died.

Lludd was then ready to deal with the dragons. His careful measurements proved that the centre of the island of Britain was at Oxford, and there he caused the pit to be dug, with the vessel of mead in it, hidden by the satin covering. Having made everything ready, he watched and soon saw the dragons appear. For a long time they fought desperately in the air, then they fell down together on to the satin cloth and, drawing it after them, subsided into the mead. Lludd waited until they were quite silent and then pulled them out, folded them carefully in the wrapping and took them to the district of Snowdon, where he buried them in the strong fortress whose remains, near Beddgelert, are still called Dinas Emrys. After this the terrible shriek was not heard again until Merlin had them dug up five hundred years later, when they recommenced fighting, and the red dragon drove the white one out of Britain.

Last of all, Lludd prepared a great banquet in his hall and watched over it, armed, with the cauldron of water near him. In the middle of the night, he heard soft, drowsy music, such as nearly put him to sleep, but he kept awake by repeatedly dipping himself in the cold water. Just before dawn a huge man clad in armour came into the hall, carrying a basket that he began to load with the viands on the table. Like the bag in which Pwyll captured Gwawl, its holding capacity seemed endless. However, the man filled it at last and was carrying it out when Lludd stopped him. They fought, and Lludd conquered the man of magic and made him his vassal. Thus the 'Three Plagues of Britain' came to an end.

Lludd, in changing from god to king, seems to have lost most of his old mythological attributes. Even his daughter Creiddylad is taken from him and given to another of the ancient British deities. Why Lludd, the sky god, should have been confounded with Llyr, the sea god, is not very apparent, but it is certain that Creiddylad of the early Welsh legends and poems is the same as Geoffrey's Cordeilla and Shakespeare's Cordelia. The great dramatist was ultimately indebted to the Celtic mythology for the groundwork of the legend that he wove into the tragic story of King Lear. 'Leir', as Geoffrey calls him in

Historia Regum Britanniae, was the son of Bladud, who built Caer Badus (Bath) and perished, like Icarus, as the result of an accident with a flying machine of his own invention. Having no sons, but three daughters, Gonorilla, Regan and Cordeilla, he thought in his old age of dividing his kingdom among them. But first of all he decided to make a trial of their affection for him with the idea of giving the best portions of his realm to the most worthy. Gonorilla, the eldest, replied to his question of how much she loved him, 'that she called heaven to witness, she loved him more than her own soul'. Regan answered 'with an oath, "that she could not otherwise express her thoughts, but that she loved him above all creatures"'. But when it came to Cordeilla's turn, the youngest daughter, disgusted with her sisters' hypocrisy, spoke after a quite different fashion. "'My father," said she, "is there any daughter that can love her father more than duty requires? In my opinion, whoever pretends to it, must disguise her real sentiments under the veil of flattery. I have always loved you as a father, nor do I yet depart from my purposed duty, and if you insist to have something more extorted from me, hear now the greatness of my affection, which I always bear you, and take this for a short answer to all your questions; look how much you have, so much is your value, and so much do I love you."' Her enraged father immediately bestowed his kingdom upon his two other daughters, marrying them to the two highest of his nobility, Gonorilla to Maglaunus, Duke of Albania,[1] and Regan to Henuinus, Duke of Cornwall. To Cordeilla he not only refused a share in his realm but even a dowry. Aganippus, King of the Franks, married her, however, for her beauty alone.

Once in possession, Leir's two sons-in-law rebelled against him and deprived him of all regal authority. The sole recompense for his lost power was an agreement by Maglaunus to allow him maintenance, with a bodyguard of sixty soldiers. But after two years, the Duke of Albania, at his wife Gonorilla's instigation, reduced them to thirty. Resenting this, Leir left Maglaunus and went to Henuinus, the husband of Regan. The Duke of Cornwall at first received him honourably but before a year was out compelled him to discharge all his attendants except five. This sent him back in a rage to his eldest daughter, who this time swore that he should not stay with her unless he would be satisfied with one serving man only. In despair, Leir resolved to through himself upon the mercy of Cordeilla and, full of contrition for the way he had

[1] Alba, or North Britain.

treated her and of misgivings as to how he might be received, took ship for Gaul.

Arriving at Karitia,[1] he sent a messenger to his daughter, telling her of his plight and asking for her help. Cordeilla sent him money, robes and a retinue of forty men, and as soon as he was fully equipped with the state suitable to a king, he was received in pomp by Aganippus and his ministers, who gave the government of Gaul into his hands until his own kingdom could be restored to him. This the king of the Franks did by raising an army and invading Britain. Maglaunus and Henuinus were routed and Leir replaced on the throne, after which he lived three years. Cordeilla, succeeding to the government of Britain, 'buried her father in a certain vault, which she ordered to be made for him under the River Sore, in Leicester ['Llyr-cestre'], and which had been built originally under the ground to the honour of the god Janus. And here all the workmen of the city, upon the anniversary solemnity of that festival, used to begin their yearly labours.'

Exactly what myth is retold in this history of Leir and his three daughters we are hardly likely ever to discover, but its mythological nature is clear enough in the light of the description of the underground temple dedicated to Llyr, at once the god of the subaqueous, and therefore subterranean, world and a British Pluto or Dis Pater connected with the origin of things, like the Roman god Janus with whom he was apparently identified.

Ten kings or so after this (for any more exact way of measuring the flight of time is absent from Geoffrey's History) we recognise two other British gods upon the scene. Brennius (that is, Bran) disputes the kingdom with his brother Belenus. Clearly this is a version of the ancient myth of the twin brothers, Darkness and Light, which we have seen expressed in so many ways in Celtic mythology. Bran, the god of death and the underworld, is opposed to Belenus, god of the sun and health. In the original, lost myth they probably alternately conquered and were conquered – a symbol of the alternation of night and day and of winter and summer. In Geoffrey's History, they divided Britain, Belenus taking 'the crown of the island with the dominions of Loegria, Kambria, and Cornwall, because, according to the Trojan constitution, the right of inheritance would come to him as the elder', while Brennius, as the younger, had 'Northumberland, which extended from the River Humber to Caithness'. But flatterers persuaded Brennius to ally himself with the King of

[1] Now Calais.

Lear and Cordelia, from a painting by Ford Madox Brown

the Norwegians and attack Belenus. A battle was fought in which Belenus was
conqueror, and Brennius escaped to Gaul, where he married the daughter of
the Duke of the Allobroges and on that ruler's death was declared successor to
the throne. Thus firmly established with an army, he invaded Britain again.
Belenus marched with the whole strength of the kingdom to meet him, and
the armies were already drawn out opposite to one another in battle array
when Conwenna, the mother of the two kings, succeeded in reconciling
them. Not having one another to fight with, the brothers now agreed upon a
joint expedition with their armies into Gaul. The Britons and the Allobroges
conquered all the other kings of the Franks and then entered Italy, destroying
villages and cities as they marched to Rome. Gabius and Porsena, the Roman
consuls, bought them off with large presents of gold and silver and the promise of a yearly tribute, whereupon Brennius and Belenus withdrew their army
into Germany and began to devastate it. But the Romans, now no longer taken
by surprise and unprepared, came to the help of the Germans. This brought
Brennius and Belenus back to Rome, which, after a long siege, they succeeded
in taking. Brennius remained in Italy, 'where he exercised unheard-of tyranny

over the people'. (One may take the whole of this veracious history to be the result of a patriotic desire to make out the Brennus who actually did sack Rome, in 390 BC a Briton.) Belenus, the other brother, returned to England. As Geoffrey says, 'he made a gate of wonderful structure in Trinovantum, upon the bank of the Thames, which the citizens call after his name Billingsgate to this day. Over it he built a prodigiously large tower, and under it a haven or quay for ships. . . . At last, when he had finished his days, his body was burned, and the ashes put up in a golden urn, which they placed at Trinovantum, with wonderful art, on the top of the tower above mentioned.' He was succeeded by Gurgiunt Brabtruc,[1] who, as he was returning by way of Orkney from a raid on the Danes, met the ships of Partholón and his people as they came from Spain to settle in Ireland.

Llyr and his children, large as they bulk in mythical history, were hardly less illustrious as saints. The family of Llyr Llediath is always described by the early Welsh hagiologists as the first of the 'Three chief Holy Families of the Isle of Britain'. The glory of Llyr himself, however, is only a reflected one, for it was his son, Bran the Blessed, who actually introduced Christianity into Britain. Legend tells us that he was taken captive to Rome with his son Caradawc (who was identified for the purpose with the historical Caratacus) and the rest of his family and remained there seven years, during which time he became converted to Christianity and spread it enthusiastically on his return. Neither his son Caradawc nor his half-brother Manawydan exactly followed in his footsteps but their descendants did. Caradawc's sons were all saintly, while his daughter Eigen, who married a chief called Sarrlog, lord of Caer Sarrlog (Old Sarum), was the first female saint in Britain. Manawydan's side of the family was less adaptable. His son and his grandson were both pagans, but his great-grandson obtained Christian fame as St Dyfan, who was sent as a bishop to Wales by Pope Eleutherius and was martyred at Merthyr Dyvan. After this, the saintly line of Llyr increases and flourishes. Singularly inappropriate persons are found in it – Mabon, the Gallo-British Apollo, as well as Geraint and others of King Arthur's court.[2]

---

[1] The same fabulous personage, perhaps, as the original of Rabelais' Gargantua, a popular Celtic god.

[2] The genealogies and families of the saints of the island of Britain are contained in the Iolo manuscripts. They were copied by Iolo Morganwg in 1783 from the Long Book of Thomas Truman of Pantlliwydd in the parish of Llansannor in the Vale of Glamorgan.

It is so quaint a conceit that Christianity should have been, like all other things, the gift of the Celtic Hades, that it seems almost a pity to cast doubt on it. The witness of the classical historians sums up, however, dead in its disfavour. Tacitus carefully enumerates the family of Caratacus and describes how he and his wife, daughter and brother were separately interviewed by the Emperor Claudius but makes no mention at all of the chieftain's supposed father, Bran. Moreover, Dio Cassius gives the name of Caratacus's father as Cunobelinus – Shakespeare's Cymbeline – who, he adds, had died before the Romans first invaded Britain. The evidence is wholly against Bran as a Christian pioneer. He remains the grim old god of war and death, 'blessed' only to his pagan votaries and especially to the bards, who probably first called him Bendigeid Vran and whose stubborn adherence must have been the cause of the not less stubborn efforts of their enemies, the Christian clerics, to bring him over to their own side by canonisation.

They had an easier task with Bran's sister, Branwen of the 'Fair Bosom'. Goddesses, indeed, seem to have withstood the process better than gods – witness 'Saint' Brigit, the 'Mary of the Gael'. The British Aphrodite became, under the name of Brynwyn or Dwynwen, a patron saint of lovers. As late as the fourteenth century, her shrine at Llandwynwyn in Anglesey was the favourite resort of the disappointed of both sexes, who came to pray to her image for either success or forgetfulness. To make the result the more certain, the monks of the church sold Lethean draughts from her sacred well. The legend told of her, recorded in the Iolo manuscripts, is that, having vowed herself to perpetual celibacy, she fell in love with a young chief called Maelon. One night, as she was praying for guidance in her difficulty, she had a vision in which she was offered a goblet of delicious liquor as a draught of oblivion, and she also saw the same sweet medicine given to Maelon, whom it at once froze into a block of ice. She was then, for her faith, offered the granting of three boons. The first she chose was that Maelon might be allowed to resume his natural form and temperature, the second that she should no longer desire to be married, and the third that her intercessions might be granted for all true-hearted lovers so that they should either wed the objects of their affection or be cured of their passion. From this cause came the virtues of her shrine and fountain, but people no longer flock there, and the efficacious well is choked with sand. Nonetheless, she whom the Welsh bards called the 'Saint of Love' still had her occasional votaries. Country girls of the neighbourhood would seek her help when all else failed. The water nearest to the church was thought to be the best substitute for the now dry and ruined original well.

A striking contrast to this easy victory over paganism is the stubborn resistance to Christian adoption of Gwyn ap Nudd. It is true that according to the Iolo manuscripts he was once enrolled by some monk in the train of the 'Blessed Bran', but it was done in so half-hearted a way that, even now, one can discern that the writer felt almost ashamed of himself. His fame as at least a powerful fairy was too vital to be thus tampered with. Even Spenser, although, in his *Faerie Queene*, he calls him 'the good Sir Guyon . . . in whom great rule of Temp'raunce goodly doth appeare', does not attempt to conceal his real nature. It is no man but

'an Elfin born, of noble state
And mickle worship in his native land',

who sets forth the beauties of that virtue for which the original Celtic paradise, with its unfailing ale and rivers of mead and wine, would hardly seem to have been the best possible school. Except for Spenser, all authorities agree in making Gwyn the determined opponent of things Christian. A curious and picturesque legend is told of him in connection with St Collen, who was himself the great-grandson of Bran's son, Caradawc. The saint, wishing still further retirement from the world, had made himself a cell beneath a rock near Glastonbury Tor in Gwyn's own 'island of Avilion'. It was close to a road, and one day he heard two men pass by talking about Gwyn ap Nudd and declaring him to be King of Annwn and the fairies. St Collen put his head out of the cell and told them to hold their tongues and that Gwyn and his fairies were only demons. The two men retorted by warning the saint that he would soon have to meet the dark ruler face to face. They passed on, and not long afterwards St Collen heard someone knocking at his door. On asking who was there, he got the answer: 'I am here, the messenger of Gwyn ap Nudd, King of Hades, to bid thee come by the middle of the day to speak with him on the top of the hill.' The saint did not go, and the messenger came a second time with the same message. On the third visit, he added a threat that if St Collen did not come now it would be the worse for him. So, a little disquieted, he went but not unarmed. He consecrated some water and took it with him.

On other days the top of Glastonbury Tor had always been bare, but on this occasion the saint found it crowned by a splendid castle. Men and maidens, beautifully dressed, were going in and out. A page received him and told him that the king was waiting for him to be his guest at dinner. St Collen found Gwyn sitting on a golden chair in front of a table covered with the rarest dainties and wines. He invited him to share them, adding that if there was anything he especially liked it should be brought to him with all honour.

'I do not eat the leaves of trees,' replied the saint, who knew what fairy meats and drinks were made of.

Not taken aback by this discourteous answer, the King of Annwn genially asked the saint if he did not admire his servants' livery, which was a motley costume, red on one side and blue on the other.

'Their dress is good enough for its kind,' said St Collen.

'What kind is that?' asked Gwyn.

'The red shows which side is being scorched, and the blue shows which side is being frozen,' replied the saint, and, splashing his holy water all round him, he saw castle, serving men and king vanish, leaving him alone on the bare, windy hilltop.

Gwyn, last of the gods of Annwn, has evidently by this time taken over the functions of all the others. He has the hounds that Arawn once had – the *Cwn Annwn*, 'dogs of hell', with the white bodies and the red ears. We hear more of them in folklore than we do of their master, although even their tradition died out with the spread of 'civilisation'. We are not likely to find another Reverend Edmund Jones, who published a book entitled *A Relation of Apparitions of Spirits in the County of Monmouth and the Principality of Wales* in 1813 in which he insisted on belief in them in case, by closing our minds to such manifest witnesses of the supernatural world, we should become infidels. Still, even in the early twentieth century people were ready to swear that they had heard them sweeping along the hillsides on stormy nights as they pursued the flying souls of unshriven men or unbaptised babes. The tales told of them curiously agree. Their cry is like that of a pack of foxhounds but softer in tone. The nearer they are to a person the less loud their voices seem and the farther off they are the louder. But they are less often seen than heard, and it has been suggested that the sounds were the cries of migrating bean geese, which are not unlike those of hounds in chase. The superstition is widely spread. The *Cwn Annwn* of Wales are called in North Devon the 'Yeth' (Heath or Heathen) or 'Yell' Hounds, and on Dartmoor the 'Wish' Hounds. In Durham and Yorkshire they are called 'Gabriel' Hounds, and they are known by various names in Norfolk, Gloucestershire and Cornwall. In Scotland it is Arthur who leads the Wild Hunt, and the tradition is found over almost the whole of western Europe.

Not many folktales have been preserved in which Gwyn is mentioned by name. His memory has lingered longest and latest in the fairy-haunted Vale of Neath, so close to his 'ridge, the Tawë abode . . . not the nearest Tawë . . . but that Tawë which is the farthest'. But it may be understood whenever the king of the fairies is mentioned. As the last of the greater gods of the old mythology, he has been endowed by popular fancy with the rule of all the varied fairy population of Britain, so far, at least, as it is of Celtic or pre-Celtic origin. For some of the fairies most famous in English literature are Germanic. King Oberon derives his name, through the French *fabliaux* from Elberich, the dwarf king of the *Niebelungenlied*, although his queen, Titania, was probably named out of Ovid's *Metamorphoses*. Puck, another of Shakespeare's 'fays', is merely the personification of his race, the 'pwccas' of Wales, 'pookas' of Ireland, 'poakes' of Worcestershire and 'pixies' of the West of England. It is Wales that preserves the most numerous and diverse collection of fairies. Some of them are beautiful, some hideous, some kindly, some malevolent. There are the gentle damsels of the lakes and streams, called Gwragedd Annwn, and the fierce and cruel mountain fairies known as the Gwyllion. There are the household sprites called Bwbachod, like the Scottish and English 'brownies'; the Coblynau, or gnomes of the mines (called 'knockers' in Cornwall); and the Ellyllon, or elves, of whom the pwccas are a branch. In the North of England the spirits belong more wholly to the lower type. The bogles, brownies, killmoulis, redcaps and their like seem little akin to the higher, Aryan-seeming fairies. The Welsh bwbach, too, is described as brown and hairy, and the coblynau as black or copper-faced. We shall hardly do wrong in regarding such spectres as the degraded gods of a pre-Aryan race, like the Irish leprechauns and pookas, who have nothing in common with the still beautiful, still noble figures of the Tuatha Dé Danaan.

Of these numberless and nameless subjects of Gwyn, some dwell beneath the earth or under the surface of lakes – which seem to take, in Wales, the place of the Gaelic 'fairy hills' – and others in Avilion, a mysterious western isle of all delights lying on or just beneath the sea. Dyfed has kept the tradition most completely. The story goes that there is a certain square yard in the hundred of Cemmes in that county which holds the secret of the fairy realm. If a man happens to set his feet on it by chance, his eyes are opened and he can see that which is hidden from other men – the fairy country and commonwealth – but the moment he moves from the enchanted spot he loses the vision and can never find the same place again. That country is upon the sea and not far from shore. Like the Irish paradise of which it is the counterpart it may sometimes be sighted by sailors. The 'Green Meadows of Enchantment' were for long an article of faith among Pembrokeshire and Caermarthenshire sailors and evidently not without some reason. In 1896 a correspondent of the *Pembroke County Guardian* sent in a report made to him by a certain Captain John Evans to the effect that one summer morning, while sailing up the Channel and passing Grassholm Island (the scene of the entertaining of Bran's head), in what he had always known as deep water, he was surprised to see to windward of him a large tract of land covered with a beautiful green meadow. It was not, however, above water but two or three feet below it, so that the grass waved or swam about as the water rippled over it in a way that made one who watched it feel drowsy. Captain Evans had often heard of the tradition of the fairy island from old people but admitted that he had never hoped to see it with his own eyes. As with the 'Hounds of Annwn', one may suspect a quite natural explanation. Mirage is at once common enough and rare enough on our coasts to give rise to such a legend, and it must have been some such phenomenon as the *Fata Morgana*, a mirage in the Strait of Messina attributed to the sorcery of Morgan le Fay, which has made sober men swear so confidently to ocular evidence of the Celtic Paradise, whether seen from the farthest western coasts of Gaelic Ireland or Scotland, or of British Wales.

Part 3

Survivals of the Celtic Paganism

Chapter 27

SURVIVALS OF THE CELTIC PAGANISM INTO MODERN TIMES

The fall of the Celtic state worship began earlier in Britain than in her sister island. Neither was it Christianity that struck the first blow but the rough humanity and stern justice of the Romans. That people were more tolerant, perhaps, than any the world has ever known towards the religions of others and gladly welcomed the Celtic gods – as gods – into its own diverse pantheon. A friendly Gaulish or British divinity might at any time be granted the so-to-speak divine Roman citizenship and be assimilated to Jupiter, to Mars, to Apollo or to any other properly accredited deity whom the Romans deemed him to resemble. It was not against the god but against his worship at the hands of his priests that Roman law struck. The colossal human sacrifices of the druids horrified even a people who were far from squeamish about a little bloodshed. They themselves had abolished such practices by a decree of the senate before Caesar first invaded Britain in the year 55 BC and, according to the Greek geographer and historian Strabo, could not therefore permit within their empire a cult that slaughtered people in order to draw omens from their death agonies. Druidism was first required to be renounced by those who claimed Roman citizenship. Then it was vigorously put down among the less civilised tribes. Tacitus tells us how the Island of Mona (Anglesey) – the great stronghold of druidism – was attacked, its sacred groves cut down, its altars laid level and its priests put to the sword. Pliny, recording how the Emperor Tiberius had 'suppressed the druids', congratulates his fellow countrymen on having put an end, wherever their dominion extended, to the monstrous customs inspired by the doctrine that the gods could take pleasure in murder and cannibalism. The practice of druidism with its attendant barbarities, abolished in Britain wherever the long Roman arm could reach to strike, took refuge beyond the northern Wall among the savage Caledonian tribes who had not yet submitted to the invader's yoke. Naturally, too, it remained untouched in Ireland. But before the Romans left Britain, it had been completely destroyed everywhere except among 'the Picts and Scots'.

Christianity, following the Roman rule, completed the ruin of paganism in Britain, so far at least as its public manifestations were concerned. In the sixth century, the monkish writer Gildas is able to refer complacently to the ancient British religion as a dead faith. 'I shall not,' he says, 'enumerate those diabolical idols of my country, which almost surpassed in number those of Egypt, and of which we still see some mouldering away within or without the deserted temples, with stiff and deformed features as was customary. Nor will I cry out upon the mountains, fountains, or hills, or upon the rivers, which now are subservient to the use of men, but once were an abomination and destruction to them, and to which the blind people paid divine honour.' And with the idols fell their priests. The very word 'druid' became obsolete and is scarcely mentioned in the earliest British literature although druids are prominent characters in the Irish writings of the same period.

The secular arm had no power in Scotland and Ireland, so consequently the battle between paganism and Christianity was fought upon more equal terms and lasted longer. In the first country, St Columba, and in the second, St Patrick are the personages who, at any rate according to tradition, beat down the druids and their gods. Adamnan, Abbot of Iona, who wrote his *Vita Columbae* in the last decade of the seventh century, describes how, a century earlier, that saint had carried the Gospel to the Picts. Their king, Brude, received him contemptuously, and the royal druids left no heathen spell unuttered to thwart and annoy him. But, as the power of Moses was greater than the power of the magicians of Egypt, so St Columba's prayers caused miracles more wonderful and more convincing than any wrought by his adversaries. Such stories belong to the atmosphere of myth which has always enveloped heroic men; the essential fact is that the Picts abandoned the old religion for the new.

A similar legend sums up the life work of St Patrick in Ireland. Before he came, Cromm Cruach had received from time immemorial his yearly toll of human lives. But St Patrick faced the gruesome idol. As he raised his crozier, we are told, the demon fell shrieking from his image, which, deprived of its soul, bowed forward to the ground.

It is far easier, however, to overthrow the more public manifestations of a creed than to destroy its inner vital force. Cromm Cruach's idol might fall but his spirit would survive – a very Proteus. The sacred places of the ancient Celtic religion might be invaded, the idols and altars of the gods thrown down, the priests slain, scattered or banished, and the cult officially declared to be extinct, but, driven from the important centres, it would yet survive outside and around them. The more civilised Gaels and Britons would no doubt accept the purer gospel and abandon the gods they had once adored, but the peasantry – the bulk of the population – would still cling to the familiar rites and names. A nobler belief and a higher civilisation come, after all, only as surface waves upon the great ocean of human life. Beneath their agitations lies a vast slumbering abyss of half-conscious faith and thought to which culture penetrates with difficulty and in which changes come very slowly.

We have already shown how long and how faithfully the Gaelic and Welsh peasants clung to their old gods in spite of all the efforts of the clerics to explain them as ancient kings, to transform them into wonder-working saints or to ban them as demons of hell. This conservative religious instinct of agricultural populations is not confined to the inhabitants of the British Islands. Modern Greeks long believed in nereids, in lamias, in sirens and in Charon, the dark ferryman of Hades. Descendants of the Romans and Etruscans also held that the old Etruscan gods and the Roman deities of the woods and fields lived in the world as spirits. The high altars of the 'Lord of the Mound' and his terrible kin were levelled and their golden images and great temples left to moulder, but the rude rustic shrine to the rude rustic god still received its offerings. It is this shifting of the care of the pagan cult from chief to peasant, from court to hovel and, perhaps, to some extent from higher to lower race, that serves to explain how the more primitive and uncouth gods have tended so largely to supplant those of higher, more graceful mien. Aboriginal deities thrust into obscurity by the invasion of higher foreign types came back to their own again.

For it seems plain that we must divide the spiritual population of the British Islands into two classes. There is little in common between the 'fairy', strictly so called, and the unsightly elf who appears under various names and guises, as pooka, leprechaun, brownie, knocker or bogle. The former belongs to such divine tribes as the Tuatha Dé Danaan of Gaelic myth or their kin, the British gods of the Mabinogion. The latter owes his origin to a quite different, and much lower, kind of imagination. One might fancy that Neolithic man made him in his own image.

Nonetheless, immemorial tradition wonderfully preserved the essential features of the Celtic nature gods. The fairy belief of later centuries hardly differed at all from the conception that the Celts had of their deities. The description of the Tuatha Dé Danaan in the 'Dialogue of the Elders' as 'sprites or fairies with corporeal or material forms but indued with immortality' would stand as an account of prevailing ideas as to the 'good people' of later time. Nor did the Irish and Welsh fairies of popular belief differ from one another. Both alike lived among the hills, although in Wales a lake often took the place of the 'fairy mound'. Both, although they warred and married among themselves, were semi-immortal. Both coveted the children of men and would steal them from the cradle, leaving one of their own uncanny brood in the mortal baby's stead. Both could lay men and women under spells. Both delighted in music and the dance, and lived lives of unreal and fantastic splendour and luxury. Another point in which they resembled one another is in their tiny size, but this would seem to be the result of the literary convention originated by Shakespeare. In genuine folktales, both Gaelic and British, the fairies were pictured as being of at least mortal stature.

But Aryan or Iberian, beautiful or hideous, they eventually vanished from belief. The secluded valleys in which men and women might still live in the old way and dream the old dreams more and more became open to the modern world of rapid movement and rapid thought. The rapid developments of the nineteenth and twentieth centuries have perhaps done for them for good. What lone shepherd or fisherman will ever see again the vision of the great Manannán? Have the stableboys of today still any faith left in Fionnbharr? Is Gwyn ap Nudd often thought of in his own valleys of the Tawë and the Nedd? It would be hard, perhaps, to find a whole-hearted believer even in his or her local pooka or parish bogle.

It is the ritual observances of the old Celtic faith that have better weathered and will longer survive the disintegrating influences of time. There are no hard names to be remembered. Things may still be done for 'luck' which were once done for religion. Customary observances die very slowly, held up by an only half-acknowledged fear that unless they are fulfilled 'something may happen'. We shall get, therefore, more satisfactory evidence of the nature of the Celtic paganism by examining such customs than in any other way.

We find three forms of the survival of the ancient religion into quite recent times. The first is the celebration of the old solar or agricultural festivals of the spring and autumn equinoxes and of the summer and winter solstices. The second is the practice of a symbolic human sacrifice by those who have forgotten its meaning and only know that they are keeping up an old custom, joined with late instances of the actual sacrifices of animals to avert cattle plagues or to change bad luck. The third consists of many still-living relics of the once universal worship of sacred waters, trees, stones and animals.

Whatever may have been the exact meaning of the Celtic state worship, there seems to be no doubt that it centred on the four great days in the year that chronicle the rise, progress and decline of the sun and therefore of the fruits of the earth. These were: Beltane, which fell at the beginning of May; Midsummer Day, marking the triumph of sunshine and vegetation; the Lughnasadh, the feast of Lugh, when, in August, the turning point of the sun's course had been reached; and the sad Samhain, when the sun bade farewell to power and fell again for half a year under the sway of the evil forces of winter and darkness.

Of these great solar periods, the first and the last were, naturally, the most important. The whole Celtic mythology seems to revolve upon them as upon pivots It was on the day of Beltane that Partholón and his people, the discoverers and, indeed, the makers of Ireland, arrived there from the Otherworld, and it was on the same day, three hundred years later, that they returned whence they came. It was on Beltane day that the Gaelic gods, the Tuatha Dé Danaan and after them the Gaelic men first set foot on Irish soil. It was on the day of Samhain that the Fomorii oppressed the people of Nemedh with their terrible tax, and it was again at Samhain that a later race of gods of light and life finally conquered those demons at the Battle of Magh Tuireadh. Only one important mythological incident – and that was one added at a later time! – happened upon any other than one of those two days. It was upon Midsummer Day, one of the lesser solar points, that the people of the goddess Danu took Ireland from its inhabitants, the Fir Bholgs.

The mythology of Britain preserves the same root idea as that of Ireland. If anything uncanny took place, it was sure to be on May Day. It was on 'the night of the first of May' that Rhiannon lost and Ternyon Twryf Vliant found the infant Pryderi, as told in the first of the Mabinogion. It was 'on every May eve' that the two dragons fought and shrieked in the reign of 'King' Lludd. It is on 'every first of May' until the day of doom that Gwyn ap Nudd fights with Gwythyr ap Gwreidawl for Lludd's fair daughter, Creiddylad. And, according to the *Morte D'Arthur*, it was when she was 'a-maying' in the woods and fields near Westminster that the same Gwyn or Melwas, under his romance name of Sir Meliagraunce, captured Arthur's queen, Guinevere.

The nature of the rites performed upon these days can be surmised from their pale survivals. They are still celebrated by the descendants of the Celts, although it is probable that few of them know – or would even care to know – why May Day, St. John's Day, Lammas and Hallowe'en are times of ceremony. The first – called Beltane in Ireland, Bealtiunn in Scotland, Shenn da Boaldyn in the Isle of Man and Galan-Mai (the Calends of May) in Wales – celebrates the waking of the earth from her winter sleep and the renewal of warmth, life and vegetation. This is the meaning of the Maypole, now rarely seen in our streets although Shakespeare tells us in *Henry VIII* Act 5, scene 3 that in his time the festival was so eagerly anticipated that no one could sleep upon its eve. At midnight the people rose and, going to the nearest woods, tore down branches of trees with which the sun, when he rose, would find doors and windows decked for him. They spent the day in dancing round the Maypole with rude, rustic mirth, man joining with nature to celebrate the coming of summer. The opposite of it was the day called Samhain in Ireland and Scotland, Sauin in Man and Nos Galan-gaeof (the Night of the Winter Calends) in Wales. This festival was a sad one: summer was over and winter, with its short, sunless days and long, dreary nights, was at hand. It was the beginning, too, of the ancient Celtic year, and omens for the future might be extorted from dark powers by uncanny rites. It was the holiday of the dead and of all the more evil supernatural beings. 'On November eve', says an old North Ceredigion proverb, 'there is a bogey on every stile.' The Scots have even invented a special bogey – the *Samhanach* or the goblin that comes out at the time of Samhain.

The sun god himself is said to have instituted the August festival called Lughnasadh (Lugh's commemoration) in Ireland, Lla Lluanys in Man and Gwyl Awst (August Feast) in Wales, and it was once of hardly less importance than Beltane or Samhain. It is noteworthy, too, that the first of August was a great day at Lyons – formerly called Lugudunum, the *dún* (town) of Lugus.

The midsummer festival, on the other hand, has largely merged its mythological significance in the Christian Feast of St John.

The characteristic features of these festivals give certain proof of the original nature of the great pagan ceremonials of which they are the survivals and travesties. In all of them bonfires are lighted on the highest hills and the hearth fires solemnly rekindled. They form the excuse for much sport and jollity. But there is yet something sinister in the air; the 'fairies' are active and abroad, and one must be careful to omit no prescribed rite if one would avoid kindling their anger or falling into their power. To some of these still-half-believed-in nature gods offerings were made down to a comparatively late period. When Thomas Pennant wrote his *Tour in Scotland and Voyage to the Hebrides* in the eighteenth century, it was the custom on Beltane day in many Highland villages to offer libations and cakes not only to the 'spirits' who were believed to be beneficial to the flocks and herds but also to creatures like the fox, the eagle and the hoodie crow which so often molested them. According to Martin Martin in his *Description of the Western Islands of Scotland*, the first published account of life in the Hebrides, written in the late 1690s, at Hallowe'en (the Celtic Samhain) the natives of the Hebrides used to pour libations of ale to a marine god called Shony, imploring him to send seaweed to the shore. In honour, also, of such beings, curious rites were performed. Maidens washed their faces in morning dew, with prayers for beauty. They carried sprigs of the rowan, that mystic tree the scarlet berries of which were the ambrosial food of the Tuatha Dé Danaan.

In their original form these now harmless rural holidays were undoubtedly religious festivals of an orgiastic nature worship such as became so popular in Greece in connection with the cult of Dionysus. The great 'lords of life' and of the powers of nature that made and ruled life were propitiated by maddening invocations, by riotous dances and by human sacrlfice.

The bonfires that fill so large a part in the more modern festivals have been casually mentioned. Originally they were no mere *feux de joie* but had a terrible meaning that the customs that are connected with them preserve. At the Highland Beltane, a cake was divided by lot and whoever drew the 'burnt piece' was obliged to leap three times over the flames. At the midsummer bonfires in Ireland all passed through the fire – the men when the flames were highest, the women when they were lower and the cattle when there was nothing left but smoke. In Wales, on the last day of October, the old Samhain, there was a slightly different and still more suggestive rite. The hilltop bon-fires were watched until they were announced to be extinct. Then all would race headlong down the hill, shouting a formula to the effect that the devil would get the hindmost. The devil of a new belief is the god of the one it has supplanted. In all three instances the custom was no mere meaningless horse-play but a symbolic human sacrifice.

A similar observance, but of a more cruel kind, was kept up in France upon St John's Day until forbidden by law in the reign of Louis XIV. Baskets contain-ing living wolves, foxes and cats were burned on the bonfires under the aus-pices and in the presence of the sheriffs or the mayor of the town. Julius Cae-sar had noted the custom among the druids of constructing huge wickerwork images, which they filled with living men and set on fire, and it can hardly be doubted that the wretched wolves, foxes and cats were ceremonial substitutes for human beings.

An ingenious theory was invented after the introduction of Christianity with the purpose of allowing such ancient rites to continue with a changed meaning. The passing of persons and cattle through flame or smoke was ex-plained as a practice that interposed a magic protection between them and the powers of evil. This homoeopathic device of using the evil power's own sacred fire as a means of protection against himself somewhat suggests that seething of the kid in its mother's milk which was reprobated by the Levitical law, but no doubt pagan 'demons' were considered fair game. The explanation, of course, is an obviously and clumsily forced one; it was the grim druidical phi-losophy that – to quote Caesar – 'unless the life of man was repaid for the life of man, the will of the immortal gods could not be appeased' that dictated both the national and the private human sacrifices of the Celts, the shadows of which remain in the leaping through the bonfires and in the numerous re-corded sacrifices of cattle within quite recent times.

In the later nineteenth century Laurence Gomme, in his *Ethnology in Folk-lore*, collected many instances of the sacrifices of cattle not only in Ireland and Scotland but also in Wales, Yorkshire, Northamptonshire, Cornwall and the Isle of Man. 'Within twenty miles of the metropolis of Scotland a relative of Professor Simpson offered up a live cow as a sacrifice to the spirit of the mur-rain.' In Wales, when cattle sickness broke out, a bullock was immolated by being thrown down from the top of a high rock. Generally, however, the wretched victims were burned alive. In 1859 an Isle of Man farmer offered a heifer as a burnt offering near Tynwald Hill to avert the anger of the ghostly occupant of a barrow that had been desecrated by opening. Sometimes, even, these burnt oblations were offered to an alleged Christian saint. The registers of the Presbytery of Dingwall for the years 1656 and 1678 contain records of the sacrifices of cattle upon the site of an ancient temple in honour of a being whom some called 'St Mourie' and others, perhaps knowing his doubtful character, 'ane god Mourie'. At Kirkcudbright, it was St Cuthbert, and at Clynnog in Wales it was St Beuno, who was thought to delight in the blood of bulls.

Such sacrifices of cattle appear mainly to have been offered to prevent plague among cattle. Man for man and beast for beast was, perhaps, the old rule, but among all nations, human sacrifices have been gradually commuted for those of animals. According to Laurence Gomme, the family of the O'Herlebys in Ballyvorney, County Cork, used in olden days to keep an idol, 'an image of wood about two feet high, carved and painted like a woman'. She was the goddess of smallpox, and to her a sheep was immolated on behalf of anyone seized with that disease.

The third form of Celtic pagan survival is found in numerous instances of the adoration of water, trees, stones and animals. Like the other 'Aryan' nations, the Celts worshipped their rivers. The River Dee received honours as a war goddess with the title of Aerfon, while the Ribble, under its name of Belisama, was identified by the Romans with Minerva. Myths were told of them, as of the sacred streams of Greece. The Dee gave oracles as to the results of the perpetual wars between the Welsh and the English. As its stream encroached either upon the Welsh or the English side, so one nation or the other would be victorious. The Tweed, like many of the Greek rivers, was credited with human descendants. That the rivers of Great Britain received human sacrifices is clear from the folklore concerning many of them. Deprived of their expected offerings, they are believed to snatch by stealth the human lives for which they crave. 'River of Dart, River of Dart, every year thou claimest a heart,' runs the Devonshire folksong. The Spey, too, requires a life yearly, but the Spirit of the Ribble is satisfied with one victim at the end of every seven years.

Evidence, however, of the worship of rivers is scanty compared with that of the adoration of wells. 'In the case of well-worship,' says Laurence Gomme, 'it may be asserted with some confidence that it prevails in every county of the three kingdoms.' He finds it most vital in the Gaelic counties, somewhat less so in the British and almost entirely lacking in the Germanic southeast. So numerous, indeed, are 'holy wells' that several monographs have been written solely upon them. In some cases these wells were resorted to for the cure of diseases; in others to obtain change of weather or 'good luck'. Offerings were made to them to propitiate their guardian gods or nymphs. Pennant tells us that in olden times the rich would sacrifice one of their horses at a well near Abergeleu to secure a blessing upon the rest. Fowls were offered at St Tegla's Well near Wrexham by epileptic patients, but in later years the well spirits had to be content with much smaller tributes – such trifles as pins, rags, coloured pebbles and small coins.

With sacred wells were often connected sacred trees, to the branches of which rags and small pieces of garments were suspended by their humble worshippers. Sometimes, where the ground near the well was bare of vegetation, bushes were artificially placed beside the water. The same people who venerated wells and trees would pay equal adoration to sacred stones. In his book *Progress of the Reformation in Ireland* Lord Roden, describing in 1851 the island of Inniskea off the coast of Mayo, asserts that a sacred well called 'Derrivla' and a sacred stone called 'Neevougi', which was kept carefully wrapped up in flannel and brought out at certain periods to be publicly adored, seemed to be the only deities known to that lone Atlantic island's then three hundred inhabitants. It sounds incredible, but there is ample evidence of the worship of fetish stones by quite modern inhabitants of our islands. According to Martin Martin in his *Description of the Western Islands*, the Clan Chattan kept such a stone in the Isle of Arran. It was believed, like the stone of Inniskea, to be able to cure diseases and was kept carefully 'wrapped up in fair linen cloth, and about that there was a piece of woollen cloth'. Similarly, too, the worship of wells was connected with the worship of animals. At a well in the 'Devil's Causeway', between Ruckley and Acton in Shropshire, lived, and perhaps still live, four frogs who were, and perhaps still are, believed to be 'the devil and his imps' – that is to say, gods or demons of a proscribed idolatry. In Ireland such guardian spirits are usually fish – trout, eels or salmon thought to be endowed with eternal life. The genius of a well in Banffshire took the form of a fly, which was also said to be undying but to transmigrate from body to body. Its function was to deliver oracles; according to whether it seemed active or lethargic, its votaries drew their omens. It is needless to multiply instances of a still surviving cult of water, trees, stones and animals. Enough to say that it would be easy. What concerns us is that we are face to face in Britain with living forms of the oldest, lowest, most primitive religion in the world – one that would seem to have been once universal, and which, crouching close to the earth, lets other creeds blow over it without effacing it and outlives all of them.

It underlies the three great world religions and still forms the real belief of perhaps the majority of their titular adherents. It is characteristic of the wisdom of the Christian Church that, knowing its power, it sought rather to sanctify than to destroy it. What once were the Celtic equivalents of the Greek 'fountains of the nymphs' were consecrated as 'holy wells'. The process of so adopting them began early. St Columba, when he went in the sixth century to convert the Picts, found a spring that they worshipped as a god. He blessed it, and, according to Adamnan's *Life*, 'from that day the demon separated from the water'. Indeed, he so sanctified no less than three hundred such springs. Sacred stones were equally taken under the aegis of Christianity. Some were placed on the altars of cathedrals, others built into consecrated walls. The animal gods either found themselves the heroes of Christian legends or, where for some reason such adoption was hopeless, were proclaimed 'witches' animals' and dealt with accordingly. Such happened to the hare, a creature sacred, according to Julius Caesar, to the ancient Britons but now in bad odour among the superstitious. The wren, too, is hunted to death upon St Stephen's Day in Ireland. Its crime is said to be that it has 'a drop of the de'il's blood in it', but the real reason is probably to be found in the fact that the Irish druids used to draw auguries from its chirpings.

Some attempt has been made in this volume to draw a picture of the ancient religion of our earliest ancestors, the Gaelic and the British Celts. We have shown what can be gathered of the broken remnants of a mythology as splendid in conception and as brilliant in colour as that of the Greeks. We have tried to paint its divine figures and to retell their heroic stories. We have seen them fall from their shrines and yet, rising again, take on new lives as kings or saints or knights of romance, and we have caught fading glimpses of them surviving as the 'fairies', their rites still cherished by worshippers who hardly knew who or why they worshipped. Of necessity this survey has been brief and incomplete. Whether the great edifice of Celtic mythology will ever be wholly restored one can only speculate. Its colossal fragments are perhaps too deeply buried and too widely scattered. But even as it stands ruined, it is a mighty quarry from which poets yet unborn will hew spiritual marble for houses not made with hands.

Appendix

Dictionary of the Celts

A

ABERFFRAW
The seat of the ancient kings of Gwynedd in southwest Anglesey where the the marriage took place of Branwen, sister of Bran the Blessed, and Matholwch,. King of Ireland. *See* Chapter 18.

ABRED
In Welsh Celtic mythology a name given to the Otherworld. *See also* Annwn.

ABUNDANCE *see* STONE OF ABUNDANCE.

ACHREN
A name for the Otherworld.

AED (1)
In Irish Celtic mythology, the second child and first son of Lir and Aobh. With his siblings, Fionuala, Fiachtra and Conn, he was turned into a swan by his stepmother, Aoife (1). *See also* Chapter 11.

AED (2) *see* IBHELL; MONGAN.

AEDA
In Irish Celtic mythology, Aeda was a dwarf at the court of Fergus Mac Leda. He was taken by the bard, Eisirt, to the court of Iubdan, the king of the diminutive Faylinn, to prove that there was a race of supposed giants elsewhere.

AED ABRAT
In Irish Celtic mythology, Aed Abrat was the father of Fand and Li Ban.

AEDH (1)
In Irish Celtic mythology, one of the three sons of Miodhchaoin. He was killed

in his attempt with his brothers to avenge the death of their father by the three sons of Tuireann. *See also* Chapter 8.

AEDH (2)
In Irish Celtic mythology, a royal suitor for Bebhionn's hand. Bebhionn was killed by him after she sought help from Fionn. *See* Chapter 15.

AENGHUS *see* OENGHUS.

AEÍ, PLAIN OF
In Irish Celtic mythology, the Plain of Aeí was where the two bulls, Donn Cuailgne and Finnbhenach, had their epic fight described in the Táin Bó Cuailgné. *See* Chapter 12.

AERFON
In Welsh Celtic mythology, a war goddess associated with the River Dee.

AES SÍDHE *see* SÍDH.

AFAGDDU
In Welsh Celtic mythology, Afagddu was the son of Cerridwen. He was so ugly that his mother sought to give him intellectual skills that would compensate for his unattractive appearance but by strange circumstances they were transferred to Taliesin (*see* Chapter 23).

AGALAMH NA SENÓRACH
'The Dialogue of the Elders', a tract contained in thirteenth- and fourteenth-century manuscripts that relates the history of Ireland in terms of the activities of the Fianna and the Tuatha Dé Danaan.

AGNOMAN
In Irish Celtic mythology, the father of Nemedh.

AICHLEACH
In Irish Celtic mythology, there are various stories relating to the death of Fionn Mac Cumhaill. According to one of these, he was murdered by Aichleach during a rebellion of the Fianna.

AIDIN

In Irish Celtic mythology, Aidin was the wife of Oscar. She died of grief following his death in the Battle of Gabhra. Oisín, Oscar's father, buried her on Ben Edar and raised over her a great dolmen that still stands there, made of ten huge blocks of stone with a capstone estimated to weigh 70 tons.

AILBHE

In Irish Celtic mythology, the youngest daughter of Ailioll of Arran and foster daughter of Bodb Dearg. Her sisters, Aobh and Aoife, both married Lir. *See* Chapter 11.

AILEACH

The place in County Donegal where in Irish Celtic mythology Ith encountered the three kings, Mac Cuill, Mac Cécht and Mac Greine, the successors of Nuada. The Grianan of Aileach is a huge circular stone fort dating from the second century BC and built for the O'Neill High Kings of Ireland. It is said to be the burial place of Nuada.

AILILL (1)

In Irish Celtic mythology, Ailill is the brother of Eochaidh who fell madly in love with Etain, his sister-in-law (*see* Chapter 11).

AILILL (2)

In Irish Celtic mythology, Ailill was the husband of Medb, queen of Connacht, she being generally held to be the more dominant partner. Ailill's ownership of Finnbhenach, the White-horned Bull of Connacht, although the bull had been born into her herd, made Medb extremely jealous and to compensate for this ownership she sought to acquire Donn Cuailgne, the great Brown Bull of Ulster. This was the origin of the Táin Bó Cuailgne, the Iliad of he Celts (*see* Chapter 12).

AILINN

In Irish Celtic mythology, the granddaughter of a King of Leinster who fell in love with Baile, heir to the Ulster throne. They feature in the story of 'Baile of the Honeyed Speech', a tale of tragic love. *See* Chapter 13.

AILIOLL OF ARRAN
In Irish Celtic mythology, the natural father of Aobh, Aoife and Ailbhe who were fostered by Lir. *See* Chapter 11.

AILLEN *see* FIONN MAC CUMHAILL; SAMHAIN.

AINÉ *or* **AYNIA**
In Irish Celtic mythology, queen of the fairies of South Munster, the divinity into whom the mother goddess Danu dwindled after the fall of the Tuatha Dé Danaan. *See* Chapter 16.

AINGE *see* GAIBLE.

AINLE
In Irish Celtic mythology, Ainle was one of the brothers of Naoise who feature in the story of Naoise and Deirdre. *See also* Chapter 14.

AIRCELTRAI
In Irish Celtic mythology, the sídh of Oghma.

AIREMH
In Irish Celtic mythology, Airemh, 'The Ploughman', is the epithet acquired by Eochaidh as a result of introducing a new method of ploughing acquired from watching the followers of Midhir. *See also* Chapter 11.

AIRMID
In Irish Celtic mythology, Airmid was the daughter of Dian Cécht who followed in her father's profession. She assisted her father at the 'spring of health where a dead or wounded member of the Tuatha Dé Danaan was brought back to life or health. She and her brother, Midach, were responsible for giving Nuada his silver hand, which enabled him to be reinstated as the king of the Tuatha Dé Danaan. *See also* Chapter 7.

AIRT 'THE LONELY'
Airt, a high king of Ireland, was the father of Cormac. In Irish Celtic mythology, he features in the story of 'Baile of the Honeyed Speech' (*see* Chapter 13). He acquired his epithet as he had lost Connlai, his brother.

AITHERNE
In Irish Celtic mythology, a bard who stole from Midhir his 'Three Cranes of Denial and Churlishness'. *See* Chapter 5.

ALBA
The ancient name for Scotland.

ALBANACTUS *see* KAMBER; LOCRINUS.

AMAETHON
In Welsh Celtic mythology, the god of agriculture, the son of Dôn and brother of Gwydion and Govannan. *See also* Chapters 22, 24.

AMHAIRGHIN *or* **AMAIRGEN**
In Irish Celtic mythology, Amhairghin, whose name exists in various variants, was a warrior and a bard. He is said to have been a son of Mil and to have been part of the expedition of the Sons of Mil Espaine that invaded Ireland. Being a bard, he was considered to have good powers of judgement and was asked by the then inhabitants of Ireland, the Tuatha Dé Danaan, to settle a dispute between them and the Sons of Mil Espaine as to who should rule Ireland (*see* Chapter 10).

ANA
In Irish Celtic mythology, one of the variant names of Danu.

ANEURIN
A sixth-century Welsh bard. The Book of Aneurin is one of the 'Four Ancient Books of Wales'. It was written in the late thirteenth century and is said to contain the poems of Aneurin. The other Ancient Books of Wales are those of Carmarthen, Taliesin and Hergest.

ANGUISH, ANGUISSANCE
In Welsh Celtic mythology the names under which Arawn appears in Arthurian legend.

ANIMALS
In Celtic mythology and beliefs, animals, both domesticated and wild, played

a significant part. Shape-changing was an intrinsic part of Celtic legend, and the shapes that people or gods adopted or were forced to adopt were those of animals. For example, the nephews of Fionn Mac Cumhaill were turned into hounds.

Stags and boars were important wild animals in Celtic culture, and horses, pigs, rams, bulls and dogs, especially hunting hounds, were important domesticated animals.

Archaeological excavations have revealed evidence of animal sacrifice to the various gods. *See also* Chapter 27.

ANNA
The name used by Geoffrey of Monmouth to describe Aranrhod.

ANNWN
In Welsh Celtic mythology, Annwn was the Otherworld realm ruled over by Arawn. Both Ireland and the Isle of Man would have been identified as Annwn. Arawn features in an early Welsh poem, 'Preiddeu Annwn', which describes a journey to Annwn to capture a magic cauldron. This is thought to have influenced the quest for the Holy Grail, prominent in Arthurian legend. *See also* Chapters 19, 22, 23.

ANOETH *see* OETH AND ANOETH.

ANU *see* DANU.

AOBH
In Irish Celtic mythology, Aobh was the eldest foster daughter of Bodb Dearg and the wife of Lir. She bore him four children. On her death, Lir married her sister, Aoife (1), and she was so jealous of her husband's love for the children of his previous marriage that she turned them into swans for nine hundred years. See Chapter 11.

AOIBHINN
In Irish Celtic mythology, Aoibhinn was queen of the fairies of North Munster. *See* Chapter 15.

AOIFE (1)

In Irish Celtic mythology, Aoife was a foster daugher of Bodb Dearg and sister of Aobh. She was the second wife of Lir. and was so jealous of Lir's four children by his first marriage that she turned them into swans for nine hundred years (*see* Chapter 11). It is said that her foster father, Bodb, was so angry with her for doing this that he turned her into a raven, a bird associated with doom and death. Another legend indicates that she was turned into a crane, which was then killed by Manannán Mac Lir and that he used the skin of the crane to make a bag in which to carry his treasures.

AOIFE (2) *or* AIFE

In Irish Celtic mythology, Aoife was the name of the great rival of Scáthach who taught Cúchulainn war skills. While studying with Scáthach, Cúchulainn defeated Aoife in battle. Later they became lovers, the result of the union being a son, Connlai. *See also* Chapter 12.

ARANON

In Irish Celtic mythology, one of the Sons of Mil Espaine. As they were approaching Ireland he climbed to the top of the ship's mast to obtain a better view and, falling off, was drowned.

ARANRHOD

In Welsh Celtic mythology, Aranrhod was a daughter of Don and the sister of Gwydion fab Don, to whom she was also married. She had two sons at one birth, Dylan, who leapt into the sea, and Lleu Llaw Gyffes (*see* Chapter 18). Malory integrated Aranrhod into Arthurian legend as Morgawse, and Geoffrey of Monmouth calls her Anna.

ARAWN

In Welsh Celtic mythology, Arawn was the king of Annwn, the Welsh Otherworld. He is best known in legend for his association with Pwyll, lord of Dyfed. One day when Pwyll was out hunting he saw a strange pack of hounds, seemingly without an owner, overcoming a stag. He chased off the hounds and set his own hounds to the stag. Arawn then appeared and told Pwyll that he had done him a great insult by chasing off his hounds and that he would have to be recompensed in some way. It was agreed that to make up for the insult Pwyll would try to kill Hafgan, Arawn's deadly rival, with whom he is said to have had an annual contest. In order to do this, Pwyll was to assume the shape of Arawn and go to live in Annwn for a year while Arawn was to take on the form of Pwyll and go to rule Dyfed for a year. *See* Chapters 19, 22. He was subsumed into the Arthurian legends as Anguish or Anguissance, King of Scotland or Ireland, and into Geoffrey of Monmouth's *Historia Regum Britanniae* as Augusel.

ARBETH *or* NARBETH

In Welsh Celtic mythology, Arbeth was the chief court of Pwyll. *See* Chapter 19.

ARDAN

In Irish Celtic mythology, Ardan was one of the brothers of Naoise who feature in the story of Naoise and Deirdre. *See* Chapter 14.

AREGETLÁMH

'He of the silver hand', in Irish Celtic mythology an epithet applied to Nuada.

ARGOED LLWYFAIN *see* URIEN.

ARTAIUS

A Gaulish god of agriculture whom the Romans identified with Mercury. The Celtic form would have been Artur.

ARTHUR

Arthur was associated with Celtic mythology, although he was a historical figure from around the fifth or early sixth centuries, after the Romans left Britain in the period that is known as the Dark Ages. In the Arthurian saga, centred on the adventures of the Knights of the Round Table, Arthur is a medieval king. There appear to be no contemporary Celtic references to Arthur, either as a historical or as a legendary figure, although he did become involved in the story of Culhwch and in the story of the journey to Annwn to acquire the enchanted cauldron (*see* Chapter 18). Arthur is associated with Celtic myth but this may have been a postdated association or a confusion of two personages, Artur, a Celtic version of Artaius, and an historical chief. It is likely that he came to power in the dying days of the Celts and that the stories surrounding him grew as they were driven farther and farther from their native land. *See* Chapters 23, 24, 25, 26.

ARTUR (1)
In Irish Celtic mythology, one of the sons of Nemedh who fought against the Fomorii.

ARTUR (2) *see* ARTAIUS.

AUGUSEL *see* ARAWN.

AURELIUS
A half-real, half-mythical British king who ordered Merlin to construct Stonehenge.

AVALLON *or* **AVALLACH**
The name given by the Britons of Somerset to a god of the Otherworld, equivalent to the Welsh Gwyn ap Nudd. His realm was called Ynys Avallon, 'Avallon's Island'.

AVALON *or* **AVILION**
In Celtic mythology an island paradise in the western seas, its origin lying in Ynys Avallon. It was adopted into Arthurian legend as the place to which Arthur was taken after he was mortally wounded. It was later identified with Glastonbury.

AYNIA *see* AINÉ.

B

BADB

In Irish Celtic mythology, Badb was an Irish war goddess. She is depicted both as a single goddess and as one aspect of a triple goddess, the other two aspects being Nemain and Macha (*see* Chapter 5). The dwindling of the mythology resulted in Badb, Macha and Nemain becoming banshees who wail over the deaths of those not necessarily found in battle. *See also* Chapter 9.

BADON

In Arthurian legend the site, possibly near Bath, of one of Arthur's battles. *See* Chapter 24.

BAILE

In Irish Celtic mythology, Baile was an heir to the Ulster throne who fell in love with Ailinn, the granddaughter of a King of Leinster. They feature in the story of 'Baile of the Honeyed Speech', a tale of tragic love. *See* Chapter 14.

BALLYMOTE, BOOK OF

One of the source books for Irish Celtic myths. Compiled by monks from previous documents or accounts, it dates from the end of the fourteeenth century. *See also* Ogham.

BALOR OF THE EVIL EYE

In Irish Celtic mythology, Balor of the Evil Eye was the king of the Fomorii. A giant and monster with one eye, he was greatly feared. It was said that the eyelid over his one eye was so huge and heavy that it had to be levered open by several men. When it was open it was a source of destruction since it could kill anyone, including whole armies, that Balor looked upon.

Since it had been forecast that Balor would be killed by his own grandson, he was at pains to make sure that no man got near his daughter, Ethlinn, whom he locked away in the Glass Tower on Tory Island or possibly in a cave.

Cian succeeded in gaining entrance to where Ethlinn was and seduced her. The story varies as to whether she had one child by him or triplets. The legend that indicates triplets tells how Balor threw the babies in the sea, only one escaping. In either event, Ethlinn had a surviving son by Cian, and in time the prophecy concerning Balor's grandson came true. The child was Lugh, and it was he who killed Balor by putting out his one eye with his slingshot. He drove it right through the back of his head and killed many of the Fomorii as well. Balor's corpse is then said to have been hung on a sacred hazel tree where it dripped poison and split in two. His Welsh counterpart was Yspaddaden. *See also* Chapters 5, 9, 16.

BANBHA

In Irish Celtic mythology, the wife of Mac Cuill and one of the three goddesses who promised help to the Sons of Mil Espaine in return for having the country named after her, the other goddesses being Eriu and Fótla. *See* Chapter 10.

BAN OF BENWYCK

One of the names under which Bran the Blessed appears in Malory's *Morte D'Arthur*. *See* Chapter 25.

BANSHEE *see* BEAN SÍDHE; SÍDH.

BAOISGNE *see* CLANN BAOISGNE.

BARD *or* FILI (*plural* FILIDH)

A poet, often one who was attached to a royal court. He was a very learned person as well as being a poet, knowing much about heroic tales and genealogies as well as poetic metres, and often having the gift of prophesy. They fulfilled the function of poets, seers and royal advisers, and were often highly trained, many being trained in a special school for several years before being allowed to practise their art.

BARDSEY ISLAND

An island off the westernmost point of Caernarvonshire, in Arthurian legend said to be the scene of Myrddin's or Merlin's final imprisonment in a tomb of airy enchantment.

339

BEALTIUNN
A variant spelling of Beltane.

BEANN GHULBAN
In Irish Celtic mythology, Beann Ghulban was a monstrous boar without ears or a tail that originally had been born as a human child to the wife of Donn. It was so named from the area where it roamed near Sligo. It was placed under a *geis* or bond by its father, Roc, to kill Diarmaid ua Duibhne, and duly did this when Diarmaid was out hunting with Fionn (*see* Chapter 15).

BEAN SÍDHE
In Irish Celtic mythology, Bean Sídhe was a female fairy or spirit that became attached to a particular family. Known in English as banshee, it was said that she would set up an eerie wail when a member of the family was going to die. *See also* Sídh and Chapter 16.

BEBO
In Irish Celtic mythology, Bebo was the wife of Iubdan and so the queen of Faylinn. She went with her husband to Ulster to visit what to the diminutive people of Faylinn was a race of giants, Iubdan having been put under a *geis* or bond by Eisirt to go there. They were held captive there. *See* Chapter 13.

BÉCUMA
In Irish legend, Bécuma was the wife of Conn 'the Hundred-Fighter', high king of Ireland. She had an affair with Gaiar. *See* Chapter 15.

BEDWYR
In Welsh Celtic mythology and adopted in Arthurian legend, Bedwyr, the swiftest of men, was a companion of Culhwch and the one who returned the spear to Yspaddaden, wounding him in the knee. *See also* Chapter 24.

BELENUS *or* BELENOS *or* BEL
In Gaulish Celtic mythology, Belenus was a god who was associated with light, the word *bel* meaning 'bright'. He was also associated with the sun and with healing and later became linked with the classical god Apollo. *See* Chapters 18, 25.

BELI
In Welsh Celtic mythology, Beli was the father of Lludd and Llefelys. He is also said to have been the husband of Don.

BELTANE *or* **BELTAINE** *or* **BELTENE**
One of the four great annual Celtic festivals was Beltane. It was celebrated on 1 May and marked the beginning of the Celtic summer. It was named after Belenus and was associated with bonfires that were lit on the night before the festival. The ordinary household fires would be extinguished and the druids would light bonfires, supposedly using torches lit by the rays of the sun. The festival was associated with regeneration and regrowth after the ravages of winter.

BENDIGEID VRAN *or* **BENDIGEIDFRAN** *see* BRAN THE BLESSED.

BHUILG *see* FIR BHOLG.

BÍLE
In Irish Celtic mythology, the equivalent of Beli and Belenus. He is also said to be a possible husband of Danu (who is never named), and therefore father of the gods, or the son of Bregon and brother of Ith and father of Mil. *See also* Chapter 5.

BLACK BOOK OF CARMARTHEN *see* CARMARTHEN, BLACK BOOK OF.

BLADUD
According to Geoffrey of Monmouth the father of Leir (Lear) who built Caer Badus (Bath) and died as the result of an accident with a flying machine of his own invention. *See* Chapter 26.

BLATHNAD *or* **BLATHNAT**
In Irish Celtic mythology, Blathnad was the daughter of Midhir and wife of Cú Roí. She entered into a conspiracy with Cúchulainn to murder Cú Roí, who had shamed Cúchulainn. After his death she was pulled to her death over a cliff.

BLODEUWEDD

In Welsh Celtic mythology, Blodeuwedd was a beautiful maiden whose name translates as 'flower face'. She was created out of oak, broom and meadowsweet by Gwydion and Math to be the bride of Lleu Llaw Gyffes to circumvent the curse that was put on him by his mother, Aranrhod, that he should never marry a mortal woman until she herself found him one, which she had no intention of doing.

Blodeuwedd was unfaithful to Lleu with Gronwy Pedbyr, and they planned to murder Lleu, but he could be killed only under certain strange conditions. She found out from Lleu what these conditions were, in particular what stance he had to adopt before he could be killed. Gronwy tried to kill Lleu with a spear but succeeded only in wounding him, and Gronwy was killed by him. Blodeuwedd was turned into an owl and became an outcast. *See also* Chapter 18.

BLUE-GREEN

In Irish Celtic mythology, the name of the spear used by Conall Cearnach.

BOANN

In Irish Celtic mythology, Boann was the mother of Oenghus by the Daghda. Oenghus was brought up by Midhir. Boann helped Oenghus in his search for his dream maiden (*see* Chapter 11).

She was said to be a water goddess and to have given her name to the River Boyne (*see* Chapter 5).

BOAR

In Celtic mythology and culture, the boar was important. Boars were admired for their ferocity and were associated with war. Helmets used in war were often adorned with crests in the shape of boars, and war trumpets with boar heads were common. The boar motif is often presented with the dorsal bristles raised, indicating that it is in attacking mood.

Like the stag, the boar was used as a symbol of hunting and it was also associated with feasting

Pork was popular for feasts, particularly with the Irish Celts, both in the mortal world and the Otherworld.

Boars also played a part in Celtic legend (*see* Chapters 14, 24).

BODB

In Irish Celtic mythology, Bodb was king of the Sídhe of Munster whose swineherd became one of the magic bulls of the Táin Bó Cuailgne (*see* Chapter 12).

BODB DEARG

In Irish Celtic mythology, Bodb Dearg, 'Bodb the Red', is said by some sources to have been the son of the Daghda and to have succeeded him as father of the gods in opposition from others. According to one source, he was the father of Aobh, but other sources indicate that she was his foster daughter. He is said to have identified the dream woman of Oenghus as Caer and took him to her. On alternate years she became a swan and Oenghus himself turned into a swan and flew away with her. Bodb Dearg was also involved in battles with the Fianna. *See* Chapters 11, 15.

BOGEY *or* **BOGLE**

With the coming of Christianity, Celtic mythology gradually dwindled into a system of fairies, elves, etc; a bogle was an evil or mischievous spirit.

BOGS

In Celtic mythology and culture, bogs were important. Votive offerings to the gods were often deposited in bogs. Perhaps it was thought that bogs, which are treacherous in that the ground above them can appear quite firm although underneath they are swampy and dangerous, contained spirits that had to be appeased. Cauldrons were often deposited in bogs, and a particularly fine example of this is the Gundestrup Cauldron, and parts of wagons and carts have also been retrieved from bogs. Bogs also seem to have been used for animal and human sacrifice, as remains of animals and humans have been uncovered from them. *See* Lindow Man.

BOND *see* GEIS.

BONE PRISON *see* OETH AND ANOETH.

BOOK OF ANEURIN *see* ANEURIN, BOOK OF.

BOOK OF BALLYMOTE *see* BALLYMOTE.

BOOK OF INVASIONS *see* LEABHAR GABHALA EIREANN.

BOOK OF LECAN *see* LECAN, BOOK OF.

BOOK OF LEINSTER *see* LEABHAR GABHALA EIREANN.

BOOK OF LISMORE *see* LISMORE, BOOK OF.

BOOK OF TALIESIN *see* TALIESIN.

BOOK OF THE DUN COW
A name given to an eleventh-century book that contains an account of the Táin Bó Cuailgne. The book was traditionally said to have been written on the skin of a favourite animal belonging to St Ciaran. Its scribe was Maelmuiri, who died in 1106 at the hands of robbers. *See also* Chapter 12.

BORS
In Arthurian legend one of the names given in Malory's *Morte D'Arthur* to Myrddin. *See* Chapters 23, 25.

BOUDICCA *or* **BOADICEA**
In British history, Boudicca was a warrior queen. She was the wife of Prasutagas, the leader of the Iceni tribe. Her husband had succeeded in retaining some degree of autonomy from the Romans, but when he died the Romans plundered the royal goods, raped the daughters of Prasutagas and Boudicca, and flogged Boudicca. Boudicca then raised a spirited campaign against the Romans and met with some success until she was eventually defeated in battle. She is said to have taken poison after the defeat.

BOYNE, RIVER
A river in Ireland that rises in the Bog of Allen in County Kildare and flows into the Irish Sea near Drogheda. In Irish Celtic mythology, it is one of the 'twelve chief rivers of Ireland' the waters of which were to be denied to the Formorii (*see* Chapter 7), and its existence is the result of the disobedience of the goddess Boann (*see* Chapter 5).

BRAN (1)
In Irish Celtic mythology, Bran was the son of Febal and was lured away to the

Otherworld by the vision of a beautiful woman. He set out to find her, taking with him his three foster brothers and twenty-seven warriors and encountering various adventures similar to those of Mael Dúin (*see* Chapter 16). *See also* Chapter 11.

BRAN (2)

In Irish Celtic mythology, Bran was also the name of one of the sons of Tuireann, who was born to her when she had been turned into a wolfhound by the mistress of her husband, Illan. Both Bran and his brother, Sgeolan, were born as wolfhounds and became the faithful hounds of Fionn Mac Cumhaill.

BRAN THE BLESSED *OR* BENDIGEID VRAN *OR* BENDIGEIDFRAN

In Welsh Celtic mythology, Bran the Blessed, was the son of Llyr, the brother of Branwen and Manawydan, and the half-brother of Efnisien and Nisien. He is best known for the expedition that he led to Ireland to rescue his sister Branwen from her husband, the Irish king, Matholwch (*see* Chapter 19).

BRANDEGORE OR BRANDEGORIS, KING

In the *Morte D'Arthur* the personage with whom Malory identifies Bran the Blessed.

BRANDEL OR BRANDILES

In the *Morte D'Arthur* the personage with whom Malory identifies Bran the Blessed.

BRANDUBH *see* MONGAN.

BRANWEN

In Welsh Celtic mythology, Branwen was the sister of Bran the Blessed and wife of Matholwch. It was Matholwch's ill-treatment of her that led to Bran's invasion of Ireland and to his death and the destruction of most of his followers. Like Bridget, she was easily assimilated into the Christian saints. *See* Chapter 20.

BREASAL

In Irish Celtic mythology, Breasal was the king of Hy-Breasal (*see* also Chapter 11).

BREGON
In Irish Celtic mythology, Bregon was the father of Bíle and Ith and grandfather of Mil.

BRENNIUS, KING
In his *Historia Regum Britanniae* the personage with whom Geoffrey of Monmouth identifies Bran the Blessed (*see* Chapter 26). He was possibly an early historical king.

BRES
In Irish Celtic mythology, there was more than one person called Bres, and they tend to become confused. The best-known one is the Bres who took over from Nuada when he lost an arm in battle and had to abdicate as king of the Tuatha Dé Danaan. Bres was part Fomorii on his father's side, his father being Elatha, and part Tuatha Dé Danaan on his mother's side, his mother, Eri, having had an affair with Elatha. Bres was a bad and tyrannical ruler. He was forced to abdicate in favour of Nuada, who had had a silver arm fitted by Dian Cécht, and defected to the Fomorii. This led to the second Battle of Magh Tuiredh. He was captured in the battle but was released by the Tuatha on condition that he gave them advice on agriculture. *See* Chapters 7, 8, 9.

BRIAN
In Irish Celtic mythology, one of the three sons of Tuireann, brother of Iuchar and Iucharba, who killed Cian. *See* Chapter 8.

BRIAREUS
In Arthurian legend, the guard of Myrddin or Merlin in his final imprisonment on Bardsey Island.

BRICRIU
In Irish Celtic mythology, Bricriu was an Ulster champion who was famous for his malice and love of mischief in the way that the Welsh Efnisien was. He is said to have given a feast for the men of Ulster and the men of Connacht. There was much competition to carve the meat at such a feast, as this honour traditionally went to the most notable warrior present. In order to cause trou-

ble, Bricriu secretly persuaded three of the notable warriors all to claim this honour, the three warriors being Cúchulainn, Conall Cerneach and Laoghaire Buadhach. The three were sent to Medb to have their claim judged, and she judged in favour of Cúchulainn, but the other two refused to accept the decision. They were then all three sent to Cú Roí Mac Dairi, the king of Munster. He also decided in favour of Cúchulainn.

Legend also has it that Bricriu was asked to judge the contest between Donn Cuailgne and Finnbhenach, but he was trampled to death by the two fighting bulls.

BRIDE *see* BRIDGET.

BRIDGE OF THE CLIFF
In Irish Celtic mythology, one of the obstacles Cúchulainn had to surmount on his journey to the island of Scáthach. *See* Chapter 12.

BRIDGET *or* **BRIDE**
The name by which Brigit is known in her representation as a Christian saint.

BRIGIT *or* **BRIGID**
In Irish Celtic mythology, Brigit seems to have been one of the goddesses who was both a single goddess and a triple goddess. Her name meant 'exalted one', and she was associated with healing, fertility, crafts, poetry and learning. According to one legend, she was the daughter of the Daghda and may have been the wife of Bres and mother ot Ruadan. When Ruadan returned home to die, his parents mourned for him, thus inventing keening.

As well as being a pagan goddess, Brigit became a Christian saint who took over some of the traditions and associations of the goddess as well as her name. *See also* Chapter 16.

BRI LEITH
The sídh or underground kingdom of Midhir, identified with Slieve Golry, near Ardagh in County Longford. It was to there that Midhir took Etain (*see* Chapter 11).

BROWN BULL OF ULSTER *see* DONN CUAILGNE.

BROWNIE

With the coming of Christianity, Celtic mythology gradually dwindled into a system of fairies, elves, etc; a brownie was a helpful spirit who did good deeds, especially household chores, at night.

BRUGH

In Irish Celtic mythology, a fairy palace, particularly associated with Oenghus, who, by trickery, obtained the Brugh na Boínne, 'the Brugh on the Boyne' (identified with Newgrange), from his father, the Daghda. *See* Chapter 11.

BRUTUS

In Romano-British Celtic mythology, Brutus is said to have been the founder of the British people. The great-grandson of the Trojan Aeneas, he is supposed to have landed at Totnes in Devon and to have subjugated the giants who then inhabited the country.

BRYNWYN

One of the two names by which Branwen is known in her representation as a Christian patron saint of lovers. The other name is Dwynwen.

BUARAINECH

In Irish Celtic mythology, the father of Balor.

BUINNE THE RUTHLESS RED

In Irish Celtic mythology, one of the sons of Fergus, who with his father and brother pursued Deirdre and Naoise. *See* Chapter 14.

BULL

In Celtic mythology and culture, the bull was important. It was a symbol of strength and virility as well as aggression, the latter symbolised by its horns, which were often depicted in carvings, figurines, etc, in exaggerated form. Bull heads were sometimes used as handles for buckets, and bull statuettes seem to have existed from the seventh century BC.

Bull sacrifice appears to have been common among the Celts, and examples are depicted on the silver Gundestrup Cauldron. The bull was also associated with other Celtic rituals. At the Tarbhfeis, which took place to chose a high king of Ireland, a bull was slain and its flesh eaten and its blood drunk by a druid, who then went to sleep and was supposed to dream of the person who was to be high king.

In mythology, the most famous legend involving a bull is contained in the Táin Bó Cuailgne, the story of how Donn Cuailgne, the famous great brown bull of Ulster, was taken by Medb of Connacht.

BWBACH (*plural* BWBACHOD)
With the coming of Christianity, Celtic mythology gradually dwindled into a system of fairies, elves, etc; a bwbach was a helpful spirit similar to a brownie. *See also* Chapter 26.

C

CADBURY *see* SOUTH CADBURY CASTLE.

CADER IDRIS
Literally 'chair of Idris', a mountain ridge in Gwynedd that features in a popular tradition that whoever dares to spend a night alone on it will be found in the morning either inspired or mad.

CAER (1)
In Irish Celtic mythology, Caer was the daughter of Ethal Anubal with whom Oenghus fell in love after dreaming of her (*see* Chapter 11).

CAER (2)
The Welsh word for a fort or castle.

CAER LOYW *see* MABON.

CAIRBRE
In Irish Celtic mythology, there are several people called Cairbre, but the best known is the son of Cormac Mac Airt and a king of Ireland. He went to war with the Fianna after he had refused to pay a tribute to them and destroyed them at Gabhra. He killed Oscar in single combat but was himself mortally wounded.

CALATIN
In Irish Celtic mythology, Calatin and his twenty-seven sons were killed by Cúchulainn. His wife bore him six monstrous children posthumously, and Medb looked after them while they learned magic skills so that they could help her defeat Cúchulainn. They later used their magic art against Cúchulainn and marched against him in the battle that led to his death. *See also* Chapter 12.

CAMLUAN

In Arthurian legend, they mythical battle at which Arthur was wounded. *See* Chapter 22.

CAOILTÉ

In Irish Celtic mythology, a hero of the Fianna and cousin of Fionn. *See* Chapter 15.

CARACTACUS *see* CARATACUS.

CARADAWC

In Welsh Celtic mythology, Caradawc was a son of Bran the Blessed. When his father set out for Ireland to challenge Matholwch for his treatment of Branwen, he left Caradawc with six companions in charge of his kingdom. When news of Bran the Blessed's death reached his kingdom, Caswallan ousted Caradawc and took over. Caradawc and his companions were killed by Caswallan. *See also* Chapter 20.

CARATACUS *or* **CARACTACUS**

The chief of a British Celtic tribe called the Catuvellauni was Caratacus.. He led a campaign against the Roman invaders but he was handed over to his Roman enemies by Cartimandua, the queen of the Brigantes. He is said to have been taken to Rome, where he was pardoned by the emperor Claudius.

CARMARTHEN, BLACK BOOK OF

One of the 'Four Ancient Books of Wales'. It was written in the late twelfth century. In it is contained a poem concerning Gwyn ap Nudd as a god of war and death from whom a prince named Gwyddneu Garanhir seeks protection as well as an account of the last resting places of the Welsh gods and demigods and other stories (*see* Chapters 16, 20, 21). The other Ancient Books of Wales are those of Aneurin, Taliesin and Hergest.

CARRIDWEN *see* CERRIDWEN.

CARTIMANDUA

The queen of the Brigantes tribe who is said to have handed Caratacus over to the Romans was Cartimandua.

CASWALLAWN

In Welsh Celtic mythology, Caswallan led a revolt against Caradawc. *See* Chapter 20.

CATHBAD *or* CATHBHADH

In Irish Celtic mythology, Cathbad, whose name has various variant spellings, was a druid at the court of Conchobar Mac Nessa. He is said to have been the father of Deichtire and so the grandfather of Cúchulainn. It was Cathbad who is said to have forecast that Deirdre would be very beautiful but that she would bring grief and destruction to Ireland. *See also* Chapters 12, 13.

CAULDRON

A recurrent theme in Celtic mythology is the cauldron. The Daghda had an inexhaustible cauldron from which no one went away hungry. Bran the Blessed gave Matholwch a magic cauldron that could heal the wounded and revive the dead. Midhir also owned a magic cauldron. Evidence has been uncovered on several archaeological sites of cauldrons. The Celts had a habit of preserving cauldrons by burying them in lakes and bogs, often as votive offerings to the gods. Of these the most famous is the splendid Gundestrup Cauldron.

CELTIC LANGUAGE

The Celtic languages formed a group that was a branch of the Indo-European family of languages. They are sometimes divided into *Continental Celtic*, now extinct languages spoken from about 500 BC to AD 500 from the Black Sea to Iberia, and *Insular Celtic*, which is usually further divided into *Brythonic* or *British Celtic* and *Goidelic* or *Irish Celtic*. Goidelic Celtic is often referred to by philologists as *Q-Celtic* and Brythonic Celtic as *P-Celtic* because of a sound change that took place from *q* to *p* in the Brythonic languages. Compare, for example, Irish *ceann* with Welsh *pen*, both meaning 'head'. It is believed these two linguistic groups began to go their separate ways around two and a half thousand years ago. Goidelic Celtic is the source of Irish and Scottish Gaelic and also the source of the now little used Manx Gaelic.

CELTS

The Celts were first recorded by the Greeks as *Keltoi*, deriving perhaps from a native word meaning 'hidden people'. This association with concealment may have come from the fact that, although writing was known to them and, indeed, was used, for example, on gravestones and pottery from early times, they did not commit any of their history or legends to writing until about the sixth century AD. The Celts are thought to have been under some form of prohibition by their druids not to commit things to writing, writing being a kind of taboo.

It is thought that they originated in central Europe, in the basin of the Danube, the Alps and parts of France and Germany around 1200 BC. They were originally farmers but became pioneers of iron-working. Around the sixth century BC they are thought to have spread into Spain and Portugal. Over the next few hundred years they spread into Britain, northern Italy, Greece and the Balkans. Unlike the Romans, the Celts never formed an empire, being essentially a tribal people. In the first century BC they were defeated by the Romans and by Germanic tribes and were virtually confined to Ireland, England and Wales. The Roman invasion of Britain in AD 43 further depleted them, and the arrival of the Anglo-Saxons in the fifth century pushed them into the far corners of Britain. Thus, in time, the Celtic civilisation was destroyed by the Romans and by the expansion of the Germanic tribes. It survived most energetically in Ireland, which was not invaded by the Romans. *See also* Hallstatt; La Tène.

CENN CRUIACH *see* TIGERNMAS.

CERMAIT
In Irish Celtic mythology, another name for Oghma.

CERRIDWEN *OR* **CARRIDWEN**
In Welsh Celtic mythology, Cerridwen was the mother of a very ugly son, Afagddu, and a very beautiful daughter, Crearwy. To compensate Afaggdu for his extremely unattractive features, Cerridwen set out to give him the gifts of wisdom, inspiration and universal knowledge by making a special brew in a cauldron. Inadvertently, however, these skills were transferred to Taliesin (*see* Chapter 23). Cerridwen, as befits her role in the story, is said to have been the keeper of the cauldron in the Otherworld, the cauldron in which inspiration and knowledge were brewed. She was associated with the sow, a symbol of fecundity.

CETHÉ
In Irish Celtic mythology, one of the sons of Dian Cécht. *See* Chapter 8.

CETHLENN
In Irish Celtic mythology, the wife of Balor.

CHARIOTS
Of great importance to the Celts were chariots, especially for use in war. They were also important as religious transport, with goddesses often being depicted as riding on them. An indication of how important chariots and carts were to the Celts is the fact that the elite of Celtic society were often buried with their chariots, carts or wagons. This is evident in the Hallstatt Period.

CIAN
In Irish Celtic mythology, Cian was the son of Dian Cécht, the god of medicine. He had a cow, which was stolen by Balor, and he went to retrieve it from the island of Tory. While he was there he found his way into the Glass Tower in which Balor had imprisoned his daughter Ethlinn so that no man could get near her. He was trying to avert a prophecy that he, Balor, would be killed by his own grandson. Cian is said to have seduced Ethlinn, who bore him a son called Lugh who did indeed kill Balor. *See also* Chapters 8, 15.

CIARAN, ST *see* ISLAY.

CIGFA
In Welsh Celtic mythology, Cigfa was the wife of Pryderi. She and Pryderi had various adventures along with Manawydan and Rhiannon. *See* Chapter 20,

CIL COED *see* LLWYD.

CILGWRI, OUSEL OF
In Welsh Celtic mythology, an ancient bird with great knowledge. *See* Chapter 23.

CILYDD
In Welsh Celtic mythology, Cilydd was the husband of Goleuddydd and father of Culhwch.

CIRCLE

In Celtic culture, the circle motif, particularly the concentric circle, was important. It may, like the wheel, have been associated with the sun, and it may also have been a symbol of eternity.

CLANN BAOISGNE

In Irish Celtic mythology, the family that was headed by Cumhaill, Fionn's father. Clann Baoisgne were defeated in battle at Cnucha (now Castleknock, near Dublin) by Clann Morna, led by Goll and Cumhaill was killed by Goll Mac Morna. Clann Baoisgne, led by Fionn, was then involved with the pursuit of Diarmaid before being finally defeated by Clann Morna at the Battle of Gabhra. *See* Chapter 15.

CLANN MORNA

In Irish Celtic mythology, the family that was headed by Goll Mac Morna and who defeated Clann Baoisgne at Cnucha. They were also involved in the troubles of Diarmaid before finally defeating Clann Baoisgne at the Battle of Gabhra. *See* Chapter 15.

CLIODNA

In Irish Celtic mythology, Cliodna was a queen of Munster.

CLUD

In Irish Celtic mythology, probably the goddess of the River Clyde and mother of Gwawl fab Clud.

COBLYNAU

With the coming of Christianity, Celtic mythology gradually dwindled into a system of fairies, elves, etc; the coblynau were gnomes of the mines. *See also* Chapter 26.

COLUMBA, ST *or* COLUMCILLE *see* IONA; ISLAY and Chapter 27.

CONAIRE MÓR

In Irish Celtic mythology, Conaire Mór was, according to some sources, the son of Eochaidh Airemh and his own daughter – for details of how this came

355

to be, *see* Midhir. Various bonds (*see* geis) were placed upon him at his birth, but he chose to ignore them. In particular he ignored warnings not to go to Da Derga's Hostel and he met his death there. *See* Chapter 11.

CONALL CEARNACH *or* CERNACH

In Irish Celtic legend, there are several people called Conall and they tend to become confused with each other. Of these, Conall Cearnach, also known as Conall of the Victories, is the best known. He was one of the three warriors who vied for the honour of carving the roast meat at the feast of Bricriu.

Conall Cearnach is sometimes confused with Connlai, also sometimes known as Conall, who was the child of Cúchulainn by Aoife (2). When Connlai went to Ireland, he was challenged to fight by Conall Cearnach. *See* Chapter 15.

CONAN

In Irish Celtic mythology, Conan Mac Morna or Conan 'the Bald' was one of the Fianna and depicted as their comic character (*see* Chapter 14).

CONANN MAC FEBAR

In Irish Celtic mythology, Conann Mac Febar was a king of the Formorii who built the Glass Tower.

CONCHOBAR MAC NESSA

In Irish Celtic mythology, Conchobar Mac Nessa was the son of Nessa. She was the wife of the giant Fachtna, but, according to one legend, Fachtna might not have been Conchobar's father. Instead, he might have been the natural son of the druid Cathbad.

Conchobar became king of Ulster when Nessa would agree either to marry Fergus Mac Roth or have an affair with him only if he would agree to her son becoming king for a year in his place. At the end of the year, Conchobar refused to give up the throne and Fergus went into exile. Conchobar had at his court of Emain Macha, a group of highly trained warriors, the Red Branch.

Conchobar married Deirdre, but she eloped with Naoise and they were pursued by Conchobar (*see* Chapter 15). *See also* Chapters 12, 16.

CONN (1)

In Irish Celtic mythology, one of the three sons of Miodhchaoin. He was killed in his attempt with his brothers, Corc and Aedh, to avenge the death of their father by the three sons of Tuireann. *See also* Chapter 8.

CONN (2)

In Irish Celtic mythology, the younger son of Lir and Aobh. With his siblings, Aed, Fionuala and Fiachtra, he was turned into a swan by his stepmother, Aoife (1). *See also* Chapter 11.

CONN (3)

In Irish legend, Conn 'the Hundred-Fighter' was high king of Ireland and father of Connlai (2) and Airt and grandfather of Cormac. *See* Chapter 14.

CONNACHT

In Irish Celtic legend, Connacht was one of the five provinces into which the Fir Bholg divided Ireland. Traditionally it was the great rival and enemy of Ulster. Medb of Connacht fought a war against Ulster to acquire Donn Cuailgne, the great brown bull of Ulster. *See also* Táin Bó Cuailgne.

CONNLAI

In Irish Celtic mythology, Connlai, sometimes known as Conall, possibly from confusion with Conall Cearnach, was the son of Cúchulainn and Aoife (2). He grew up to be a great warrior and eventually went to Ireland, where he killed Conall Cearnach but was then killed by his father, Cúchulainn. *See* Chapter 12.

CONNLAI (2) *see* CONN (3).

CORANAID

In Welsh Celtic mythology, the Coranaid were a group of small people who could overhear everything, no matter how low it was whispered. They were one of three plagues that disturbed the reign of Lludd. Lludd and his brother Llefelys devised a plan to poison them (*see* Chapter 26).

CORC

In Irish Celtic mythology, one of the three sons of Miodhchaoin. He was killed in his attempt with his brothers, Aedh and Conn, to avenge the death of their father by the three sons of Tuireann. *See also* Chapter 8.

CORMAC MAC AIRT

In Irish Celtic mythology, Cormac Mac Airt appears in various stories, although he is also supposed to have been a historic king around the middle of the second century. He is said to have been the father of Cairbre and of Grainne.

CREARWY

In Welsh Celtic mythology, the daughter of Cerridwen (*see* Chapter 22).

CREIDDYLAD

In Welsh Celtic mythology, the daughter of Llud over whom Gwyn and Gwythyr fought an annual duel (*see* Chapter 18).

CREIDHNE

In Irish Celtic mythology, Creidhne was one of a triad of craft gods, Creidhne being a metal-worker. With the other two, sometimes described as his brothers and called Goibhniu and Luchtaine, he worked extremely quickly to make and repair the weapons of the Tuatha Dé Danaan. The weapons were magical, in that anyone wounded by any of them would not recover. *See also* Chapter 7.

CROMM CRUACH

In Irish Celtic mythology, a gold idol on the Plain of Adoration (Magh Slécht) that was worshipped by Tigernmas. Human sacrifices were made to it.

CU

In Irish Celtic mythology, Cu was one of the sons of Dian Cécht. *See* Chapter 8.

CÚCHULAINN

In Irish Celtic mythology, Cúchulainn is the epitome of the warrior hero. There are many legends about him, and sometimes these become confused. He is said to be the son of Deichtire but probably not by her husband, Sualtam. Instead he may have been the son of Lugh, although some say that Conchobar Mac Nessa was his father. He was originally named Sétanta. Although married to Emer, Cúchulainn was also involved with several other women.

One of these was Fand. He is said to have rejected sexual advances made to him by Morrigan and to have incurred her hostility thereafter. *See also* head. *See* Chapters 12, 13.

CULHWCH

In Welsh Celtic mythology, Culhwch was the son of Cilydd and Goleuddydd. When his mother died, his father married again, although his mother had begged him not to and had tried to arrange that he would not. His stepmother wanted Culhwch to marry her daughter and, when he refused, she was furious and put a curse on him that the only woman that he could marry was Olwen, the daughter of the giant Yspaddaden. *See* Chapter 24.

CÚ ROÍ MAC DAIRI

In Irish Celtic mythology, Cú Roí Mac Dairi was a king of Munster and a sorcerer. He was involved in several legends relating to Cúchulainn (*see* Chapter 12).

CWM CAWLWYD, OWL OF

In Welsh Celtic mythology, a bird with great knowledge. *See* Chapter 24.

CWN ANNWN

In Welsh Celtic mythology, 'dogs of hell' the hounds belonging to Arawn.

D

DA DERGA'S HOSTEL

In Irish Celtic mythology, Da Derga's Hostel was owned by a Leinster chief. A hostel was a place where travellers were always welcome, and Da Derga's Hostel was the place to which Conaire Mór insisted on travelling, having broken a *geis* or bond by so doing (*see* Chapter 11).

DAGHDA *or* DAGDA, THE

In Irish Celtic mythology, the Daghda, whose name meant 'the good god' and which has various variants, was a father-god and the chief of the Tuatha Dé Danaan. He was the son of Eladu.

He is often depicted as a very large man wearing peasant garb, in particular a short tunic that reveals his buttocks. The Celts may have chosen to present him in this way to emphasise his sexuality and fertility. According to legend, the Daghda always carried a gigantic club that had magical powers and also had a magic cauldron and a magic harp (*see* Chapter 5). As his possession of an inexhaustible cauldron suggests, the Daghda was associated with abundance. Although he was a very powerful figure, being the chief of the Tuatha, he was not presented as a very attractive but as fat and gross with a prodigious appetite for food as well as sex, and this is demonstrated by a legend relating to an attempt by the Fomorii to increase their chances of success at the second Battle of Magh Tuiredh (*see* Chapter 9). The Tuatha Dé Danaan defeated the Fomorii, but they themselves were conquered by the Sons of Mil Espaine. After their defeat, the Tuatha Dé Danaan were assigned the underground part of Ireland while the Sons of Mil Espaine ruled the upper part of the country (*see* Chapter 11).

DAIRE (1)

In Irish Celtic mythology, was a ruler of Cualgne who became owner of the Donn Cuailgne, the Brown Bull of Ulster (*see* Chapter 12).

DAIRE (2)

In Irish Celtic mythology, Daire was a son of Fionn Mac Cumhaill. Legend has it that he was swallowed by a monster but succeeded in hacking his way out of the creature's stomach, thereby releasing other people who had also been swallowed.

DANA *see* DANU.

DANI

Dani was one of the last Celtic kings to rule at Tara before the arrival of St Patrick. He led a military campaign into Britain and then into Europe. He was struck by lightning when he was storming a tower in the Rhine valley.

DANU *or* **DANA**

In Irish Celtic mythology, Danu was a mother-goddess and the mother of the Tuatha Dé Danaan. *See* Chapters 5, 6, 7.

DEALGNAID

In Irish Celtic mythology, Dealgnaid was the wife of Partholón. She is said to have accompanied him to Ireland. She was the mother of Rury, who is said by some to have been the son of her husband, Partholón, but may have been the son of Topa, the manservant of Partholón, whom Dealgnaid seduced.

DECAPITATION *see* HEAD, THE.

DEICHTIRE *or* **DEICHTINE**

In Irish Celtic mythology, Deichtire is said to have been the daughter of the druid Cathbad and the mother of Cúchulainn, perhaps by the god Lugh, although she was married to Sualtam, an Ulster chieftain, and some sources say that Cúchulainn was his son. Some sources indicate that she was the daughter or sister of Conchobar Mac Nessa.

DEIRDRE *or* **DERDRIU**

In Irish Celtic mythology, Deirdre was the subject of a prophesy by the druid Cathbad. He forecast that she would become the fairest woman in all of Ireland but that she would bring death and destruction to the country. Because of the second part of this prophecy, some people wanted to have her killed at birth. However, Conchobar Mac Nessa, hearing of the prophecy of her beauty, decreed that she should live and that he would marry her when she came of age. When she did come of age, she did not want to marry Conchobar, who was by that time quite old, and wanted to marry Naoise instead and she eloped with him. *See* Chapter 14.

DEMNA

In Irish Celtic mythology, Demna was the original name of Fionn Mac Cumhaill (*see* Chapter 15).

DERDRIU

In Irish Celtic mythology, a variant name for Deirdre.

DESTINY, STONE OF *see* STONE OF DESTINY.

'DIALOGUE OF THE ELDERS' *see* AGALAMH NA SENÓRACH.

DIAN CÉCHT

In Irish Celtic mythology, Dian Cécht was the god of healing, often depicted as a giant leech. He was especially active during the two Battles of Magh Tuiredh (*see* Chapter 7). His son Midach and daughter Airmid were also healers, and when Midach showed such a gift for healing that Dian Cécht was afraid of having his own reputation surpassed, he killed him.

DIARMAID

In Irish Celtic mythology, there are several people called Diarmaid, but the most famous of these is Diarmaid ua Duibhne, who was the son of Donn and is said to have been either the foster son or grandson of Oenghus. He received a spot, known as the 'love spot', on his forehead from a mysterious maiden who said that any woman who saw this spot would instantly fall in love with him. He is said to have been extremely handsome, and Grainne fell in love with him, although she was engaged to be married to the elderly Fionn Mac Cumhaill. Diarmaid and Grainne eloped, leading to Fionn's great pursuit of them (*see* Chapter 15).

DINAS EMRYS

In Welsh Celtic mythology, the place near Beddgelert in Gwyned where Llud buried the dragons he had ousted (*see* Chapter 24). In Arthurian legend it was here that Elen, Myrddin's wife, later built a fortress (*see* Chapter 21).

DINNSENCHUS

An ancient topography preserved in the twelfth-century Book of Leinster that contains information on places connected with Irish Celtic mythology. *Dinnseanchus* is the modern Irish word for 'topography'.

DISSULL

In Welsh Celtic mythology, a giant with a beard from which a leash is made for Mabon's hounds (*see* Chapter 24).

DIWRNACH

In Welsh Celtic mythology, the owner of the cauldron that was one of the treasures of Britain (*see* Chapter 24).

DOBHAR

In Irish Celtic mythology, the king of Sicily from whom the sons of Tuireann had to obtain his two horses (*see* Chapter 8).

DOMNU

In Irish Celtic mythology, Domnu was a Formorian goddess and mother of Indech. *See also* Chapter 6.

DON

In Welsh Celtic mythology, Don was the Welsh equivalent of the Irish Danu. She is said to have been the daughter of Mathonwy, and so the sister of Math, and the wife of Beli. Her children include Gwydion and Aranrhod. *See also* Chapter 18.

DONN

There are various people called Donn in Irish Celtic mythology. Of these, one is the god of death. Another was one of the Sons of Mil Espaine, and he is sometimes identified with the god of death. In terms of the invasion of Ireland by the Sons of Mil Espaine, he is better known as Eber Donn.

Donn was also the name of the father of Diarmaid ua Duibhne.

DONN CUAILGNE

In Irish Celtic mythology, Donn Cuailgne was the name of the great Brown Bull of Ulster. It was at the centre of the Táin Bó Cuailgne, the legend of how Medb tried to get hold of it and caused a war between Ulster and Connacht. The bull was finally captured and was taken to Medb's camp, where it had a terrible fight with Finnbhenach, the White-horned Bull of Connacht, during which Finnbhenach was killed and torn to pieces. After that, Donn Cuailgne went back to Ulster, where it died.

DOWTH

An important prehistoric passage grave near Drogheda in County Louth, forming part of the Brugh na Bóinne (*see* Chapter 11).

DRUID

In Celtic culture, a druid was a priest. The name druid is thought to have come from *drus*, the ancient name for the oak tree, which was sacred to the druids. As well as being priests, the druids were teachers, poets, philosophers, seers and judges. Druids represented the most powerful force in Celtic society. Druids were extremely highly trained and this rigorous training could go on for as long as twenty years.

DÚN

The word for 'fort' or 'fortress' in the various Celtic languages.

DURROW *see* ILLUMINATED GOSPELS.

DWYNWEN

One of the names by which Branwen is known in her representation as a Christian patron saint of lovers. The other name is Brynwyn.

DYFED

In Welsh Celtic mythology, the realm over which Pwyll reigned (see Chapter 21).

DYLAN EIL TON

In Welsh Celtic mythology, Dylan Eil Ton was a golden-haired boy who was the first of the two sons to be born to Aranrhod when she was taking the virginity test for the post of foot-holder to Math. At the moment of his birth he made for the sea where he was able to swim like a fish. 'Eil ton' indicates 'son of the wave'.

E

EASAL

In Irish Celtic mythology, the King of the Golden Pillars from whom the sons of Tuireann had to obtain his seven pigs (*see* Chapter 8).

EBER *or* **EBER DONN**

In Irish Celtic mythology, Eber was one of the leaders of the expedition undertaken by the Sons of Mil Espaine to Ireland. He killed Mac Cuill, but he himself was dead before his brother, Eber Finn, and Eremon quarrelled over who should rule Ireland.

EBER FINN

In Irish Celtic mythology, Eber Finn was one of the leaders of the expedition made by the Sons of Mil Espaine to Ireland. He was the brother of Eber Donn and after the latter's death became involved in a dispute with Eremon over who should be ruler of Ireland. Amhairghin decreed that Eremon should rule first and that Eber Finn should become ruler on the death of Eremon. Eber Finn refused to accept this judgement, and Ireland was divided into two realms, the southern ruled by Eber Finn and the northern by Eremon. However, before long war broke out and Eber Finn was killed. Eremon became king of all Ireland which he ruled from Tara.

ECHTRAI *or* **EACHTRA**

In Irish Celtic mythology, echtrai referred to a class of adventure legends usually relating to a mortal's journey to the Otherworld, made either by crossing several tracts of water or by entering a sídh. *See* immram.

EDAIN *see* **ETAIN**.

EDAIN ECHRAIDHE see **HORSES**.

EDEYRN

In Welsh Celtic mythology, .a brother of Gwyn ap Nudd.

EFNISIEN

In Welsh Celtic mythology, Efnisien was the brother of Nisien and the half-brother of Bran the Blessed, Branwen and the rest of the children of Llyr. He was known as a mischief-maker, and his brother Nisien was known as a peacemaker. When Matholwch went from Ireland to Wales to seek the hand of Branwen in marriage, Efnisien inflicted terrible disfigurement on the hundred horses that Matholwch had brought with him. Matholwch took his revenge by ill-treating Branwen when he got her to Ireland. Bran the Blessed was angry at his sister's treatment and formed an expedition to go to Ireland to rescue her where again Efnisien wreaked havoc and war ensued, leading to the death of Bran (*see* Chapter 20).

EFRAWG *see* PEREDUR.

EGGARDON *see* HILL FORT.

EIRE

The name given to southern Ireland today is Eire. The name derives from the goddess Eriu.

EISIRT

In Irish Celtic mythology, Eisirt was the bard at the court of Iubdan, king of the Faylinn, a diminutive people (*see* Chapter 13).

EITHNE *see* ETHLINN.

ELADU

In Irish Celtic mythology, Eladu was the father of the Daghda.

ELAINE

In Arthurian legend, the name accorded to Elen by Sir Thomas Malory in the *Morte D'Arthur*.

ELATHA
In Irish Celtic mythology Elatha was a Fomorii leader and father of Bres by Eri. Bres later became king of the Tuatha Dé Danaan (*see* Chapter 5).

ELAYNE
In Arthurian legend, one of the names accorded to Elen.

ELCMAR
In Irish Celtic mythology, Elcmar was the foster-father of Oenghus.

ELEN
In Welsh Celtic mythology, Elen was the daughter of Eudaf, from whom the kings of Cornwall are supposed to be descended. In Arthurian legend she is described as the wife of Myrddin or Merlin.

ELFFIN
In Welsh Celtic mythology, Elffin was the boy who found the leather bag containing Taliesin in his father's fish weir, where Cerridwen had thrown it. He it was who named Taliesin because of his 'radiant brow' (*see* Chapter 23).

ELLYLLON
With the coming of Christianity, Celtic mythology gradually dwindled into a system of fairies, elves, etc; the ellyllon were elves. *See also* Chapter 26.

EMAIN MACHA
The seat of the kings of Ulster was known as Emain Macha, which was the centre of the Red Branch. It is supposed to have been established by Macha, hence its name. It was the court of Conchobar Mac Nessa. It has been identified as being at Navan, near Armagh.

EMER
In Irish Celtic mythology, Emer was the daughter of Forgall and the wife of Cúchulainn (*see* Chapters 12, 14).

EMRYS
An epithet of Myrddin or Merlin.

EOCHAIDH AIREMH

In Irish Celtic mythology, Eochaidh Airemh married the reincarnation of Etain and then refused to return her to Midhir, her husband in her original form (*see* Chapter 11).

EPONA

In Gaulish Celtic mythology, Epona was one of the more important deities. Epona derives from the Celtic word for 'horse' and she was a horse goddess. Since horses were of particular importance to the Celts, in terms of transport, war and economics, it follows that the cult of a horse goddess was an important part of their beliefs. Epona is always depicted with horses. In some representations she is shown riding side-saddle and in others she is standing or sitting between two or more horses. She is also often shown with a symbol of fertility or abundance, for example a basket of fruit or corn. Her horse is always a mare, and this is sometimes shown with a foal, representing fertility and regeneration. Epona also seems to have been associated with healing, particularly water healing, being venerated at some Gaulish spring sanctuaries. She is also thought to have been associated with death, and it has been suggested that perhaps she was a guide and guardian to those of her devotees who were entering the next world.

ERC

In Irish Celtic mythology, Erc features in a legend in which he is said to have killed Cúchulainn. He joined forces with Medb and the monstrous children of Calatin and marched in battle against Cúchulainn (*see* Chapter 12).

EREMON

In Irish Celtic mythology, Eremon was one of the Sons of Mil Espaine who invaded Ireland. On the death of Eber (Donn) he had a quarrel with Eber Finn over who should rule Ireland. The country was first divided between them but war broke out and Eber Finn was killed. Eremon thus became the first king to rule over all Ireland.

ERI

In Irish Celtic mythology, Eri was one of the Tuatha Dé Danaan and the mother of Bres by Elatha.

ERIN

One of the three ancient names of Ireland derived from the goddess Eriu (*see* Chapter 10). The others were Banba and Fótla.

ERIU

In Irish Celtic mythology, Eriu was the goddess who gave her name to Ireland (*see* Chapter 10).

ETAIN *or* EDAIN

In Irish Celtic mythology Etain was the daughter of Ailill. Midhir fell in love with her and sought her hand in marriage, using the auspices of Oenghus to intercede on his behalf (*see* Chapter 11).

ETHAL ANUBAL

In Irish Celtic mythology, Ethal Anubal was a prince of Connacht and the father of Caer (*see* Chapter 11).

ETHLINN *or* EITHNE *or* ETHNE

In Irish Celtic mythology, Ethlinn was the daughter of Balor. Because of a prophecy that he would be killed by his grandson, Balor had her confined in a tower, probably the Glass Tower. Cian succeeded in entering the tower and having a relationship with Ethlinn. There are variations on the legend. According to one source, she bore one son, whom Balor ordered to be drowned, but the boy was saved and fostered by Manannán Mac Lir. The boy was Lugh, and he fulfilled the prophecy. According to another source, she gave birth to triplets and all but one was drowned, the surviving child being brought up by Cian. *See also* Chapter 15.

ETHNE *see* RONAN.

F

FACHTNA

In Irish Celtic mythology, Fachtna was the king of Ulster and the husband or lover of Nessa. According to some sources, he was the father of Conchobar Mac Nessa.

FAILINIS

In Irish Celtic mythology, the hound whelp of the King of Ioruaidhe that the sons of Tuireann had to obtain (*see* Chapter 8).

FALGA

In Irish Celtic mythology, a name of the Isle of Man.

FALIAS

In Irish Celtic mythology, Falias was one of the four great cities of the Tuatha Dé Danaan before they went to Ireland. The Stone of Destiny came from Falias. The other cities were Finias, Gorias and Murias.

FAND

In Irish Celtic mythology, Fand was a daughter of Aed Abrat and sister of Lí Ban. She was the wife of Manannán Mac Lir who deserted her so she had an affair with Cúchulainn (*see* Chapter 14).

FAYLINN

In Irish Celtic mythology, the Faylinn were the diminutive people who were ruled over by Iubdan (*see* Chapter 13).

FEBAL

In Irish Celtic mythology, Febal was the father of Bran (1).

FEDLIMID
In Irish Celtic mythology, Fedlimid was a bard at the court of Conchobar.

FENIUS FARSA
In Irish Celtic mythology, the first Irishman (*see* Chapter 10).

FERDIA
In Irish Celtic mythology, Ferdia was a friend of Cúchulainn who sided with Medb and was goaded into single combat with Cúchulainn (*see* Chapter 12).

FERGUS
In Irish Celtic mythology, Fergus was one of the two sons of Fionn. He became the bard and ambassador of the Fianna.

FERGUS MAC LEDA
In Irish Celtic mythology, Fergus Mac Leda was the king of Ulster at the time that Iubdan and his wife went from Faylinn to visit Ulster to see for themselves what was to them a race of giants (*see* Chapter 13).

FERGUS MAC ROTH
In Irish Celtic mythology, Fergus Mac Roth was a king of Ulster. He agreed to give up his throne for a year to Conchobar Mac Nessa, but at the end of the year Conchobar refused to give the throne up, and, in any case, he had proved to be a popular king. At first Fergus served Conchobar, but he was disgusted when Conchobar broke his word to Naoise and defected to Medb, the queen of Connacht, and took part in the Táin Bó Cuailgne on the side of the men of Connacht. Fergus Mac Roth was the tutor and foster father of Cúchulainn, and fulfilled his promise to him never to confront his foster son in battle, thus having to leave Medb's army. *See* Chapter 12.

FER-SÍDHE *see* SÍDH.

FERREX
In British Celtic mythology, Ferrex was a son of Gorboduc and Judon and the brother of Porrex. Porrex and Ferrex had a quarrel over the succession, and Porrex plotted to ambush Ferrex. He, however, found out about this and es-

caped to Gaul to raise an army. This attempt to save his life was in vain, as Porrex killed him on his arrival back in Britain. Judon went mad on hearing of the death of Ferrex and hacked Porrex to pieces. Thus, on the death of Gorboduc, there was no one left to continue the line of descent, a line supposed to have come down from Brutus.

FIACHA (1)
In Irish Celtic mythology, Fiacha was an exile from Ulster who fought on the side of Connacht in the Táin Bó Cuailgne.

FIACHA (2)
In Irish Celtic mythology, Fiacha was a son of Conchobar.

FIACHADH *see* KNIGHTS.

FIACHTRA
In Irish Celtic mythology, Fiachtra was a daughter of Aobh and Lir. She was one of the four children of Lir who were turned into swans by their stepmother, Aoife (*see* Chapter 11).

FIANCHUIVÉ
In Irish Celtic mythology, Fianchuivé was an island in what is now called the Irish Sea. The sons of Tuireann had to obtain a cooking spit from the woman who lived on the island (*see* Chapter 8).

FIANNA
In Irish Celtic mythology, the Fianna were a group of warriors who formed a military elite who guarded the high king of Ireland. At one point they were led by Fionn Mac Cumhaill (*see* Chapter 15).

FIDCHELL
In Celtic legends, a game of chess often features, especially as a method of settling disputes. Although it is usually translated in the legends as 'chess', the game being referred to in Irish legends is usually fidchell, a board game resembling chess, said to have been invented by Lugh. The Welsh equivalent of the game was gwyddbwyll.

FILI *see* BARD.

FINDABAIR *or* **FINDABAR** *or* **FINDBHAIR**
In Irish Celtic mythology, Findabair was the daughter of Medb and Ailill. Her hand in marriage was the reward for the champion who could defeat Cúchulainn, but none could and she died of shame.

FINEGAS
In Irish Celtic mythology, Finegas was a druid who caught the salmon of knowledge (*see* Chapter 15).

FINIAS
In Irish Celtic mythology, Finias was one of the four great cities of the Tuatha Dé Danaan before they went to Ireland. Nuada's great sword came from Finias. The others were Falias, Gorias and Murias.

FINNBHENACH
In Irish Celtic mythology, Finnbhenach was the White-horned Bull of Connacht. It was born into the herd owned by Medb but transferred itself into the ownership of Medb's husband, Ailill. Medb was jealous of her husband's ownership of such a fine bull and decided that she must have Donn Cuailgne, the great Brown Bull of Ulster, in order to outrival her husband. She invaded Ulster and a war took place (*see* Chapter 12).

FIONNBHARR
In Irish Celtic mythology, one of the Tuatha Dé Danaan to whom the Daghda gave Sídh Meadha (Knockma) after their defeat by the Sons of Mil Espaine. He and his wife, Oonagh, had seventeen sons. With the dwindling of the mythology Fionnbharr and Oonagh became the king and queen of the fairies.

FIONN MAC CUMHAILL
In Irish Celtic mythology, Fionn Mac Cumhaill, sometimes anglicised as Finn mac Cool, was one of the most celebrated heroes. His story is told in Chapters 15 and 16.

FIONUALA
In Irish Celtic mythology, Fionuala was the oldest child and first daughter of

Lir and Aobh. With her siblings, Aed, Fiachtra and Conn, she was turned into a swan by her stepmother, Aoife (1) (*see* Chapter 11).

FIR BHOLG *or* FIRBOLG
In Irish Celtic mythology, Fir Bholg was the name given to the leaders of the invasion of Ireland after the Nemedians. The name translates as 'bag men', and, according to one legend, they got their name because at one point they were slaves, perhaps in Thrace, and during their enslavement had to carry bags of soil from the fertile part of the country to the rocky, barren part. Another source suggests they took their name from a god, Bhuilg. They are said to have divided Ireland into five provinces. The Tuatha Dé Danaan ended the Fir Bholg's rule of Ireland when they defeated them at the first Battle of Magh Tuiredh.

The vanquished Fir Bholg are said to have fled to Aran, but another source indicates that the Tuatha Dé Danaan let them keep the Irish province of Connacht. *See also* Chapter 6.

FIRE
The veneration of fire was important to the Celts. Bonfires were lit both at the festival of Beltane on 1 May and at the festival of Samhain on 1 November. The Celts may have thought of fire as the earthly element that corresponds to the sun in the sky. Wheel-rolling also played a part in the Celtic fire rituals, the wheels being set ablaze and rolled downhill. Another reported Celtic fire ritual suggests that the Celts went in for human sacrifice. Images in the human shape and made of wicker were supposedly filled with sacrificial animals and people and set alight.

FOLLACH *see* TIGERNMAS.

FOMORII *or* FOMHOIRE *or* FOMOIRE *or* FOMORIANS
In Irish Celtic mythology, the Fomorii, a name that appears in various variant spellings, were a race of demonic beings, many of whom were half-human, half-monster. Their name has been translated both as 'sea giants' and as 'under-demons', and they are thought to have had their home under the sea. They fought against Partholón when his forces invaded Ireland and were defeated by him, supposedly going into exile in the Hebrides and the Isle of Man. How-

ever, legend has it that they returned after Nemedh's arrival in Ireland. They subjugated the Nemedians and extorted terrible tributes from them. The Nemedians rebelled but were defeated, and the few survivors fled, possibly to Greece or Thrace – the Fir Bholg may be descendants of these survivors.

The next of the conflicts involving the Fomorii was against the Tuatha Dé Danaan. At first both the Fomorii and the Tuatha Dé Danaan inhabited Ireland, the Fomorii having quite a small part of it. Hostilities broke out between the Fomorii and the Tuatha Dé Danaan, and the second Battle of Magh Tuiredh took place (*see* Chapter 9). Both sides suffered heavy losses, but the Tuatha won and the remnants of theFomorii people driven from Ireland.

FORGALL
In Irish Celtic mythology, Forgall was the father of Emer, who married Cúchulainn. Forgall was not keen on the union and made it a condition of the marriage that Cúchulainn went out of the country to study war skills at the house of Scáthach (*see* Chapter 12).

FOSTERING
In Celtic culture, fostering was common. Children would be fostered in the home of a druid, chief, scholar or monk from about the age of seven in order tobe educated. They would learn about poetry, music and literature and often the skills necessary for warfare.

FÓTLA
One of the three ancient names of Ireland derived from the goddess Eriu (*see* Chapter 10). The others were Banba and Erin.

G

GABALGLINE
In Irish Celtic mythology, Gabalgline was an ancient blind seer whom Medb consulted when she wished to have details of the illness that had rendered the men of Ulster unfit for battle (*see* Chapter 12).

GABHRA *or* **GOWRA**
In Irish Celtic mythology, the Battle of Gabhra, known also as Gowra, was the last great battle in which the Fianna took part. It led to the loss of their supremacy in Ireland and to the death of most of them. The battle was instigated by Cairbre, who was intent on curbing the power of the Fianna. Oscar, who was in command of the Fianna, killed Cairbre but was himself killed.

GAE-BHOLG
In Irish Celtic mythology, Gae-Bholg was the famous spear belonging to Cúchulainn that was given to him by Scáthach (*see* Chapter 12).

GAELS
In Irish Celtic mythology, the Gaels were said to have been the descendants of the Sons of Mil Espaine, who defeated the Tuatha Dé Danaan to become rulers of Ireland and the first human inhabitants of Ireland. In modern times the name is given to the inhabitants of Ireland and to the inhabitants of parts of Scotland, specifically those who speak Gaelic.

GAIAR
In Irish Celtic mythology, Gaiar was a son of Manannán. He had an affair with Bécuma (*see* Chapter 15).

GAILIOIN *or* **GALIOIN**
In Irish Celtic mythology, the Gailioin was one of the three companies that

made up the descendants of Nemedh, who came from Greece and invaded Ireland. *See also* Laighin.

GALAHAD, SIR
In Welsh Celtic mythology, Galahad was originally known as Gwalchafed, which translates as the 'falcon of summer'. In the medieval Arthurian legend, Galahad went in quest of the Holy Grail. *See also* Chapter 25.

GALAN MAI
In Welsh Celtic culture, Galan Mai was the equivalent of the Irish Beltane. Like Beltane, Galan Mai was held on 1 May.

GALIAN
The ancient name for Leinster was Galian. *See* Laighin.

GAN CEANACH
With the coming of Christianity, Celtic mythology gradually dwindled into a system of fairies, elves, etc; Gan Ceanach was a spirit who whispered thoughts of love in the ears of young women.

GAUL
Usually Gaul is thought of as corresponding to France, but the Gaul of the ancient Celts also included Switzerland and Belgium. As the Romans gradually conquered Gaul, some of the Celts were assimilated into Roman culture, some migrated, and many were killed.

GAVIDJEEN GO
In Irish Celtic mythology, the worker who was recommended by Gobhan to complete the work on Balor's palace (*see* Chapter 16).

GAWAIN *or* GAUVAIN, SIR
In Arthurian legend, the name given to Gwalchmei (*see* Chapter 25).

GEIS (*plural* GEASA)
In Celtic mythology and culture, a geis was a kind of bond that people were placed under. If someone placed under such a bond broke it, he or she would

either die or face extreme dishonour. The geis usually took the form of a pro-hibition of some kind.

GEOFFREY OF MONMOUTH

The base text for many of the stories in the medieval Arthurian saga is *Historia Regum Britanniae*, 'history of the kings of Britain'. It was written by Geoffrey of Monmouth (*c.*1100–*c.*1155), a Welsh cleric of Breton origin. *See also* Chapters 18, 23, 26.

GIANTS

In the legends of Celtic mythology, giants occur quite frequently. Traditionally giants could not be overcome by physical force because of their sheer size but had to be overcome by trickery or magic. Britain was supposed to have been ruled by a race of giants until the arrival of Brutus.

In the legends of the Celts, the word 'giant' appears not only to have been used in the sense of a huge person, many times the size of a normal person and often very ugly, but also in the sense of a person who has extraordinary talents and is thus superior to the ordinary person.

Particularly notable giants are Bran the Blessed (see Chapter 20) and Yspaddaden Penkawr (*see* Chapter 24).

GIANTS' RING *see* MYRDDIN; STONEHENGE.

GILDAS

There is little in the way of written historical accounts relating to the Celts. One of the few extant records is *De Excidio Et Conquestu Britanniae*, 'On the Ruin and Conquest of Britain'. This is often attributed to Gildas, who is thought to have moved from what is now Strathclyde to go and live in Wales where he became a monk. The work with which he has been credited, al-though his authorship has been disputed, was probably written between AD 516 and 547. The work is part history and part mythology, but it describes the invasion of Britain and the annihilation or mass migration of the Celts. He is also credited with the authorship of an open letter of rebuke to the secular and ecclesiastical Celts, *Epistola Gildae*.

GIRALDUS CAMBRENSIS *see* ITINIERARIUM CAMBRIAE.

GLAS GHAIBHNENN

In Irish Celtic mythology, Glas Ghaibhnenn was a magic cow that was stolen by Balor. He took it to Tory Island, but Cian went in pursuit and rescued the cow.

GLASS TOWER *or* GLASS CASTLE

In Irish Celtic mythology, the Fomorii are said to have built a glass tower or castle, also known as Conan's Tower, on Tory Island. The Nemedians stormed the island and castle, and killed Conan Mac Febar, the king of the Fomorii. Balor is said to have imprisoned his daughter in the Glass Tower.

GLASTONBURY TOR

In Irish Celtic mythology, the hill at Glastonbury in the Vale of Avalon in Somerset, known as Glastonbury Tor, was said to be the home of Gwyn ap Nudd and to have been a kind of gate between the mortal world and the Otherworld. Celtic hermits occupied cells on the slopes of the hill. The Celtic name for Glastonbury Tor was Ynys Wittrin, meaning 'island of glass'. *See also* hill sites.

GLENN ETIVE

In Irish Celtic mythology, the place to where Deirdre and Naoise fled (*see* Chapter 14).

GLUNEU

In Welsh and Irish Celtic mythology, Gluneu was one of the seven survivors of the expedition that was mounted by Bran the Blessed, to go to Ireland and retrieve Branwen, who was being ill-treated by her husband, Matholwch. The other survivors included Pryderi. *See* Chapter 20.

GOAT

In Celtic mythology and beliefs, the goat was a representation of fertility. A goat is sometimes depicted as accompanying the Romano-Celtic god Mercury, and the goat seems in some aspects to have been interchangeable with the ram, also a representation of fertility. Like the ram, the goat also had associations with aggression, particularly sexual aggression. Horned gods were a common part of Celtic culture. Often these horns were representations of ram's horns and often they were representations of deer antlers but sometimes they were goat's horns.

GOBHAN SAER
In Irish Celtic mythology, 'Goibhniu the Architect', an epithet of Goibhniu (*see* Chapter 16).

GODEU
In Welsh Celtic mythology, a name for the Otherworld. The name was also given to the battle fought by Gwydion, the 'Battle of the Trees', to secure three boons for mankind – the dog, the deer and the lapwing. *See also* Annwn and Chapter 22.

GOFANNON
In Welsh Celtic mythology, Gofannon is a divine smith and the Welsh equivalent of the Irish Goibhniu. He is said to have struck the blow that killed his nephew Dylan Eil Ton, the son of Aranrhod, although other reasons are also given for his death.

GOIBHNIU
In Irish Celtic mythology, Goibhniu was a smith god. He was a member of a triad of craft gods who were associated with the Tuatha Dé Danaan, the other two being Creidhne and Luchtaine. The three craft gods were responsible for making and repairing the magic weapons of the Tuatha Dé Danaan, which inflicted wounds from which no one could recover. Goibhniu is said to have been the host at feasts in the Otherworld at which people who partook of a special ale became immortal. *See also* Chapter 7.

GOLEUDDYDD
In Welsh Celtic mythology, Goleuddydd was the wife of Cilydd and mother of Culhwch (*see* Chapter 24).

GOLL MAC MORNA
In Irish Celtic mythology, Goll Mac Morna was the leader of the Fianna before Fionn Mac Cumhaill. He is said to have slain Cumhaill, Fionn's father, in order to gain leadership of the Fianna, and he is said to have later killed a son of Fionn's. According to legend, he was present at the wedding feast of Fionn Mac Cumhaill and Grainne (*see* Chapter 15) and was one of those not drugged by Grainne when she went off with Diarmaid ua Duibhne.

GOOSE

To the Celts, the goose symbolised war and protection, and geese were sometimes buried with the dead bodies of warriors. The Celtic war deities were sometimes depicted as being accompanied by geese.

GORBODUC

In British Celtic mythology, Gorboduc was a king of Britain who was supposed to be a descendant of Brutus. He was the husband of Judon and the father of Porrex and Ferrex. Porrex killed Ferrex, and Judon killed Porrex in a fit of grief at the loss of her son Ferrex. Thus when Gorboduc died there was no successor and the supposed line from Brutus died out.

GOREU

In Arthurian legend, a cousin of Arthur who rescued him from the bone fortress of Oeth and Anoeth. *See also* Chapter 24.

GORIAS

In Irish Celtic mythology, Gorias was one of the four great cities of the Tuatha Dé Danaan before they went to Ireland, the others being Falias, Finias and Murias. Lugh brought his invincible sword from Gorias.

GOSPELS, ILLUMINATED *see* ILLUMINATED GOSPELS.

GOWRA *see* GABHRA.

GRAIL

According to some sources, the cup that Jesus drank from at the Last Supper was known as the Holy Grail. According to other sources, the Holy Grail was the cup that was used to catch the blood from the wound inflicted by the centurion Longinus on Jesus as he hung upon the cross. Joseph of Arimathea is said to have arrived in Glastonbury in the first century AD. He is said to have brought the Holy Grail with him together with two bottles containing the blood and sweat of Jesus. The Grail was handed down from generation to generation and then became the centre of a quest that was central to the Arthurian saga, Galahad eventually finding it. However, the basis of the idea of a quest for some kind of vessel appears to have come from Celtic traditions.

It may be connected with the journey to the Otherworld to find a magical cauldron. *See also* Chapter 25.

GRAINNE

In Irish Celtic mythology, Grainne was the beautiful daughter of Cormac Mac Airt, a high king. She became betrothed to Fionn Mac Cumhaill when he was already old. During the wedding feast that took place the night she was due to marry Fionn, Grainne drugged most of the company and placed Diarmaid under a geis to elope with her and they were pursued by Fionn and his Fianna (*see* Chapter 15).

GRANNOS

In Gaulish Celtic mythology, Grannos was a god of healing who possibly became assimilated with the classical god Apollo. He is often depicted in conjunction with Sirona, who is regarded as being his consort.

GRASSHOLM *see* GWALES.

GREAT FURY

In Irish Celtic mythology, one of the swords that belonged to Manannán Mac Lir. Manannán gave it to Diarmid to help him in his flight from Fionn (*see* Chapter 15).

GREY OF MACHA

In Irish Celtic mythology, the war horse of Cúchulainn (*see* Chapter 12).

GRIANAINECH

In Irish Celtic mythology, 'Sunny-faced', the epithet of Oghma.

GRIANÁN OF AILEACH *see* AILEACH.

GRONWY PEDBYR

In Welsh Celtic mythology, Gronwy was the lover of Blodeuwedd. Together they tried to kill her husband, Lleu Llaw Gyffes, but Gronwy was killed by Lleu (*see* Chapter 18).

GROVE

Although the Celts sometimes built temples for the worship of their gods, they very often used natural landscape features as the centre of their worship. Sacred groves were common places of worship with the Celts, the druids being in charge of this worship. Many trees were sacred to the Celts, and a group of these was regarded as being even more sacred.

GUANHAMARA

A name used by Geoffrey of Monmouth for Gwenhwyfar.

GUINEVERE *see* GWENHWYFAR.

GUNDESTRUP CAULDRON

One of the most impressive of all the Celtic relics that have come to light is the Gundestrup Cauldron. It was found in 1891 in a bog at Vesthimmerland in Jutland by a man cutting peat. Made of almost pure silver, it was probably originally gilded and would have been a ceremonial vessel. It holds more than twenty-eight gallons and consisted of a base plate and five inner and seven outer panels. Before the cauldron was buried, the silver panels had been dismantled. The panels appear to depict some kind of mythological narrative, with gods, people and animals portrayed. Several of the figures are well-known Celtic cult figures. One of the panels shows three bulls about to be slaughtered, while others show more exotic animals, such as lions, leopards and elephants. Several goddesses are depicted, and among these is a female deity flanked by wheels, as though she were travelling in a cart. One of the panels depicts a procession of Celtic foot-soldiers and cavalry.

There is controversy about the date and origins of the cauldron. One suggestion is that it was made between the fourth and third centuries BC and that it was made in Romania or Thrace. It is thought to have been wrought by several silversmiths. Although many of the symbols depicted are obviously Celtic in origin, many do not seem to have a parallel in the Celtic art of Western Europe. There is speculation that either craftsmen from southeast Europe made the cauldron for more northern Celts or else that the cauldron had been stolen from Gaul by Celtic invaders. It was quite usual for cauldrons and other artefacts to be buried in water as a votive offering. It also might have been hidden for safety.

GUYNAS
One of the variant spellings used in Sir Thomas Malory's *Morte D'Arthur* for Gwyn ap Nudd.

GWALCHAFED *see* GALAHAD.

GWALCHMEI
In Welsh Celtic mythology, 'Falcon of May', the nephew of Arthur and one of the warriors who accompanies Culhwch. In Arthurian legend he appears as Sir Gawain. *See* Chapters 23, 24, 25.

GWALES
In Celtic mythology, the name of the island, Grassholm, where the seven survivors of the war between Bran and Matholwch spent forty years entertaining Bran's head

GWAWL FAB CLUD
In Welsh Celtic mythology, Gwawl fab Clud was the suitor whom Rhiannon rejected to marry Pwyll. The story of how he tried to marry Rhiannon after all is told in Chapter 19.

GWEDDW
In Welsh Celtic mythology, the owner of Gwynn Mygdwn, the only horse that could carry Mabon (*see* Chapter 24).

GWEIR
A form of the name Gwydion.

GWENBAUS
One of the variant spellings used in Sir Thomas Malory's *Morte D'Arthur* for Gwyn ap Nudd.

GWENHWYFAR *or* **GUINEVERE**
In Arthurian legend the wife of Arthur (*see* Chapter 25).

GWERN
In Welsh Celtic mythology, Gwern was the son of Branwen and of Matholwch,

king of Ireland. The sovereignty of Ireland was bestowed on him to avoid battle between Bran the Blessed and Matholwch. However, the boy was cast into a fire by Efnisien, and the battle between Matholwch and Bran the Blessed began (*see* Chapter 20).

GWERN ABWY, EAGLE OF
In Welsh Celtic mythology, a bird with great knowledge. *See* Chapter 24.

GWINAS
One of the variant spellings used in Sir Thomas Malory's *Morte D'Arthur* for Gwyn ap Nudd.

GWION BACH
In Welsh Celtic mythology, Gwion was the son of Gwreang. According to legend, Taliesin was Gwion reincarnate (*see* Chapter 24).

GWLÂD YR HÂV
In Welsh Celtic mythology, the 'Land of Summer', i.e. the Otherworld or Annwn.

GWLGAWD GODODIN
In Welsh Celtic mythology, the owner of a mystic drinking horn that was one of the treasures of Britain (*see* Chapter 24).

GWRAGEDD ANNWN
In Welsh Celtic mythology, spirits of the lakes and streams.

GWREANG
In Welsh Celtic mythology, Gwreang was the father of Gwion Bach, who became Taliesin (*see* Chapter 23).

GWREIDAWL
In Welsh Celtic mythology, Gwreidawl was the father of Gwythyr.

GWRHRYR
In Welsh Celtic mythology, Gwrhryr was one of the party formed to help Culhwch in his quest for Olwen. Gwrhryr was chosen because he could inter-

pret the language of animals and so could ask them for directions. *See* Chapter 24.

GWRI

In Welsh Celtic mythology, Gwri was the name given to Pryderi by Teyrnon when the baby turned up on his doorstep (*see* Chapter 19).

GWRNACH

In Welsh Celtic mythology, a giant who owned a magic sword that he would not let out of his own keeping as it was destined to die by it (*see* Chapter 24).

GWYAR

In Arthurian legend, the sister of Arthur and mother of Gwalchmei.

GWYDDBWYLL *see* FIDCHELL.

GWYDION FAB DON

In Welsh Celtic mythology, Gwydion fab Don was a magician and a poet and the son of Don. It was Gwydion who killed Pryderi in single combat by using his magical powers. *See* Chapters 18–24.

GWYL AWST

The harvest festival of the Welsh Celts, like the Lughnasadh.

GWYLLION

In Welsh Celtic mythology, cruel mountain fairies.

GWYN AP NUDD

In Welsh Celtic mythology, Gwyn ap Nudd was a king of the Otherworld. He abducted Creiddylad, even although she was engaged to be married to another man, Gwythyr, the son of Gwreidawl. It was agreed that Gwyn and Gwythyr should fight an annual combat and whoever won the combat that took place on doomsday would be the winner (*see* Chapter 18).

GWYN DUN MANE

In Welsh Celtic mythology, Gwyn Dun Mane was a cow that Culhwch had to obtain for Yspaddaden (*see* Chapter 24).

GWYNGELLI
In Arthurian legend a companion who helped catch the boar Twrch Trwyth (*see* Chapter 24).

GWYNN MYGDWN
In Welsh Celtic mythology, a horse owned by Gweddw that was the only horse that could carry Mabon (*see* Chapter 24).

GWYNWAS
A variant form of Gwyn.

GWYTHYR AP GWREIDAWL *see* GWYN AP NUDD.

H

HAFGAN

In Welsh Celtic mythology, Hafgan, whose name means 'summer white', was the rival and opponent of Arawn, king of Annwn (*see* Chapter 19).

HAG OF HELL

In Celtic mythology, the Hag of Hell was as a woman of supernatural powers who appears in the story of Culhwch and Olwen (*see* Chapter 24).

HALLOWEEN

Also known as All Hallows Eve, this is a festival still celebrated on the night of 31 October, now mainly by children. Traditionally it is associated with witches and warlocks, who are said to roam around freely then. It is the equivalent of the ancient Celtic festival of Samhain, also celebrated on the night of 31 October, which in the old Celtic calendar marked the beginning of the year.

HALLSTATT

A village in Upper Austria, Hallstatt is situated by a lake in the region known as Salzkamergut, whose capital is Salzburg. Salzkamergut means 'the place of good salt' and Salzburg means 'salt town', indicating the importance of salt to the area. Salt is thought to have been mined at Hallstatt more than two and a half thousand years ago, some of the early salt miners having been Celts – the word *hall* is Celtic for salt. Austria is one of the oldest Celtic territories in Europe and the area around Hallstatt was one of the main Celtic settlements in Austria. There were important excavations in the second part of the nineteenth century (*see* Hallstatt Excavations) and Hallstatt has become not only a village famous for its Celtic connections but a term given to indicate a stage of development of Celtic culture and civilisation wherever it was found (*see* Hallstatt Period).

HALLSTATT EXCAVATIONS

In 1846, George Ramsauer, the director of the Hallstatt State Salt Mine, discovered on a hill above the village of Hallstatt a vast prehistoric cemetery situated under some curiously shaped grass-covered mounds. He conducted investigations on many of these ancient graves, which were about two and a half thousand in number, and the results of these investigations attracted the interest of the Academy of Sciences in Vienna. A team of professional investigators was sent from there to Hallstatt in 1876 and began exhaustive excavations in the area. Their discoveries put the Celts on the map, so to speak, since before that the ancient map of Europe had been dominated by the Greek and Roman civilisations. The Hallstatt excavations produced tangible evidence of another civilisation whose people had a fixed habitation and were farmers and traders, reminding historians that the Greeks and Romans had referred to trade with a people who lived in areas of Central Europe and who were called Keltoi. The grave goods retrieved from the ancient cemetery at Hallstatt indicated that at that stage of their development the Celts were an iron-using people who had moved on from the Bronze Age. Many finely decorated vessels, weapons and horse trappings, all made of iron, were brought to the surface, as were pieces of leather clothing, shards of pottery, wooden utensils and dishes, and the remains of food. The excavations at Hallstatt have proved to be of immense importance in piecing together the culture of this ancient people, who were the Celts. So important were these excavations that the village gave its name to the Hallstatt Period or Hallstatt Culture, a means of assessing and indicating the stage of development of the civilisation of the Celts generally.

HALLSTATT PERIOD *OR* HALLSTATT CULTURE

These terms do not simply refer to the connection between the Celts and the Austrian village of Hallstatt. Instead, they are used in standard archaeological parlance to indicate a means of assessing the stage of development and time span of Celtic civilisations, wherever these were situated geographically. The style of the artefacts excavated at the Hallstatt Excavations has been used as a standard by which to assess the age and level of development and sophistication of other Celtic settlements, the other major standard being referred to as the La Tène Culture, named after a Swiss lakeside settlement. It is difficult to give exact dates in connection with things that happened so long ago, and there is some variation among historians of the dates that should be ascribed to the Hallstatt Period. Roughly speaking, it can be regarded as stretching from about 750 BC until about 450 BC.

HAMMER-GOD

One of the important Gaulish Celtic divinities was the Hammer-god. A representation of him has been found on many stone monuments and bronze figurines. He is usually depicted with a kind of hammer with a long shaft and a mallet-type head and a small vessel, such as a pot or goblet. Frequently he is represented as bearded and as wearing a short belted tunic and a heavy cloak. Sometimes he appears alone and sometimes he is part of a couple. The Hammer-god appears to have had several associations. He seems to have been connected with healing, as his statue frequently is situated at the sites of healing springs, and he was also in some parts of Gaul, such as Burgundy, associated with wine and grapes. He is also associated with the sun and with earthly prosperity.

HARP

The Irish harp is referred to extensively in Celtic myths and legends, and there are examples of it depicted on Celtic stone carvings dating from the eighth and ninth centuries in Ireland and in the west of Scotland. However, there are only fourteen surviving instruments and fragments of instruments from the whole of the early period during which the traditional form of the Irish harp flourished. The lack of concrete information is further exacerbated by the fact that the makers of the traditional Irish harps were not in the habit of either signing the instruments or dating them. What is known is that the Irish harps were of a heavier and bulkier construction than harps in other countries and, perhaps from the twelfth century, were strung with brass. There were two distinct forms of European harp by the fourteenth century, one being the sturdily built Irish harp and the other being a lighter, more delicate instrument commonly referred to as the Gothic or Romanesque harp. Legend has it that the harp came into being after a woman fell asleep on the seashore and heard the wind blowing through the sinews of the skeleton of a whale that was lying near her. On hearing her story, her husband made a wooden frame and equipped it with whale sinews to make the first harp. A less romantic account of the origins of the harp suggests that the instrument was brought to Ireland from Greece.

HAWTHORN, CHIEF OF GIANTS
In Arthurian legend the name by which Yspaddaden Penkawr is known (*see* Chapter 24).

HEAD, THE
The head was particularly revered by the ancient Celtic peoples. To them it was much more important than the heart, which was revered by other civilisations. The Celts regarded the head as housing the soul and even seem to have believed that the head could function without the rest of the body. It is probably for that reason that the ancient Celts are said to have decapitated enemies killed in battle and carried the heads from the battlefield, often attached to the necks of their horses. They would then display the heads on posts outside their settlements or nail them up on their houses, as some hunters now hang up stags' heads as trophies. The greater the owner of the head had been, the more honour went to the Celtic warrior who displayed the head as a trophy. It is also said that the Celts sometimes preserved the heads of some of their more important foes by embalming them in cedar oil and storing them in chests. Evidence of the Celtic habit of severing heads and keeping them as trophies was discovered by the Romans when they defeated the Celtic tribe, the Salii. They found a sanctuary, constructed by the Salii at Entremont in Provence, that was dedicated to the cult of the severed head. There were examples of carved heads but they also found the remains of actual human heads. Human skulls and severed heads were also found in stone pillars at Roquepertuse in Bouches-du-Rhône.

The head, as befitting something that was of such importance to the Celts, features frequently in Celtic mythology. In one of the legends associated with Cúchulainn, he is set upon by twelve enemy warriors but succeeds in defeating all of them at once and cuts off their heads. He then set up twelve stones in the ground and impaled one of the heads on each stone. Other legends demonstrate the supposed ability to function without its missing body. For example, in the Welsh legend of Bran the Blessed, when Bran is mortally wounded in his war against Matholwch, the Irish king, he asks his followers to decapitate him and take his head back home from Ireland. During the long voyage back, his head, according to the legend, was able to eat, drink and talk, just as it had done when he was alive and it was attached to his body (*see* Chapter 20). In later more civilised times when the macabre practice of decapitation had been abandoned by the Celts, the cult of the head remained important to them. This is obvious from the many stone carvings of heads that have been discovered in the areas in which the Celts flourished. Some of these were located at sacred places, such as temples, shrines or sacred wells, as though the carved head was acting as a protector. The head was also used to decorate more everyday things. Various excavations have revealed buckets and bowls with representations of the human head acting as handles.

HEFEYDD HEN

Hefeydd in Welsh mythology was the father of Rhiannon, the wife of Pwyll. He was known as Hen, meaning 'old' or 'ancient', in view of his advanced years (*see* Chapter 19).

HEILYN

In Welsh Celtic mythology, Heilyn was one of only seven Britons who survived the terrible war in Ireland between Matholwch and Bran the Blessed. Heilyn is said to have opened the magic door through which the seven survivors escaped from the Island of Gwales, having spent eighty years there on their way back from Ireland after the war (*see* Chapter 20).

HEININ

In Welsh Celtic mythology, Heinin was the chief bard at the court of King Arthur at the time when Taliesin arrived.

HELIG AP GLANNOWG

In Welsh Celtic mythology, Helig was the ruler of a kingdom in the sixth century. It is said to have been situated about ten miles out to sea from Colwyn Bay. From the nineteenth century there have been claims of sightings of the ruins of Helig's palace.

HELVETII

The Helvetii were a Celtic tribe who tried to migrate across Gaul to establish settlements on the Atlantic coast, having been driven out of their settlements in what is now Germany. Julius Caesar feared that their presence would interfere with his plans for settling and controlling Gaul, and he and his army attacked and inflicted a terrible, bloody defeat on the Helvetii at Armecy.

HERGEST, RED BOOK OF

The largest of the 'Four Ancient Books of Wales'. It was written in the four-teenth and fifteenth centuries. In it is contained Welsh translations of the British Chronicles, many triads – verses celebrating famous traditional persons or things, ancient poems attributed to Llywarch Hen and the Mabinolgi, from which large parts of Welsh Celtic mythology were worked into romantic form, notably the romance of Culhwch and Olwen (*see* Chapter 24). The other Ancient Books of Wales are those of Aneurin, Carmarthen and Taliesin.

HERNE THE HUNTER

In British Celtic mythology, Herne was the name of a giant with antlers on his head. According to legend, Herne in modern times lives in Windsor Great Park.

HIGH CROSS

The Celtic high cross is a well-known part of Celtic culture, and there are several examples of these situated in Britain and Ireland, for example on Iona and Islay in Scotland, at Kilmalkedar in Ireland and Llantwit Major in Wales (*see* Houelt Cross). Some of these freestanding crosses are thought to be twelve hundred years old or more. The early high crosses were often quite plain and undecorated, but many of the later ones were richly carved. Such carvings include the knotwork typical of Celtic culture, spiral patterns or patterns consisting of raised bosses, the latter perhaps included as symbols of the sun, which was a source of worship for the early Celts. Other subjects for carving included animals or mythical beasts and biblical scenes. Celtic high crosses were often constructed to indicate a meeting place, perhaps within a monastery, rather than to indicate a burial place.

HILL FORT

In Britain in the Iron Age a favourite place of occupation of the Celts was the hill fort. Such a settlement enabled them to observe the land below and to look out for any approaching danger, such as a marauding army. Some of the hill forts occupied by the Celts predate their arrival in Britain. A number of the sites that the Celts used had been in existence since Neolithic times, and the Celts reinforced their security rather than starting them from scratch. Instead of using high wooden fences to keep the settlement livestock in and any invaders out, the Celts made huge earthen ramparts that can still be seen in some of the areas of Britain that they inhabited. Some of the finest of the Celtic hill forts are located in western and southern Britain, and a particularly fine example is Maiden Castle near Dorchester in Dorset. Consisting of a vast enclosed area of over forty acres, it is the largest Celtic hill fort dating from the Iron Age in Europe. Fortunately, a number of the Celtic hill forts are still in a good state of preservation today – another fine example being at Eggardon, situated at the extremity of a long chalk ridge that crosses the south of England, *don* or *dun* being Celtic for 'fort', and so the historian, both professional and amateur, is able to get quite a good idea of what the Celtic hill fort was actually like. The entrance to the hill fort, as can be seen clearly at Maiden Castle, was a labyrinth-like series of earthen ramparts designed both to confuse and repel any potential invaders, although they had little effect on the Roman army when it invaded Britain in AD 43. The hill forts were constructed near ready sources of water such as dew ponds. Security and defence were, of course, important aspects of the Celtic hill forts, but they were certainly not simply military settlements. The hill forts acted as a kind of general headquarters for the local tribe of the area, for peaceful as well as warlike purposes. They functioned also as religious centres, and the Roman invaders often continued to observe the religious associations of the hill forts after they had taken them over, perhaps afraid of the Celtic deities wreaking vengeance on them. In many cases the hill forts also functioned as centres where the Celtic craftsmen could practise their art and produce goods.

HILL SITES *or* TORS

The early people, including the Celts, often made use of hills in their religious ritual. The sun often featured in their worship, and a hill was the perfect place from which to observe its rising and setting. The view of this would have been even more dramatic if the surrounding countryside were flat, and perhaps it is for this reason that the Celts and other early peoples were attracted to the hills or mounds that rise from the otherwise flat surrounding land in parts of the south of Britain. So important were such hills or mounds considered to be that some of them were man-made, notably the huge hill site at Silbury Hill in Wiltshire. This is the largest man-made hill site in western Europe and is said to be over four thousand years old. Some other hill sites were naturally occurring hills that had been amplified by man-made additions. Some of the hill sites connected with early religious ritual are surrounded by a kind of ridging or terracing, and various theories have been put forward to account for this. One theory suggest that the ridging marks the remains of a prehistoric processional maze by which the worshippers made their way to the top of the hill. Another theory suggests that the ridging is simply evidence of early agricultural methods. One of the best-known hill sites is Glastonbury Tor.

HIR ATRYM AND HIR ERWN

In Welsh Celtic mythology, Hir Atrym and Hir Erwn feature in the legend of Culhwch and Olwen (*see* Chapter 24). They were two brothers who had absolutely insatiable appetites. They could eat vast quantities of food that was provided for them and then they would lay bare the land around them as well.

HOCHDORF

The village of Hochdorf is situated in southern Germany near the Black Forest. Its claim to fame in terms of the Celts lies in the fact that in the late 1970s a Celtic burial mound was discovered and investigated by Dr Jorg Biel, an archaeologist from Baden-Württemberg. The burial mound was found to conceal a vast burial chamber built for a Celtic prince thought to have been buried around 550 BC. The excavations at Hochdorf are important in the history of Celts because of the sheer scale of the findings and because of the state of preservation of these, the grave site showing no signs of having been robbed or vandalised. The Celts, as was the case with other ancient peoples, believed that a dead person had to be supplied with the necessities of life in the afterworld, and the excavators found not only evidence of these but the remains of an elaborate cart that had been buried with the prince. The things deemed necessary for the prince's afterlife, including domestic utensils, drinking horns and weapons and a large bronze cauldron for holding honey mead, together with the other grave goods and grave clothes and trappings, shed much light on the lifestyle of an important Celtic warrior of the period. Most importantly, the sumptuousness of the clothes and the quantity and nature of the gold jewellery and trappings provided for the body of the prince certainly emphasised that the Celts were not a simple unsophisticated, poverty-stricken people, at least if you were one of their aristocracy.

HOLY GRAIL *see* GRAIL.

HORNS

Many Celtic deities that otherwise had a human form were represented as having horns or antlers, whether these were of the bull, goat, ram or stag variety. Early horned sculptures have been found, and Iron Age coins show representations of horned beings, while bucket mounts consisting of horned heads have also come to light. Horned deities were particularly popular among the Brigantes in Britain. Although most horned gods are represented as men, some dressed as warriors, female horned deities are portrayed at Icklingham in Suffolk and Richmond in Kent. Animals were extremely important in the Celtic culture and so perhaps this association between human deity and horn is not surprising. The horns are thought to have been symbolic of aggression, virility and fertility.

HORSES

As is obvious from the grave goods that have been retrieved from burial sites, the Celts were great horsemen and they used horse-drawn chariots to great effect in their battles against their foes. Their high regard for the horse is demonstrated by the effigies and carvings of horses that have been discovered at various Celtic sites throughout Europe, including the large-scale hillside horse carvings, often in chalk soil, of which the White Horse of Uffington near Oxford is a prime example. The horse was not held in regard by the Celts for its role in battle but for its associations with speed, beauty, sexual potency and fertility. Such was the importance of the horse in Celtic culture that horse sacrifices and ritual practices concerning dead horses were common. Some of the Iron Age burial sites were found to contain not only people, such as princes or charioteers, but chariots or wagons and horses, aids to the journey into the next world.

The importance of the horse to the Celts is also manifested in their habit of representing deities on horseback. These mounted gods were often depicted in the guise of warriors. Some of the pre-Roman Celtic sanctuaries in southern Gaul were decorated with stone images of mounted warriors, and mounted warrior gods were particularly worshipped by the Catuvellauni and the Corieltauvi tribes of eastern Britain. The Celts in Gaul worshipped the horse goddess, Epona, who may be identified with Edain Echraidhe in Ireland and Rhiannon in Wales. The image of Epona is found depicted on several hundred stones in what was Gaul. Epona also found favour with the Romans, and she was worshipped by them also, often being associated in Roman times with corn, fruit and, later, fertility.

HOUELT CROSS
Houelt Cross is an example of a Welsh Celtic high cross. It is situated at Llantwit Major.

HOUSES
In lowland Britain in the Iron Age the most usual form of Celtic dwelling was the round house. These round houses were built round a central pole with a timber frame secured to vertical posts, radiating out from this. The walls were low and made from wattle and daub, and the roof was thatched. Groups of round houses were built together forming villages and were often accompanied by animal shelters and storerooms of a structure similar to that of the houses. Reconstructed Celtic round houses can be seen in the Welsh Folk Museum at St Fagans, near Cardiff.

HUNTER GOD
Hunting was extremely important to the Celts, as it was to all early peoples, this being the basis of their survival. Thus it is not surprising that the Celtic culture extends its range of deities to hunter gods. These are distinguishable by their weapons and sometimes by their dress. For example, a hunter god might be represented as carrying a bow and a quiver of arrows, often with a representation of a dog beside him. Although the purpose of a hunt is obviously to kill an animal, the hunter gods appear to have been on the side of the hunted as well as the hunter. The hunter gods are frequently depicted as being accompanied by live animals of the kind liable to be hunted, and they are sometimes represented as wearing horns, suggesting an affinity between hunter god and animal of prey.

HWICCE
Hwicce was an ancient Celtic kingdom covering roughly the territory now covered by Gloucestershire and Worcestershire. Its capital was Deerhurst.

HY-BREASAL *or* HY-BREASIL *or* HY-BRASIL
In Irish Celtic mythology, Hy-Breasal was an island off the west coast of Ire-

land that was visible above the water only once every seven years. According to legend, the island would rise to the surface of the water permanently if it came into contact with fire and would then become an earthly paradise. The island is said to have been ruled by Breasal. As with all legends, various forms of Celtic legends become confused with each other, and one legend has it that Manannán Mac Lir, the son of Lir, was responsible for the sinking of Hy-Breasal under the sea. Legend often also becomes confused with fact, although the fact is usually somewhat hazy. So it is that Hy-Breasal is recorded as having being a real place. When explorers travelled to South America and discovered Brazil, they thought that they had found Hy-Breasal, although early cartographers thought that it was in southwest Ireland, where legend had placed it.

I

IALONUS

In Gaulish Celtic mythology, Ialonus was a deity associated with cultivated fields. He is thought also to have been associated with glades, since *ialo* means 'glade'.

IANUARIA

In Gaulish Celtic mythology, Ianuaria was a female deity who was venerated at the sanctuary of Beire-le-Châtel in Burgundy. Very little is known about her history or associations, although a small stone statuette depicting a young girl with curly hair, thought to be a representation of the goddess, was found at the sanctuary. The statuette is clad in a pleated coat and is holding a set of pipes, and from this latter fact it has been deduced that Ianuaria might have been associated with music, although it might be assumed that her primary association was with healing, the sanctuary at Beire-le-Châtel being dedicated to healing.

IATH N' ANANN

This was an ancient name for Ireland and may be derived from *Anu* or *Ana*, an alternative form of Danu, a mother-goddess.

IBERIA

The Celts are thought to have had extensive settlements in Iberia, which consists of Spain and Portugal, perhaps from as early as 900 BC. According to Irish legend, the Celts who colonised Ireland came from Spain. The Celts in Iberia became involved in the war between Carthage and Rome and paid a heavy price for this involvement. The Carthaginian general Hamilcar Barca invaded the southern coast of Iberia and his son, Hannibal, decided to launch an attack on Rome through the territory of the Celts. The Celts formed an alliance with Hannibal and the Romans took their revenge on them after the fall of Carthage in 197 BC. The Romans conquered and colonised the Iberian Celts and often treated them extremely savagely. Servius Sulpicius Galba even massacred the Celts after they had surrendered in 151 BC. War between the Celts and Romans in Iberia continued until the middle of the first century BC. After that the Celts seem gradually to have become assimilated into the Roman way of life.

ICENI

The Iceni were an ancient British tribe and one of the leading tribes of the East Anglian area of England. It is particularly famous for one its queens, Boudicca. She was the wife of Prasutagus. The Iceni allied themselves with the Trinovantes to mount attacks against the Roman invaders under the leadership of Boudicca and had three notable victories before being routed by the Romans.

ICOVELLAUNA

In Gaulish Celtic mythology, Icovellauna was a deity who was worshipped in the area around Metz and Trier. She is said to have presided over the healing spring of Sablon at Metz and is therefore associated with healing. No representations of the goddess have been uncovered.

IDRIS

In Welsh Celtic mythology, Idris was a giant who is said to have been skilled in poetry, astronomy and philosophy. His home was on the mountain of Cadair Idris in Gwynedd.

ILBHREACH

In Irish Celtic mythology, Ilbhreach was a son of Manannán. After the Daghda gave up his leadership of the Tuatha Dé Danaan, Ilbhreach was one of the five aspirants for the leadership. During the war that followed he fought with Caoilte against Lir (*see* Chapter 12).

ILLANN THE FAIR

In Irish Celtic mythology, Illann was one of the sons of Fergus Mac Roth, who with his father and brother pursued Deirdre and Naoise (*see* Chapter 14).

ILLUMINATED GOSPELS

These gospels, colourfully, intricately and painstakingly decorated by Celtic monks over a long period of time, are rightly considered to be one of the most important legacies that the Celtic culture has given us and indeed are considered a major contribution to the art world generally. The monks, of course, used only natural pigments to produce their brilliant blues, greens, yellows, and so on. The three finest extant examples are respectively the Book of Kells and the gospel books of Lindisfarne and Durrow.

IMBAS FOROSNAI

In Irish Celtic mythology, this was a rite based on the fact that knowledge and sagacity could be imparted to someone who chewed the raw flesh of the thumb. Fionn Mac Cumhaill is said to have done this after he had burned his thumb while cooking the salmon of knowledge or wisdom and thus to have acquired his knowledge and wisdom.

IMBOLC *or* IMBOLG

This was one of the four Celtic festivals, the others being Samhain, Beltane and Lughnasadh. It was celebrated on 1 February. It is associated with the lactation of ewes. The festival was also associated with the Irish goddess Brigit. Subsequently this pagan festival was taken over by the Christian church as one of their festivals, the feast day of St Bridget.

IMMORTALITY

The Celts believed in the immortality of the soul and they were one of the first European people to hold such a belief. It was not a theory of reincarnation but a belief based on the fact that when a person died he or she simply changed places or worlds. This was why the Celts put not only bodies in graves but all the appurtenances necessary to sustain life, the notion being that the person would need all of this in the Otherworld. The Celts seem to have believed in an constant exchange of souls taking place between this world and the Otherworld. Because they believed not only that a death in this world was the means of sending a soul to the Otherworld but that a death in the Otherworld was the means of bringing a soul to this world, the Celts are said to have mourned birth and celebrated death.

IMMRAM

This was the name given to the two main classifications of ancient Irish literature, the other being echtrai. Immram referred to a tale concerning a long voyage, usually a fantastic voyage to an island kingdom, whether this was inhabited by humans or supernatural beings. A classic example is the voyage of Mael Dúin (*see* Chapter 17). The echtrai referred to a tale involving a journey made by a human or humans to a supernatural land either by crossing many tracts of water or by gaining entrance through a sídh or burial mound.

INDECH

In Irish Celtic mythology, a son of Domnu and a Formorii king and father of Octriallach. He was killed at the second Battle of Magh Tuireadh by Oghma (*see* Chapter 9).

INFANT BURIAL

There is some evidence of rituals involving dead babies in the Celtic culture, although whether the babies all died naturally or whether some were the result of human sacrifice is not known. It is thought that interred infants may have been regarded as a means of propitiating the gods or as a means of conferring a blessing. Certainly it has been ascertained that the corpses of babies were included in the foundations of shrines and sanctuaries. At a shrine in Cambridge, dead babies were buried wearing shoes that were several sizes too big for them, perhaps because it was felt that the babies would go on growing in the Otherworld.

INGCÉL

In Irish Celtic legend, Ingcél was a monster with a single eye that contained three pupils, and he is said to have been the son of the king of Britain. He went into exile in Ireland and joined forces with the foster brothers of Conaire Mór, the high king, and some other dissidents. They made plundering raids in Ireland and Britain and killed Ingcél's father, mother and brothers. Ingcél and the band of marauders attacked Da Derga's Hostel and in the attack Conaire was killed (*see* Chapter 11).

INTERPRETATIO CELTICA

This is a term used to describe the fusion of the Celtic and Roman religious cults. As a result of this fusion, Roman gods to some extent were accepted into the Celts' own set of beliefs. Roman gods were sometimes given a Celtic title also, such as Jupiter Taranis. The converse of this process by which the Romans regarded some of the Celtic gods as part of the Roman culture – for example, the Romans named the Celtic goddess Sulis of Bath Sulis Minerva by a hybridisation process – is known as *Interpretatio Romana*, a term that was used by Tacitus.

INVASION MYTHS

In Irish Celtic mythology, invasion myths feature rather than creation myths. They are included in the Book of Invasions (*see* Leabhar Gabhala Eireann).

IOLDANACH

In Irish Celtic mythology, an epithet for Lugh, meaning 'Master of All Arts'.

IONA

St Columba, or Columcille as he is known in Gaelic, established a Celtic Christian community at the Hebridean island of Iona, having travelled there as a missionary from Ireland in AD 563. The community dwelt in 'beehive huts', the remains of some of which can be seen on the island today. It is hardly surprising, then, that Iona is rich in tangible evidence of its association with the Celts and Celtic Christianity. There is much of interest there to anyone interested in the history of the Celts. Notably it is rich in Celtic high crosses, although history suggests that there were originally many more but that most of these were destroyed by the Vikings who invaded the island from around the seventh century AD. There are today three fine examples of freestanding crosses. One is St Martin's Cross, which dates from the ninth century AD and stands five metres in height. It has various biblical scenes carved on the front of the cross, which is made of a hard volcanic stone. The back of the cross is richly carved with 'boss and serpent designs', the serpents probably pointing to a pagan influence incorporated into Christian art and worship. Another example of a freestanding Celtic cross on Iona is St John's Cross, which is situated outside the west door of the abbey. It is in fact a cast of the original cross, which dates from the late eighth century AD and has been removed for preservation and repair. Another high cross on the island is of a later date than the other two. It is McLean's Cross, which is a disc-headed crucifixion cross, having a carving depicting the Crucifixion in the centre of the round head. Tall and extremely slender, the high cross has carved panels of intricate design stretching right down the shaft.

It is not only high crosses for which Iona is noted in Celtic history. The island is also the site of the Well of Healing. Situated close to the summit of Dun-I, a granite outcrop about ninety metres in height, it takes the form of a large cleft in the rock filled with extremely cold water. Dedicated to St Columba, the well is thought to have been in use during his lifetime. Pilgrims seeking a cure from the well would climb to it if their disability allowed. Otherwise, water from it would be brought down to them.

Iona is not only associated with the Celts from the time of Columba. It has earlier Celtic connections with the druids. Indeed, the early Gaelic name for Iona was Innis na Druineach, which translates as the Isle of the Druids. There is today a thriving religious community on Iona, founded in the 1930s by Dr George MacLeod on the site of the Benedictine Abbey that was built in the Middle Ages over the foundations of Columba's original monastic settlement.

IORUAIDHE

In Irish Celtic mythology, Ioruaidhe was a kingdom, the ruler of which was the owner of a hound that could not be defeated in a fight. It could catch any wild beast that it came across and it could turn to wine any water that it bathed in. Capturing this hound and taking it to Ireland was one of the tasks imposed on the sons of Tuireann as a punishment for having killed Cian. The brothers took the king of Ioruaidhe captive and offered to let him go free only on condition that they were given the hound (*see* Chapter 8).

IRISH HARP *see* HARP.

ISEULT *see* TRISTAN AND ISEULT.

ISLAY

The Scottish Hebridean island of Islay is rich in evidence of Celtic culture from the megalithic and early Christian periods. A particularly good example of this is sited at Kildalton, where a well-preserved early Celtic wheel cross dating from around AD 800 is located. The cross is about nine feet in height and has carved on it in high relief an example of the 'nest of eggs' symbol, which appears also on St John's Cross on Iona. The significance of this symbol can only be speculated on. It has been suggested that it may be a symbol relating to the druids' worship of the sun or nature. Another suggestion is that it denotes the Holy Trinity, but its true nature is lost in the mists of time. Another fine example of the Celtic craftsmanship is to be found on Islay at Kilnaver. This is the site of a Celtic high cross eight and a half feet high and dating from around AD 850. The carvings on it, although difficult to make out, bear a resemblance to those on the high cross at Kells in County Meath in Ireland. At Kilchonan, also on Islay, is a fine example of a freestanding disc-headed cross, dating from around the late fourteenth century, and examples of some elaborately carved grave slabs. Islay is supposed to have had connections with St Columba (see Iona). According to tradition, his tutor in Ireland, St Ciaran, settled in the Rhinns of Islay and died there in AD 548.

ISLE OF MAN

There were Irish Celtic missionaries in the Isle of Man from the fifth century AD onwards, and Celtic carvings, such as the eighth-century Calf of Man Crucifixion slab, testify to their presence. However, the island was more heavily influenced by the Vikings who invaded and occupied it in the tenth century. An interesting piece of hybridisation took place between Celtic and Viking culture. Sculptures were created by the Vikings that incorporated the Celtic high cross framework and some of the symbols and patterns associated with these, such as knotwork, but also incorporated representations of characters from Norse sagas and Scandinavian runes. In Irish Celtic mythology, the Isle of Man is particularly associated with Lugh.

ITALY

In the fourth century BC, the Celts expanded their area of settlement from Gaul to Italy. They were a warlike nation, and around 390 BC they invaded Rome. The Romans were, however, able to get their revenge in the second and first centuries BC when they moved into Gaul and forced the Celts to move north.

ITH

In Irish Celtic legend, Ith was one of the Sons of Mil Espaine, who were the first human rulers of Ireland. As the name suggests, these invaders are supposed to have come from Spain and legend has it that Ith caught sight of Ireland from the top of a Spanish tower and set out to visit it (*see* Chapter 10).

ITINIERARIUM CAMBRIAE

The Norman-Welsh chronicler and cleric, Giraldus Cambrensis (*c.*1146– *c.*1223) wrote *Itinerarium Cambriae* after he had journeyed through Wales in 1188 with the archbishop of Canterbury. It is an important source book of Welsh legend as the author recorded everything he was told by the local people, however unlikely.

IUBDAN

In Irish Celtic legend, Iubdan was the elfin king of Faylinn and husband of Queen Bebo. He and his wife visited the realm of Ulster to see the humans who dwelt there, having been put under a bond by Eisirt, his bard, to do so (*see* Chapter 13).

IUCHAR

In Irish Celtic legend, Iuchar was the son of Tuireann and the brother of Brian and Iucharba. The three brothers killed Cian whose son Lugh decided to take vengeance on them (*see* Chapter 8).

IUCHARBA

In Irish Celtic legend, Iucharba was the son of Tuireann and the brother of Brian and Iuchar (*see* Chapter 8).

IWERIADD

In Welsh Celtic mythology, Iweriadd was one of the two wives of Llyr. The other was Penardun.

J

JOSEPH OF ARIMATHEA

According to legend, Christianity reached Britain with the arrival of Joseph
Arimathea, said to be the uncle of Jesus, in the first century AD. He is supposed
to have brought with him the cup that was used at the Last Supper and this
was later known as the Holy Grail, becoming the subject of several quests.
Joseph is said to have founded a Christian settlement at Glastonbury and to
have buried the cup from the Last Supper there. The holy thorn tree there is
said to have grown as a result of Joseph's planting his staff in the ground.

JUDON

In British Celtic mythology, Judon was the wife of Gorboduc, a king of Britain
who was said to be a descendant of Brutus. She was the mother of two sons,
Ferrex and Porrex. Ferrex was killed by his brother and Judon then murdered
Porrex. Judon and Gorboduc had no other children and neither of their dead
sons had heirs, so the line of descent from Brutus died out.

JUPITER

The Roman god was adopted by the Celts into their own cult. He was often
given a Celtic epithet, as Jupiter Taranis, Taranis being the Celtic thunder god.

K

KACMWRI

In Arthurian legend, a servant of Arthur.

KAI

In Welsh Celtic mythology, a warrior who accompanies Culhwch (*see* Chapter 24). He appears in Arthurian legend as Sir Kay (*see* Chapter 23).

KAMBER

In British Celtic mythology, Kamber was the son of Brutus and brother of Locrinus and Albanactus. After his father died, he became king of Wales, Locrinus became king of England and Albanactus became king of Scotland. Kamber helped Locrinus to defeat the Huns after they had killed Albanactus.

KAY, SIR *see* KAI.

KELLS, BOOK OF

Celtic Christianity is associated with beautifully executed illuminated gospels, painstakingly crafted by Celtic monks. The best known of these is the Book of Kells, which is located in the library of Trinity College in Dublin, it having been presented to the college during Cromwell's reign. The Book of Kells takes its name from an early monastery of this name in County Meath. According to tradition, the Book of Kells was executed on Iona and was taken to the monastery of Kells for preservation from the raids of the Vikings, but the first actual written reference to it is in the *Annals of Ulster* for 1006. There reference is made to it having been stolen from the monastery and retrieved after several months with the gold removed from it. It dates from the late eighth century AD and is profusely decorated with symbols relating not only to the Celts, such as the famous knotwork, but to the Picts and the Anglo-Saxons, with some evidence also of a Byzantine influence. Like other illuminated manuscripts, the Book of Kells has been illustrated with highly coloured, naturally occurring pigments, chiefly blue, green, yellow and red-brown. It is considered to be one of the finest legacies of the Celts.

KELTOI

The Greeks and Romans gave the name of Keltoi to the northern tribes of barbarians who threatened them from parts of western and central Europe. The word may be the origin of the word Celt.

KEY

Several representations of Celtic goddesses feature a key. It is thought that the key may be symbolic of the ability of a particular goddess to open the gates that lead to the Otherworld and so allow those who worship her to pass from one life to another.

KILCHONAN see ISLAY.

KILDALTON CROSS see ISLAY.

KILLARAUS

In Irish Celtic legend, this is the mountain in County Kildare from which Myrddin transported the ring of stones known as the Giant's Ring. He is said to have re-erected this at Stonehenge.

KILLMOULIS

With the coming of Christianity, Celtic mythology gradually dwindled into a system of fairies, elves, etc, which included the killmoulis.

KILMALKEDAR

An unusual Celtic cross is located in a churchyard at Kilmalkedar on the Dingle Peninsula in Kerry in Ireland. The top of the cross is in the form of a squared head and is called the Sundial Cross, it having been thought to have acted as a primitive sundial. It dates from the late seventh or early eighth century.

KNIGHTS

The idea of elite groups of warriors was part of Irish Celtic legend before King Arthur and his Knights of the Round Table came on the scene (see Chapter

23). The Fianna were the members of an elite bodyguard who guarded the high kings of Ireland, founded in 300 BC by Fiachadh, the high king (*see* Chapter 15). There was also an Ulster military elite called the Red Branch, whose greatest champion was Cúchulainn. This group of warriors was founded by Ross the Red of Ulster (*see* Chapter 12).

KNOCKERS

The Cornish equivalent of the coblynau. *See also* Chapter 26.

KNOTWORK

This is one of the most common designs on Celtic crosses and other forms of sculpture. As the name suggests, it involved designs based on knots.

KNOWTH

An important prehistoric passage grave near Drogheda in County Louth, forming part of the Brugh na Bóinne (*see* Chapter 11).

KYLEDYR WILLT

In Welsh Celtic mythology, Kynedyr Wyllt was the chief huntsman with Mabon in the hunt for Twrch Trwyth (*see* Chapter 24).

KYNDDELIG

In Welsh Celtic mythology, Kynddelig was the guide for the hunting of Twrch Trwyth (*see* Chapter 24).

L

LABHRA
An alternative name for Dian Cécht.

LABHRAIDH LOINGSECH
In Irish Celtic mythology and originally named Maon or Moen (meaning 'dumb'), Labhraidh Loingsech was a king of Leinster who is supposed to have reigned around 268 BC.

LABRAID LUATHLAM AR CLEB
In Irish Celtic mythology, Labraid Luathlam ar Cleb, 'Labraid of the Quick Hand', was the ruler of Magh Mell and husband of Lí Ban (*see* Chapter 15).

LAEG *or* LOEG
In Irish Celtic mythology, Laeg was charioteer to Cúchulainn, charioteers being important figures in Celtic culture. He is said to have been with Cúchulainn during his final battle and to have thrown himself in front of a spear thrown at his master, although Cúchulainn ultimately met his doom in the battle (*see* Chapter 12).

LAIGHIN (1)
Galian was renamed Laighin before it became Leinster. One suggestion as to why it was so named is that it was named after the Gauls who went to Ireland with Labhraidh Loingsech to recover his kingdom.

LAIGHIN (2)
In Irish Celtic mythology, the name Laighin is also applied to the Gailioin, one of the three companies who came from Greece and invaded Ireland. They named themselves Laighin because they settled in Leinster.

LAKES

Water was important in Celtic culture, and lakes held a particular significance. They were regarded as holy places through which gods could be reached. Many treasures, such as spears, swords, shields, brooches, horse and vehicle fittings, tools and cauldrons were deposited in these sacred lakes, there being archaeological evidence for this in the sites that have been excavated. For example, at the La Tène site in Switzerland treasures were retrieved from a bay at the eastern end of Lake Neuchâtel.

LAMHFADA

In Irish Celtic mythology, an epithet applied to Lugh, meaning 'Long-handed' or 'Far-shooter'.

LANCELOT *see* LAUNCELOT.

LAND OF ILLUSION

In Welsh Celtic mythology, a name for Dyfed.

LAND OF PROMISE *see* TÍR TAIRNIGIRIB.

LAND OF SUMMER *see* GWLÂD YR HÂV.

LAND OF THE LIVING *see* TÍR NAN BEO.

LAND OF THE YOUNG *see* TÍR NA OG.

LANHERNE CRUCIFIXION CROSS

A number of freestanding crosses can be found in Cornwall, the Cornish cross being shorter and squatter than those of Ireland, Scotland and Wales. One of the best examples of the Cornish Celtic cross is the Lanherne Crucifixion Cross, which dates from the tenth century AD. It has a pattern of interlacing and is dedicated to someone called Runhol, who may or may not have been the sculptor.

LAOGHAIRE

In Irish Celtic legend, there are several people of the name Laoghaire. One of these was a historical king of Ireland who was on the throne at the time that St Patrick arrived in Ireland (*see* Chapter 16).

LAOGHAIRE BUADHACH

In Irish Celtic mythology, 'Laoghaire the Battle-winner', a friend of Cúchulainn (*see* Chapter 12).

LA TÈNE

A few kilometres outside Neuchâtel in Switzerland, on Lac de Neuchâtel is located La Tène. In 1858, following unusually low water levels in the lake, there were uncovered remains that were to be categorised as belonging to the second great period of Celtic culture, as Hallstatt was the first. As was the case with Hallstatt, La Tène became a standard archaeological method of categorising the stages of Celtic culture. La Tène Period or La Tène Culture represents Celtic civilisation at the time of its maximum development from about the fifth century BC until the time of the Roman occupation. The artefacts found at La Tène were considerably more delicate, more sophisticated and more indicative of wealth and power than those of the Hallstatt Culture, showing that the Celts had moved on.

LAUNCELOT *or* LANCELOT

In Arthurian legend one of the Knights of the Round Table and lover of Guinevere. He appears late in legend, taking the place of Medrawt but was possibly based on a sun god. *See also* Chapter 25.

LEABHAR GABHALA EIREANN

This is a book dealing with the various mythological invasions of Ireland and as such is a mythical history of Ireland, being also known as the *Book of Invasions*. It survived in various ancient forms, principally in the form of the *Book of Leinster*, dating from the twelfth century. A version of the book was compiled from several ancient manuscripts now no longer extant by Micheal O Cleirigh (*c.*1575–*c.*1645). When the *Book of Invasions* is referred to, it is usually this translation that is meant. The invasions dealt with in the book include the pre-Flood journey by Cesair. It also includes the invasion of Partholón, who, with his followers, defeated the Fomorii, a race of half-human monsters, and the invasion of Nemedh, after whose death the Fomorii returned.

The next invasion dealt with is that of the Fir Bholg, who were accompanied by the Gailioin and the Fir Dhomhnann, all three of these tribes being the descendants of the Nemedh. The fifth invasion mentioned is that of the Tuatha Dé Danaan, also descended from the Nemedh, and the sixth is that of the Sons of Mil Espaine, or the Milesians, who defeated the Tuatha Dé Danaan. Eventually the two sides worked out an agreement by which the Milesians ruled the part of the land above ground and the Tuatha Dé Danaan ruled the underground part.

LECAN, BOOK OF
One of the source books for Irish Celtic myths. Compiled by monks from previous documents or accounts, it dates from the fifteenth century.

LECAN, YELLOW BOOK OF
One of the source books for Irish Celtic myths. Compiled by monks from previous documents or accounts, it dates from the end of the fourteeenth century.

LEINSTER
In Irish Celtic mythology, Leinster was one of the five provinces into which the Fir Bholg divided Ireland. *See* Laighin.

LEINSTER, BOOK OF *see* LEABHAR GABHALA EIREANN.

LEODEGRANCE
In Arthurian legend a name given to Bran the Blessed (*see* Chapter 25).

LEPRECHAUN
With the coming of Christianity, Celtic mythology gradually dwindled into a system of fairies, elves, etc. Lugh became a fairy craftsman, Lugh Chromain, and his name gradually became Leprechaun and dwindled further to include mischievous elves, often with a hoard of treasure.

LÊR *see* LIR.

LEVARCHAM
In Irish Celtic mythology, Deirdre's teacher (*see* Chapter 14).

LIA FÁIL *see* STONE OF DESTINY.

LÍ BAN

In Irish Celtic mythology, Lí Ban was the wife of Labraid Luathlam ar Cleb and sister of Fand. She invited Cúchulainn to help slay three Fomorii, promising him Fand as a lover in return (*see* Chapter 14).

LIMB VOTIVE

It was a custom of the Celts to present models of diseased limbs to deities at the various healing shrines and sanctuaries. Sometimes these were in wood and sometimes they were in stone. Models of organs other than arms or legs, such as breasts, heads, eyes and internal organs, were also presented. The idea obviously was that if a votive limb or other organ was given to a god or goddess then he or she would cure the actual limb or organ of any disease. Evidence of the practice of limb or organ votives has been found at various excavated sites. The offering of models of limbs and organs to deities for healing purposes was not confined to the Celts, it being found in various other early cultures.

LINDISFARNE *see* ILLUMINATED GOSPELS.

LINDOW MAN

In August 1984 part of a human body was uncovered in a peat bog at Lindow Moss in Cheshire. The body was that of a young man and it was face down in a crouching position and painted in different colours. He was naked apart from an armlet of fur. The young man, who became know as Lindow Man, had probably been placed in the bog around the fourth century BC. Lindow Man is thought to be evidence of the Celtic practice of human sacrifice. He had been hit on the head and garotted, and he looked as though he had been pushed from the back into the bog. His stomach contents revealed the presence of mistletoe pollen, suggesting that the young man may have featured in some form of druid sacrifice. *See* Tollund Man.

LIR *or* **LÊR**

In Irish Celtic mythology, Lir was the sea god, the equivalent of the Welsh god Llyr. He was the father of Manannán who became in turn the sea god. He married Aobh and the children whom he had by her were turned into swans for nine hundred years by Aoife (1), his second wife, because she was jealous of Lir's love for them (*see* Chapter 11).

LISMORE, BOOK OF
One of the source books for Irish Celtic myths. Compiled by monks from previous documents or accounts, it dates from the fifteenth century.

LITTLE FURY
In Irish Celtic mythology, one of the swords that belonged to Manannán Mac Lir. Manannán gave it to Diarmid to help him in his flight from Fionn (*see* Chapter 15).

LLA LLUANYS
The Celtic harvest festival of the Isle of Man, like the Lughnasadh.

LLEFELYS
In Welsh Celtic mythology, Llefelys was the son of Beli and brother of Lludd. He was the ruler of Gaul and helped his brother, who was ruler of Britain, to get rid of the three plagues (*see* Chapter 26).

LLEU LLAW GYFFES
In Welsh Celtic mythology, Lleu Llaw Gyffes was a warrior god who may have some form of association with the Irish god Lugh (*see* Chapters 18, 22, 23).

LLUDD *or* **NUDD**
In Welsh Celtic mythology, Lludd was the son of Beli and the brother of Llefelys. He ruled Britain while Llefelys ruled Gaul, and during that time three plagues beset Britain (*see* Chapter 26). *See also* Chapters 18, 23, 24, 25.

LLUDD LLAW EREINT
In Welsh Celtic mythology, Lludd Llaw Ereint was the equivalent of Nuada. He was the father of Creiddylad, and it has been suggested that she was the original of Cordelia, the daughter of King Lear. He is sometimes confused with Lludd, and sometimes their legends are run together.

LLWYD
In Welsh Celtic mythology, Llwyd was the son of Cil Coed and the friend of

Gwawl. To avenge Pwyll's treatment of Gwawl, Llwyd put a curse on Dyfed and took Rhiannon and her son Pryderi prisoner. They were rescued by Manawydan. *See* Chapter 21.

LLWYR
In Welsh Celtic mythology, Llwyr was the son of Llwyryon and owner of a magic pot (*see* Chapter 24).

LLYCHLYN
In Welsh Celtic legend, Llychlyn was the name for Scandinavia or Norway , meaning 'land of lakes'. It is the equivalent of the Irish Lochlann. It has also been suggested that it was a name for the Otherworld.

LLYN CERRIG BACH
A lake on the island of Anglesey that was sacred to the Celts was Llyn Cerrig Bach. Metal votive gifts dating from between the second century BC and the first century AD have been recovered. Many of these are associated with warfare and the aristocracy, suggesting that Celtic chiefs travelled to it to present votive gifts.

LLYR
In Welsh Celtic mythology, Llyr was cognate with the Irish god Lir. He is thought to have been the original of Shakespeare's King Lear (*see* Chapter 18).

LOCH
In Irish Celtic mythology, Loch was the son of Mofebais. He was a champion warrior of Connacht who refused to fight Cúchulainn because he did not wish to fight a youth without a beard (*see* Chapter 12).

LOCHLANN *see* LLYCHLYN.

LOCRINUS
In British mythology, Locrinus was a son of Brutus and brother of Albanactus and Kamber. After his father died, he became the ruler of England and Albanactus became ruler of Scotland.

LOT OR LOTH

In Arthurian legend Lot was the King of Orkney, based on Llud. His wife was the mother of Mordred (Medrawt) by Arthur. She was also the mother of Gawain (*see* Chapter 25).

LUCHTAINE *or* LUCHTA *or* LUCHTAR

In Irish Celtic mythology, Luchtaine was one of a triad of craft gods, Luchtaine being a wright or carpenter. With the other two, sometimes described as his brothers and called Goibhniu and Creidhne, he worked extremely quickly to make and repair the weapons of the Tuatha Dé Danaan. The weapons were magical, in that anyone wounded by any of them would not recover. *See also* Chapter 7.

LUGAID

In Irish Celtic mythology, the son of Cú Roí who led the forces against Cúchulainn (*see* Chapter 12).

LUGH

In Irish Celtic mythology, Lugh was one of the more important of the gods. He was associated with light and the sun, and was also the god of arts and crafts. He is cognate with the British and Gaulish god Lugus and the Welsh god Lludd. Lughnasadh is named after him. There are various accounts about his origins, and he is said to have become ruler of the gods after Nuada, king of the Tuatha Dé Danaan, having demonstrated that he was capable of many skills and earning the name Samildanach, meaning 'of many skills'. As king of the Tuatha Dé Danaan, he led them into the Second Battle of Magh Tuiredh. In the battle he often took the form of someone with a single arm and a single eye. The Fomorii were defeated, and Lugh killed Balor in single combat with a sling. *See* Chapters 7, 8, 9

LUGHNASADH

The Celts had four major festivals. One was Lughnasadh, which was held on 1 August and was the Celtic harvest festival. It was so called because it was the feast of the god Lugh. Later it became the Christian festival of Lammas. The other three major festivals were Samhain, Imbolc and Beltane.

LUGUS

In British and Gaulish Celtic mythology, Lugus was a god who gave his name to various place names in several lands, such as Lyons and Leiden. He is cognate with the Irish god Lugh and the Welsh Lludd and is associated with the Roman god Mercury.

LYONESSE

In British Celtic mythology, Lyonesse is said to have been a land off the south coast of Cornwall, famous for housing the remnants of the court of Arthur after the death of the king. The sea is said to have rushed over the land to prevent people following his knights.

M

MABINOGI

In Welsh literally 'the Four Branches of the Mabinogion', popularly known as the Mabinogion.

MABINOGION

In Welsh Celtic mythology, Mabinogion is one of the most important source texts. It is based on two earlier manuscripts, *The White Book of Rhydderch* (1300–1325) and *The Red Book of Hergest* (1375–1425). It consists of four tales concerning Pwyll, Branwen, Manawydan fab Llyr and Math fab Mathonwy. Later versions include the story of Culhwch and Olwen (*see* Chapter 24).

MABON

In Welsh Celtic mythology, Mabon was the son of Modron. Legend has it that he was abducted from his mother when he was three days old and was incarcerated at Caer Loyw, which in the legend was synonymous with the Otherworld. Culhwch rescued him from captivity and in return he helped Culhwch find Olwen and assisted him in fulfilling the tasks that needed to be accomplished before Culhwch could claim Olwen in marriage (*see* Chapter 24).

MAC CÉCHT

In Irish Celtic mythology, Mac Cécht was one of the Tuatha Dé Danaan at the time of the invasion of Ireland by the Sons of Mil Espaine, who defeated the Tuatha. A son of Oghma, he was the husband of the goddess Fótla or Fodla. He was killed by Eremon. *See* Chapter 10.

MAC CUILL

In Irish Celtic mythology, Mac Cuill was one of the Tuatha Dé Danaan at the time of the invasion of Ireland by the Sons of Mil Espaine who defeated the

Tuatha. He was the husband of the goddess Banbha or Banb and was killed by Eber. *See* Chapter 10.

MAC GREINE
In Irish Celtic mythology, Mac Greine was one of the Tuatha Dé Danaan rulers at the time of the invasion of Ireland by the Sons of Mil Espaine. The Tuatha were defeated by them. A son of Oghma, Mac Greine was the husband of the goddess Eriu, who gave her name to Eire or Ireland. He was killed by Amhairghin. *See* Chapter 10.

MACHA
In Irish Celtic mythology, Macha was a goddess who is sometimes taken to be one deity and sometimes taken to be three. She was associated with war, fertility and the prosperity of Ireland, and is also associated with horses. As a goddess associated with fertility, she was regarded as being a mother-goddess. As a war goddess she did not actually take part in battles but was present in the field and used her powers to help one side or the other (*see* Chapter 5).

MAC KINEELY
In Irish Celtic mythology, a brother of Goibhniu and owner of a cow that was stolen by Balor (*see* Chapter 16).

MAC MOINEANTA
In Irish Celtic folklore, Mac Moineanta became king of the fairies but was supplanted by Fionnbharr.

MAC OC
In Irish Celtic mythology, 'Song of the Young', an epithet applied to Oenghus.

MAC SAMTHAINN
In Irish Celtic mythology, a brother of Goibhniu and owner of a cow that was stolen by Balor (*see* Chapter 16).

MACSEN WLEDIG
The Roman emperor Maximus was known as Macsen Wledig in Welsh Celtic tradition. He is said to have married a Celt named Elen. According to one tra-

dition the emperor's standard, which showed a dragon on a purple background, was the origin of the Welsh red dragon banner.

MAELCEN
In Irish Celtic mythology, a druid who brought about the death of Cormac (*see* Chapter 15).

MAEL DÚIN
In Irish Celtic mythology, Mail Dúin was the central character of one of the immram or invasion tales. He was the son of a nun who, according to legend, was raped by his father, Ailill, who was said to have come from Aran. Mail Dúin with some companions set out on a voyage to find a group of raiders from overseas who had murdered his father. The immram tells of their adventures on the voyage (*see* Chapter 16).

MAELMUIRI
The name of a scribe of the Tain Bó Cuailgne (*see* Chapter 2).

MAELON
In Welsh Celtic mythology, Maelon was a young chief with whom Branwen fell in love (*see* Chapter 26).

MAENOR ALUN AND MAENOR PENARDD
In Welsh Celtic mythology, the sites of two battles in which Pryderi was defeated (*see* Chapter 22).

MAEVE *SEE* MEDB.

MAGA
In Irish Celtic mythology, Maga was a daughter of Oenghus who married Ross the Red and later Cathbad the Druid.

MAGH MELL
In Irish Celtic mythology, 'the Plain of Happiness', where some of the Tuatha Dé Danaan went to following their defeat (*see* Chapter 11). One of its rulers was Labraid Luathlam ar Cleb.

MAGH MON
In Irish Celtic mythology, 'the Plain of Sports' (*see* Chapter 11).

MAGH RATH
In Irish Celtic mythology, 'the Plain of Prosperity', the site of a battle (see Chapter 5).

MAGH SLECHT
In Irish Celtic mythology, 'the Plain of Adoration' where Cromm Cruach was sited (*see* Chapter 4).

MAGH TUIREDH *or* MOYTURA
In Irish Celtic mythology, 'the Plain of Towers', which was the site of two famous battles. The first battle was fought between the Tuatha Dé Danaan under Nuada against the Fir Bholgs. Nuada's forces won, but he himself was badly wounded (*see* Chapter 6). The second battle was between Nuada's forces and the Fomorii (*see* Chapter 9).

MAIDEN CASTLE *see* HILL FORT.

MALORY, SIR THOMAS
An English writer who lived in the 15th century. He translated, largely from French sources, *Le Morte D'Arthur*, a collection of Arthurian legends, printed by Caxton in 1485. The work includes several episodes, e.g. the quest for the Holy Grail, that have been recycled by generations of authors, for example, Tennyson and T. H. White. The author has been traditionally identified with a Warwickshire knight of that name but the attribution is doubtful.

MAN, ISLE OF *see* ISLE OF MAN.

MANANNÁN MAC LIR
In Irish Celtic mythology, Manannán Mac Lir was the son of Lir. Like his father, he was a sea god and is associated with sea journeys to the Otherworld. Traditionally he is supposed to have lived on the Isle of Man, of which he was the first king, although he is also supposed to have lived in Tír Tairnigirib, the Otherworldly Land of Promise. He is associated with the Welsh deity Mana-

wydan fab Llyr. His wife was Fand. He is usually shown as wearing a green cloak, perhaps one that seemed to change colour when it caught the light. He had the ability of shape-changing and is supposed to have used this skill to father mortal children, such as Mongan. The sea was very important to Ireland, and Manannán Mac Lir was an important god, being able, for example, to create storms to wreck invading ships. He was also associated with trickery and sorcery, and is supposed to have given Lugh magical gifts to help Nuada and him fight the Fomorii. *See* Chapters 5, 8

MANAWYDAN FAB LYR

In Welsh Celtic mythology, Manawydan fab Lyr was the son of Llyr. He may be the Welsh equivalent ofManannán Mac Lir, although there is not an exact parallel and there is no evidence that he was considered to be a god of the sea. He is said to have been the brother of Bran the Blessed and Branwen, and possibly a cousin of Pryderi. He is also said to have been the husband of Rhiannon. Manawydan and Pryderi with their wives, Cigfa being Pryderi's wife, are said to have been at their palace at Arbeth in Dyfed when a peal of thunder was heard and a mist fell. When the mist cleared, the land was barren, with no crops, cattle or people apart from the four in the palace. One legend has it that after some time roaming in the forests living off what they could find in the way of food, the four went to England. After a series of adventures they returned to Dyfed (*see* Chapter 21).

MAON *see* LABHRAIDH LOINGSECH.

MAPONOS

In Celtic mythology, a sun god of Gaul and Britain identified with Mabon.

MARCH AP MEIRCHION

In Welsh Celtic mythology, a prince of the underworld whose pig Arthur attempted to obtain unsuccessfully (*see* Chapter 23). In Arthurian legend he appears as King Mark of Cornwall.

MARK

In Arthurian legend, Mark was King of Cornwall, husband of Iseult and uncle of Tristan (*see* Chapter 23).

MATA

In Irish Celtic mythology, Mata was a hundred-legged and four-headed monster that was captured by the Daghda (*see* Chapter 5).

MATH FAB MATHONWY

In Welsh Celtic mythology, Math fab Mathonwy was, as his name indicates, the son of Mathonwy. He had great powers of magic and was able to make people change shape. He may also have been associated with fertility.

Math and Gwydion fab Don made for Lleu Llaw Gyffes Blodeuwedd, a woman made of flowers (*see* Chapter 18).

MATHGAN

In Irish Celtic mythology, the chief sorcerer to the Tuatha Dé Danaan (*see* Chapter 7).

MATHOLWCH

In Welsh Celtic mythology, Matholwch was a king of Ireland who married Branwen in an attempt to promote good relations between Ireland and Wales, and who received a magic cauldron from Branwen's brother, Bran the Blessed. At the wedding feast he was insulted by Efnisien, Branwen's half-brother, and in revenge mistreated Branwen, which led to war (*see* Chapter 20).

MEDB

In Irish Celtic mythology, Medb, whose name has several variants and is sometimes anglicised as Maeve, was a goddess queen of Connacht. Her name means 'she who intoxicates' and is related to the word 'mead'. She is said to have been the wife of nine Irish kings, and only someone who was her mate could be a true king of Ireland. In all her various marriages she was the dominant partner. Her promiscuity suggests fertility and she also appears to have been regarded as a goddess of sovereignty.

Perhaps the most famous legend involving Medb is that in which she sets out to get possession of the great Brown Bull of Ulster, known as Donn Cuailgne (*see* Chapter 12).

MEDICINE

The Celts, particularly the Irish, were renowned for their medical skills, and during the Dark Ages the Irish medical schools were renowned throughout

Europe. The oldest surviving medical manuscripts in Irish date from the early fourteenth century. In Irish Celtic mythology, Dian Cécht was the god of medicine.

MEDRAWD
In Welsh Celtic mythology, the nephew of Arthur and lover of Gwenhwyvar and possibly based on Dylan. In Arthurian legend he appears as Mordred (*see* Chapter 23).

MEICHE
In Irish Celtic mythology, Meiche was the son of Morrigan. He was killed by Dian Cécht because it was prophesied that he would bring disaster to Ireland. When he was dead, his body was cut open to reveal three hearts, one for each aspect of his mother, and according to one legend each of these hearts had a serpent growing in it. Two of the hearts were burnt but the third escaped and its huge serpent did indeed threaten disaster to Ireland but it too was killed by Dian Cécht (*see* Chapter 5).

MELEAUS *or* MELIAS DE LILE, MELIAGAUNCE, MELIAGRAUNCE, MELWAS
In Arthurian legend names under which Gwyn ap Nudd appears (*see* Chapter 25).

MENW
In Welsh Celtic mythology, one of the warriors who accompanied Culhwch (*see* Chapter 24).

MERLIN
In Welsh Celtic mythology, Merlin was a wizard who played a major part in the Arthurian legends. The Welsh form of his name was Myrddin, and a character of this name played a part in Welsh mythology before Arthur and his knights came to the fore. Geoffrey of Monmouth describes Merlin and his exploits in *Libellus Merline* (Little Book of Merlin) which was written around AD 1135 and incorporated into his *Historia*. See Chapters 23, 24.

MERMAIDS/MERMEN
As in several other cultures, especially those associated with the sea, mer-

maids and mermen, creatures that are half-human, half-fish, feature significantly in Celtic culture. Mermaids are represented as being beautiful and enticing creatures, although they are not always benevolent. Mermen are usually much uglier with small piggy eyes, red noses and green hair. Cornwall is particularly rich in mermaid lore. According to one legend a mermaid spirited away a squire's son from Zennor.

MESGEDRA
In Irish Celtic mythology, a King of Leinster (*see* Chapter 11).

MESS BUACHALLA
In Irish Celtic mythology, the granddaughter of Etain and Eochaid and mother of Conaire Mór (*see* Chapter 11).

MIDACH
In Irish Celtic mythology, Midach was a son of Dian Cécht who followed in his father's profession. He and his sister, Airmid, were responsible for giving Nuada his silver hand, which enabled him to be reinstated as the king of the Tuatha Dé Danaan. He was killed by his jealous father (*see* Chapter 7).

MIDHIR
In Irish Celtic mythology, Midhir lived in the sídh of Bri Leith, one of the underground kingdoms of the gods when they had been driven from Ireland by the Sons of Mil Espaine. The most important story of Midhir concerns his courtship of Etain (*see* Chapter 11).

MIL
In Irish Celtic mythology, Mil was the son or grandson of Bregon and the ancestor of the first human rulers of Ireland, who were known as the Sons of Mil Espaine. He was the brother or nephew of Ith, who led an invasion expedition from Spain to Ireland but was killed by the Tuatha Dé Danaan. After Ith's body was returned to Spain, Mil organised another invading trip to Ireland. He did not reach it but his sons did, and they attempted to carry out the conquest of Ireland (*see* Chapter 10).

MILCHRU *see* PATRICK.

MIL ESPAINE, SONS OF *OR* MILESIANS

In Irish Celtic mythology, the Sons of Mil Espaine were the sons and descendants of Mil. They landed in Ireland on the feast of Beltane under the leadership of Amhairghin. The invaders defeated the Tuatha Dé Danaan (*see* Chapter 10). The Tuatha Dé Danaan, having been defeated, deprived the invaders of milk and corn in an attempt to retrieve their land. In the end, the two sides decided to divide the land between them, the Tuatha Dé Danaan getting the underground part. The part above ground went to the Sons of Mil Espaine, Eremon, a son of Mil, ruling the northern half of the country and Eber Finn, one of the leaders of the Sons of Mil Espaine, ruling the southern part. Later north and south went to war, Eber Finn was killed and Eremon became ruler of the whole kingdom, becoming the first human king to rule the whole of Ireland.

MINERVA *see* SULIS.

MIODCHAOIN

In Irish Celtic mythology, Miodchaoin was a warrior and friend of Cian, who lived on a hill. He was placed under a geis never to permit anyone to shout from the summit of the hill. Miodchaoin had a fight with the three sons of Tuireann when they arrived at the hill to complete the last of the tasks imposed on them by Lugh as their punishment for murdering Cian. Miodchaoin was killed and the three sons were barely alive after the fight. As they were dying, they succeeded in giving three weak shouts from the hill, thereby fulfilling the last of their punishment tasks. They then begged Lugh to heal them of their fatal wounds but he refused and all three died (*see* Chapter 8).

MISTLETOE

The Celts, particularly druids, were much connected with the partially parasitic plant mistletoe. It seems to have been regarded as a cure for barrenness if it was mixed in a drink, and it is likely to have been used in fertility rites. The oak tree on which mistletoe grows was sacred to the druids. They used oak trees to form sacred groves and they used oak branches in sacred rites. When Lindow Man was discovered, he was found to have mistletoe pollen in his stomach, causing speculation that he had taken part in some form of druidic human sacrifice.

MOANER *see* OCHAIN.

MODEL WEAPONS
A tradition that the Celts shared with other early peoples was that of making small replicas of weapons, such as swords, spears and shields, and tools, such as axes and wheels. They were used as votive offerings to the gods and as grave goods to accompany dead people on their way to the Otherworld. Some appear to have been worn as talismans by the living. Often great trouble was taken to make the model as close to the original as possible.

MODRON
In Welsh Celtic mythology, Modron, whose name means 'mother', was the mother of Mabon. Her name is thought to be a form of the Gaulish Matrona, and she is considered to have been a mother-goddess (*see* Chapter 23).

MOEN *see* LABHRAIDH LOINGSECH.

MOFEBAIS *see* LOCH.

MOLMOTIUS *see* PINNER.

MONGÁN
An historical king who ruled at Moylinny on Lough Neagh and died around AD 625. Mongán is also said to be a reincarnation of Fionn Mac Cumhaill, and parallels have been drawn between the legend of Mongán and the Arthurian legend.

MORC
In Irish Celtic mythology, a king of the Formorii at the time of the war with the children of Nemedh (*see* Chapter 6).

MORDRED *see* MEDRAWD.

MORGAN LE FAY *see* MORGEN.

MORGAWSE
The name under which Aranrhod was absorbed into Arthurian legend by Sir Thomas Malory in the *Morte D'Arthur*.

MORGEN

In Welsh Celtic mythology, Morgen was a druidic goddess who had nine sisters and may have associations with Modron. Various claims have been made for her, such as that she could fly on artificial wings, that she could change her shape and that she had great powers of healing, but there is a good deal of confusion surrounding her. She is thought to have been the original of the Morgan Le Fay of the Arthurian legend.

MORRIGAN OR MORRIGU

In Irish Celtic mythology, the .i.Morrigan;Morrigan was one of a group of Irish war goddesses who can be thought of as a single goddess or as a triple goddess. The war goddesses did not actually take part in battles but they were present in the field and used their powers to help one side or the other (*see* Chapter 5). Morrigan was also associated with sexuality and fertility, this last association making her a mother-goddess. In addition, she is said to have had powers of prophesy and the ability to cast spells. In her capacity of war goddess, she helped the Tuatha Dé Danaan at the Battles of Magh Tuiredh (*see* Chapter 9). Her sexuality is emphasised in the legend of how she made overtures to Cúchulainn but was rejected by him, thereby ensuring that she bore him a terrible grudge (*see* Chapter 13).
Morrigan is also known for her ability in shape-changing. She frequently took the shape of a crow or a raven.

MORTE D'ARTHUR see MALORY, SIR THOMAS.

MOTHER-GODDESS

The concept of abundance and fertility was important in Celtic culture. Various goddesses were associated with this concept, being regarded as divine earth-mothers, often being referred to as *matronae* in Gaul and the Rhineland. Such goddesses can often function both as single goddesses and as triple goddesses. Mother-goddesses are often depicted on sculptures as wearing long garments and sometimes have one breast bared. They are often accompanied by some kind of symbol of fertility, such as babies, fruit or loaves, and are often presented in groups, although single images of mother-goddesses are also common.

In Irish Celtic mythology, the mother-goddess is prominent. They are often triple goddesses, being associated with other concepts as well as fertility. Macha and Morrigan are cases in point.

MOUNTAINS

As is the case with lakes, mountains were important in Celtic worship. For example, in the mountainous regions of Gaul a number of gods associated with high places were venerated. The Celtic god of the sky was also associated with mountains since they rose from the earth high into the boundaries of his kingdom.

MOUNT BADON *see* BADON.

MOYTURA *see* MAGH TUIREDH.

MUIREDACH, CROSS OF

One of the finest of the Irish high crosses is the Cross of Muiredach, situated in the early Celtic settlement of Monasterboice near Drogheda. The main sculpture on the circular head on the west side is an elaborate Crucifixion scene and on the east side is an elaborate Last Judgement scene. Some of the other carving is open to interpretation, some regarding it as depicting various events in Christ's life and others regarding it as depicting events relating to the Vikings, which had taken place around the ninth century just before the cross was erected.

MUIRTHEMNE, PLAIN OF

A part of County Louth between the Boyne and Dundalk. In Irish Celtic mythology, it is particularly associated with Cúchulainn.

MUNSTER

In Irish Celtic mythology, Munster was one of the five provinces into which the Fir Bholg divided Ireland, Munster itself being divided into two parts, North Munster and South Munster. Munster is supposed to derive its name from Eocho Mumho, tenth king in succession from Eremon.

MURIAS

In Irish Celtic mythology, Murias was one of the four great cities of the Tuatha

Dé Danaan before their arrival in Ireland, the others being Falias, Finias and Gorias. The magic cauldron of the Daghda is said to have come from Murias.

MYRDDIN

In Welsh Celtic mythology, Myrddin was the original Welsh name of Merlin, who was the wizard in the Arthurian legends. There are many legends about him, some of them conflicting. He is supposed to have been the offspring of a nun and an evil spirit, thereby making him a fatherless child. Other traditions ascribe various fathers to him.

One Welsh tradition suggests that Myrddin was not one person but three incarnations of the same person. The situation is made more confusing by the fact that historically there appears to have been not only one Myrddin but two. One was Myrddin Wyllt, who lived in Scotland, and one was Myrddin Emrys, who lived in Wales. It is the latter who became the Arthurian Merlin. *See* Chapters 23, 25.

N

NAGES

At Nages near Nimes in Provence there was a Celtic shrine of which a lintel survives. It is particularly interesting because it has a carved stone frieze on which are depicted a number of severed heads alternating with galloping horses. It calls to mind the practice of Celts of collecting the scalps of their defeated enemies and attaching them to their horses when riding away from battles.

NAKED WARRIORS

In the Celtic world it was a custom of warriors to strip naked before rushing into battle, for example, against the Romans, or to engage in single combat. It has been suggested that this made them at one with nature and so increased their life force.

NANTOSVELTA

In Gaulish Celtic mythology, Nantosvelta was a goddess often associated with Sucellus as part of the divine couples. Her name, generally being taken to mean 'winding river', suggests that she is a water goddess but she is sometimes depicted as carrying the model of a house on a pole, suggesting that she is also associated with hearth and home. She is sometimes shown carrying a pot, which has been taken, like the cauldron, as a symbol of regeneration. Associated with prosperity and abundance, she also has connections with death, as is suggested by the presence of a raven in several of her representations.

NAOISE

In Irish Celtic mythology, Naoise was the one of the three sons of Usna. He attracted the attention and love of Deirdre, who had been told by friends that he had the physical attributes that she sought – black hair, white skin and red cheeks but she was betrothed since birth to Conchobar Mac Nessa. They eloped and were pursued by Conchobar (*see* Chapter 14).

NARBETH *see* ARBETH.

NEAGH, LOUGH
A lake in County Antrim, the largest lake in the British Isles. In Irish Celtic mythology, it is one of the 'twelve chief lakes of Ireland' the waters of which were to be denied to the Formorii. *See* Chapter 7.

NEMAIN *or* NEMHAIN
In Irish Celtic mythology, Nemain was a war goddess like Macha and the Morrigan. Although the war goddesses did not themselves take part in battles, they often showed their influence, for example by striking terror into one of the armies. Nemain's name means 'frenzy', and she was famous for causing panic among warriors. In the war between Connacht and Ulster, she stirred up such terror in the men of Connacht that a hundred of them are said to have died of fright (see Chapter 12).

NEMEDH *or* NEMED
In Irish Celtic mythology, Nemedh was the leader of the third invasion of Ireland. The previous inhabitants who had come to Ireland with Partholón had been destroyed by a plague (*see* Chapter 6). When Nemedh died, his people were defeated and subjugated by the Fomorii. They rebelled, and the Fomorii king was killed but only thirty of Nemedh's followers survived and they left Ireland looking for somewhere to settle.

NEMEDIANS
In Irish Celtic mythology the Nemedians were the followers of Nemedh.

NEMETON
In Celtic times, a nemeton was a sacred grove, the Celts having a special veneration for woodlands.

NEMETONA
In Romano-Celtic mythology, Nemetona was a goddess associated with groves, her name being formed from nemeton. An association between her and Nemain has been suggested.

NEMHAIN *see* NEMAIN.

NENNIUS

A Welsh historian who wrote his *Historia Britonum* about the year 800. He derived his authority from various sources – ancient monuments and writings of Britain and Ireland (recording in the latter the legend of Partholón). His account of Arthur states that he lived in the sixth century and was not a king, his ancestry being less noble than that of many other British chiefs, but nevertheless because of his great talents he was chosen as their leader against the Saxons, whom he defeated in twelve battles, the last being at Mount Badon.

NESSA

In Irish Celtic mythology, Nessa was the mother of Conchobar Mac Nessa, either by her husband, Fachta, or by the druid Cathbad. She was the lover of Fergus Mac Roth.

NEWGRANGE

An important prehistoric passage grave near Drogheda in County Louth, forming part of the Brugh na Bóinne (*see* Chapter 11).

NIALL NOIGIALLACH

In Irish Celtic mythology, Niall Noigiallach was called 'Niall of the Nine Hostages'. He is considered by some to have been a historical figure as well as having featured in legend. He was the founder of the fifth Irish province and established his capital at Tara. His descendants were the Ui Neill, and they gained control over the central and northern parts of Ireland. In legend they have sometimes become synonymous with the Sons of Mil Espaine.

NIAMH

In Irish Celtic mythology, Niamh was the daughter of Manannán Mac Lir and she became the lover of Oisín (*see* Chapter 15).

NIMUE

In Arthurian legend a name accorded to Rhiannon (*see* Chapter 25).

NISIEN

In Welsh Celtic mythology, Nisien was the brother of Efnisien and half-brother of Bran, Branwen and the other children of Llyr. He was a peacemaker and mediator (*see* Chapter 20)..

NODENS *or* **NUDENS**
The Roman equivalent of Nudd (*see* Chapter 18).

NOS GALAN-GAEOF
The Welsh equivalent of Samhain.

NUADA ARGETLÁMH
In Irish Celtic mythology, Nuada was a leader of the Tuatha Dé Danaan. He lost an arm in the first battle of Magh Tuiredh, even although he owned a sword from which no one could escape. Because no one who was physically imperfect could be king of the Tuatha, he had to abdicate in favour of Bres. Later, the giant leech, Dian Cécht, fitted him with an artificial silver arm and he became known as 'Nuada of the Silver Hand'. Bres was forced to abdicate and Nuada was reinstated. During the subsequent war, Nuada, who was afraid of Balor, gave up his kingdom to Lugh who killed Balor in single combat. *See* Chapters 5, 6, 7.

NUDD *see* LLUDD.

NUDENS *see* NODENS.

NUMBERS
In Celtic mythology, numbers played a significant part. The odd numbers were particularly important, notably three, five, seven, nine and seventeen. Of the even numbers, twelve was important.

NYNNIAW
In Irish Celtic mythology, a son of Beli and one of two kings of Britain, the other being his brother Peibaw. They quarrelled over ownership of heaven and the stars and went to war (*see* Chapter 18).

O

OAK

In Celtic culture, the oak tree had sacred connections, being associated with the druids. Indeed, it has been suggested that the word 'druid' might be derived from the root *dru*, meaning oak. The druids used oak trees to form sacred groves and used oak branches in some of their rites. Mistletoe, also used in druidic ritual, grows on oak trees. The oak was revered for its strength and its longevity, and was sometimes thought of as being representatives of the Tree of Life, which linked the mortal world with the Otherworld. Oak trees were associated with the sky, and solar gods and many of the Celtic images and carvings that have been uncovered in archaeological excavations have been found to be made of wood from oak trees, showing the regard in which these were held. Many of the Celtic sailing ships were made of oak, making these particularly durable. Oak was also used to build bridges and plank-built houses. In the Celtic Christian era, churches and monasteries in Ireland were often constructed near oak trees.

OCEAN

In Irish Celtic mythology, the name of a black-maned heifer owned by the Daghda (*see* Chapter 7).

OCHAIN

In Irish Celtic mythology 'the Moaner', the magic shield belonging to Conchobar Mac Nessa. When its owner was in danger, it gave out a moaning sound.

OCHALL OCHNE

In Irish Celtic mythology, king of the Sídhe of Connacht whose swineherd was in eternal rivalry with the swineherd of Bodb (*see* Chapter 12).

OCTRIALLACH

In Irish Celtic mythology, the son of Indech. He discovered the healing spring of the Tuatha Dé Danaan (*see* Chapter 9).

OENGHUS *or* AENGHUS

In Irish Celtic mythology, Oenghus was a god of love. He was a son of the Daghda, his mother being Boann. There are several legends associated with Oenghus. In one, he dreams of a young woman whom he does not recognise and with whom he falls in love. He discovers she is Caer, daughter of Ethal Anubal. She changes shape every other year and becomes a swan. The only time that Oenghus can get together with Caer is when she has the shape of a swan, and so he changes himself into a swan and flies off with her. In another legend, Oenghus helps Midhir marry Etain (*see* Chapter 11). In yet another legend, Oenghus helps Diarmaid, whom Oenghus had fostered, and Grainne against Fionn Mac Cumhaill (*see* Chapter 14).

OETH AND ANOETH

In Welsh Celtic mythology, a bone prison built in Gower by Manawyddan (*see* Chapter 18). Arthur also spent time in it (*see* Chapter 23).

OGHAM

The earliest form of Irish writing, Ogham is frequently referred to in Irish Celtic mythology. Legend has it that it was the invention of Oghma. In fact, it is thought to have been developed in the third and fourth centuries AD, although there have been claims that it was in use as early as the first century BC. The majority of existing examples of Ogham are to be found on stones, some in Scotland, some in Wales, but most in Ireland. About a third of all the stones showing Ogham are to be found in County Kerry. The script takes the form of a series of lines or notches and may be related to some, now lost, system of druidic writing. The fourteenth-century Book of Ballymote discusses Ogham and its characters and contains legends about the origins and uses of Ogham. The Ogham script is sometimes known as the Tree Alphabet because each letter takes the name of a tree. *See also* Chapter 5.

OGHMA *or* OGMA

In Irish Celtic mythology, Oghma was the god of eloquence and literature. He was given the titles of Grianainech, referring to the fact that he had a sunny countenance, and Cermait, referring to the fact that he had a honeyed mouth. In legend, the invention of Ogham, the early Irish script, is ascribed to him (*see* Chapter 5).

He was one of the Tuatha Dé Danaan, and under the rule of Bres he was humiliated by being made to collect firewood (*see* Chapter 7). He is depicted as a warrior and a poet, and sometimes as a guide of the dead to the Otherworld. He is the Irish equivalent of the Gaulish god Ogmios.

OGMIOS

In Gaulish Celtic mythology, Ogmios was the equivalent of the Irish Celtic god Oghma. He was often depicted as an old man carrying a club and bow. Because of the latter fact and because he was also depicted sometimes as being very muscular, he has been associated with the classical hero Hercules. He was the god of eloquence and poetry and was described by the Greek writer Lucian of Samosata as being depicted being followed by a happy group of people whose ears were attached to his tongue by thin chains. Like Oghma, he is sometimes associated with guiding the dead to the Otherworld.

OGYRVRAN

In Arthurian legend a name given to Bran the Blessed.

OISÍN *or* OSSIAN

In Irish Celtic mythology, Oisín was the son of Fionn Mac Cumhaill and Sadb and the father of Oscar. His mother was changed into a deer by a druid, and when he was found by his father he called him Oisín, meaning 'fawn'. He is said to have grown up to be a great warrior and a great poet. According to legend, Niamh fell in love with him and took him to live in the Otherworld. When he thought that he had been with her long enough, he decided to return to his home, but in fact he had been away for three centuries. He was warned by Niamh not to dismount from the white horse that she gave him for his journey, but he ignored this warning when he stopped to help some peasants who were trying to move a very heavy stone. At his dismounting he became a very old man on the verge of death instead of the young man that the magic of Niamh and the Otherworld had preserved him as. He is said to have been taken to St Patrick, whose scribes recorded what he said before he died. *See also* Chapter 15.

OLWEN

In Welsh Celtic mythology, Olwen, whose name translates as 'white track', perhaps because four white trefoils are said to have sprung up wherever she walked, was the daughter of the chief giant, Yspaddaden. Culhwch had been advised that she was the only woman for him, and he set out to find her, a task that proved arduous (*see* Chapter 24).

OONAGH

In Irish Celtic mythology, Oonagh was the wife of Fionnbharr.

ORAL TRADITION

The Celtic tradition was essentially an oral one, and it was not until early Christian times that the Celts were to be found recording things in writing in their own language, whether this was legend, history, poetry or law. This inclination towards an oral tradition was not because of lack of education on the part of the Celts but seems to have been a matter of choice. That the Celts were capable of writing things down is shown by the various inscriptions associated, for example, with gravestones, of the kind, written in the characters of Latin and Greek, that have been found in Italy and Spain and linked to the Celtic culture.

Julius Caesar commented on the phenomenal amount of material memorised by the Celts and on the fact that the Celts seemed to think that it was improper to commit things to writing. This dislike of the written word may have been associated with their religion. Certainly the Celts seem to have been associated with secrecy and mystery. It has been suggested that when the Greeks gave the name of Keltoi to the Celts they were simply putting on record a form of the name with which the Celts referred to themselves and which meant 'secret people'.

The oral tradition is obviously a source of frustration to historians because it has added considerably to the mystique of the Celts and to the difficulty in establishing facts about them as a people. Most of the legend and history that was eventually recorded in writing had been handed down orally for a thousand years, obviously varying as the handing-down process went on.

ORAN

The brother of St Columba (*see* Iona) was known as Oran. He is said to have volunteered to die so that Columba could consecrate with a burial the ground on which he wished to build his chapel.

ORDOVICES

One of the tribes that supported Caratacus against the Roman invaders was a northern Welsh tribe known as Ordovices.

OSCAR

In Irish Celtic mythology, Oscar was the son of Oisín. He was a mighty warrior and distinguished himself by killing a huge boar that many others had failed to catch. Oscar killed three kings in his first battle. He was in charge of a powerful battalion called 'The Terrible Broom', so called because it swept its enemies before it. He was married to Aidin, who died of a broken heart when he was mortally wounded in the Battle of Gabhra. *See also* Chapter 15.

OSLA BIG KNIFE

In Arthurian legend, a companion of Arthur in the pursuit of Twrch Trwyth.

OSSIAN *see* OISÍN.

OTHERWORLD

In Celtic mythology, Otherworld was, among other things, a name for the place where people's souls went after death to be reborn, it being part of the Celtic doctrine to believe in the immortality of the soul. On the night of the feast of Samhain, the Otherworld was said to be visible to mankind and its gates were opened wide. Legend has it that the inhabitants of the Otherworld then wreaked vengeance on any inhabitants of the mortal world who had done them wrong during their lives. Mortalhumans could travel to the Otherworld while they were still alive but, although they retained their youth while they were there, they aged to theiractual age when they returned. This was the fate that befell Oisín when he went to live with Niamh and then returned.

The Otherworld was also the land of the gods. The Irish Otherworld of the gods consisted of a series of sídhe (*see* sídh), each with its own inexhaustible cauldron designed for perpetual feasting. The sídhe were the dwelling places of the Tuatha Dé Danaan and were thought of as lying underneath the country of Ireland. The Tuatha were allotted this underground world by the Sons of Mil Espaine, the first mortals to rule Ireland.

In Welsh Celtic mythology the Otherworld was known as Annwn.

The Otherworld was often perceived as being located on an island or islands to the west of Wales or Ireland and was not only the land of the dead but the land of youth, the land of happiness or the land of the promise. However, some mortals, when visiting it when still alive, such as Cúchulainn, experienced the dark side of it and encountered monsters and other horrors.

To the Cornish Celts, the Otherworld was the Gower peninsula and Lundy island, to the Welsh Annwn was Ireland, while Britain was the Otherworld to the Irish, and both Irish and Welsh saw the Isle of Man as a little Otherworld.

OWAIN

Historically, Owain was the son of Urien. Although he is thought to have lived after the traditional Arthurian period – he is said to have defeated the British heavily in AD 593 – in Welsh Celtic mythology Owain has passed into Arthurian legend along with his father. In legend, he is said to have been the son of Urien and Arthur's sister, Morgan Le Fay.

P

PARTHOLÓN *OR* PARYTHOLON

In Irish Celtic mythology, Partholón was said to have been the son of Sera and the leader of one of the invasions of Ireland. Some ascribe the second invasion to him and others the third. With his companions, the Parthalians, he is said to have defeated the Fomorii and forced them into exile in the Hebrides and the Isle of Man. He and his people are then said to have cleared four plains and created seven lakes, as well as introducing brewing of ale and crafts, establishing the first hostel and establishing laws. Partholón is thus credited with bringing civilisation to Ireland.

According to one legend, Partholón murdered his father and mother. He and his followers are said to have been wiped out by a plague, with only Tuan Mac Stern surviving. *See also* Chapter 6.

PATRICK, ST

The patron saint of Ireland is Patrick. There are various legends about him, and although he is a historical figure, the legends have tended to obscure the facts. He is said to have been born in South Wales, the son of a Christian deacon who was a Roman citizen and a man of considerable means. Patrick is said to have been captured by a group of Scoti, Irish raiders, who attacked his father's country estates. He was taken to Ireland, where he was taken into slavery, his master perhaps being an Antrim chief called Milchru. Six years later, guided by a dream, he walked a long way until he reached a harbour. From there a merchant ship is said to have taken him across the sea to a country that was possibly France, where he may have studied to become a monk.

After some time he is said to have returned to Britain, where he became a deacon and a priest. He was made a bishop and went to Ireland as a missionary. In this capacity he travelled as far as Cashel in the south and Ulster in the north, concentrating his efforts on converting the chiefs. He established a bishop's see at Armagh, where he is said to be buried, having died at Saul in Ireland. However, another theory suggests that he died at Glastonbury, where he had become abbot.

One of the legends involving St Patrick concerns the conversion of Oisín (*see* Chapter 15) while another legend relates to Cúchulainn (*see* Chapter 16) and he is said to have destroy Cromm Cruaich (*see* Chapter 27).

Some literary works of St Patrick remain extant – *Confessio*, a kind of auto-biography written in rather crude Latin, and a letter addressed to a British chieftain who had carried off as slaves some Irish Christians. His writings give almost no exact dates and almost no geographical detail. There is some disagreement about his date of birth. Some ascribe to the theory that he was born around AD 389, became a slave in 405, returned to Ireland in 432 and died in 461. Others think he was captured in the 430s, returned to Ireland between 450 and 460, and died soon after 491.

PEIBAW *see* NYNNIAW.

PELEUR
In Arthurian legend a name for Pryderi..

PELLEAS OR PELLES
In Arthurian legend a name for Pwyll (*see* Chapter 25)..

PENARDUN
In Welsh Celtic mythology, Penardun is said to have been the daughter of Don and the wife of Llyr. One legend has it that she was the mother of Manawydan fab Lyr, Branwen and Bran the Blessed. Another has it that she was not the mother of Bran and Branwen, ascribing their birth to Iweriadd. Penardun is said to have later borne Nisien and Efnisien to Eurosswydd (*see* Chapter 18).

PENDARAN DYFED
In Welsh Celtic mythology, Pendaran Dyfed is a swineherd who is the foster father of Pryderi (*see* Chapter 19).

PERCIVAL
In Arthurian romance, the character based on Peredur (*see* Chapter 25).

PEREDUR

In Welsh Celtic mythology, Peredur was the son of Efrawg. He is the model of Percival of the Arthurian legends, who went on quests to find the Holy Grail. *See* Chapters 23, 25.

PERILOUS GLENS

In Irish Celtic mythology, one of the obstacles Cúchulainn had to surmount on his journey to the island of Scáthach. *See* Chapter 12.

PHALLUS

In Celtic culture the phallus was a symbol of maleness and of fertility. The Celtic male deities were frequently depicted as having exaggeratedly large phalluses, indicating the Celts' preoccupation with fertility. In the northern parts of Britain, representations of naked gods of war were often shown with horns and with extremely large erect phalluses.

PICTS

This is the name given to the people who inhabited northern Britain in Roman times. Their name is first recorded around AD 297 in a Latin poem. The name means 'painted people' and was given to them by the Romans because they painted their bodies before going into battle in order to give them a fierce appearance. They appear to have been a confederation of several northern tribes.

There is some dispute as to whether the Picts, or at least all of them, were Celtic in origin, although it is acknowledged that their original name for themselves was Priteni, which is Celtic in origin, that some of the recorded tribal names are Celtic in origin and that some of them appear to have spoken a Celtic language. There is also dispute about where the Picts originally came from. Bede indicates that they came from Scythia, a region nowadays part of the Ukraine, but the medieval Irish poet Mael Mura of Othain indicates that they came from Thrace. There is also some dispute as to whether or not they preceded the ancient Britons.

PIGS

The Celts appear to have held pigs in high regard. There are frequent references to them in Celtic legend, often connected with some form of magic. For example, Easal, King of the Golden Pillars, gave to the sons of Tuireann seven magic pigs that could be killed and eaten and yet be still alive next day (*see* Chapter 8). People who ate the flesh of any of these pigs were said to be immune to disease.

PILLAR CROSSES
The high crosses that were very popular with the Celts had their origins in pillar crosses. The early pillar crosses were standing stones with designs carved on them, and they gradually evolved over several hundred years into the great intricate high crosses.

PILLARS
In Celtic culture, pillars played a large part. Sometimes they were made of wood and sometimes of stone. They were frequently erected at places that were regarded as being sacred. They may have been regarded by the Celts as representations of trees, several of which were also held to be sacred. The pillars were often very tall and many of them depicted carvings of various kinds.

PINNER
In British Celtic mythology, Pinner was a king of England who was defeated and killed by Molmotius, who was set on expanding the kingdom of Cornwall, which he had inherited from his father.

PISEAR
In Irish Celtic mythology, the king of Persia from whom the sons of Tuireann had to obtain his poisoned spear (*see* Chapter 8).

PIXIES
With the coming of Christianity, Celtic mythology gradually dwindled into a system of fairies, elves, etc; the pixies were the fairies of the West of England. *See also* Chapter 26.

PLAIN OF ILL-LUCK
In Irish Celtic mythology, one of the obstacles Cúchulainn had to surmount on his journey to the island of Scáthach. *See* Chapter 12.

POAKES
With the coming of Christianity, Celtic mythology gradually dwindled into a

system of fairies, elves, etc; the poakes were the fairies of Worcestershire. *See also* Chapter 26.

POOKA
With the coming of Christianity, Celtic mythology gradually dwindled into a system of fairies, elves, etc; the Pooka is a fairy who leads travellers astray in Ireland. *See also* Chapter 26.

PORREX
In British Celtic mythology, Porrex was a prince of Britain. According to Geoffrey of Monmouth, he was a descendant of Brutus and was the son of Gorboduc and Judon. Porrex had a brother, Ferrex, with whom he quarrelled over the right of succession. Ferrex, nervous of his brother's hostile intentions, fled to Gaul and returned with an army. This, however, did not save him, as he was defeated and killed. Their mother, Judon, was so distraught at the loss of her younger son that she went mad and hacked Porrex to pieces as he lay sleeping. Thus both the potential heirs to the throne were dead, and, when Gorboduc himself died, the line descending from Brutus died out.

PRASUTAGUS
In British Celtic mythology, Prasutagus was the husband of Boudicca. He was the chief of the tribe Iceni, who were under Roman rule in Britain but had retained a degree of autonomy. After his death, the Romans took advantage of the situation and pillaged possessions that had belonged to Prasutagus and his family. They also are said to have had Boudicca flogged and to have raped her daughters. Their actions made Boudicca anxious for revenge, and she led a rebellion against the Romans. The rebellion was a spirited one and met with some initial success, but in the end it proved unsuccessful.

PRYDEIN
In British Celtic mythology, Prydein is said to have been a king of Cornwall who conquered the rest of Britain after Porrex's death. Some sources indicate that Britain may be named after him.

PRYDERI
In Welsh Celtic mythology, Pryderi was the son of Pwyll and Rhiannon, born

after his parents had almost given up hope of Rhiannon conceiving. When Pryderi was just a few days old, he mysteriously disappeared (*see* Chapter 19). Pryderi is said to have been a member of the expedition led by Bran the Blessed to Ireland to retrieve Branwen (*see* Chapter 20) and was one of the seven survivors. On the death of his father, Pryderi became lord of Dyfed, and Rhiannon, Pwyll's widow, married Manawydan fab Llyr. By that time Pryderi had married Cigfa. Pryderi, Cigfa, Manawydan and Rhiannon had various adventures (*see* Chapter 21).

PRYDWEN
In Arthurian legend, the name of Arthur's ship (*see* Chapter 24).

PWCCAS
A branch of the ellyllon.

PWYLL
In Welsh Celtic mythology, Pwyll was a prince of Dyfed whose chief court was at Arbeth. For the various legends concerning Pwyll *see* Chapter 19. Pwyll married Rhiannon and they had a son, Pryderi.

R

RAM

In Celtic culture, the ram was a common image. It was associated with the Romano-Celtic version of Mercury, as was the original classical god, Mercury. Small figures of rams belonging to the cult of Mercury have been found in parts of Britain and Gaul. The ram was associated in the Celtic world with war cults. Some of the Celtic war gods in northern Britain were found depicted with ram horns, rams being associated with aggression and often sexual in nature. Some of the war gods not only wore ram's horns but also were naked, suggesting virility and fertility as well as aggression and belligerence. Artefacts containing ram motifs have been uncovered by archaeologists at various Celtic sites, including La Tène. For example, a flagon might have ram head motifs for handles.

RAVEN

Traditionally ravens were associated with darkness but were also associated with prognostication, and the raven is frequently credited with prognostic powers in Irish Celtic literature. For example, they are said to have warned Lugh of the approach of the Fomorii. The raven was also associated with battle, gloating over the bloodshed or foretelling the outcome of the battle. Badb, a war goddess, frequently took the shape of a raven when she was present at a battle. The appearance of Badb in raven guise was often taken as an prognostication that someone was going to die.

RED BOOK OF HERGEST *see HERGEST, RED BOOK OF.*

RED BRANCH

In Irish Celtic mythology, the Red Branch was the collective name given to the group of heroic warriors at the court of Conchobar Mac Nessa. There is some difference of opinion as to the origin of the name. Some think that it came from the fact that they had their regular gatherings in a red room in the palace at Emain Macha. Other sources have it that Ross the Red of Ulster gave his name to the group. *See* Chapter 12.

REDCAPS
With the coming of Christianity, Celtic mythology gradually dwindled into a system of fairies, elves, etc; the redcaps were of this order. *See also* Chapter 26.

RED JAVELIN
In Irish Celtic mythology, one of the spears that belonged to Manannán Mac Lir. Manannán gave it to Diarmid to help him in his flight from Fionn (*see* Chapter 15).

REDYNVRE, STAG OF
In Welsh Celtic mythology, a bird with great knowledge. *See* Chapter 24.

RETALIATOR
In Irish Celtic mythology, the sword that belonged to Manannán Mac Lir and never failed to slay.

RHEINHEIM
In 1954 the burial place of a Celtic princess was uncovered at Rheinheim. She had been buried with a great deal of jewellery made of gold, bronze, amber and coral. As well as having been supplied with food and drink for her journey to the next world, she had been supplied with a mirror. The grave goods point to the belief of the Celts that the dead person was simply moving from one world to another and would have need of worldly goods. She is thought to have been buried in the fourth century BC.

RHIANNON
In Welsh Celtic mythology, Rhiannon was the daughter of Hefeydd Hen and extremely beautiful. Her name means 'great queen', and she became the wife of Pwyll. Legend has it that Pwyll saw Rhiannon riding by on a fine white horse and fell instantly in love with her. He sought her hand in marriage and, although they eventually did marry, things did not go smoothly. For the story of the events leading to their wedding and after the birth of their son, Pryderi,

see Chapter 19. Rhiannon, after Pwyll's death, married Manawydan fab Llyr. For her adventures with him, *see* Chapter 21. Rhiannon is associated in legend with horses and this has led to her being associated with Epona, the Celtic horse goddess.

RHINNON RHIN BARNAWD
In Welsh Celtic mythology, the owner of magic bottles in which no drink ever turned sour (*see* Chapter 24).

RHONABWY
In Welsh Celtic mythology, a man-at-arms of Madawc, son of Maredudd, whose brother, Iorweth, rose in rebellion against him. Rhonabwy is sent with other troops to put Iorwerth's rebellion down. One night he has a dream in which he foresees the Battle of Mount Badon (*see* Chapter 24).

RIENCE
In Arthurian legend the name by which Urien appears in Sir Thomas Malory's *Morte D'Arthur* (*see* Chapter 25).

RITUAL DAMAGE
As was the case with the peoples of the classical world, the Celts often deliberately broke or damaged things that were being offered as votive gifts to the gods. This was true of such things as pieces of pottery, but it was even more true of weapons. Thus, broken swords, etc, have been uncovered at former shrines to the gods and have been retrieved from burial chambers. It is as though whatever was offered as a gift to a god had to be rendered useless for earthly use before it was acceptable to a deity.

RIVERS
Water generally was important to the Celts and rivers were often regarded as having their own spirit or river god. It was a common practice to throw valuable weapons, body armour, coins and jewellery into rivers as offerings to the river spirit or river god.

ROSMERTA
In Gaulish and British Celtic mythology, Rosmerta was a goddess associated

with material wealth and prosperity. Indeed, her name means 'great provider'. She was the patron saint of merchants. She is associated with the Roman god Mercury, who became a Romano-Celtic god, and images of her accompanied by him were quite common, both carrying a purse and caduceus, which were associated with Mercury. It is quite possible that Rosmerta predated the Romano-Celtic Mercury. At any rate, images of her appeared unaccompanied by him. She was sometimes depicted as carrying a basket of fruit or cornucopia, symbols of plenty, and sometimes as carrying a churn or a bucket and ladle. The bucket, like the cauldron, may be a symbol of regeneration.

ROSS THE RED

In Irish Celtic mythology, Ross the Red was a king of Leinster. He is thought by some to have given his epithet to the Red Branch, although another reason given for this is that the group had their meetings in a red room. He married Maga, daughter of Oenghus.

ROUND HOUSES *see* HOUSES.

RUADAN

In Irish Celtic mythology, Ruadan was a son of Bres and the goddess Brigit. He wounded the smith god Goibhniu at the second Battle of Magh Tuiredh, but was mortally wounded in combat by the smith god with one of his magical weapons. His mother pleaded with Goibhniu to let her son be healed by Dian Cécht and so live, but in vain. Brigit went to the battlefield to mourn for her son, and her lamentations are supposed to be the first 'keening' to be heard in Ireland.

RUMHOL *see* LANHERNE CRUCIFIXION CROSS.

S

SAAR *or* SABIA *see* SADB.

SACRIFICE, HUMAN

There is little definite archaeological evidence that the Celts went in for human sacrifice. There are certainly examples of what appear to be abnormal burials, but a distinction must be made between people who died naturally and were then subjected to some form of religious ritualistic activity and people who were ritually killed. There is much evidence of abnormal burial practices but whether this was or was not a follow-on from natural death or sacrificial ritual murder is by no means clear. For example, the infants who were buried as foundation deposits at shrines, sometimes having been first decapitated, might have died naturally or they might have been murdered.

Lindow Man, however, the young man who had been poleaxed, garrotted and had his throat cut before being buried in a bog, seems to point to ritual murder, but, of course, ritual murder might have been administered as a punishment rather than as a form of human sacrifice.

Although archaeological evidence does not seem to point very clearly at the practice of human sacrifice among the Celts, the writings of some Mediterranean commentators does draw attention to such a practice, particularly among the druids. Strabo, a Greek writer, described the druidic practice of stabbing victims and using their observations of their dying struggles to prophesy what was going to happen in the future.

SADB *or* SAAR *or* SABIA

In Irish Celtic mythology, Sadb was turned into a fawn by a druid. Fionn Mac Cumhaill came across her when he was out hunting. Sadb took on her mortal form and became Fionn's mistress or wife. The druid discovered that she was no longer a fawn and turned her back into this form. Fionn then lost track of her, but one day he came across a naked boy who had been raised in the form of a fawn. He realised that the boy was his son by Sadb and called him Oisín, which meant 'little fawn'.

SALII *see* HEAD.

SALMON OF KNOWLEDGE

In Irish and Welsh Celtic mythology, the salmon was a symbol of wisdom and knowledge. One story involving salmon concerns Fionn Mac Cumhaill (*see* Chapter 15).

SALT

In several Celtic sites in Europe the wealth of the inhabitants was based on salt. The famous site at Hallstatt, the excavation of which greatly increased our knowledge of the Celts, was named after a salt-mining settlement in Upper Austria.

SAMHAIN

One of the four major Celtic festivals, Samhain was celebrated on 1 November and on the night that preceded it, making it in terms of time the equivalent of the modern Halloween. A pastoral festival, Samhain marked the passing of one pastoral year and the beginning of another year. At the time of Samhain, the livestock were brought in from the fields, some to be slaughtered for food and others to be kept for breeding purposes during the festival. Samhain was also the time when the usual barriers between the mortal world and the Otherworld were suspended. At Samhain there were great gatherings at Tara, and people met to feast and take part in fairs, markets and horse races. It was thought that spirits from the Otherworld could freely visit the mortal world and that mortals could see and penetrate the Otherworld. This connection between Samhain and the supernatural corresponds to the connection between witches and other supernatural forces and Halloween. Ritual fires were lit but only after all fires were extinguished and relit from a ceremonial fire lit by the druids.

Samhain was a time of great significance to the Celts, and their legends reflect the strange and important things that happened on the festival. For example, it was the time that the people of Nemedh had to pay their annual tribute to the Fomorii, a tribute that was extremely crippling, consisting as it did of two-thirds of their corn, wine (some legends say milk) and children. It was also the date of the second battle of Magh Tuiredh.

SAMHANACH

In Scots Celtic mythology, a goblin that appears at Samhain.

SAMILDANACH

In Irish Celtic mythology, an epithet applied to Lugh, meaning 'of many skills'.

SAUIN

In Celtic culture, Sauin was the equivalent of the Irish Samhain. Sauin was held on 1 November.

SCÁTHACH

In Irish Celtic mythology, Scáthach was a prophetess and great warrior. She is supposed to have run a kind of military school at which she passed on her skills in war to her pupils. One of her pupils was Cúchulainn, to whom she is said to have given Gae-Bholg, an invincible spear (*see* Chapter 12).

SCEOLAN *see* SGEOLAN.

SCEPTRE

Various archaeological excavations have revealed objects that appear to have been sceptres or maces. Frequently these have come to light at temple sites, and it is thought that they were part of the regalia of the priests. Some of these spectres or maces were quite plain but others were quite elaborate, with carvings relating to the cult of a particular divinity, such as the sun god.

SCOTA

In Irish Celtic mythology, the woman from whom the Gaels were descended (*see* Chapter 10).

SEANCHAN TORPEIST

In Irish Celtic mythology, the chief bard of Ireland in the seventh century. He is said to have obtained permission from the saints to call Fergus Mac Roth back from the dead to recount what happend in the Tain Bó Cuailgne.

SEARBHÁN

In Irish Celtic mythology, Searbhan was a one-eyed giant who was sent to guard a magic rowan tree that had grown from a berry that had accidentally been let fall by one of the Tuatha Dé Danaan. He was of a terrible appearance, and everyone was terrified of him, particularly as it was said that the only way that he could be killed was by three blows from his own iron club. He was eventually killed by Diarmaid ua Duibhne (*see* Chapter 15).

SEDANTA *see* SÉTANTA.

SEMION

In Irish Celtic mythology, Semion was the son of Stariat. The Fir Bholg are said to have been descended from him.

SENACH

In Irish Celtic mythology, Senach was a warrior against whom Cúchulainn did battle and won.

SENCHA

In Irish Celtic mythology, Sencha was the chief judge and poet of Ulster at the time of Conchobar Mac Nessa.

SEN MAGH

In Irish Celtic mythology, 'Old Plain', the original plain of Ireland. It was to here that the race of Partholón went to die (*see* Chapter 6).

SEQUENA

In Gaulish Celtic mythology, Sequena was the goddess of the source of the River Seine, which takes its name from her. A sanctuary to her was uncovered near the source and votive offerings found. She is said to have been associated with the duck.

SERA

In Irish Celtic mythology, Sera was the father of Partholón (*see* Chapter 6). According to some sources, it was not Partholón but Sera who was the husband of Dealgnaid.

SÉTANTA *or* SEDANTA
In Irish Celtic mythology, Sétanta was the boyhood name of Cúchulainn. While he still bore this name he performed his first noted heroic deed when he defeated all fifty youths who were in the service of Conchobar Mac Nessa (*see* Chapter 12).

SGEOLAN *OR* SCEOLAN
In Irish Celtic mythology, Sgeolan was one of the two faithful hounds of Fionn Mac Cumhaill, the other one being Bran (2) (*see* Chapter 15).

SHANNON, RIVER
The main river in Ireland, rising in County Cavan and flowing through several lakes into the Atlantic Ocean near Limerick. In Irish Celtic mythology, it is one of the 'twelve chief rivers of Ireland' the waters of which were to be denied to the Formorii (*see* Chapter 7) and its existence is the result of the disobedience of the goddess Sianon (*see* Chapter 5). It also features in the Tain Bó Cuailgne (*see* Chapter 12).

SHAPE-CHANGING
A very common motif in Celtic mythology and religion was shape-changing or shape-shifting, in line with Celtic belief that the soul is immortal. Divinities could turn themselves into the shape of their choice at will. For example, Morrigan and Badb frequently appeared in the form of crows or ravens to warriors in battle. Gods or people with supernatural powers could turn other people into other shapes, often animals, frequently as a punishment. Twrch Trwyth in Welsh mythology was turned into a boar from having been a king. Sometimes the act of shape-changing is the result of jealousy on the part of the person or god bringing about the metamorphosis. Tuireann was turned into a wolfhound by the druid mistress of her husband Illan when she was pregnant because she was jealous of Tuireann, and the children of Lir were changed into swans by their stepmother because she was jealous of her father's love for them.

SHENN DA BOALDYN
In Celtic culture, the equivalent on the Isle of Man of the Irish Beltane. It was celebrated on 1 May.

SHONY

In Hebridean Celtic mythology, a god of the sea who was offered libations at Samhain.

SÍDH (*plural* **SÍDHE**)

In Irish Celtic mythology, each member of the Tuatha Dé Danaan was assigned part of the underground realm that was given to them when they were defeated by the Sons of Mil Espaine, and each part was called a *sidh*, the word meaning a mound or hill. Later the word was used not just to refer to the dwelling place of a god. Every god was a *Fer-Sidhe*, a 'Man of the Hill', every goddess a *Bean–Sidhe*, a 'Woman of the Hill' (the banshee of popular legend), and the *Aes Sidhe*, 'the People of the Hills' became the name of the gods collectively and was shortened to *Sidhe*.

SILBURY HILL *see* HILL SITES.

SIONAN *or* **SINAINN**

In Irish Celtic mythology, Sionan was the granddaughter of Lir. She is associated with the River Shannon, which is said to be named after her (*see* Chapter 5).

SIRONA

In Gaulish Celtic mythology, Sirona was a goddess whose name means 'star', although there is no evidence that she played any kind of celestial part in Celtic belief. She was particularly associated with healing shrines and was often depicted in association with Grannos, who may have been assimilated with the classical god Apollo. Although Sirona was depicted as the consort of Grannos or Apollo, she is thought to have existed as an independent divinity before the Romano-Celtic period. She was associated with regeneration and fertility as well as with healing.

SKY

In Celtic mythology and belief, sky deities appear to have existed separately from sun deities, the sky god having ascendancy over all the elements associated with the sky and being a champion of light and life as opposed to the forces of darkness and death. The classical sky god Jupiter was assimilated into the Celtic range of deities.

SMITH

The art of the smith was of importance to the Celts, not least because they forged the weapons so essential to an essentially warlike people. The art of taking a lump of stone or ore and fashioning into something essential to war, such as a spear, was held in such high regard that smiths were sometimes credited with supernatural powers. There is some archaeological evidence pointing to a kind of smith cult. Particularly in northern parts of Britain, such as Durham and Yorkshire, there have been uncovered potsherds that are decorated with the tools associated with smiths. In addition, a bronze image of a smith was discovered at Sunderland, and a site in Northumberland produced a complete figure of a smith god applied to a vessel made of pottery. He is depicted as standing over an anvil with, in one hand, an ingot held in a pair of tongs and in the other hand a hammer, the tools of his trade. The shard of pottery depicting this is thought to date from around the second century AD. There are various examples of divine smiths in Celtic mythology. In Irish legend, Goibhniu, for example, fashioned magical weapons for the other gods and also appeared as Gobhan Saer, 'Goibhniu the Architect'. The equivalent of Goibhniu in Welsh Celtic mythology was Gofannon.

SNAKE

In Celtic mythology and belief, the snake was associated with fertility and with healing and also with the Otherworld. Sirona, for example, a Gaulish goddess associated with healing, is depicted with a serpent twined round her arm. Because of the rippling movement of the snake, it is often associated with water. In one of the tales of the hero Fionn Mac Cumhaill, he is recorded as being skilled at killing water snakes. There are various tales relating to snakes or serpents in Celtic mythology. A famous one relates to Meiche, the son of Morrigan. It was prophesied that he would bring great disaster to Ireland. He was born with three hearts, one for each manifestation of his mother, and each of these hearts contained a serpent. These were revealed when he was killed and cut open by Dian Cécht. Two of them were burnt, but one legend has it that the third escaped and grew into a huge serpent that was later killed by Dian Cécht. Thus the prophesy of wholesale disaster for Ireland was averted.

SONS OF MIL ESPAINE *see* MIL ESPAINE, SONS OF.

SOUTH CADBURY CASTLE

There are the remains of an Iron Age fortified town at South Cadbury in Somerset. It appears to have been a centre of Celtic religious activity, and of particular interest is the body of a young man, which was buried in the rear of the bank. This seems to have been interred either as a token of good luck or as an act of propitiation to the gods, but it is not clear whether his death was accidental or whether it was an act of human sacrifice. Whether or not the Celts engaged in human sacrifice is the subject of dispute, and the young man might simply have died in battle or as a result of natural causes. On the other hand, the site was found to contain evidence of animal sacrifice, with the remains of young domestic animals such as piglets, calves and lambs.

South Cadbury Castle is also considered as a possible site for Camelot (*see* Chapter 23.

SPIRIT OF IRELAND

The actual identity of the 'Spirit of Ireland', also known as the 'Sovereignty of Ireland' or 'the Sovranty of Ireland', is subject to uncertainty and confusion. That this being was female in form and that she embodied the very essence of Ireland is not in doubt. As such, she was one of the most important Irish deities. The ritual surrounding her is also a bit shadowy, but she is held to have had the right to confer the status of king and to have a ritual mating with the successful candidate. Some sources indicate that the spirit of Ireland was personified as Medb, and others that she was the personification of the most beautiful woman in Ireland, such as Edain Echraidhe (*see* horses). Another source has it that the spirit of Ireland was Banbha (*see* Eriu).

SPLENDID MANE

In Irish Celtic mythology, the horse that belonged to Manannán Mac Lir. Manannán. It could travel at great speed over land or sea. He lent it to Lugh who in turn lent it to the sons of Tuireann (*see* Chapter 8).

SPRINGS

Water was generally important to the Celts, but of special importance to them were springs, which were considered to have healing powers. Because springs by their very nature well up from below the ground, they were often credited with supernatural associations, as though they provided a link between the mortal world and the Otherworld. During the Romano-Celtic period the concept of the healing spring was developed to an even greater extent. At that point the Celtic goddess Sirona, who was associated with healing, became known also as a consort of the classical god Apollo. One of the interesting features of the healing springs of the Romano-Celtic period was the presentation of model votive offerings of the part of the body that was suffering from disease. Thus, if the model of a diseased arm was presented as a votive offering to the god or goddess who was the spirit of the spring, the hope was that the arm would become whole.

SRENG

In Irish Celtic mythology, Sreng was a Fir Bholg warrior who was despatched as an ambassador to have talks with the Tuatha Dé Danaan when they landed with their invading force in Ireland. He spoke to Bres, the spokesman of the Tuatha Dé Danaan, who suggested that Ireland should be divided between the Fir Bholgs and the Tuatha. The Fir Bholg rejected this suggestion, leading to the first Battle of Magh Tuiredh. Although the Fir Bholgs gained some initial success when Sreng and Nuada fought in single combat and Sreng severed Nuada's arm, the Fir Bholgs were eventually soundly defeated (*see* Chapter 6).

STAG

The stag was important in Celtic mythology and beliefs. The stag was a symbol of virility, dignity, speed and aggression. It also had additional associations. The antlers of the stag were symbolic of the branches of a tree, and trees were sacred to the Celts. The shedding of their antlers, in common with the shedding of their leaves by trees, was a symbol of regeneration. Stags and deer play a significant part in Celtic mythology, as is evident in the legend of Pwyll's encounter with Arawn, when he chased away Arawn's hounds, which were in pursuit of a stag, and in penance had to change forms and countries with Arawn for a year (*see* Chapter 19). *See also* white stag.

STAG OF REDYNVRE *see* REDYNVRE, STAG OF.

STARIAT *see* SEMION.

STARN

In Irish Celtic mythology, Starn was a son of Sera and brother of Partholón.

STONEHENGE

According to Celtic mythology, .i.Myrddin;Myrddin is said to have had Stone-henge built with stones brought from Ireland. In Ireland, they had formed the Giants' Ring on Mount Killaraus. According to legend, the stones had been carried by giants who originated in Africa and who were the first inhabitants of the earth (*see* Chapter 23).

STONE OF DESTINY OR LIA FÁIL

In Irish Celtic mythology, one of the treasures of the Tuatha Dé Danaan. It was said to have come from Galias and afterwards fell into the hands of the early kings of Ireland (*see* Chapter 6).

STRETTWEG

At Strettweg in Austria was discovered a unique bronze wagon model. It is thought to date from the seventh century BC and thus belongs to the early Celtic period or Hallstatt culture. The model comprises a platform on four wheels, at each end of which is an image of a stag with antlers. In the centre stands a woman carrying a flat bowl on her head, and she is surrounded by a group of cavalrymen and infantrymen with spears and shields. It is thought that this might represent a ritual hunt.

SUALTAM

In Irish Celtic mythology, Sualtam was the mortal father of Cúchulainn. The night before his wedding to Deichtire, the god Lugh carried her off and slept with her, and Sétanta (Cúchulainn) was later born. When Medb invaded Ulster in quest of the great brown bull of Ulster, Sualtam tried to rouse the men of Ulster to action. He then turned his horse, the Grey of Macha, so angrily and suddenly that the sharp rim of his shield cut off his head. The severed head then continued to call out a warning to the men of Ulster until the curse that Macha had placed on them was lifted and they were once again men of action (*see* Chapter 12).

SUCCAT

Either the childhood name or the nickname of St Patrick was Succat.

SUCELLUS

In Gaulish Celtic mythology, Sucellus, which translates as 'good striker', was a god who is often depicted as carrying a long-handled mallet, has a wine cask or drinking vessel near, and is often accompanied by a dog.

SULIS

The name of the goddess who presided over the healing spring at Bath was Sulis. When the Romans came to Britain they converted the healing springs at Bath into a large bath house and built a temple, but the site of the springs is thought to have been sacred to healing long before their arrival. Sulis was one of the British Celtic water deities and, as befits her association with Bath, was a goddess of healing. The Romans held Sulis in such regard that they named the town that is now Bath after her, the Roman name for it being Aquae Sulis. From the time of the arrival of the Romans, Sulis began to be identified with the classical goddess Minerva. This hybridisation of Celtic and Roman deities was quite common, and the hybridised goddess became known as Sulis Minerva. She was the presiding goddess of the therapeutic springs at Bath in Roman times.

SUN

That the Celts venerated the sun is obvious from the motifs on various artefacts that have come to light during archaeological expeditions. Particularly common are depictions of the wheel as a solar symbol. Although it is to be expected that the Celts would be sun-worshippers since they venerated natural phenomena generally, such as water and trees, there is little evidence of sun gods in Celtic literature. The Irish god Lugh, whose name means 'shining one', who had a beautiful, radiant countenance and was associated with light, is an obvious candidate to have been a sun god. The Gaulish god Belenus was also associated with light, the word *bel* being translated as 'bright', but he was known as a god of light and healing rather than specifically as a sun god.

SUN GOD *SEE* SUN.

SWAN

In Celtic mythology and beliefs, the swan was of particular importance. In Hallstatt Europe archaeologists have uncovered model wagons, drawn by creatures resembling swans, the wagons sometimes carrying vessels. Swans were common in Celtic legend and seem to have been a favourite in shape-changing. The children of Lir were turned into swans by their stepmother because she was jealous of their father's love for them. In another legend, Midhir changes himself and Etain into swans to escape from the court of Eochaidh. In yet another, Caer, who was beloved by Oenghus, became a swan every other year and Oenghus turned into a swan to fly away with her. *See* Chapter 11.

SWASTIKA

In Celtic Europe, the swastika was a solar motif in the way that the wheel was. Swastikas have been found on stone altars and as a motif on artefacts. Sometimes it appears alone and sometimes accompanied by a wheel motif. It is thought that perhaps it was indicative of good luck as well as being a solar motif.

T

TAILLTINN

In Irish Celtic mythology, the battle at which the Sons of Mil Espaine defeated the Tuatha Dé Danaan for the second time was the Battle of Tailtinn. After it, Mac Cécht, Mac Cuill and Mac Greine became rulers of Ireland and the Tuatha Dé Danaan were given the underground portion of the country (*see* Chapter 10).

TÁIN BÓ CUAILGNE

The basis of the Táin Bó Cuailgne is the quest of Medb, queen of Connacht, for the Donn Cuailgne, the great Brown Bull of Ulster, partly because her husband, Ailill, owned Finnbhenach, the White-horned Bull of Connacht. Ulster was the traditional enemy of Medb's kingdom, and so in order to acquire the bull that she so much desired she had to raise an army with which to invade Ulster. At that time the warriors of Ulster were unfit for battle since Macha had placed a curse on them, and the only warrior who was fit to fight was Cúchulainn. He put up a spirited defence against Medb, single-handedly holding off her troops for many weeks. Eventually he was killed and the bull captured and taken to Medb's camp where it had an epic fight lasting a day and night with Finnbhenach, and the White-horned Bull was killed and torn to pieces. Later, Donn Cuailgne returned to Ulster where it died. *See* Chapter 12.

TALIESIN

In Welsh Celtic mythology, Taliesin was the son of Cerridwen, and he was born under strange, supernatural circumstances (*see* Chapter 23). Taliesin is thought not only to have been a legendary figure but also to have been a historical sixth-century figure, noted for his poetic powers. The Book of Taliesin is.one of the 'Four Ancient Books of Wales'. It is thought to have been written in the fourteenth century. The other Ancient Books of Wales are those of Aneurin, Carmarthen and Hergest.

TARA

For many centuries the most sacred place in Ireland, and the main residence of the high kings, was Tara in County Meath, the ancient site dating back to 2000 BC. It was regarded as the Celtic capital of Ireland, being an important religious and political centre, although the site of Tara is thought to have been a sacred one long before the Celts, possibly from Neolithic times. Tara features in various Irish Celtic legends. It was the capital of the Tuatha Dé Danaan and the location of the court of Conchobar Mac Nessa and thus the home of the Red Branch.

TARANIS

The Celts believed that the weather was a manifestation of the supernatural powers of their gods, and several of their divinities were personifications of natural phenomena. Thunder and storms with their noise and turbulence may have indicated a power struggle among the gods. Taranis was their thunder god. The Roman poet Lucan, who lived around the first century AD, wrote about events that occurred around the middle of the first century BC, mainly an account of the civil war between Pompey and Caesar in his poem *The Pharsalia*. He referred to a Celtic god called Taranis and described the cult surrounding the god as being very cruel. Taranis has also been equated with the Roman god Jupiter, who was often depicted brandishing a thunderbolt and has been associated with war as well as thunder. Although it has been assumed that Lucan considered Taranis to be quite an important god, only seven altars dedicated to him have been found. On the other hand, these altars are widely spread, from Britain to Gaul to Germany to Dalmatia, there being one at Chester in Britain.

TARBHFEIS

In Irish Celtic mythology, Tarbhfeis, which survives in various spellings and is translated as 'the bull feast', was a ceremony associated with the selection of the high kings of Ireland. The ceremony was held at Tara and was conducted by five druids. One had to eat the flesh of a bull and drink its blood before being put to sleep by the other four as they chanted over him. He would then have a dream about the person who was chosen to become high king. Obviously he could lie, but he was under threat of being destroyed by the gods if he did not tell the truth. The rite is said to have been outlawed by St Patrick.

TATHLUM

In Irish Celtic mythology, a 'brain-ball' that was made by mashing up the brain of a dead opponent and mixing it with lime. A brain-ball was said to be a particularly deadly missile if it was flung at someone.

TECH DUINN

In Irish Celtic mythology, Tech Duinn is said to have been the name given to an island off the southwest coast of Ireland. It was believed to be the home of Donn, the god of the dead. One legend has it that he was the son of Midhir the Proud, but another identifies him with Donn, one of the Sons of Mil Espaine, who drowned on the voyage of the Sons and was buried on the island.

TEIRNYON *see* TEYRNON.

TEIRTU

In Welsh Celtic mythology, the owner of the harp that played itself and was one of the treasures of Britain (*see* Chapter 24).

TERRIBLE BROOM

In Irish Celtic mythology, a banner for use in war that was never known to retreat a foot. It was entrusted to Oscar (*see* Chapter 15).

TETHRA

In Irish Celtic mythology, a Fomorii king, one of the leaders of the Fomorii invasion.

TEUTATES

One of the Celtic gods was Teutates, said to have been a Gaulish tribal deity. He is described as being connected with arts, journeys and trading.

TEYRNON *or* TEIRNYON

In Welsh Celtic mythology, Teyrnon was the lord of Gwent Is-Coed. He is best known as the foster father of Pryderi, whom he found on his doorstep as a baby (*see* Chapter 19).

THIRTEEN TREASURES OF BRITAIN

In Welsh Celtic mythology, the dowry required for Olwen (*see* Chapter 24).

TIGERNMAS

In Irish Celtic mythology, Tigernmas was a king who may have had some historical connections. Said to have been the son of Follach, he supposedly introduced the worship of Cromm Cruach to Ireland. This worship involved human sacrifice on the feast of Samhain. He and many of his followers are said to have been slain at one of these ritual feasts. Some sources indicate that he was credited with introducing mining and the smelting of gold into Ireland.

TIERNA OF CLONMACNOIS

Tierna was a chronicler and the abbot of Clonmacnois, a great monastic and educational centre in medieval Ireland. He died in 1088.

TÍR NA MBAN

In Irish Celtic mythology, Tír na mBan was an Otherworld country, an island that was populated entirely by women. It is said to have been visited by Bran (1) and his followers, who thought that they had left after a year but had in fact stayed for several hundred years, and by Mael Dúin (*see* Chapter 16).

TÍR NAN BEO

In Irish Celtic mythology, the 'Land of the Living' or 'Land of the Happy Dead', believed to lie far out to the west beyond the unsailed Atlantic Ocean. Both Partholón and Lugh were said to have come to Ireland from there

TÍR NA OG OR TÍR NA NOG

In Irish Celtic mythology, Tír na Og, which has various spelling variants, was an .i.Otherworld;Otherworld realm in which people are forever young. It is thus sometimes known as the 'Land of the Forever Young' and the 'Land of Youth'.

TÍR TAIRNIGIRIB

In Irish Celtic mythology, the 'Land of Promise', the home of Manannán Mac Lir, another term for the Otherworld.

TOLLUND MAN

In 1950, the body of a man, known as Tollund Man, was discovered in a peat bog in Denmark. He had been garrotted and was wearing only a leather cap and girdle, bearing a marked resemblance to the state of Lindow Man. He is thought to have been placed in the bog around 500 BC and may have been deposited there by a Teutonic tribe rather than a Celtic tribe, since some of the Teutonic tribes are thought to have shared some traditions and customs with the Celts.

TORACH *see* TORY ISLAND.

TORC
The Celtic neck ring was known as a torc. Torcs were often found round the necks of Celtic deities. A stag-antlered god, is depicted on the Gundestrup Cauldron as wearing one torc round his neck and carrying another in his hand. The same god has also been depicted with a torc hung over each antler. When worn by mortals, they were often a sign of nobility or high status. For example, the prince who was buried at Hallstatt was interred wearing a torc. Torcs were often made of gold and could be extremely heavy.

TORC TRIATH
In Irish Celtic mythology, Torc Triath was the king of the boars. It is said to have been the Irish equivalent of Twrch Trwyth, against which Culhwch was sent by Yspaddaden as one of the tasks set to win the hand of Olwen (*see* Chapter 24).

TORS *see* HILL SITES.

TORY ISLAND
In Irish Celtic mythology, the Fomorii had a stronghold on Tory Island. The name derives from the word *torach*, meaning a watchtower, and the island is sometimes referred to as Torach.

TREASURES OF BRITAIN
In Welsh Celtic mythology, the dowry required for Olwen (*see* Chapter 24).

TREE ALPHABET *see* OGHAM.

TREES
The Celts held trees to be sacred, both as individual species, such as the oak,

and as collections of trees, such as woods and groves. Trees were thought by the Celts to represent a link between the upper or mortal world and the Otherworld or lower world, the roots spreading deep into the ground and the branches reaching high into the sky. Trees were also thought of as representing the Tree of Life, and as such were regarded as being associated with fertility. The falling of the leaves of deciduous trees in the autumn and the appearance of buds and young leaves was also thought to be related to the Celts' philosophy of regeneration.

TRIAD

An aphoristic literary form that was developed in Irish and Welsh literature celebrating famous traditional persons or things. *See also* triplism.

TRI DÉ DANA

In Irish Celtic mythology, the Tri Dé Dana was the triad of gods associated with craftsmanship. They were Creidhne, Goibhniu and Luchtaine. They forged and repaired the magical weapons of the Tuatha Dé Danaan.

TRINOVANTES

This was the tribal name given to the Britons who were said to be inhabiting London, and the territory to the north of there, at the time of the second invasion of Julius Caesar in 54 BC.

TRIPLISM

The number three played an important part in Celtic culture and beliefs. Triads were common, and the concept of the triple goddess was particularly common. For example, Morrigan was a triple war goddess, as was Macha.

TRISTAN AND ISEULT

A medieval series of tales based on Celtic myth. Tristan is the nephew of King Mark of Cornwall. Tristan is escorting Iseult to Cornwall, to the castle of his uncle, King Mark, to whom Iseult is betrothed. The two drink a love potion, thinking it to be poison, and while duty requires Iseult to become Mark's queen, their love grows so strong that they cannot hide it. Mark surpasses them and Tristan is mortally wounded. His servant takes him to his castle in Brittany, and there he is joined by Iseult. The joy of seeing her saps his remaining strength and he dies in her arms. Iseult, knowing that they can only love in death, dies by his side. Parallels can be drawn with Diarmaid and Grainne and Deirdre and Naoise. *See* Chapter 23.

TRISTREM, TRYSTAN

In Arthurian legend, variant forms of Tristan.

TUAN MAC CAIRELL

In Irish Celtic mythology, Tuan Mac Cairell is said to have been the son of Starn, brother of Partholón. He is supposed to have survived the plague that destroyed most of the people of Partholón and to have been reborn as a stag. He was then reborn as an eagle and again as a salmon. When in the form of a salmon, he was eaten by his wife. She then gave birth to him in human form. Another legend has it that Tuan Mac Cairell was a reincarnation of Tuan Mac Stern, who was the nephew of Partholón. *See* Chapter 6.

TUAN MAC STERN *see* PARTHOLÓN; TUAN MAC CARELL.

TUATHA DÉ DANAAN

In Irish Celtic mythology, the gods of pre-Christian Ireland were known as the Tuatha Dé Danaan, which translates as the 'people of the goddess Danu'. When the Tuatha Dé Danaan arrived in Ireland, they fought two great battles, the first against the previous invaders, the Fir Bholg (*see* Chapter 6), and the second against the Fomorii (*see* Chapter 9). The Tuatha Dé Danaan defeated the Fir Bholg at the first Battle of Magh Tuiredh and the Fir Bholg had to hand over the kingship of Ireland to the Tuatha. The king of the Tuatha, Nuada, lost an arm in the battle and so was forced to abdicate. In his place, Bres was chosen to be leader and king, but his leadership was not a success and Nuada, having had an artificial silver arm fitted, was restored to the throne. Bres then defected to the Fomorii and raised an army against the Tuatha. Lugh became the leader of the Tuatha, Nuada having stepped down in his favour.

The second Battle of Magh Tuiredh was then fought between the Tuatha under Lugh and the Fomorii under Bres. This battle was to be decided on the result of single combat between Lugh and the giant Balor. Lugh won when he delivered a slingshot that went right through Balor's single eye and out of the back of his head to kill or injure some of the Fomorii followers.

The Tuatha were finally defeated by the invasionary force of the Sons of Mil Espaine (*see* Chapter 10), and the Tuatha were given the underground part of Ireland for their realm.

TUIREANN *OR* TUIRENN
In Irish Celtic mythology, Tuireann was the father of Brian, Iuchar and Iuchar-ba, possibly by the goddess Brigit (*see* Chapter 8).

TUIS
In Irish Celtic mythology, the King of Greece from whom the sons of Tuireann had to obtain his pig's skin (*see* Chapter 8).

TWRCH TRWYTH
In Welsh Celtic mythology, Twrch Trwyth was a fierce boar who had been a king before being transformed. In Irish Celtic mythology, Torc Triath was his equivalent. In the legend of Culhwch and Olwen, one of the tasks Culhwch had to perform to win Olwen's hand was to obtain the comb and razor, or the comb, razor and shears, that lay between the ears of the beast so that he could act as barber to Yspaddaden. With some help, he accomplished the task and the boar was forced to jump off a cliff into the sea (*see* Chapter 24).

TYLWYTH TEG
In Welsh Celtic mythology, Tylwyth Teg was the collective name given to the people of Gwyn ap Nudd. The name probably referred to spirits who were waiting to be born again rather than the dead, so can perhaps can be regarded more as a type of fairies (*see* Chapter 18).

U

UAITHNE

In Irish Celtic mythology, Uaithne was the harp of the Daghda. It was a magic instrument and would play only when it was asked to do so by the Daghda. The instrument was stolen by the Fomorii, but the Daghda discovered the theft and traced it to the feasting hall of their enemy. They then called to the instrument and it leapt forward, killing nine Fomorii in the process, and began to play a song of praise to the Daghda.

Uaithne was also the name of the Daghda's harpist.

UGAINE MOR

In Irish Celtic mythology, Ugaine Mor was a high king in the sixth century BC, although he may be partly historical. He is supposed to have ruled the whole of Ireland and part of Western Europe, particularly Gaul. On Ugaine's death, Ireland was divided into twenty-five parts among his children, and this system lasted for three hundred years.

UIGREANN

In Irish Celtic mythology, Uigreann fought Cumhaill, the father of Fionn Mac Cumhaill because of Cumhaill's abduction of Muirne. He was later killed by Cumhaill, and his sons are said to have sought vengeance for their father's death. According to some sources, each of the sons threw a spear at Cumhaill and all five were credited with killing their father's killer.

UISNEACH, HILL OF

In Irish Celtic mythology, the point at which the five provinces into which Ireland was divided met. It was formerly called Balor's Hill.

ULAID

The original Irish name for Ulster was Ulaid. It appears to have covered approximately the geographical area of the modern province. Its capital was Emain Macha.

ULSTER

In Irish Celtic mythology, Ulster was one of the five provinces into which the Fir Bholg divided Ireland. It was the great enemy and rival of Connacht (*see also* Táin Bó Cuailgne). Ulster had several heroes associated with it, principally Cúchulainn.

UNDRY

In Irish Celtic mythology, the magic cauldron of the Daghda was called Undry. It had an unlimited supply of food that was never used up, no matter how many people ate from it. No worthy person ever went away hungry from it and everyone got food from it in proportion to their merits (*see* Chapter 5).

URDDAWL BEN

In Welsh 'Venerable Head', in Welsh Celtic mythology the head of Bran the Blessed as described by Taliesin.

URIEN

Urien was an historical sixth-century AD king of Rheged who defeated the Anglo-Saxons at Argoed Llwyfain. He is said to have been the father of Owain. He was assassinated. *See* Chapter 23.

URIENCE, URIENS

Two of the names with which Urien is associated in Arthurian legend.

USNA *see* NAOISE.

UTHER BEN

In Welsh Celtic mythology, 'Wonderful Head', the head of Bran the Blessed as described by Taliesin.

UTHER PENDRAGON *or* BENDRAGON

In Arthurian legend Uther Pendragon is given as Arthur's father. He can be associated with Bran the Blessed as 'dragon' is not part of the name but a title signifying 'war leader'.

V

VIVIEN
In Arthurian legend a name accorded to Rhiannon (*see* Chapter 25).

VIX
A Celtic princess was buried in a barrow at Vix in Burgundy in France in the sixth century BC. Known as the Princess of Vix, her grave with its grave goods, which was excavated in 1953, significantly added to our knowledge of the Celts. The body of the princess was laid on a four-wheeled wagon that was adorned with gold, brooches and amber jewellery. It also contained a very large, very heavy Grecian vase. Various other valuable artefacts were buried with the princess. The lavishness of the grave goods for her journey to the Otherworld points to the fact that women in Celtic culture could achieve high rank and importance, and their nature also points to the fact that the early Celts traded with the Greeks, the Etruscans and with Rome and Burgundy.

VORTIGERN
This name means 'overlord' and may have been a title rather than a name. He is generally thought of as being a historical figure, although, as is frequently the case with Celtic historical figures, facts and legends have become somewhat jumbled. He is said to have been ruler of Britain in the fifth century AD and to have married a daughter of the rebel Roman emperor Maximus. He is mentioned by Geoffrey of Monmouth. Vortigern is said to have instigated the assassination of Constantine, king of Britain, by a Pict and to have installed Constantine's son, Constans, as a puppet king. Later he is said to have killed Constans in order to get the throne for himself. He is also said to have invited Saxons to Britain in order to rid the kingdom of the Picts, but they began to carve out territory for themselves. Vortigern is said to have fled to Wales after the murder of some British princes on Salisbury Plain. The king is said to have been burned to death in his tower, which was finally built by Ambrosius Aurelius, the rightful heir to the throne.

W

WANBOROUGH

This is the site of a Romano-Celtic temple in Surrey. The presence of three bronze chain headdresses indicates the sacred nature of the site in Celtic times, since such headdresses were worn by priests who were officiating at religious ceremonies in temples. The miniature bronze wheels that surmounted two of the headdresses suggest that they would have been worn by priests who were associated with the worship of the sun. Significant quantities of Celtic coins uncovered underneath the level at which Roman remains were found suggest that the site was sacred to the Celts before the advent of the Romans.

WAR

The Celts were a warlike people. This is obvious from the archaeological evidence that has been retrieved from various excavations. Shields, spears, etc, were a common part of the grave goods interred with the corpse to help the soul in its journey to, and life in, the Otherworld. It is also evident from the votive offerings to gods that have been uncovered from lakes, rivers, pools and bogs. These were not necessarily intended for war gods but were perhaps to be regarded as offerings to the god or spirit of the piece of water concerned. Many of the weapons so presented had been deliberately broken or damaged before being offered, perhaps because the Celts felt that such weapons had to be rendered unfit for use in this world before they would be acceptable to the god (*see* ritual damage). Miniature weapons were also often offered as gifts to the gods in shrines.

Images of warriors and of war gods were a common part of the Celtic culture. Life-size sculptures of war gods clad in full armour have been discovered in various shrines, and many Celtic coins depict male and female warriors. In the north of Britain some of the representations of war gods not only bear shields and spears to exhibit their warlike connections, but they were also depicted wearing horns, sometimes ram horns, which suggested not only aggression but sexual aggression. This was further emphasised by the fact that such depictions of war gods were often naked and had exaggeratedly large phalluses. In Irish Celtic mythology, several of the war deities were female, such as Macha and the Morrigan. Here again, the warlike qualities of the goddesses were often accompanied by attributes of sexuality and fertility.

WATER

The Celts appear to have venerated water, seeing it not only as essential to life but perhaps seeing it as having connections with the Otherworld. This would obviously be more true of forms of water that came from deep down within the earth, such as wells and springs. That water was venerated is obvious from the quantities of weapons and valuable artefacts, such as items of jewellery, coins, items of domestic life, such as cauldrons, and even animal and human sacrifices, that have been retrieved from rivers, springs, lakes, pools and wells. Rivers, lakes and so on were thought to have spirits or gods associated with them who would appreciate such votive offerings – some of them were shrines.

Water in Celtic times, as later, was thought to be a source of healing. Especially during the late pre-Roman Celtic period and the Romano-Celtic period, healing shrines grew up around natural springs that were thought to have healing powers. This association with water and natural healing powers lasted far longer than Celtic society – one has only to think of Bath and its associations with healing. *See also* Chapter 7.

WAVE-SWEEPER

In Irish Celtic mythology, the boat that belonged to Manannán Mac Lir. Manannán lent it to Lugh who in turn lent it to the sons of Tuireann (*see* Chapter 8).

WELLS

As has been pointed out at water, wells, in common with rivers, springs, lakes and pools, were venerated by the Celts. Wells were especially venerated, partly because of their supposed healing properties but also because they were perceived as forming a connection between the mortal world and the Otherworld.

WHEEL

In the Romano-Celtic period, the wheel was regarded as being a symbol of the sun, probably because the wheel, being circular, bears a resemblance to the sun with spokes radiating out from it. The Celts sometimes buried model wheels with corpses, perhaps as symbols of the sun to light the way of the dead to the Otherworld.

WHITE-HORNED BULL OF CONNACHT *see* FINNBHENACH.

WHITE MOUNT

In British Celtic mythology, the head of Bran the Blessed was buried by Manawydan fab Llyr, Pryderi and others in the White Mount, one of the major druidic sites in London. The supposed founder of London, Brutus, was also buried there. It is said that King Arthur dug up the interred head of Bran so that he himself would be the only guardian of Britain, a role to which Bran had laid claim. With this in mind, he had ordered his head to be buried facing towards France, a potential enemy of Britain. *See* Chapter 20.

WHITE STAG

To the Celts the white stag was a mystical animal thought to have come from the Otherworld originally and so was endowed with special powers. The animal features in several Celtic legends.

Y

YELLOW BOOK OF LECAN *see* LECAN, YELLOW BOOK OF.

YELLOW SHAFT
In Irish Celtic mythology, one of the spears that belonged to Manannán Mac Lir. Manannán gave it to Diarmid to help him in his flight from Fionn (*see* Chapter 15).

YNAWAG
In Welsh Celtic mythology, Ynawag was one of the seven survivors of the expedition led by Bran the Blessed against Matholwch, then king of Ireland, to rescue Branwen. He was thus part of the group who carried the head of Bran to be buried under the White Mount in London (*see* Chapter 20).

YNYS WITTRIN *see* GLASTONBURY TOR.

YSPADDADEN PENKAWR
In Welsh Celtic mythology, Yspaddaden, whose name meant 'chief giant', according to legend had such huge, heavy eyelids that they had to be propped open by metal supports before he could see anything. He was the father of Olwen, whom Culhwch wanted to marry (*see* Chapter 24).